THE HISTORY OF
WHALLEY RANGE
CRICKET & LAWN TENNIS CLUB
VOLUME I

1845-1945
The First 100 Years

Chief Author & Historian : Peter Simpson

Foreword by John Gwynne
(sports commentator and former WR cricketer)

Edited by Mike Hill
(WRC&LTC Chairman)

Published in Great Britain by Tony Brown,
4 Adrian Close, Beeston, Nottingham NG9 6FL.
Telephone 0115 973 6086. E-mail soccer@innotts.co.uk
First published 2015

© WRC&LTC 2015

All rights reserved. No part of this publication may be reproduced, stored in a retrieval system, or transmitted in any form, or by any means, electronic, mechanical, photocopying, recording or otherwise without the prior permission in writing of the Copyright holders, nor be otherwise circulated in any form or binding or cover other than in which it is published and without a similar condition including this condition being imposed on the subsequent publisher.

Cover design by Bob Budd & Peter Simpson.

Printed and bound by 4Edge, Hockley, Essex
www.4edge.co.uk

ISBN: 978-1-905891-88-7

This book is dedicated to Alf Crompton who sadly passed away during the writing of this volume of the book. Alf was President of Whalley Range Cricket & Lawn Tennis Club from 1992 to 2014.

Alfred Bernard Crompton

CONTENTS

Foreword	5
Whalley Range – A Social History	8
Early Days (1845-1878)	14
Going it Alone (1879-1892)	32
Joining Forces (1892-1899)	63
Dawn of a New Century (1900-1910)	81
On The Move (1911-1922)	104
The Old Hulmeians Connection	115
A New Beginning (1923-1929)	128
On the Way to a Century (1930-1945)	150
Tennis (1881-1945)	178
Appendix A : Notable Alumni	190
Appendix B : List of Officers	196
Appendix C : Notable Vice-Presidents	197
Appendix D : Highest Totals	198
Appendix E : Lowest Totals	199
Appendix F : Centuries	200
Appendix G : Best Bowling Performances for 1st XI	202

Foreword
by John Gwynne

John Gwynne, well known for his radio and TV sports commentaries, played for Whalley Range CC for twelve years through the '60s and into the early '70s. A former schoolteacher, he gave up that profession in 1987 to concentrate on his work in the media. A darts commentator on Sky Sports for over two decades and a familiar voice on Sky's 'Soccer Saturday' show, he was also employed by the BBC in the north west – Radio Manchester, Radio Merseyside, Radio Lancashire and television's North West Tonight – for many years as their Lancashire CCC correspondent, covering all their matches, home and away, including seven Lord's finals. He is also an entertaining after-dinner speaker and host, who has worked alongside many great and famous sports personalities. He is proud to be associated, as host, with Whalley Range Cricket and Lawn Tennis Club's annual dinner each spring and he is to be seen, invariably, at President's Day in the summer.

John flanked by two of the all-time greats, Sir Garfield Sobers and Sir Richard Hadlee
(Lancashire CCC Development Association 10th Anniversary Dinner, Old Trafford, June 1st 2004)

I played my first game for Whalley Range CC, at the age of 16, for Ralph Astin's Extra-Second XI at Arley CC in Cheshire (Whalley Range, as you will discover, didn't deal in anything less than Second Elevens), on Saturday 17 June 1961. That same morning, I had taken a hat-trick for Chorlton Grammar School 1st XI, and was offered a chance to play by a leading Whalley Range player, Doug Cannell, who was umpiring. Clearly, the Whalley Range Extra-Second team, which undertook all its matches away from home, was short of players and I was a useful late selection! The team comprised mainly former players from Withington Cricket Club, which had folded a year or two earlier and whose players had been offered the chance to stay together within the Whalley Range fold. Among them was Roy Dixon, goalkeeper of Cheshire League Buxton FC, whose son, Lee, was to become a leading player for Arsenal and England and who is now a TV soccer pundit. Another was Alf Crompton, who, until his death in the summer of 2014, served the club for over 50 years, 22 as President and to whom this book is dedicated.

There were two quite elderly men in the team, though, who had Whalley Range blood running through their veins, whose names appear in the latter chapters of this book. Ralph Astin and E. G. "Geoff" Widdows had served the club for many years as not unformidable members of the senior side, now content to ply their trade at a much lower level, continuing to play the game they clearly loved. The most striking aspect, to me, was that of Ralph Astin's pads. They were the first time I had seen the old-fashioned type, with gaps between the protective slats, just like those seen in old illustrations of players from a bygone age! Indeed, this particular teenager became all too quickly aware that he was in the company of one whose past was far more impressive than his own future was likely to be! I played on for another dozen years, before moving to South West Manchester, Denton and Denton West, before retiring in 1988, but I have been a 'Ranger' for well over 50 years now.

Whilst I had become instantly aware of this link with the past, neither I nor any of the others who took to the field that day at Arley Hall could have been aware that it was almost exactly 100 years earlier, April 1861, that the earliest reference to the club, in the Manchester Guardian, was to be found, to an 'Adjourned General Meeting, chaired by H. Dunnill, in the New Schoolroom on Chorlton Road'. I discovered this through reading this first volume of Peter Simpson's club history. Indeed, it was one of the first of hundreds of discoveries I was to make in journeying my way through this most interesting of publications. Discoveries, I am sure, you will enjoy making, too.

Like that of the 1883 appearance on the Whalley Range scoresheet of one F. Delius. Yes, the very Frederick Delius, lover of cricket and music, who was to become one of England's best known composers - if not cricketers! No doubt, his 'On Hearing the First Cuckoo in Spring' held deeper meaning for him than might have met the eye, or ear, of the non-cricketer, heralding, as that beautiful sound still does, the beginning of a new bat-and-ball campaign! Or like that of the author of more than 100 books for boys, Gunby Hadath, who, as well as performing on the College Road ground for Whalley Range, played alongside P.G. Wodehouse and Arthur Conan Doyle at Lord's. And like that of the association with twice former Prime Minister, the Rt. Hon. Sir Robert Peel, through another Whalley Range devotee, the Rev. Robert Peel Willock.

Great names from the world of international cricket, such as Archie McLaren, whose 424 for Lancashire, at Taunton in 1895, is still the highest first-class score by an Englishman; and A. G. Steel, scorer of the first international century at Lord's, find their way into this delightfully detailed history. Sporting grandees from beyond cricket's boundaries, too, have made their contributions to the great story of a great club. Champions from the athletics track, the boxing ring, the fields of rugby, football and lacrosse, all excellent cricketers, too, are highlighted in the coming chapters.

Whalley Range cricket, tennis and lacrosse are decidedly and definitively linked by association with the nearby Hulme Grammar School, provider of so many fine players to the club down the years. Those of note, amongst many others, are dutifully recorded. One I remember was B. C. K. Ballinger, who played his first match in 1933, and was the First XI captain at the time I joined the club, whose pleasant demeanour, allied to a quiet but steadfast determination, made him highly suited to the role. I might have been overawed at playing my first game under Brian Ballinger, a 1st XI 'friendly' at Middlewich during a busy Whit Week in 1962, but for the fact that this highly respected, learned and successful man made one feel completely at home and very much a part of his team. One of the famous Buckland clan, John Buckland, who made his debut in 1939, became a good friend. An outstanding wicket-keeper/batsman, he had time for everyone and was always willing to give useful advice. He was an outstanding lacrosse player who, like his uncle, G. F. Buckland, had done 40 years earlier, picked up an Olympic medal in 1948. I was never more proud than to be able to speak at John's funeral in Wrexham, in 2000.

Walter Stansby, Bill Thornton and Gordon Brookes – he of Brookes' Bakery and Mother's Pride renown – were others who played in the pre-war years, whom I came to know and admire, and were great supporters of the club. It must have been difficult for them and their peers to experience the changes which were, inevitably, to occur in the post-war years. They had joined what was, and had been since its inception, an institution catering for those of high social standing, with success in business, the arts and sport foremost amongst its membership. It is to their credit that they saw the club become more 'open' in its constituency, if not always without some reluctance, with a great degree of acceptance and dignity.

It must be remembered that, until the 1960s, Whalley Range, along with Bowdon CC, didn't play for points, although their respective opponents did so. For all that might be assumed, the club was no less competitive. Any team which overcame 'The Range' certainly had to earn their victory!

Events and occurrences, expertly researched and brilliantly described, remind one that, down the years, there have been good days and not-so-good ones too for the club. For instance, what now for Whalley Range, upon being told, only a few weeks before the 1911 season's start, that their 'home' ground was no longer available to them? What sentence for those guilty of operating, albeit in good faith, an unlawful sweepstakes scheme in 1923? But what joy and celebration on the acquisition of a new, permanent home on Kingsbrook Road, and what relief and gratitude upon receiving vital 'daily bread' from 'Mother's Pride'!

Tragedy reveals itself from time to time. Whether through death following a cycling accident, in the shape of an on-coming train at a level-crossing or by way of suicide, one cannot help but have sympathy for the victims, each of them, once, of Whalley Range. Players and members who lost their lives in the two World Wars, too, are sensitively and respectfully remembered and recalled.

As impressive as any aspect of this publication, perhaps, is the season-by-season detail of matches played, of performances made and even, on occasions, of that ever-present in the cricketer's life, the rain! Such detail, amongst which there exists poignant reference to so many key personalities, contributes to the wonderful kaleidoscope which is Whalley Range Cricket and Lawn Tennis Club.

This is the club of Gaddum, Classen, Woollam and Leroy. It is the club, too, of everyone else whose name, on its behalf, appears within these chapters. It is the club, of course, of many more, including wonderful players and great characters of the post-1945 era whose stories will appear in the next volume of this club's marvellously rich history.

It is Whalley Range!

John Gwynne

Whalley Range – A Social History
by Mike Hill

In the 1830s, Manchester was a world-wide phenomenon: the home of the industrial revolution, the workshop of the world, its factories and mills employing thousands of toiling workers, who lived in generally appalling conditions, packed into an area so concentrated that Cheetham Hill and Chorlton-on-Medlock were pastoral idylls.

One of the many visitors who came to study Victorian Manchester was Karl Marx, at the behest of his fellow German Friedrich Engels. Engels lived out in the countryside in Birch-in-Rusholme, and managed a factory in Manchester, but he was a communist and he wrote in 1844, *The Condition of the Working Class in England*. Published in 1845 – the same year the Gentlemen of Whalley Range played their first cricket matches – it is a visceral read. Manchester had a population of about 400,000, squeezed into what we would call the city centre, and its most notorious slum was Little Ireland, where Oxford Station is. Here in 200 rough-built houses, 4000 bare-footed Irish immigrants eked out a precarious living amidst the stench of the open sewer which was the River Medlock.

Engels describes a world of prostitution (his 'girlfriend' lived in a notorious slum, Angel Meadow, and supplemented her income by selling her favours), alcohol abuse, child labour, health epidemics, low wages, hard graft, and explains the political movements such as Chartism, socialism and so on. He doesn't really spend much time on the capitalist classes, except to note that they make a lot of money and live in grand houses out in the sticks. However, Manchester was a magnet for entrepreneurs and their money from throughout the UK and Europe, who were always looking for a 'deal'.

One of these wealthy capitalists, Samuel Brooks, made his money in banking and in 1836 moved into real estate, buying up for £12,000, 63 acres of land south west of the city, on Jackson's Moss, on the way to the small village of Chorlton-cum-Hardy. Here he laid out a modern estate ready for big houses, including one for himself called Whalley House (the site today of Woodlawn Court's flats). The boggy land had to be drained (it is no surprise that Moss Side, Turn Moss, Rusholme refer to residual dampness!), roads laid out between Withington Road and Upper Chorlton Road, its own police force was raised, and a toll bar was established at Brooks's Bar which took tolls until 1896.

Samuel Brooks had been born in Whalley (pronounced 'Worley' as opposed to our 'Wally'), near Blackburn, hence the name. The attraction to Manchester's growing capitalist class – and Manchester attracted fortune-seekers from across the world let alone the UK – was obvious: fresh, clean air, nice countryside with good shooting, excellent transport links to the city, houses with all the latest mod-cons, and stables for the horses. It was a major success, and later in the century, the main land-owner in the region, Lord Egerton of Tatton, sold a chunk of his land for housing too, between the original estate and the newly laid out Alexandra Park (1871).

Samuel Brooks

Here the houses were slightly smaller, aimed more at the senior manager classes and professionals rather than the owners. So Samuel Mendel built Manley Hall for £120,000 (where Manley Park is now), with two dozen staff for its 50 rooms, but his managers (who worked in Chepstow House in Manchester) might well have lived on Alexandra Road South, in a house with stables, but quarters for just three or four servants.

To the south of Whalley Range was farmland – Whalley Farm, Old Dog House Farm, Old Hall Farm and so on, and vestiges of the old feudal north west – Hough End Hall, and Barlow Hall.

Many of the families who lived in the area at the time WRCC was started in 1845, and gained traction in the '50s and '60s, were wealthy enough to send their sons away to board at the great public schools in the south. The famous Lancashire and England cricketer Archie MacLaren and two of his six brothers, for instance, all born and brought up in Whalley Range, went to Harrow in the 1880s. Samuel Brooks sent his son, later Sir William Cunliffe Brooks, 1st Baronet – barrister, banker and Conservative politician who sat in the House of Commons between 1869 and 1892 – to Rugby. But, as the social make-up of the area started to become more aspiring and professional middle-class, a local school was needed and Hulme Grammar School was founded in 1887, on open fields on Spring Bridge Road.

Catholic emancipation in 1829 allowed Catholicism – never extinguished in the north west – to emerge as a social force, and St. Bede's School on Alexandra Road began in 1878, whilst the Bishops of Salford lived next door. The photo below shows how St. Bede's looks today. By this time, trams were going up and down Alexandra Road and Upper Chorlton Road (the old tram stables are still evident on Range Road, though now flats), trains were going to Chorlton, and there was a stop too where the petrol station is on Mauldeth Road.

A photo of how St. Bede's College looks today

Whalley Range was sometimes known as Little Germany. Even a casual glance at any gazetteer from the latter half of the century will reveal many German names, and you will see them dotted throughout the first chapters of this book. In fact, Our Lady's R. C. Primary School on Whalley Road was partly housed, until the 1990s, in the former Imperial German consulate, seized during the First World War by the Custodian of Enemy Property. But there were also the French, Poles and Italians, as well as Scots, Welsh people and occasionally an Irish family. A recurring theme is the cosmopolitan nature of the area (see below).

Up to the 1st World War, life in Whalley Range for the well-to-do was pretty good. They had their schools, their churches, their sports clubs (tennis clubs abounded after 1874), lots of servants, a new park (at a cost of £60,000), lots of countryside, no nasty beerhouses, no low life, little if any crime and lots of money.

For instance, my house was built in 1900, a year before Victoria died, on the south, less built-up side of Whalley Range. The family name was Mudie, they had five children, and two Irish servants (who lived in the only two rooms without a fireplace). He worked in the family's commercial library (after the 1871 Education Act, and before public libraries, books were borrowed for a penny). His 16 year old son had started in the railway business as a clerk. The next door neighbour, called Hermann Janus, was of

German extraction, and was a shipping agent. His family had one servant. My house has a German connection too: it is called Broda, named after a hamlet in Silesia.

After the 1st World War, as the British Empire recovered partially, the area expanded its housing and most of the gaps between clusters of houses were built on, either with council estates or with private housing. These houses were smaller (no servants), had garages rather than stables, and little gardens rather than grounds. The very big houses became uneconomic to run, and started to be demolished. Hazel Green, a mansion on the College Road was so big, whole streets fitted in its back garden, whilst across the road, the original Whalley Range cricket ground became the Burford Road 'estate'.

Sunnyside, another large mansion on College Road, was the home of the MacLaren family (of whom much more anon), following their move from Royston Lodge, and so for those family members who played cricket for Whalley Range at the time, they lived literally within a cricket throw of the ground. The following graphic illustrates just how massive some of these mansions were, with close to a hundred modern houses now occupying the same ground that contained just a handful of these old mansions and their gardens.

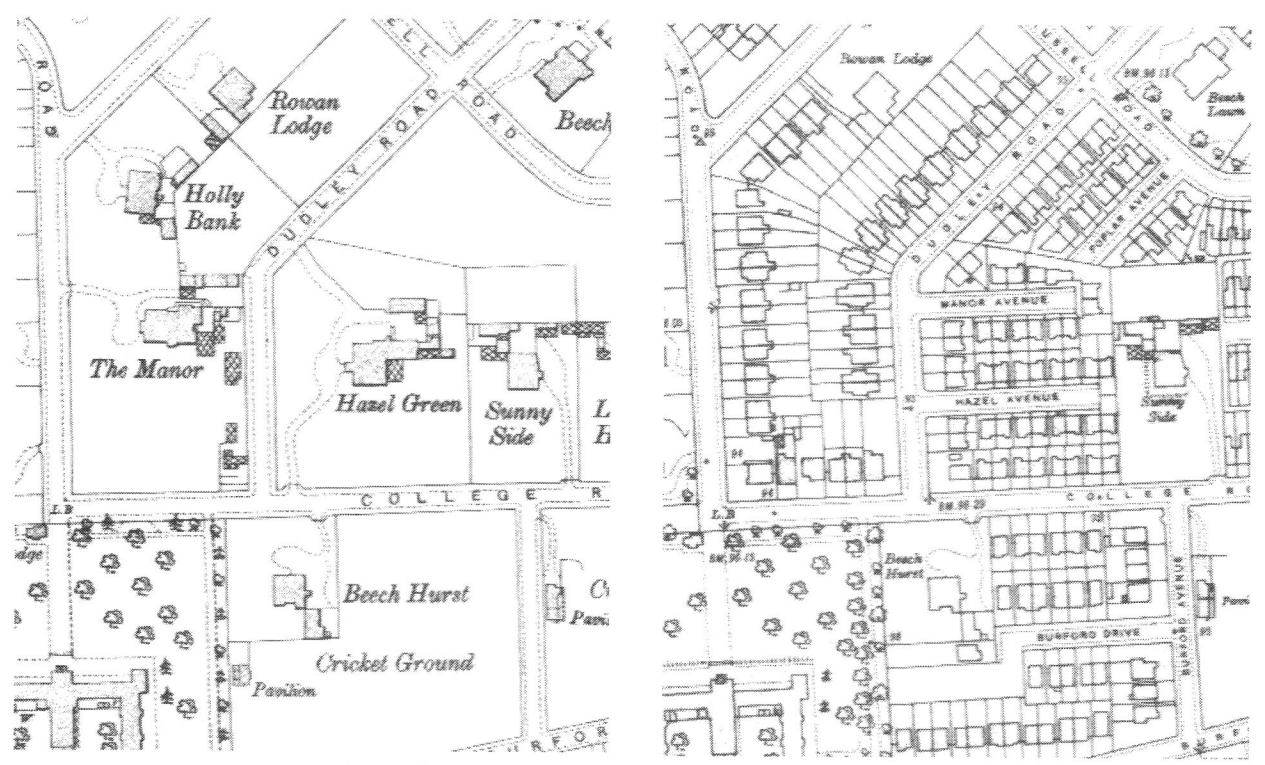

Comparison of College Road in 1907 with that of 1922

Flats also started to appear, such as Woodlawn Court on Wood Road. More schools were built and expanded – Whalley Range High School for Girls, St. Margaret's, Manley Park etc, and terraced houses were also built to house the lower middle-classes who were now as likely to work in Trafford Park as Manchester.

Between the wars, the population rose and was mainly well-off despite the Depression. The quality of life was still good: much of the old farmland became sports fields (St. Bede's PF on Withington Road, St. Margaret's PF on Brantingham Road, and of course Hough End, which was also the site of Manchester's first airport, during and after the First World War). Cars broadened horizons, but there were shops on Alexandra Road, Withington Road, a cinema, a dance hall, and Manley House's grounds were now a park as well as housing (Park Road, obviously). The Edwardian toffs were still around (though their private police force wasn't), all High Church and tennis and cricket, lacrosse and rugger and so on, but they were now rubbing shoulders with a more meritocratic middle-class, and subtly the social make-up was changing.

After the 2nd World War, some but not all of the bomb sites in the area were filled, and some of the bigger houses which fell into disrepair were demolished. The more affluent families started to move out to the modern suburbs beyond the Mersey. Some housing was taken over by landlords who divided the bigger houses up into bed-sits. The intake at William Hulme's Grammar School – as it is now called –

was drawn from a wider catchment area. Students started to move into the area as the University of Manchester grew, and in the '50s and '60s, the influx of post-war Poles and Irish families were joined by immigrants from the West Indies. A school picture at Manley Park in 1952 shows an all-white class, whilst by 1968, at St. Margaret's about a third of the kids were from the Caribbean.

When I moved in to student digs in 1981, on Grosvenor Road, the only pub in the area was The Caught on the Hop, where the Co-op is now on Withington Road. The landlord was Cornelius Ebenezer Delamore, and the clientele was Irish, West Indian and ladies of the night. A longer walk took me to the Seymour, a gigantic pub on the corner of Seymour Grove and Upper Chorlton Road, now flats. The Hop was closed in the early '90s after it was machine-gunned in a drugs war. The Whalley Hotel had its moments, though even this has now closed in recent times. There are other places to get a drink, and it is an urban myth that there can be no licensed premises in the area: Thin Lizzy's lead singer Phil Lynott's mum ran a dodgy drinking club on Withington Road in the '50s and '60s which was patronised allegedly by George Best.

Whalley Hotel

The '70s and '80s saw crime, prostitution, drugs, bail hostels, students, Old People's Homes, and continued middle-class flight. A south east Asian population started to move in too, at first into the small terraced houses around Clarendon Road, and then into the bigger houses in Whalley Range; the popularity of Chorlton amongst young professionals had a knock-on effect on the housing market in Whalley Range (or Chorlton Borders to some estate agents!), and during the boom in the '90s, houses which once were divided into flats were turned back into family houses (my house was part of a Moonies community until 1999). Gentrification had started. Social housing and private developments started to fill in the gaps on Alexandra Road.

Indeed, in 1991, the city council made a large part of Whalley Range a Conservation Area. Most vacant sites have now been built upon and development pressure has more recently turned towards applications for demolition of the old large houses and the subsequent redevelopment of their sites. Designation of the conservation area is aimed at halting this trend and actively encouraging refurbishment of what is left of the fine quality original housing stock. Several buildings in Whalley Range are individually listed by the Department of the Environment (see later).

In the 21st century, the area is generally on the up. The ethnic mix is striking: African as well as Caribbean, Indian as well as Pakistani, Eastern European as well as Western European (note the Gita Bhavan Hindu Temple, the Sikh Gurdwara opened in 2011 at a cost of £2m, the resurgent Catholic churches, the Minhaj-ul-Qur'an Central Mosque on Withington Road, and a British Muslim Heritage Centre on College Road). Over 50 separate languages are spoken in local schools. The socio-economic mix is changing too, with affluent families in houses, young professionals in

Gita Bhavan Hindu Temple

Page 11

apartments, new build on Caistor Close, nursing homes, housing associations, the gated community at the end of Arnold Road, behind Kassim Darwish Grammar School, and so on.

Listed Buildings

The most prominent building in the Whalley Range conservation area is the former Lancashire Independent College on College Road. It is a gothic-style stone building with octagonal tower and pinnacles, completed in 1843. It was converted into a residential college for the General and Municipal Boilermakers' Union, and is now the British Muslim Heritage Centre. The entrance gates and octagonal gate piers are in the same style and are also listed buildings.

St. Bede's College is an ornate red brick and terracotta building in the Italian renaissance style, which incorporates the redundant aquarium building. The eleven bays of the college form an incomplete facade as construction ceased in 1880. A chapel to the rear was added in 1898, followed by several subsequent additions.

St. Edmund's Church is a stone building with a steeply-pitched slate roof. Designed in the geometrical Gothic style, it has paired clerestory windows with tracery. The building typifies the problem of overly large premises for modern use as a church and is now apartments.

The Church of St. Margaret on Whalley Road is a stone building with a slate roof and a tall spire. It was designed in 1843 and consecrated in 1849. The architects were Locker & Newsham with N. T. P. Harrison.

Stucco villas on Withington Road

The three pairs of houses on Withington Road that are numbered 4 to 14 form a distinct group of stucco villas. The central pair are Gothic style with matching Italianate style on either side.

There are many other fine houses of a high quality which were built according to rules and restrictions set by Samuel Brooks and written into the ground leases.

2011 Census and other Information

The Manchester ward of Whalley Range includes part of historical Chorlton, and excludes parts of historical Whalley Range (including, ironically, Whalley Range Cricket and Lawn Tennis Club, the girls' High School and William Hulme's GS), which are in Fallowfield. Nonetheless, the information here is indicative of the area.

The population has risen by 12.8% in 10 years; compared to the population of England and Wales as a whole, there are proportionately more people aged 0 to 4, and 20 to 39, but fewer children and young people aged 10 to 24 and proportionately fewer residents aged 40 and over. When compared to Manchester as a whole, there is a lower proportion of people aged 15 to 34, and 60 to 79. The ward has a higher proportion in the 5 to 9, 25 to 59 and 80 to 84 age groups.

In November 2011, private residential properties accounted for 83.6% of all property, much higher than the City average of 68.7%. In all, 93.1% of properties were occupied, and 21.9% of all properties in Council Tax band C, higher than the City average of 13.7%.

Of those of working age, about 10% are unemployed, 8% are students, 13% self-employed and 69% employed as follows:

Employees 2010	Whalley Range	Manchester
Agriculture, hunting and forestry	0.3%	0.2%
Construction	1.9%	1.8%
Education	22.0%	7.4%
Electricity, gas and water supply	0.0%	0.1%
Financial intermediation	0.1%	5.7%
Health and social work	44.6%	16.2%
Hotels and restaurants	2.7%	9.4%
Manufacturing	2.9%	7.9%
Public administration and defence; compulsory social security	0.2%	1.8%
Real estate, renting and business activities	6.5%	18.8%
Transport, storage and communication	1.9%	8.1%
Wholesale and retail trade; repair of motor vehicles, motorcycles and personal and household goods	6.1%	15.2%
Other*	10.7%	7.4%
TOTAL (number)	2,295	284,480

* includes community, social and personal services activities; private households with employees and extra-terrestrial organisations and bodies

In 2009, it had a much lower proportion of children under the age of 16 in poverty than the Manchester average (26.5% compared to 39.9%), but a higher rate than the average for England as a whole. It is relatively less deprived than other parts of Manchester, although not so much as some other more affluent areas in south Manchester. On most measures of poverty, educational attainment and crime, Whalley Range is better than most of Manchester but slightly worse than the England average.

After all White groups, Pakistani is the second most dominant ethnicity in Whalley Range, making up 21.4% of the population of the area. Indian people account for 6.3% and Black Caribbean people make up 4.3%. Despite the ethnic diversity indicated in the census data, only 23% were born outside the UK.

Mike Hill

Early Days (1845-1878)

Independent Congregational College

In 1843, the Independent Congregational College was opened on the site of Moll's Field adjacent to College Road, Whalley Range. According to previous research now lost, at some point between then and 1845, Sue's Field, situated next to the College, began to be used for playing cricket by the College personnel and the Gentlemen of Whalley Range. As such, it is this year of 1845 that is generally cited as representing the birth of the Whalley Range Cricket Club, though it is highly unlikely the club existed in a format we would recognise today. Previous research also supposedly unearthed match reports in the Manchester Guardian as early as 1850, indicating that cricket was regularly played there, though sadly in these early days, the Manchester Guardian tended only to report on better established clubs such as Broughton, Longsight, Manchester, Sale, Urmston, and Western (Eccles).

As such, with regard to the current research, the earliest discovered mention of the club in the papers is from the Manchester Guardian on 13th April 1861 when there was notice of an 'Adjourned General Meeting' that was to take place in the New School Room on Chorlton Road. As can be seen below, the print is not especially clear, but it is just about discernible that H. Dunnill is listed as the President. It is believed that this is Henry Dunnill, who with business partner John Palmer, was based at 1-3 Bond Street in Manchester (off Mosley Street), and traded as Dunnill, Palmer, and Co. in the book industry in the 1850s and early 1860s.

Earliest discovered article relating to Whalley Range Cricket Club

According to Dr. Samuel Johnson's 1755 Dictionary of English Language, a club is 'an assembly of good fellows meeting under certain conditions', which probably sums up Whalley Range CC in the early and mid-Victorian period. It is doubtful they had 'members' and subscriptions, or a constitution until the 1850s, at which point, current research has illustrated the presence of a President and an Honorary Secretary. Neither of those two men – Dunnill and C. M. Barlow – appear in any of the few team lists we have, so it is possible they took on the administrative duties after their playing days in the late '40s and early '50s (Dunnill was born in 1825). It is likely that a team was raised from amongst the young 'gentlemen' of the area and their weekend guests to play one-off games from time to time, before things started to crystallise in the 1850s. At this stage, most of the working-classes did not really have the leisure time to play the game.

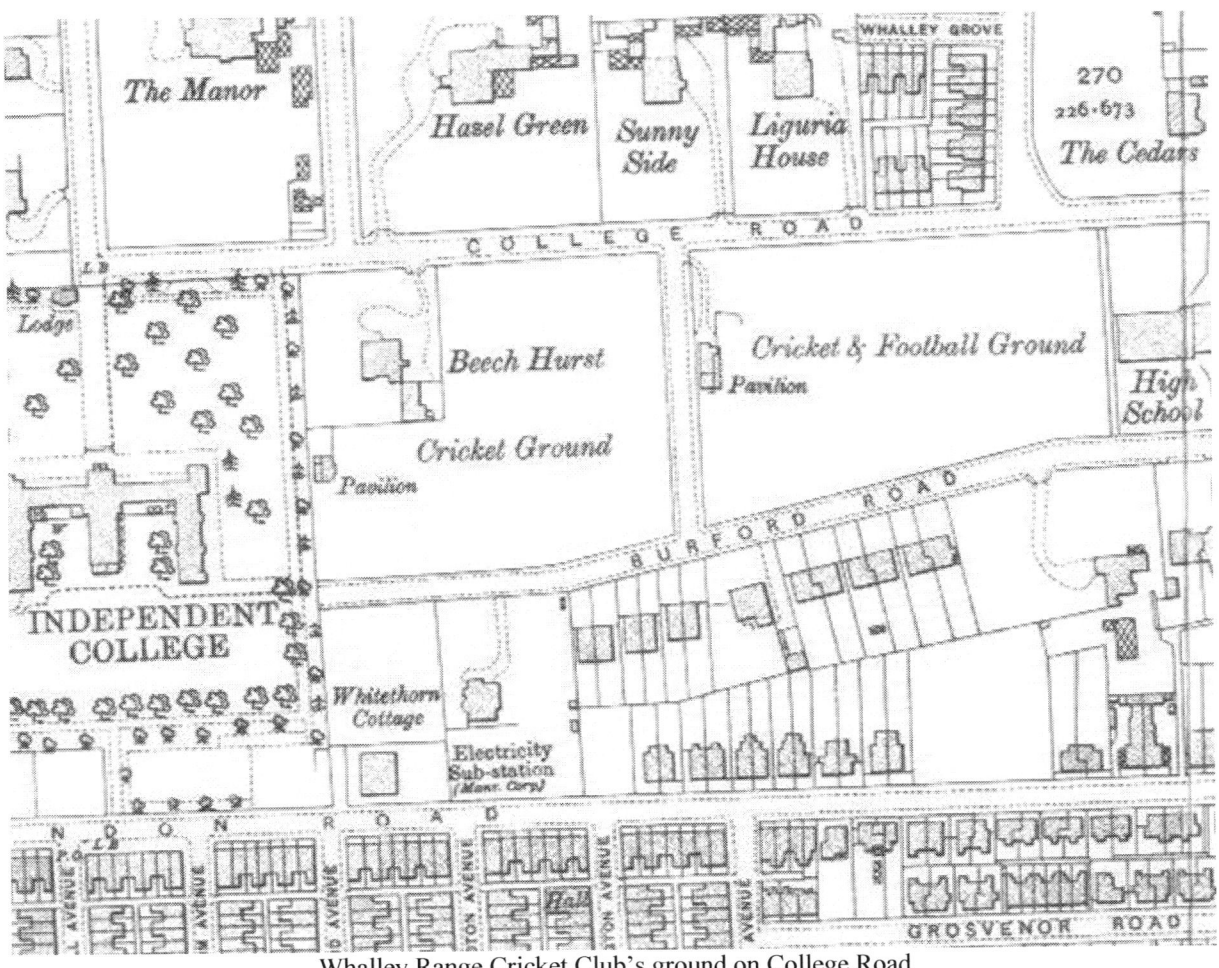

Whalley Range Cricket Club's ground on College Road

This graphic, taken from a map of Whalley Range in 1907, illustrates Whalley Range's cricket ground, situated on College Road, occupying a large part of what used to be Sue's Field, a site that would serve as their home ground for over 50 years, up until the close of the 1910 season. Note that it is the ground on the left that was used by Whalley Range Cricket Club.

It is worth taking a little time here to consider how cricket was played in this period around the middle of the 19th century. Today, we think of cricket being played on manicured squares, smooth-ish outfields and carefully prepared wickets. Modern clubs are well constituted, with regular weekend fixtures, and players have access to cars and usually their own kit. But in 1845, the lawn-mower was a very new and imperfect invention, but since most bowlers were still 'bowling' the ball underarm, a 'proper' wicket was not necessary. Some radical players were bowling round-arm (i.e. arm between hip and shoulder). Even after modern over-arm bowling was legalised in 1864, under-arm (or lob bowling) was still common, last used in a Test Match in 1910.

The outfield may well have been kept short-cropped by sheep. Players would have walked to the ground from their local houses, and some will have come on horseback or in a horse buggy (many large houses in Whalley Range still have evidence of coach houses for horses). For away matches, the horse-drawn buses into and out of town would have been used, and trains taken to some fixtures. There would have been one kit bag (familiar well into the 1970s and '80s), possibly carried by a servant to away games in advance. No wonder games often started at 2.30pm. It is also clear that many players of the time would play for more than one club in the same season. There was a particularly close relationship between Whalley Range and Manchester CC, based two miles away where White City Retail Park is now.

For the 1862 season, the first significant mention of Whalley Range Cricket Club in the local press was by way of the Classified Ads section, when C. M. Barlow, the Club's Honorary Secretary, posted advertisements stating that Whalley Range Cricket Club's opening game would take place on Saturday 12th April. The Manchester Times on Saturday 14th June provides the earliest result of a game involving Whalley Range. It should be borne in mind that the laws of cricket weren't quite as well defined as they are today, with for instance, the better teams often playing against a side comprising as many as twenty two players. Thus, we find the "Sixteen of Whalley Range" up against Didsbury, and despite having five more players than their hosts, Didsbury were victorious by 6 runs (94 v 88).

A few days later on 17th June, the Manchester Guardian reported that Whalley Range beat The Clifford 2nd XI (72 v 29) at the ground of the latter on the Saturday, and on 2nd July reported that they beat Rusholme 2nd XI by over an innings (78 v 20 & 37). One other snippet that was discovered this season was a home game involving the 2nd XI teams of both Whalley Range and Urmston. The print isn't particularly clear, though it would appear to suggest that Urmston won by 3 runs (66 v 63). What is clear though, is that Whalley Range Cricket Club was sufficiently well-established at this time, to be able to field at least two teams, which further encourages the belief that the club was active before 1860.

By 1864, it would appear that the role of Honorary Secretary had been taken up by H. Rodgers, since it was he who posted a Classified Ad announcing that the Annual Meeting of Whalley Range Cricket Club would take place on 27th January at 8pm in the School Room on Chorlton Road. Also in 1864, thankfully Whalley Range played one of the clubs that the local papers reported on, and so the following scorecard printed on 7th June provides the first evidence of the Whalley Range line-up.

Sale v Whalley Range, at Sale, June 1864

Whalley Range			Sale		
Marshall	c H. Allen	4	E. Ogden	b Dunkerly	15
Mitchell	b R. Turner	0	H. Allen	b Dunkerly	3
C. Wright	c H. Allen	5	G. Jones	b Colburn	4
H. Rodgers	b R. Turner	3	A. Ollivant	b Dunkerly	9
J. Dunkerly	b R. Turner	0	R. Turner	b Colburn	22
C. Colburn	not out	27	C. Barlow	b Dunkerly	2
H. Carver	run out	12	H. Hines	b Colburn	2
J. McLaren	c Barlow	2	E. W. Woollaston	b Dunkerly	7
J. Ludlow	b R. Turner	0	W. Turner	b Dunkerly	0
Whittaker	c A. Ollivant	0	R. Anderson	b Marshall	3
Nicholson	run out	3	A. Royle	not out	4
B 8, w 4		12	B 8, w 5, lb 1		14
Total		68	Total		85

There are a few things to note about the scoresheet. Firstly, the concept of declaring an innings was yet to materialise, and in fact wouldn't do so for another quarter of a century. Thus, weather and time permitting, the team batting first would always continue until they were all out. Likewise, the team batting second would also continue to bat until the whole team was dismissed, regardless of whether the opposition total had been surpassed or not. Matches were generally won by 'number of runs', with Sale winning by 17 runs, despite batting second. Not only would this provide more opportunity for more players to get a bat, but would allow teams to bat a second time in the event that both first innings finished early.

In the Sale line-up is Alfred Ollivant who went on to play a couple of games for Lancashire a decade later. Also worthy of note is the fact that J. Dunkerly (also spelt Dunkerley elsewhere) captured six wickets for Whalley Range. However, the most important aspect to note about the scoresheet, is the name of J. McLaren. Spelling didn't appear to be the biggest of concerns of sub-editors in these days, but this is in fact James MacLaren, who would go on to become an important figure in cricket, not least because of one of the children he'd father a few years hence.

The MacLaren Family

Like Samuel Brooks who created the Whalley Range area, James MacLaren (1845-1900) was also a success in the cotton industry, having inherited his father's business. When he was 19, he married Emily Carver, and they lived together in a large house called Royston Lodge in Whalley Range. The scoresheet dates from around this time, and as can be seen, there is also an H. Carver in the Whalley Range line-up.

Archibald Campbell MacLaren

In later years, James served as honorary treasurer to the Lancashire County Cricket Club for the best part of two decades, from 1881 until his death in 1900. He was also fond of rugby, helping establish the renowned Manchester Rugby Club, before going on to hold the position of President of the Rugby Union committee in 1882. However, as mentioned previously, his major contribution to the world of cricket was through one of his sons. James and Emily's first son was born on 4th January 1870, and as tradition dictated, was given the name James, or James Alexander MacLaren, to give him his full title. This latest James would go on to play cricket not only for Whalley Range, but would also represent Lancashire as well, as would one of the later sons, Geoffrey.

However it would be the second of their seven sons who would make the biggest impact, and leave an indelible mark on the cricketing world. Archibald Campbell MacLaren was born on 1st December 1871, and would go on to captain not only his county at cricket but also his country. In 1895, he produced one of the most stunning innings ever, amassing 424 when captaining Lancashire against Somerset. Prior to Archie's monumental effort, the highest individual score had been W. G. Grace's 344. Thus, this was the first time ever that a batsman had registered a quadruple-hundred, and to this day, is still the record score ever made by an Englishman, and what's more, an Englishman who was born in Whalley Range!

Perhaps passed down by word of mouth over several generations of cricketers, local folklore suggested that Archibald Campbell MacLaren had also played for Whalley Range Cricket Club. After all, he'd definitely been born in Whalley Range, and it was certainly known that other members of his family had played for the club down the years. Unfortunately, no concrete evidence appeared to exist to prove conclusively whether he had indeed graced the College Road ground. However it wouldn't be too long, before the research for this book would be yielding the truth behind the myth!

Sixteen of Whalley Range v Didsbury, at Whalley Range, July 1864

Whalley Range

Burd		b T. Nelson	0
McLaren	c Dodgson	b Saul	0
H. Carver	c Dodgson	b Saul	2
Macalister		b Henderson	14
Pearn		b Saul	0
Dunkerley		b T. Nelson	12
Marshall		st Crosbie	3
C. Carver		run out	1
Rowarth		b T. Nelson	2
Whittaker		b T. Nelson	0
Piercy		b T. Nelson	1
Sudlow		b Capes	16
Tarr	lbw	b Capes	3
Darwent		b Crosbie	0
Foster	c J. Nelson	b Capes	0
Suttle		not out	0
B 15, w 10			25
Total			79

Didsbury

J. Nelson		b Macalister	26
Birley		b C. Carver	1
Henderson		b Carver	3
Dodgson	c Carver	b Macalister	12
T. W. Nelson		not out	13
Saul		not out	9
B 5, lb 12			17
Total		(for 4)	81

Returning back to the 1864 season, it seems like Whalley Range Cricket Club weren't quite yet a force to be reckoned with. In the two other matches that got reported on this season, with both being played at Whalley Range, one was where their 1st XI were only up against the 2nd XI of Pendleton, though it was a match they won based on first innings scores (54 v 48), whilst for the second innings scores it is not clear whether the hosts scored 16 or 46, to which Pendleton replied with 25-3, thus possibly implying the lower total. As the previous scoresheet shows, the other game was another battle where the 'Sixteen of Whalley Range' still didn't have sufficient numbers to outmuscle a strong Didsbury team that included the classy Nelson brothers, John and Thomas Walker. This match, reported on 12th July 1864, is the earliest discovered scoresheet of a match actually played at Whalley Range. The following season, John Nelson would score a century at Old Trafford against the powerful Manchester team (that he himself often represented). As will be seen, playing at Old Trafford in front of large crowds against the Manchester and Clifford teams, was a privilege bestowed on several local clubs, including Whalley Range. A few years later, John Nelson would marry Alice Campbell Rowley, daughter of Alexander Butler Rowley, though it was a union that would eventually end in divorce. The Rowley family who feature a few times throughout the coming chapters were very important figures in the history of Lancashire CCC, with no fewer than six brothers representing the various incarnations of the county team in their embryonic years.

For the following season, again very little of Whalley Range cricket managed to make the local papers, with just two results being printed, both of which illustrated defeats. The first of these saw Whalley Range 2nd XI lose to Bowdon 2nd XI by 44 runs (79 v 35) in mid-July, whilst a week later the 1st XI responded with 37 to Sale's total of 92.

In early May 1866, another clash with Sale, played at Whalley Range, provided the next opportunity to view the Whalley Range line-up, with just three players playing in this game who'd also appeared in the Sale fixture two seasons previously, namely Mitchell, MacLaren, and Whittaker. The rest of the team comprised H. Allen, S. Burd, MacEwen, Marriott, Pearn, Rowarth, Suttle, and Worrall, with Sale again being victorious (77 v 67). For Whalley Range, only opener Mitchell and Pearn made double-figures, whilst the wickets were shared between MacLaren and Suttle, who each captured three wickets, Allen who took two, Pearn who took one, with the other Sale wicket being a 'run out'.

For the return game in July, played at Sale, the Whalley Range batsmen again failed to make much of an impression, with just Allen, coming in at number ten, making double-figures. As such, Whalley Range's total of 45 was easily surpassed by Sale, who went on to make 97. In addition to Allen, the team again comprised Burd, Pearn, Rowarth, Suttle, and Worrall. The rest of the team comprised Beckett, Laurie, Rickards, Sewell, and Wilson. The main wicket-takers were Pearn and Rowarth, who each took three, Suttle who took two, with the remaining wickets being claimed by Allen and Beckett (who is possibly J. H. Beckett who appears as Hon. Treasurer in the 1884 team photo).

Sadly, little else came to light this season, other than another couple of defeats. The first of these was the week following the first Sale clash, when Levenshulme on their home ground beat Whalley Range by 12 runs (90 v 78), and then the following week, in another away game, Whalley Range scored 40 and 28-8, whilst Pendleton totalled 75. For the 1867 season, it seems like Whalley Range were still commanding very little local press coverage with just one result managing to be discovered. This was a game played at Whalley Range in July, with the 2nd XI losing to Levenshulme 2nd XI by 28 runs.

Rowan Lodge and the Marriott family

The Marriott name continued to appear in line-ups for the Whalley Range team from 1866 to 1874, though only once was an initial provided, with an 1869 scoresheet featuring the name of H. Marriott. This is undoubtedly Hail Marriott, who was born in 1845 in London, and was the eldest son of Elizabeth and Henry Raine Marriott. The family moved up north in about 1850, where Henry Raine Marriott set up his own "home-trade" business in Manchester city centre, and also at the same time commenced a cotton-spinning business in Stockport. The following years would see H. R. Marriott prosper well, establishing himself as a much respected and successful member of the Manchester business scene, becoming a life governor of the Royal Institution, a director of the Union Bank, and a member of the Manchester Chamber of Commerce. He was for many years one of the principal members and some time churchwarden of St. Margaret's Church in Whalley Range. The Marriott family were also keen on sports, and when Manchester Lacrosse Club was formed on July 5th 1876, not only was Henry Raine Marriott their first ever President, but one of his sons, Percy Henry Marriott, was also on the committee (and later became one of the vice-presidents for Whalley Range Cricket club). Another of his sons was Ernest Edward Marriott, born

on January 15th 1857, and he went on to play rugby for England on December 13th 1875 against Ireland in Dublin. It is certainly possible that he also represented the Whalley Range cricket team, though without further corroborative evidence in the way of initials, this is not something that can be established for definite. Another son, Lewis Herbert Marriott, played rugby for the Manchester club. The 1871 Census shows the Marriott family to be residing at Rowan Lodge in Whalley Range, which can be seen in the map illustrations depicted earlier in the book. Henry Raine Marriott died in 1875, though the 1911 Census shows that Rowan Lodge was still in the occupation of the Marriott family with Percy Henry Marriott now living there with wife Mary Louisa and son Robert Denis. The ensuing photo shows how Rowan Lodge looks today, and as can be seen now forms part of the Carlton Social & Bowling Club :-

Rowan Lodge pictured today

As for the only member of the Marriott family that is known definitely played cricket for the Whalley Range club, Hail Marriott married Louisa Brook from Lincolnshire in 1870, and they later moved to the Ormskirk area, though sadly he was to die fairly young, aged just 39.

Fortunately for the 1868 season, the Manchester Guardian decided to devote a bit more attention to Whalley Range Cricket Club, and did so at an interesting stage in its history. On 28th April 1868, the Manchester Guardian provides the scoresheet of a Whalley Range team that lost against Cheetham Hill, and on 2nd June, reports on another Whalley Range defeat, this time to Longsight 2nd XI. Both games were played at Whalley Range, and though the print is not especially clear, it would appear that the home team managed just 28 in each of the games, to lose both matches fairly heavily. Later on in the season, on 1st August, the Manchester Guardian provides a scoresheet of a team called Manchester Athletic Cricket Club (who played Worsley in a game played on a Wednesday) with a similar looking line-up to that of the Whalley Range team that lost to Cheetham Hill at the start of the season, with both line-ups containing the likes of Allen, F. D. Broughton, Carver, and a certain C. G. Hulton.

The first mention of Manchester Athletic Club was at least four years previously, when it looks like its main purpose back then was indeed to cater for Athletics. However by 1868, it is clear from all of the available evidence, that not only had this Athletic Club expanded to include various other sports sections, such as rugby, but had also encapsulated what was previously the Whalley Range Cricket Club. This is further corroborated by the almost complete lack of any mention of Whalley Range Cricket Club for a number of years after 1868. Instead, we see mention of the Athletic Cricket Club in various guises, with the cricket team being listed as either Manchester Athletic, Whalley Range Athletic, or sometimes just plain Athletic, though the team's composition and the home venue being Whalley Range, would clearly indicate that this was still the Whalley Range Cricket Club. As such, the result printed on July 14th 1868 in the Manchester Guardian shows the earliest known three-figure total thus far unearthed of a Whalley Range team, with Manchester Athletic Cricket Club scoring 171 in reply to Bowdon's 61 in a game played at Whalley Range.

The Whalley Range scoresheet against Cheetham Hill at the start of the 1868 season comprised some more of the Carver clan, with both F. Carver and A. J. Carver appearing in the line-up. The former of these is Frederick William Carver, born in 1850, who married Isabella MacLaren, the sister of James MacLaren, who as mentioned earlier, married Emily Carver. Clearly a case of keeping it in the family! A. J. Carver is Alfred John Carver, born in 1853. Note that over the coming years, another F. Carver started playing, namely Frank Henton Carver, born in 1855.

The Rugby Connection

England XX for the world's first ever rugby international in 1871

Keeping with the theme of family connections, another MacLaren appearing for the cricket team in the 1869 season was William MacLaren, a cousin of James. William was born in Chorlton in 1844, and like James, was keen on both cricket and rugby. In fact, William has the distinction of playing for England in the world's first ever rugby international!

The match took place against Scotland on March 27th 1871 in Edinburgh, at Raeburn Place, which was the home ground of Edinburgh Academicals, the oldest rugby club in Scotland, having been formed in 1857. The game attracted 4000 spectators, with Scotland winning 1-0. On first glance, this would appear to be an unusual and low-scoring result for a game of rugby but the rules for scoring back then were completely different. In fact, only converted tries counted as a goal, i.e. one point in effect, with unconverted tries only coming into the reckoning in the event of the goal tally being equal. Throughout the game, England did score a try, but since they missed the conversion, then this counted for nothing, whilst Scotland crossed over the goal-line twice, one of which they managed to convert, to thus emerge victorious by a solitary goal.

Other rules for the game, were that each team comprised 20 players, and was played over two halves, with each half lasting 50 minutes. As well as William MacLaren, there were also three others from the Manchester Football Club representing England that day, namely Arthur Sumner Gibson, Richard Osborne, and Henry John Cecil Turner. This is the famous Manchester Club that William's cousin, James MacLaren, helped established in 1860, and whose home ground at this time was in Whalley Range, regularly attracting several thousand spectators. It is believed that this ground was on Chorlton Road, and so should not be confused with the College Road ground in Whalley Range used by the Manchester Athletic rugby and cricket teams. The photo shows the England team who played on this historic day, in the world's first ever rugby international. A number of Whalley Range cricketers played county and international rugby over the next decade, a further confirmation of the predominantly public school background of the membership.

The ensuing scoresheet from mid-June 1869 features both MacLarens, and was played against the Manchester Club at Old Trafford. As alluded to earlier, one of the fixtures that became firmly entrenched in the calendar back then, was that against the prestigious Manchester team, formed in 1816, who were one of the early forerunners of what was to become Lancashire County Cricket Club in 1864. Apart from the MacLaren cousins, the scoresheet contains some other notable personnel. As already mentioned, someone who represented the Whalley Range outfit during this period was a certain C. G. Hulton (or Campbell Arthur Grey Hulton to give him his full title), an extraordinary fellow of some standing, being a direct descendant of King Henry VII. Later this season (mid-August 1869), he would be making his debut for Lancashire (opening the batting against Sussex), and would follow this up with seven further appearances for his county over the ensuing decade or so, whilst also serving on the committee at one point. Having been born in Manchester on March 16th 1846, and lived a lot of the time in Whalley Range (close to the cricket ground in a house called "The Cedars" on College Road – see map earlier in this chapter), most of his cricket around this time was played for Cheetham Hill and the Manchester club, though he was still playing the odd game for Whalley Range up until 1887. Notably he was also the godfather of Archie MacLaren, thus providing Archie with his middle name. Later in life he moved down south, where amazingly he represented the Marylebone Cricket Club up until the outbreak of the First World War, by which time he was well into his late sixties. He was also a fine rugby player, and according to one report, also represented his county at this sport as well, as did J. H. Hulton.

Manchester v Athletic, at Old Trafford, June 1869

Manchester

R. Swire	c Grave	b Allen	69
C. Mason		b Allen	7
J. Midwood	hit wicket	b Grave	0
W. P. Woodcock		b Grave	24
E. Hulton		b Grave	29
E. Challender	c &	b Hulton	5
J. B. Huntingdon	c McLaren	b Allen	3
W. R. Hanley		not out	17
T. Gorton		b Allen	2
P. Okell	c Fox	b Allen	0
R. Page		b Allen	9
Extras			8
Total			173

Athletic

C. S. Watson		b Hulton	0
H. Allen	c &	b Woodcock	4
C. G. Hulton		b Swire	46
W. Grave		b Swire	41
A. P. McEwen		b Swire	0
C. J. Holliday		run out	13
J. Suttle		b Swire	10
W. McLaren	st Mason	b Hulton	4
J. McLaren	c Page	b Swire	17
W. Fox		run out	1
J. Hulton		not out	4
Extras			25
Total			165

Also appearing is one William Grave, who was born in Manchester in 1848, the second son of (Alderman) John Grave, who was Mayor of Manchester between 1868 and 1871. William was also a noted rugby player, and would represent his county in 1870, and also play for the North of England team, against the South. When the Lancashire Football (i.e. Rugby) Union was later formed in 1880, William Grave was appointed as the inaugural Hon. Sec. and Treasurer, further augmenting the Whalley Range connection, since William MacLaren was the first president!

Following the defeat by Manchester, the local press managed to capture a few other games this season, against Sale, Cheetham Hill, Hornets, and Pendlebury, none of which resulted in victory either, until their encounter with nine men of Worsley, a game which the Manchester Athletic Club, with a full complement of 11 won easily. In this particular match, the Whalley Range team featured three of the MacLaren clan, with a young David Bannerman MacLaren (born in 1853) now appearing alongside his elder brother James, and his cousin William, though coming in at number 11, he failed to trouble the scorers. Later in life, true to family tradition, he too would excel at rugby, by representing his county.

For whatever reason, Whalley Range cricket barely appeared on the radar in 1870, with just one game being reported on, a 24-run defeat to Swinton (49 v 25), that was played at Whalley Range. For the following season, Manchester Athletic made slightly more of an impression, with the results of games against Hulme (twice), Worsley, Kersal, St. Margaret's (probably the local parish church), and Manchester Clifford 2nd XI, appearing in the local press.

In the first encounter with Hulme, the print is too unclear to determine the opposition total. Sadly, the Athletic total did not benefit from such similar obfuscation, as the home team managed just 20, one of their lowest ever 1st XI totals that has come to light. For the game with Kersal in early August, the hosts were listed as "Kersal, with Baker" presumably implying that Baker had been drafted in either as a guest or professional, but despite his seven wickets, Manchester Athletic still emerged victorious, if only by a few runs. For this game, the scoresheet was provided, showing the line-up comprised, in order, J. Turner, S. Smith, G. Elliott, A. Smith, H. Carver, H. N. Pope, Mantle, W. Donald, E. Worrall, A. Leigh, and R. Walker. It seems like the stars of the team were Turner and Walker, since they were the only two to reach double figures, and between them, they captured all but one of the Kersal wickets, with Turner taking five, and Walker claiming four, whilst S. Smith, who also took two catches, captured the other wicket. It is certainly possible that R. Walker is Roger Walker, who played a couple of cricket games for Lancashire, and who also played international rugby for England, but sadly, there is not enough corroborating evidence to be able to ascertain this for definite.

Mentioned in the previous paragraph, H. N. Pope is Henry Newbery Pope, who was born in 1847 in Yeovil in Somerset. His father, Thomas Pope, was the owner of a farm in Cotleigh near Honiton, occupying 250 acres close to the Devon and Somerset border, and when his father passed away in 1876, control of the farm passed down to Henry. However, for a few years in the early 1870s, he moved up north, and during this time represented the team from Whalley Range. After returning back down south, he married Frances Ann Newbery in December 1876, and continued enjoying playing cricket for the Honiton team, and once represented the Seaton team in a game against the MCC in 1881. He became a well-known and respected figure in Devon, before passing away in 1918, aged 70.

For the following two seasons, the Athletic team again failed to warrant much press attention, with just three results being discovered in 1872 and two in 1873. The first of these was a narrow win at Sale (59 v 56), whilst the others in 1872 illustrated defeat to a team calling themselves 'The Owls', and then late in the season, in a game played at Old Trafford, they were put to the sword by Manchester Clifford who scored 193, whilst Athletic managed just 41 runs. The results for 1873 showed a heavy defeat at Didsbury in May, but the other illustrated a handsome win at Kersal in June, with Athletic scoring 110 before removing their hosts for just 37.

In the first game of the 1874 season, Athletic were actually involved in a tied game at home against Rusholme with both sides being all out for 99. As it transpired, this season would see the team commanding a lot more press coverage than in recent seasons, perhaps due in part to their fine batting display against the Manchester Club at Old Trafford, in a 12-a-side game the following Saturday. Though they would go on to lose, batting first, Manchester Athletic posted a commendable 153 with H. E. Carter top-scoring with 42, whilst B. Smith also contributed well with 36. The full complement of 12 consisted of J. M. Cowie, R. Butterworth, H. E. Carter, B. Smith, F. H. Carver, W. O. Matteson, F. W. Carver, P. W. Kessler, D. MacLaren, A. Jameson, S. Smith, and J. Turner. Born on 15th October 1853, P. W. Kessler is Philip William Kessler, a man who went on to prosper well in life, since the 1911 Census went on to list him as a Managing Director, with no fewer than four servants – namely a housemaid, a sewing maid, a parlour maid, and a cook. Later in the book it will be discovered that he had an important association with one of the more famous people who would represent the Whalley Range club, and can also be seen pictured as captain in the 1884 team photo. Born on 17th December 1854, W. O. Matteson is William Ord Matteson who back in 1871 had attended Cheltenham College and had the dubious privilege of competing against an MCC side that included Edward Mills Grace, brother of W. G. Grace.

Also mentioned in the previous paragraph is H. E. Carter, who was also a fine rugby player, and played for the Manchester Rugby Club. He also excelled at lacrosse and played in the first ever game that was played in the area between two officially organised local clubs, captaining Manchester against Broughton in January 1877. A couple of seasons later, Reverend C. C. Carter, his elder brother, would also represent the Athletic Cricket Club. They were the two youngest of 13 children, with Charles Clement Carter born on 14th June 1850 and Henry Ernest Carter (known as Harry) born on 15th April 1854, in Old Malton, Yorkshire. Charles Clement Carter played cricket for Gentlemen of Yorkshire, Cheshire, and Gentlemen of Cheshire, once playing alongside Harry for Gentlemen of Cheshire in July 1877. However, the Reverend C. C. Carter would die at the age of just 31 from consumption, on 29th November 1881, having already come close to death when he was shipwrecked in the English Channel on his way to Australia for a period of convalescence a few years earlier. Tragically, Harry Carter would also die young, on 25th February 1886, also at the age of 31.

Huyton v Athletic, at Huyton, May 1874

Huyton 1st innings				2nd innings		
E. S. Eccles	c Matteson	b Kessler	2		b Cowie	3
C. Johnson	c Smith	b Cowie	13		b Cowie	9
A. Bean		b Kessler	23	c Richardson	b Matteson	0
Pugh		b Cowie	3	c Richardson	b Cowie	1
H. Rigby	c Kessler	b Cowie	2		b Cowie	12
J. Harrison		b Cowie	13	c Richardson	b Matteson	28
E. Jackson	c Carver	b Matteson	1		b Kessler	1
Wainwright	c Kessler	b Cowie	1		b Cowie	24
Cooper		not out	4	c &	b Kessler	11
Speed		b Kessler	0		not out	1
G. Towsey		b Kessler	5	c Bulteel	b Cowie	0
Extras			24	Extras		8
Total			91	Total		98

	Athletic 1st innings			2nd innings		
E. Bulteel		b Rigby	1		b Rigby	0
R. Butterworth		b Rigby	3		not out	8
F. H. Carver		b Rigby	15		not out	4
E. P. Bowden-Smith		b Rigby	6			
W. O. Matteson	c Harrison	b Towsey	10			
H. Richardson		b Rigby	26			
J. M. Cowie	c Pugh	b Rigby	21			
P. W. Kessler		b Rigby	4			
A. M. Bulteel		b Rigby	0			
H. N. Pope		not out	0		b Harrison	2
G. H. Wood		b Rigby	0	c Jackson	b Harrison	18
Extras			4	Extras		5
Total			90	Total	(for 3)	37

The previous scoresheet is of a game against Huyton in May 1874, and provides the earliest evidence unearthed of the Bulteel brothers, Edward and his younger more noteworthy sibling Andrew Marcus, playing for the team from Whalley Range. The Bulteel family was of Huguenot descent and had arrived in England from France in the 1600s. Andrew Marcus Bulteel was born in September 1850 in Liverpool, the fourth child and second son of Andrew Hume Bulteel and his wife Catherine Chartres, with Edward having been born a couple of years earlier. The Bulteel family then moved to Chorlton-on-Medlock in Manchester. Similar to quite a few of the Athletic personnel, Andrew Marcus enjoyed rugby as well as cricket, and played not only for the Manchester Rugby club, but also represented England against Ireland in a 20-a-side rugby international, played on December 13th 1875 at Rathmines in Dublin, playing alongside Ernest Edward Marriott, in what transpired to be their one and only appearance for England, for both of them. Sadly, A. M. Bulteel died aged just 38, in Melbourne, Australia.

Also featured in this same scoresheet is Edmund Philip Bowden-Smith who was educated at Rugby School (where his father, Rev. Philip Bowden-Smith, was Assistant Master for 43 years) and once played for them at Lord's in a game against the MCC a couple of years earlier. Born in 1854, the eldest of 12 children, he went on to have a successful military career, rising to the rank of Colonel. He was also the uncle of Brigadier Philip Ernest "Bogey" Bowden-Smith CBE, who served as a cavalry officer in the British Army and was described as "one of the finest horsemen of his generation". It was these equestrian skills that saw "Bogey" representing Great Britain at the 1924 Olympics, and at the 1936 Olympics in Berlin, where as captain of the equestrian team he led them to a bronze medal in the team eventing competition. As for E. P. Bowden-Smith, it appears that he played just the one season for the Athletic cricket team. In 1881 at Wickham in Hampshire, in a marriage service conducted by his father, he married Kate Mary Moore-Miller. He lived until the age of 76, before passing away in South Kensington in Middlesex, in 1931.

Another notable name that featured during the 1874 season was that of Henry Worrall, whose elder brother Edward had also previously represented the club. Henry was born in Salford in 1851 to Henry and Martha Worrall. In April 1899, he was one of the founding members (and later Chairman of Directors) of the English Velvet and Cord Dyers' Association Ltd., which was incorporated for the purpose of amalgamating fourteen firms (including his own, Ordsall Dye Works) engaged locally in the cotton velvet and corduroy dyeing industry. Thus, Henry Worrall certainly became a very successful man in the business scene, and used his wealth very altruistically, helping establish the "Henry Worrall Infant School for Deaf Children" in Old Trafford. However he doesn't appear to have been as fortunate in his personal affairs. During the 1874 season he played alongside Arthur Benjamin Rickards (who worked as a solicitor in Manchester before moving down south to apply the same trade in the capital), and in 1878 married his twin sister, Louisa Rickards. It didn't prove to be the happiest of marriages though, and in 1895 he filed for divorce *"by reason of his wife's alleged misconduct with the Rev. Hugh William Jones, formerly curate of St. Mary's, Hulme"*! Strangely enough, it seems that divorces ran in the Rickards family, with Arthur Benjamin also getting divorced around this time. With regard to the cricket, Henry Worrall would later become President of the Whalley Range club between 1904 and 1914. Having re-married, he passed away in June 1939, aged in his late eighties.

The highest reported Athletic total that was discovered during the 1874 season was 171, against Rusholme who themselves were dismissed for just 31. However the best performance, certainly from an individual perspective, came in late June in the game against Heaton Norris Club & Ground (though note that they were also labelled as Heaton Chapel on the scoresheet), who were dismissed for 48 with J. M.

Cowie the main destroyer with eight wickets. Cowie also helped in one of the other dismissals by taking a catch off the bowling of Swan. John McRae Cowie would go on to become a fine servant for the Whalley Range club, representing them for the next quarter of a century. His brother, Thomas Scott Cowie, also played for the club at this time. It then looks like the team finished the season on a high, beating Manchester Clifford at home in September, dismissing the visitors for just 41, having posted 73 themselves.

The 1875 season was another that failed to make much of an impression on the local press, with just four results being printed for the 1st XI and one for the 2nd XI. The 2nd XI game was played in June at Bowdon, where the team from Whalley Range emerged as comfortable winners (122 v 65). At the same time, there was an equivalent 1st XI game at home against Bowdon that made the local press, but sadly the print is too unclear to ascertain the result. In August at Whalley Range, the Athletic team handsomely beat Rusholme (147 v 75), and then a week later on the same ground beat Alderley (128 v 70). The final result that was discovered was a game in September against 20th Regiment, again at home, where the opposition responded with 97-4 to the 136 posted by the Athletic team.

The following season commanded far greater coverage in the local press, and early in the year, on February 19th 1876, the following advertisement appeared in the Manchester Courier, with the upper-casing presumably indicative of the fact that the job description was quite definitely 'groundsman' as opposed to 'groundswoman' or 'boy'!

Wanted by the Athletic Cricket Club, Whalley Range, for the coming season a MAN to keep their ground in order, one with a knowledge of cricket preferred.

One of the early encounters of the season was at Old Trafford against the powerful Manchester team who, despite Cowie removing one of their openers for a duck, went on to total 147. In reply, most of the Athletic team were clearly awestruck by such salubrious surroundings, with seven of them being out for a duck, whilst two others each only made four. The team were saved from complete disaster thanks to M. J. Stewart who scored 23, and J. M. Cowie who also scored (an unbeaten) 23. Perhaps the Athletic team could take some comfort from the fact that the Manchester team comprised at least two players who'd represented the Whalley Range outfit in the past (and would do so again in the future), James MacLaren and C. G. Hulton, and as it happens, someone else who'd represent them in the future, namely Thomas Percy Bellhouse.

Athletic v 7th Hussars, at Whalley Range, May 1876

Athletic				7th Hussars			
Knapp		b Spencer	2	Lieut Graham-Smith	c Low	b Carter	9
Crankshaw		b Spencer	0	Private Barker		b Carter	0
Stewart		b Spencer	25	Lieut Phipps		b Low	26
Kessler	c Jones	b Spencer	13	Lieut Ridley	c Carter	b Low	0
Carter	c Hunt	b Spencer	7	Lieut Roper		b Carter	2
H. Carver	c &	b Spencer	3	Capt Hunt		b Carter	2
Hudson	c Baird	b Jones	8	Corp Spencer		not out	4
F. Carver		b Spencer	1	Lieut Morison		b Carter	0
Low		not out	13	Lieut Baird		b Low	0
Bowman		b Spencer	19	Private Jones		b Low	0
Pattison		b Ridley	10	Hon R. Lawley		b Low	0
Extras			18	Extras			9
Total			119	Total			52

The previous scoresheet illustrates a game this season against 7th Hussars, where not content with each taking five wickets, J. C. Low and Carter took the only catches as well. This provided the opportunity for 7th Hussars to bat a second time, and this time they fared slightly better, scoring 66. The team from Whalley Range were thus victorious by an innings and 1 run.

Stewart appeared to be main star with the bat in 1876, scoring 47 in a 34-run win over Free Wanderers (140 v 106), 35 not out in the second innings against Huyton, and 68 in a 26-run victory at Birkenhead Park. He also scored 40 out of a total of 90 against Manchester Clifford in another game played at Old Trafford, with David MacLaren now playing for the opposition. J. M. Cowie was another batsman to notch a half century this season with 54 in the return game with Manchester Clifford. Cowie was also one of the two main stars with the ball, along with H. E. Carter, who together monopolised affairs in the field in the first innings against 7th Hussars. There were several other occasions where one or other, or sometimes both, captured five wickets, and in the match with Lymm in June, Carter took eight wickets as Lymm were bowled out for 67 in reply to Athletic's 79.

As alluded to earlier, Reverend C. C. Carter also played for the club this season. In fact, it seems that the club attracted quite a few men of the cloth around this time, including Reverend Thomas Lloyd Knapp, who was later the vicar of St. James's Church in Oldham, whilst his brother, William Kenyon Knapp, would also play 2nd XI cricket for the club a couple of seasons hence.

With an influx of new talent, it seems Whalley Range cricket was very much in the ascendancy in 1877, with of the 17 matches that were reported on, only five ended in defeat, one was drawn, whilst of the remaining victorious encounters, there were some notable scalps. The first of these scalps occurred in mid-May when Manchester Clifford came to Whalley Range and were soundly beaten, being dismissed for just 43 in reply to the hosts' total of 115, of which Edward Kessler (born in 1855, and the younger brother of P. W. Kessler) top-scored with 40. The first reported defeat of the season came in a Thursday game at the end of May, when in spite of 53 from James MacLaren, Athletic could only muster 85 in total, with nobody else in double-figures. The following week saw Athletic losing again, this time against Cheetham Hill 2nd XI, against whom they only managed a paltry 26. Following an easy win against Boughton Hall, Emeris scored 75 away at Rusholme in mid-June, in the one drawn game of the season.

The next game at Whalley Range, played on Saturday 23rd June 1877, was a very significant one in the history of the club. It was against Alderley Edge and it was a game that the hosts won easily. Batting first, the hosts posted 159 with Kessler top-scoring with 35, before the opposition were quickly removed for just 30 with Carter taking six wickets and two catches. At their second attempt, the opposition fared slightly better, finishing on 57-5, with Cowie claiming another four wickets to go with the four that he had captured in the first innings. However, the most important aspect of this game, was that batting at number three for Athletic was someone called Steel who scored 20, and took a wicket in the opposition's second innings. Whether this was A. G. Steel or F. L. Steel is not possible to say with absolute certainty, though it is more likely to be the former, and both would certainly represent the Whalley Range outfit later in the season.

The Steels – WRCC and LCCC

Allan Gibson Steel

The Steels were an amazing set of seven sporting brothers from Liverpool, where their father Joseph was a ship-owner. Four of them represented Lancashire, and one went on not only to represent England, but also to captain them as well, with this particular brother being none other than Allan Gibson Steel!

A. G. Steel was a remarkable cricketer, who in his day was reckoned by many to be the equal of the legendary W. G. Grace. He was born on 24th September 1858, and made his first-class debut for Lancashire in the 1877 season, having excelled at Marlborough College. His education continued at Trinity Hall, Cambridge, where he was an instant star in the University cricket team, topping the bowling averages.

He played in the first ever Test Match played in England at The Oval in 1880, and played in the famous test defeat in 1882, the aftermath of which saw the creation of The Ashes trophy. He went on the 1882-1883 tour of Australia and topped both the batting and the bowling averages over the whole tour.

In 1884 he made his highest Test score of 148 against Australia, and being the first ever Test Match century scored at Lord's, his name will forever head the honours board. He captained his country in 1886, as Australia were whitewashed 3-0. His last Test was in 1888, again as captain.

Later in life, he was rewarded with the position

of President of the Marylebone Cricket Club for the 1902 season. Away from cricket, he was admitted a barrister at Inner Temple in 1883 and practised in Liverpool. He became a King's Council in 1901 and Recorder of Oldham in 1904.

The other Steel brother who would play for the Whalley Range team during the 1877 season was Frederick Liddell Steel who was born on 10th December 1854. Amazingly, despite being an immensely talented bowler, he never represented his county, unlike four of his younger brothers. Following the 1877 season, he didn't play for Whalley Range again, until his brother E. E. Steel started playing for the club in 1885.

Ernest Eden Steel was born on 25th June 1864, and as evidenced later in the book, would make an even bigger impact than A. G. Steel on the Whalley Range Cricket Club, by which time he'd also made his Lancashire debut. The other two brothers to represent the county were Douglas Quintin Steel (born 1856) and Harold Banner Steel (born 1862).

In the 1884 season, in one remarkable game played in mid-July (at Aigburth) in Liverpool, the home town of the Steel family, it was as though Lancashire wanted to pay homage to the Steels, and included all four of A. G. Steel, D. Q. Steel, H. B. Steel, and E. E. Steel.

Returning back to the 1877 season, the Athletic team then suffered a drastic dip in form losing three games in fairly quick succession, to Kersal, Manchester Clifford, and Cheetham Hill, with a string of low scores. They made 65 against Kersal, 77 against Manchester Clifford, and were sent packing for just 42 at Cheetham Hill with nobody able to reach double-figures.

The defeat to Manchester Clifford mentioned above, was another significant encounter this season, since this game played on Saturday 7th July 1877 at Old Trafford featured the earliest discovered inclusion of D. A. Bannerman in the line-up. Born into the famous Bannerman dynasty on April 10th 1857, sadly David Alexander Bannerman's life would end in tragic circumstances. Aged 28 he married Edith Mary Armitage in July 1885.

However, the following year, in early September 1886 (different reports quote both the 2nd and 3rd September), he was involved in some playful antics with a friend, at the swimming baths of the Manchester Swimming Club situated on Blackfriars Street in Salford. Chased round the baths, D. A. Bannerman slipped and fell heavily against a wooden partition, badly cutting his knee against an earthenware spittoon. Sadly, it was the injuries to his knee that then caused his death a few weeks later on 18th November.

The introduction of penicillin was still over 50 years away, so it could well have been that sepsis had taken hold. Just five days after his burial on 22nd November, his widow gave birth to his son. Thus David Alexander Bannerman would never know of the wondrous achievements of David Armitage Bannerman, who would go on to become one of the world's most prominent ornithologists, writing countless books on his favourite subject, before being recognised with many awards, including an OBE, and the vice-presidency of the RSPB.

David Armitage Bannerman

The Bannerman Family

As already mentioned, there was a strong connection between the Carver and MacLaren families, but there was an even stronger bond between the Bannerman and MacLaren clans, with several marriages between the two stretching back throughout their Scottish ancestry.

With regard to David Alexander Bannerman, the member of the family who played cricket for the club, his grandfather was David Bannerman (c1783-1829), who was also the grandfather of James MacLaren (1845-1900).

The surname Bannerman derives from the family's ancestors having had the privilege to carry the royal standard banners in the 10th and 11th centuries.

In the early 19th century, Henry Bannerman, a prosperous Perthshire farmer, sent his eldest son David to Manchester, to test the prospects of success in the cotton trade, where he initially set up in partnership with Peter MacLaren. A year or two of successful trading was enough

David Bannerman (c1783-1829)

to convince Henry to give up his farm and take the whole of his family to join David, and renew the business experiment on a larger scale.

Following the death of Henry in 1823, it was his eldest son David who then took over the business. However, he died at the early age of 46 in 1829, leaving three sons and two daughters. One was also called David, born in about 1827, who would presumably have known very little of his father. It was he who then became the father of David Alexander Bannerman, born in 1857, who in a fateful case of history repeating itself, would have a son, David Armitage Bannerman, who as previously mentioned, would also sadly not get to know his father.

Of the two daughters referred to above, one was Lilias Alexander Bannerman, and she married James MacLaren (1810-1870), who was the son of Peter MacLaren (David's original business partner), and Louisa Bannerman (David's sister), as the links between the two families became ever more entwined! It was this James MacLaren who would go on to become the grandfather of Archibald Campbell MacLaren.

As well as Louisa, David had several other sisters, including Isabella, who further cemented the ties between the two families by marrying Peter's brother, James MacLaren (1781-1866). However, his most notable sister was Janet Bannerman (1791-1873), who married Sir James Campbell of Stracathro (1790-1876), who was Lord Provost of Glasgow in the early 1840s, and together they produced two sons who would both go on to become very prominent politicians.

The first of these sons was Sir James Alexander Campbell (1825-1908) who in 1880 was elected MP for Glasgow and Aberdeen Universities. As a Conservative, he was very much opposed to the policies of his younger and more famous brother, Sir Henry Campbell-Bannerman GCB (1836-1908), who went on to become leader of the Liberal Party between 1899 and 1908, and Prime Minister of the UK from 1905 to 1908. Known colloquially as "CB", he was a firm believer in free trade, Irish Home Rule, and the improvement of social conditions. He has been referred to as "Britain's first and only, radical Prime Minister". He also twice served as Secretary of State for War.

The ensuing simplified family tree illustrates just the salient aspects of the connections between the illustrious Bannerman, MacLaren and Carver clans.

Sir Henry Campbell-Bannerman (1836-1908)

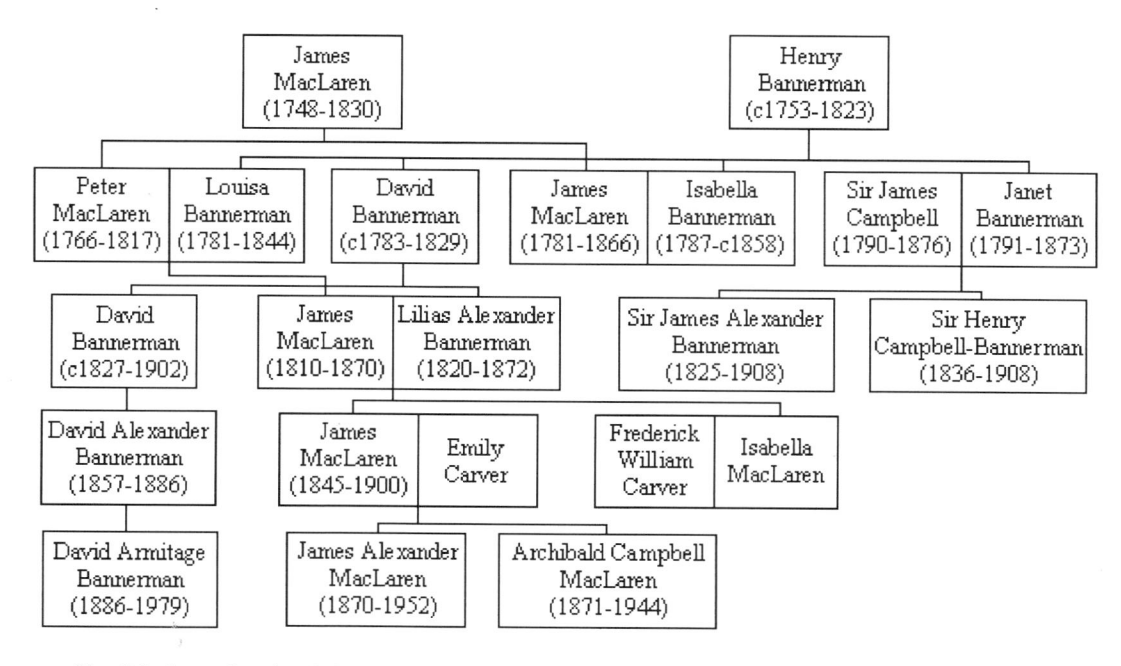

Simplified tree showing links between salient personnel of Bannerman, MacLaren, and Carver families

Of the remaining seven games in the season that were reported on, the team from Whalley Range won all seven, with some superb performances. The first of these was a consummate victory at Alderley Edge where the home team were dismissed for 101 with Kessler taking 6 wickets. It was Kessler who then starred with the bat, scoring an unbeaten 64 as Athletic replied with 160-6, whilst Cowie scored 47.

Between Thursday 2nd and Saturday 4th August, 18-year-old A. G. Steel was making his debut for Lancashire, and on the opening day top-scored with 87. It was an innings that set Lancashire well on their way to a convincing victory over Sussex by an innings and 31 runs. Two days later, on the Bank Holiday Monday, A. G. Steel and his elder brother F. L. Steel were playing for the Athletic club in a 12-a-side game against the Western Club. The two brothers had played against Western earlier in the season, playing for Liverpool, and it would appear that A. G. Steel had learnt well from the encounter, since not only did he score a brilliant century this time round, scoring 115 out of a total of 186, he followed this up by capturing five Western wickets as well! As such, the first known century to be scored for the club from Whalley Range, was scored by someone who heads the honours board at Lord's and who would also become a future England cricket captain!

Western v Athletic, at Eccles, Monday 6th August 1877

Athletic

S. K. Douglas		b Fletcher	0
D. MacLaren		b C. Pilkington	1
Kessler		b C. Pilkington	11
A. G. Steel	c Royle	b Fletcher	115
Hulton		b Briggs	23
F. L. Steel		b Briggs	0
Carter	c Knowles	b Blair	3
Cowie		b Briggs	6
Carver		b Fletcher	13
Jameson		b Eccles	2
Jones		b Eccles	2
Low		not out	4
Extras			6
Total			186

Western

A. Pilkington		b Carter	2
Smith		b Carter	16
Briggs	c Kessler	b Cowie	10
Royle		b Carter	0
E. K. Douglas	c Carter	b F. L. Steel	37
Eccles	st Hulton	b A. G. Steel	21
Cooke		b Cowie	8
Potter		not out	18
Blair		b A. G. Steel	4
C. Pilkington	st F. L. Steel	b A. G. Steel	4
W. MacLaren	c Kessler	b A. G. Steel	0
Fletcher	c Jones	b A. G. Steel	1
Extras			8
Total			129

Bowdon, admittedly with a couple of players missing, were the next team to suffer from a rejuvenated Athletic team, as they were thrashed by 98 runs, with H. E. Carter scoring 78 out of a total of 161, after Cowie with six wickets and Carter with the other two had helped dismiss Bowdon for 63. This was yet another seminal moment this season in the history of the club, since the game witnessed the first known appearance of another incredible character to represent the club.

The Boxing Connection

Thomas Percy Bellhouse

The game against Bowdon on Saturday 11th August 1877 was the first time that the name of Bellhouse was seen adorning the line-up for the Whalley Range outfit. Thomas Percy Bellhouse was born in 1856, the son of Thomas Taylor Bellhouse, who himself had represented the prestigious Manchester Cricket Club. In fact his father had been Treasurer and Secretary in 1849-50 and again in 1858-59, and part of the committee that brought about the amalgamation of the Manchester Club and Lancashire County Cricket Club in 1880. About the time that Thomas Percy Bellhouse was born, the firm of David Bellhouse and Son built the pavilion at the Old Trafford ground. David Bellhouse was Thomas Percy's grandfather. However, Thomas Percy Bellhouse's main claim to fame is with regard to boxing, winning the inaugural Amateur Boxing Association Middleweight Championship in 1881. He also became secretary of the Manchester Amateur Gymnastic Club, a club devoted to boxing.

Carter was in fine form again the following weekend, taking seven wickets with Cowie claiming the other three as the once-mighty Western Club were beaten again, this time being sent packing for just 55, a total that Carter beat on his own, scoring 59 out of 114. Carter then took a further six wickets in the ensuing game, with three for Cowie and a run out accounting for the other wickets in a total of just 43 for Kersal Club & Ground, as the Athletic Club claimed another victory.

Thus, the team from Whalley Range went into their clash with the Manchester Club in fine form, and even with Bellhouse and MacLaren playing for Manchester in this game, having previously played for Athletic just weeks prior, there was no stopping Carter, at least with the ball. His seven wickets, including those of Bellhouse and MacLaren, managed to restrict Manchester to a total of 113. Admittedly Carter then failed with the bat, being out for a duck, but with 52 from Mellor and 47 from Shelmerdine, the Athletic team overhauled the Manchester total, finishing on 138, for a superb win over one of the bigger clubs at the time. With Carter not playing in the next game, it was left to Cowie to inflict most of the damage on Levenshulme, as his six wickets helped dismiss them for 57. In this match played at Whalley Range, the home side then responded with 70, as they continued on their winning ways, and gained revenge for their loss to them earlier in the season.

In 1878, as the team seemed to continue in the same vein of form in which they'd finished the previous season, we see the name of A. M. Nesbitt (or Alfred Mortimer Nesbitt to give him his full title) appearing on the scoresheet for the first time, a player who would contribute much to Whalley Range cricket over the coming seasons. The first match that was reported on showed Athletic easily beating South Manchester in a game played at Withington.

At the end of May, opener Nesbitt scored 52 out of 96 against Rusholme, before the opposition were routed for just half of that total with Cowie taking seven wickets. Then on the first day of June, we see the appearance of some interesting names. Playing for Athletic 2nd XI was W. R. Richardson, who would continue to play cricket for the Whalley Range team over the coming decade or so, and of whom more will be elaborated on in a later chapter, since he was a fine all-round sportsman who not only played in the club's first tennis tournament, but also excelled in another sporting arena. At the same time, playing at home for the 1st XI against Western, we see the name of Buckland, who is undoubtedly related to later generations of the Buckland clan. This is probably James Edward Buckland, who would have been about 30 at the time, and who would go on to father four sons, most of whom would also play cricket for the club. All four sons would also excel in the sport of lacrosse.

The highlights during the rest of June, were Carter and Cowie both claiming five wickets in a comfortable win over Kersal, whilst against Alderley Edge it was the turn of G. A. H. Jones to claim a five-wicket haul, before the Athletic team went sailing past their target thanks to 76 from opener A. M.

Nesbitt in a total of 219 in reply to the hosts' score of 76. This was the earliest discovered report of the Whalley Range team surpassing 200.

In July, A. M. Nesbitt notched another fifty, scoring 72 out of a total of 155 against Boughton Hall from Chester, whilst fellow opener H. C. Barnes-Lawrence also performed well scoring 37. Not only did Nesbitt and Barnes-Lawrence open together, but they also worked together at this time, as schoolmasters at Manchester Grammar School. Born in 1852, Herbert Cecil Barnes-Lawrence in later life went on to become deputy headmaster at Giggleswick Grammar School, before moving on to being headmaster at the Perse School, Cambridge. He also came from quite a prestigious family who made their fortune in the East India Company. One of his younger brothers was Captain Lionel Aubrey Walter Barnes-Lawrence, who at one point held the position of Harbour Master in Hong Kong, a prestigious role at the time.

Following a draw in the return game with Rusholme (in which E. Kessler scored 41, and Nesbitt an unbeaten 30) came a superb batting display against Bowdon, rattling up 255. It was opener Nesbitt who again led the way with 75, his third score in the 70s in four games, whilst E. Kessler chipped in with 40, and A. S. Jameson, batting at number ten, contributed 38. Bowdon then had little time left to bat, closing on 22-1. The following weekend, G. A. H. Jones captured six wickets against Cheetham Hill, though they weren't enough to prevent Athletic slipping to a 25-run defeat.

Having set new record totals during the season already, it seems like the Athletic team were determined to aspire to even greater heights, with the first game in August seeing the team from Whalley Range break the 300 barrier, with a superb total of 307 against The Wanderers.

Athletic v The Wanderers, at Whalley Range, Saturday 3rd August 1878

Athletic

A. M. Nesbitt	c Pinto-Leite	b Watkin	110
E. Kessler		b Gartside	1
A. S. Jameson	c &	b Gartside	12
H. C. Barnes-Lawrence		b Davies	61
J. M. Cowie	lbw	b Watkin	12
R. Hunt	lbw	b Pope	25
J. Bury		b Davies	7
G. A. H. Jones		b Gartside	13
H. Lindley		b Gartside	10
J. W. Botsford	lbw	b Davies	2
W. R. Farquhar		not out	0
Extras			54
Total			307

It perhaps went without saying that the total owed a lot to the prolific A. M. Nesbitt, who recorded the earliest discovered century scored by a home player at Whalley Range. Also in the runs, was his fellow schoolmaster, H. C. Barnes-Lawrence, who scored 61, whilst the next best contribution came from Extras which amounted to a sizeable 54. Unfortunately there was then no time left for the opposition to bat.

August continued with a good victory over Western at Eccles. Batting first, Athletic posted 157, with opener Cowie scoring 36, whilst Jones, coming in at number eight, top-scored with an unbeaten 41. Cowie's fine day continued as his five wickets helped bowl out Western for 113, with only two of their players making doubles figures. This left enough time for Athletic to bat again, and by the close of play they'd made 91-7.

Then on Saturday 24th August, the Athletic players travelled to Old Trafford, and batting first, performed so well that they managed to prevent the illustrious Manchester team from actually getting to bat themselves! It was an extraordinary effort against a team that comprised Bellhouse, Hillkirk, Hargreaves, and Openshaw, the last three of whom are all believed to have represented Lancashire. By batting all afternoon, as seen in the ensuing scoresheet, Whalley Range again managed to surpass the 300 barrier. Opening the innings in this game was R. Hunt, who regularly appeared for the Whalley Range team this season, and over the coming years. Since during this season, he occasionally appeared alongside C. G. Hulton, and there was a definite connection between C. G. Hulton and Roger Hunt in rugby circles, then it seems very probable that the R. Hunt who played for Whalley Range was indeed the Roger Hunt who played international rugby for England.

Even though he only played the occasional game of cricket for the club, a conspicuous name that also appeared in the scoresheet for this game, is that of Hon. K. St. Lawrence. This is in fact Capt. Hon.

Thomas Kenelm Digby St. Lawrence, who was born on December 12th 1855, the second son of the 3rd Earl of Howth, which was a title of some distinction in Ireland. The St. Lawrence family descended from Christopher St. Lawrence who was elevated to the Peerage of Ireland as Baron Howth in about 1425. Sadly, the elder brother and Capt. Hon. K. St. Lawrence of the 5th Dragoon Guards, who died on May 8th 1891, aged just 35, were both without issue and the title died out in 1908.

Manchester v Athletic v, at Old Trafford, Saturday 24th August 1878

Athletic

G. A. H. Jones	st Hargreaves	b Hillkirk	19
R. Hunt	c Bellhouse	b Hillkirk	47
J. M. Cowie	c Barnett	b Perera	25
J. Style	c Barnett	b Henderson	41
E. Kessler	c Miller	b Hillkirk	22
W. J. Mackeson	st Hargreaves	b Hillkirk	37
Hon. K. St. Lawrence	st Hargreaves	b Barnett	32
H. E. Carter		not out	67
J. Bury	c Openshaw	b Barnett	5
H. Eller		b Pountney	2
W. R. Farquhar	st Hargreaves	b Barnett	4
Extras			21
Total			322

On the last day of August, Athletic then scored 151 at Kersal. Opener Headley scored 57, whilst Cowie contributed 42 before being run out. Headley was described as Captain Headley, presumably implying he really was a captain outside of cricketing circles, since it certainly wasn't the tradition at this time to signify who the cricket captains were. Kersal's reply had barely started (21-0) before being curtailed by the weather, one presumes.

A fortnight later, the Athletic team were in the runs again, scoring over 250 runs for at least the fourth time this season, as they amassed 280 at home against South Manchester. The top scorers were Harry Carter with an unbeaten 72, E. Kessler with 54, whilst opener A. M. Nesbitt was next best with 37. Also in the line-up for the Athletic team this day was S. H. Fourdrinier who was someone else who would appear in the inaugural Whalley Range tennis club tournament just a few years hence.

Thus, two of the most prominent stars for the Whalley Range club during this early chapter in the club's existence were A. G. Steel and A. M. Nesbitt, the scorers of the two earliest discovered centuries for the club. However it is not believed that the two ever met each other during this period, at least not in a cricketing environment, with A. G. Steel playing just the occasional game for the club in 1877, whilst A. M. Nesbitt didn't make his debut until the following year. Thus it seems quite extraordinary that their paths would cross on a cricket field on the opposite side of the globe a few years later.

In a Land Far Far Away

Alfred Mortimer Nesbitt had many relations who were famous artists, including his older brother Sidney Pearce Nesbitt. Having been a schoolmaster at Manchester Grammar School, he then emigrated to Australia in 1882, to take up the role of headmaster at the recently established Toowoomba Grammar School, situated just to the south-west of Brisbane in Queensland, a position he held until 1887.

As mentioned earlier, A. G. Steel was part of the England team whose famous loss to Australia in 1882 had inspired the creation of The Ashes trophy, and was part of Ivo Francis Walter Bligh's England party that then toured Australia in 1882-1883 and reclaimed The Ashes winning the official test series 2-1. During the tour, Ivo Bligh's XI (England in modern parlance) played a 2-day game against Queensland XVIII at the Eagle Farm Racecourse in Brisbane, on 2nd February 1883. In Queensland's total of 62 in their first innings, A. G. Steel had the amazing figures of 41.3 overs, 21 maidens, 10 wickets, 28 runs, including the wicket of A. M. Nesbitt! Queensland were blown away again in their second innings with none of the 18 players able to get into double-figures, as A. G. Steel again wreaked havoc, taking 9-16 as the hosts were dismissed for just 49. One has to imagine that having both played for the Whalley Range club in the 1870s, the two must have conversed with each other down under, perhaps regaling stories of their centuries for their former club!

Going It Alone (1879-1892)

For the 1879 season, changes were very much afoot, with Whalley Range Cricket Club severing its ties with the Athletic Club, and re-establishing itself in its own right. With regard to the cricket itself, the team was much the same, though there were some new faces, notably F. D. Gaddum, a tall left-hander who would serve the club admirably over the coming years.

Frederick Ducange Gaddum was born in South Manchester on 28th June 1860, to George Henry Gaddum and Sophia Susannah Gaddum, with some sources stating his birthplace as Didsbury though others quoted it as being Withington. He was initially educated at Uppingham, before moving on to Rugby, where he played cricket between 1877 and 1878. He then studied at St. John's College, Cambridge where he was a member of the University cricket team 1880-82, winning his blue in 1882. In the 1880 university team, he played alongside future England stars in the form of Ivo Bligh, and former Whalley Range player, A. G. Steel. In addition to the ten first-class matches he played for his university, F. D. Gaddum was then selected to represent Lancashire against Kent at Old Trafford in June 1884, under the captaincy of A. N. Hornby. However, picked mainly as a bowler, he failed to make too much of an impression, and so this would prove to be his one and only appearance for his county.

Frederick Ducange Gaddum

One of the early season fixtures for Whalley Range was the encounter with the Manchester Club at Old Trafford, on May 3rd. Following on from their amazing efforts the previous season, it was a game that the Whalley Range team won well, replying with 131 (H. E. Carter 43), after Manchester had made 90, with each of G. A. H. Jones and H. E. Carter capturing four wickets. Again, the success was all the more remarkable because of the many Lancashire players (past, present, and future) who were playing in the Manchester side, namely C. G. Hulton, W. E. Openshaw, J. R. Hillkirk, S. H. Swire, and Edmund Butler Rowley, the latter of whom represented his county 81 times over a 15-year period. Also playing for Manchester that day, were Thomas Percy Bellhouse and James MacLaren.

Inspired by such heroics the previous weekend, Whalley Range scored 251 at home against a strong Western outfit, with A. M. Nesbitt top-scoring with 80, whilst J. Style made an unbeaten 59. Having opposed them the previous weekend, also representing Whalley Range again in this game, for what would appear to have been his swansong appearance for the club, was James MacLaren, though he was run out for just 3. Opening the innings for Western were W. E. Openshaw and C. G. Hulton who had also opposed Whalley Range the previous weekend, though neither troubled the scorers much again. The final Western total was 88, presumably all out, though only ten players were listed, with H. E. Carter again claiming four wickets. In late May, Whalley Range put in a solid batting performance against Bowdon, thanks mainly to an unbeaten 58 from E. Kessler, though again it is unclear whether Whalley Range forged victory against a depleted team or whether the game actually ended as a draw, with the visitors on 102-8, in reply to the hosts' total of 150.

In mid-June Whalley Range's recent run of good form was halted with defeat to Rusholme despite dismissing them for just 86. However for Whalley Range, only opener H. C. Barnes-Lawrence with 36 made much of an impression, as the hosts collapsed to 73 all out, allowing Rusholme to bat again and make 60-3. The following weekend witnessed a draw against a Castleton team that included James MacLaren, though Whalley Range had much the better of the game, with opener H. C. Barnes-Lawrence again performing well, scoring 46, whilst A. M. Nesbitt top-scored with 51 in a total of 164, before the visitors replied with 65-7.

At the end of June came a minor setback at Cheetham Hill with a 24-run defeat, in a game which saw the earliest known appearance of J. G. Denison for Whalley Range. The Reverend Joseph Glasson Denison was a member of a famous and old Manchester family, which gave its name to Denison Road, in Rusholme. A branch of the family settled in Toronto, in Canada where there is still a Denison Avenue and a Denison Square. Denison later became the first captain of Didsbury Golf Club in 1891.

The corresponding 2nd XI fixture at Whalley Range featured another player who was possibly making his debut for the club. Though generally listed as E. F. Woodforde, Edward Woodforde didn't actually have a middle name, with the middle initial merely alluding to his original surname of Ffooks. The Ffooks family originated from the South of England, where the name still survives to this day, along with its original incarnation of Fooks. With both Edward's father and his elder brother having the first name Woodforde, the family chose to adopt this forename as their replacement surname as well. Both Edward and his brother, Woodforde Beadon Woodforde (who would also go on to play cricket for Whalley Range) also enjoyed rugby, with Edward representing both the Manchester Club and Lancashire, whilst his brother played for the Clifton Club in Bristol, prior to his move up north.

The start of July witnessed a comprehensive thrashing by Western, who still eager perhaps to avenge their recent defeats, really taught Whalley Range a lesson, dismissing them for just 47 in their first innings and a pitiful 24 in their second attempt, to register victory by the not inconsiderable margin of an innings and 77 runs. For this match, even though he'd already played for Whalley Range this season, and would also do so later in the season, Gaddum actually appeared for the Western team, and was one of the guys inflicting most of the damage on his fellow team-mates, taking 11 wickets over the two innings! At least the 2nd XI team were victorious in the corresponding game at Whalley Range with C. Schofield capturing seven wickets, whilst both John and James Botsford prospered with the bat.

The Jewellery Connection

One of the Botsford brothers had first played for the club the previous season, but with both having the same initials, it is impossible to determine which one with absolute certainty. However, the Western game does seem to be the first instance of them playing alongside each other. John William Botsford was the elder brother, born in 1857, with James Wall Botsford born two years later. Two other younger brothers, Charles Wright Botsford (born in 1867), and Arthur Botsford (born in 1870), would also go on to represent the club in later years. One of their elder sisters, Sarah Ann, would later marry one of their team mates, G. A. H. (George Albert Hamilton) Jones, in 1890. Their father, who was also called John William Botsford, was a goldsmith and originally had his own jewellery business in Manchester city centre, in St. Ann's Square, before going into partnership with Thomas Ollivant in Exchange Street, to form the highly regarded jewellery firm of Ollivant and Botsford Ltd in 1854. At one point they also had premises in Paris, and made timepieces for the Admiralty. The business was very much a family affair, so following the death of John William Botsford (senior) in 1880, the company continued to prosper through his sons, and was still extant in the 1980s, before being swallowed up by the Mappin & Webb group.

John William Botsford

Whalley Range cricket continued in July 1879 with victory over a strong Bowdon side, with Rev. J. G. Denison cheaply removing both Leese brothers (Ernest and Sir Joseph Francis Leese, both of whom represented Lancashire), thus restricting the hosts to exactly 100. Whalley Range then coasted past their target for the loss of just three wickets, courtesy of an unbeaten 59 from J. M. Cowie and 33 from A. M. Nesbitt. In the corresponding 2nd XI fixture at Whalley Range, A. B. Rickards scored an unbeaten 66 out of a total of 151. The 2nd XI's fine form was still very much in evidence the following week with Alderley Edge 2nd XI removed for just 23 with W. H. Radford taking seven wickets.

Over the rest of the season, Whalley Range had further games against Castleton, Rusholme, Kersal (twice), Alderley Edge, Longsight, and a team called The Garrison, with a fair few of the games ending in draws, presumably because of the weather. Just one of the games resulted in a Whalley Range victory, against Alderley Edge (109 v 103), thanks mainly to 48 from J. M. Cowie. In other games, Whalley Range were well-positioned before being thwarted by either time or the weather. In reply to Castleton's 144 (G. A. H. Jones 6 wickets), Whalley Range were 79 without loss at the close, with H. C. Barnes-Lawrence just short of his fifty on 47 not out, whilst against The Garrison who didn't get to bat, Whalley Range were coasting on 150-4 with E. Kessler scoring 47, and Gaddum an unbeaten 39.

Just as it had the previous year, Whalley Range's season in 1880, got off to a great start with a game against Manchester Cricket Club, on May 1st at Old Trafford. Batting first against a strong hosts' line-up that again included Thomas Percy Bellhouse and James MacLaren, Whalley Range totalled a hugely impressive 247. All of G. A. H. Jones, A. Jones, and E. Kessler reached 30, but the main contribution came from H. C. Barnes-Lawrence who amassed 84, before running out of partners. In reply, at the close of play, Manchester were 118-7.

The season continued in fine form with a thumping win at Huyton on a Monday in mid-May with the visitors amassing 202, thanks to 69 from Rothwell, 40 from Openshaw, and 38 from A. Jones, before G. A. H. Jones with five wickets helped remove Huyton for just 78. With enough time remaining to bat again, Huyton prospered slightly better second time around, finishing on 105-7.

Sadly, over the rest of the season, the number of defeats outweighed the number of victories. The two most amazing and closest games came within two days of each other in the second half of the season. On the Saturday, in a low-scoring affair against Bowdon, Whalley Range dismissed the visitors for just 43 with Cowie wreaking havoc with seven wickets. However in reply, when Whalley Range's final wicket fell, they had only just managed to reach their target, being all out for 44, with only Kessler with 11 managing to make double figures. Amazingly, on the Bank Holiday Monday at the start of August, Whalley Range's next game was also decided by the smallest of the margins. The game was also noteworthy because this was the first recorded instance of Edward and Woodforde Beadon Woodforde playing alongside each other. Whalley Range batted first at Eccles and posted a mediocre 98. However, G. A. H. Jones quickly removed three of the first four Western batsmen for ducks on his way to a five-wicket haul. However when the final Western batsman was run out, the Western total stood on 99, as they too crept past their target by just one run, thanks mainly to an unbeaten 48 from Stewart Keith Douglas, who had previously made a one-off guest appearance for the Whalley Range club in 1877 (when A. G. Steel had scored his century) against Western, when he'd been up against his younger brother Evelyn Keith Douglas, though like so many guests he'd failed to trouble the scorers on that occasion.

Other notable performances throughout the season included Kessler scoring an unbeaten 52 in a drawn game at Longsight in June, whilst the previous weekend witnessed J. M. Cowie capture a six-wicket haul away at Bowdon to ensure victory. Towards the end of the season, it was G. A. H. Jones inflicting most of the damage with the ball, taking six wickets against Alderley Edge, and all five of the Rusholme wickets to fall, though both of these games ended in defeat.

Someone who played occasionally for Whalley Range during the 1880 season was William McLachlan, where the McLachlan clan was quite a renowned sporting family. Admittedly William never performed particularly well in his handful of appearances for Whalley Range, but on his day was a really good batsman, as he showed a few seasons hence when he scored 157 for Didsbury in a large opening partnership with his brother Alfred Peter who scored 71. Another brother, Albert Edwin, also played in this game. Both William and Alfred Peter also played against the touring Australians during the 1880 season, representing Stockport. William continued to play into the 1900s, where in one particular game for Didsbury, all of the top four batting order was occupied by McLachlans, with William now joined by his son Frederick as the opening batsmen, whilst his two other sons, Robert and Peter, occupied the next two positions!

The early part of the 1881 season witnessed F. D. Gaddum taking four wickets for Whalley Range against Sale in late April, though the game eventually fell victim to the weather. A fortnight later, he was again taking four wickets, but this time against an England XI, playing for Cambridge University. Later in May, John McRae Cowie captured six wickets in a 40-run win over Longsight, whilst on the same day, his brother Thomas Scott Cowie was top-scoring in a 2nd XI game. However, that top score was a mere 5 in a sorry total of just 18 at Cheetham Hill. Also playing in this game were Joseph Arthur Railton (born 1856) and his younger brother Alan, who being born in late August 1865, was just 15 at this point, but in later years, would represent Lancashire at hockey. The family home was Harewood Lodge on Carlton Road in Whalley Range, and their father, also called Joseph Arthur Railton, was a very prominent figure in Manchester circles, being at one point the chairman of the Union Bank of Manchester, before becoming a city magistrate for over thirty years. Interestingly enough, and furthering the close associations within the club, the brothers had an elder sister Emily, who had married David Bannerman MacLaren back in 1875.

The cricket continued in 1881 with G. A. H. Jones capturing six wickets the next week, as Sale were routed for just 42, and in the next game, against Huyton at Huyton Lane, he took 11 wickets in the match, including seven in the first innings as the home side made just 51. During July the runs really began to flow, for both the 1st and 2nd XIs. Against Rusholme the 1st XI amassed 208, thanks mainly to 59 from T. P. Bellhouse, though they were on the receiving end in the next game as Castleton finished on 234-3, with J. Style having earlier made 62 in a Whalley Range total of 129. The following weekend it was the turn of the 2nd XI to really shine, with the following scoresheet illustrating a superb century for Edward Woodforde at Castleton :-

Castleton 2nd XI v Whalley Range 2nd XI, at Castleton, Saturday 23rd July 1881

Whalley Range 2nd XI

E. Woodforde	b C. P. Butterworth	117
H. B. Fawssett c Healey	b C. P. Butterworth	3
C. Schofield	b Bretherton	22
T. S. Cowie	b Bretherton	0
W. H. Radford c Healey	b J. Leach	0
C. A. Sharp	run out	7
J. M. Rippon	b C. P. Butterworth	7
W. B. Harvey	run out	5
A. Railton	b C. P. Butterworth	26
D. J. Fitzgerald	b C. P. Butterworth	8
J. A. Railton	not out	0
Extras		19
Total		214

Just five days after Woodforde's century, on a Thursday afternoon, came an incredible knock by Alfred Mortimer Nesbitt, as he rattled up his second recorded century for the club. Considering whom the opposition were, one wonders whether Nesbitt was running the risk of getting arrested for wasting police time, as he smashed them all round the Whalley Range ground, on his way to a brilliant 150, leaving the City Police very little time left in which to bat. With just 10 men, Whalley Range amassed 292 before the opposition closed on 33-4 :-

Whalley Range v City Police, at Whalley Range, Thursday 28th July 1881

Whalley Range

A. M. Nesbitt	run out	150
H. C. Barnes-Lawrence	b Tomlinson	3
J. W. Botsford	b Barber	20
J. M. Cowie c Lomas	b Barber	10
G. A. H. Jones c Durrans	b Tomlinson	0
W. R. Richardson	run out	15
C. Schofield	b Durrans	73
W. H. Radford	b Barber	4
E. Woodforde	b Durrans	5
C. Kendal	not out	9
Extras		3
Total		292

Before July had finished, Nesbitt was in the runs again, scoring 91 against Manchester, as Whalley Range again broke through the 200 barrier, finishing on 206. In reply the visitors were struggling on 45-5 when time ran out. A conspicuous name in the home line-up for this game was that of Capt. E. C. B. Rawlinson. Edward Cuthbert Brookes Rawlinson had risen to the position of Captain whilst in the Bengal Army, and was now the Deputy Chief Constable of Manchester (1881-1887) under Charles Malcolm Wood, the latter of whom would command the City Police cricket team against Whalley Range two years hence.

The rest of the season wasn't quite as enthralling, though there were further noteworthy performances with the likes of J. M. Cowie and G. A. H. Jones adding to their list of 5-wicket hauls, whilst G. F. E. (George Frederick Ellinthorpe) Burton took six wickets against Western.

For the 1882 season, Whalley Range seemed to have a very strong side most of the time, comprising the likes of A. M. Nesbitt, H. C. Barnes-Lawrence, J. M. Cowie, T. P. Bellhouse, P. W. Kessler, G. A. H. Jones, and most notably, W. G. Mills. Walter George Mills had previously played for Lancashire, making six appearances between 1871 and 1877, and had also played against the touring Australians in 1880, whilst playing for an oversized Stockport team. Thus, following on from a fairly successful previous season, one would have thought that Whalley Range might have prospered better than they did during the 1882 season,

Walter George "Salter" Mills

though there were some fine individual performances, especially in the bowling department.

The first of these notable bowling efforts was that of J. M. Cowie who captured eight wickets against Western in June, though having beaten their reputable opponents the previous month, this time the game ended in a draw.

Another bowler to claim an eight-wicket haul this season was F. D. Gaddum, who did so in the August Bank Holiday fixture against Kersal, to help dismiss the opposition for 68 in reply to Whalley Range's total of 111. This allowed time for Whalley Range to bat a second time and rattle up 168-4, thanks mainly to 66 from T. P. Bellhouse who'd been promoted up the order after top-scoring in the first innings with 31 despite batting at number ten.

Later in August came the earliest discovered occurrence of a Whalley Range bowler capturing nine wickets in an innings. In fact, judging by the scoresheet below, one assumes J. M. Cowie claimed all of the first nine City Police wickets to fall, before Henry Barnard Fawssett (a commercial traveller from Lincolnshire) arrested his onslaught by capturing the tenth. Whalley Range had earlier posted 133 with A. Blaikie top-scoring with 44. Blaikie had started the season in the 2nd XI team, but a score of 55 before being run out (or "thrown out" as it was described on this particular occasion) against Western 2nd XI in May, helped secure promotion to the first team.

Whalley Range v City Police, at Whalley Range, Saturday 19th August 1882

City Police

Thefrid		b J. M. Cowie	1
Tomlinson		b J. M. Cowie	8
Smith	c T. S. Cowie	b J. M. Cowie	3
Grayshon	c C. H. Scott	b J. M. Cowie	2
Durrans	st A. M. Saunders	b J. M. Cowie	0
Rawlinson		b J. M. Cowie	25
Stroud		b J. M. Cowie	0
Barber		b J. M. Cowie	0
Wood	c &	b J. M. Cowie	0
Stander		b H. B. Fawssett	8
Burrows		not out	2
Extras			3
Total			52

The following weekend saw W. G. Mills score 51 out of 180 against Kersal, but the visitors desperately clung on for a draw, finishing on 39-9, despite Mills adding to his fifty with five wickets. The next game witnessed another superb bowling performance this season with G. A. H. Jones claiming eight wickets in a drawn game with Alderley Edge at the start of September. The season concluded with a tight win over South Manchester, and so 1882 did finally transpire to be a reasonable season for Whalley Range (with the number of wins eventually equalling that of losses), though sadly this proved to be A. M. Nesbitt's last season for the club, with him emigrating to Australia to further his academic career (as noted in the previous chapter).

The 1883 season should have kicked off at Old Trafford for the Whalley Range team, but the inclement weather put paid to their customary game with the Manchester Club. Thus the season got going the following week in early May, when Bowdon were the visitors to Whalley Range. It was a game where Whalley Range seemed to be cruising to victory, before some stubborn resistance from the visitors' lower order meant the winning margin was a mere 10 runs, in what would appear to have been a 10-a-side game. However, the most important aspect of this game, is that it witnessed the debut appearances of two very esteemed characters, since at number nine in the Whalley Range line-up was R. P. Willock, whilst one of the openers was a certain F. Delius.

The Music Connection

The composer Frederick Delius was born in Bradford in 1862, the fourth child of the German wool merchant Julius Delius and his wife Elise. Throughout his life, Fred's main passions were cricket and music. In fact it was his passion for the former that in a way helped further his love of the latter. In his younger days, whilst walking from a cricket field, he and his brother were playing around with the stumps, using them as spears. Unfortunately, one of them, thrown with great force, stuck in Fred's head, resulting in a very serious wound. The ensuing convalescence proved to be a

Frederick Delius, pictured in later life

lengthy affair, much of which Fred spent engrossed at the piano. With regards to music, Frederick went on to become one of the country's greatest ever composers, though naturally, considerably less is known of his cricketing exploits. Between 1874 and 1878, he attended Bradford Grammar School, where it is believed he would have played cricket for the school. His education continued at the International College in Isleworth and in his last year there, he won the cricket prize for the best average during the term. In 1882, Fred played cricket for the Bradford-based W. A. Dawson's XI, and in 1884, Fred was sent to Florida in the United States to manage an orange plantation.

In between times however, in 1883, Fred was sent to work for his uncle Theodore in Manchester. Thus, with such a distinctive name, and with all other criteria matching perfectly, the "F. Delius" who conspicuously appeared on the scoresheets for Whalley Range in the 1883 season, is undoubtedly Frederick Delius continuing to enjoy the game that he loved.

His music was influenced greatly by his time in the USA, and was championed in Britain by Sir Thomas Beecham from 1907 (Beecham had been with the Halle Orchestra in Manchester). The Manchester Guardian's music critic, Sir Neville Cardus (yes, the cricket writer) was a great fan as well, though by the time he knew Delius well, tertiary syphilis was killing Delius (a disease he contracted in the 1880s – hopefully not in Manchester!)

Further proof connecting Frederick Delius to Whalley Range and Bradford later emerged with the following article illustrating that Delius was actually associated with the Kessler family prior to the start of the 1883 cricket season. The article relates to the wedding of Emma Wechmar (born and bred in Bradford) to George Herman Averdieck, where F. Delius was best man, and W. Kessler (i.e. Philip William Kessler one assumes, as opposed to his father William) was one of the groomsmen. Other research indicated that the Averdieck, Kessler, and Delius families knew each other through their associations within the cotton and wool industries. The complete text of the article from the Leeds Times, dated 10th March 1883, read as follows :-

A wedding which excited some interest took place at Horton-lane Chapel, on Wednesday morning. Miss Emma Wechmar, daughter of Mr. W. M. Wechmar, 8, Spring-bank-place, Manningham, was married to Mr. G. H. Averdieck, son of Mr. H. Averdieck, of Knottfield, Rawdon. The chapel was decorated, and the ceremony was witnessed by a large congregation. The Rev. Dr. Campbell officiated. The bride was given away by her father. The best man was Mr. F. Delius, Manchester, the groomsmen Mr. W. Kessler, Manchester, and Mr. Rudolf Kissell, New York; and the bridesmaids Miss T. Wechmar, Miss Averdieck, and the Misses Hutchison. Among the wedding party were Mr. and Mrs. Hutchison, London; Mr. and Mrs. Averdieck; Mr. and Mrs. Schlesinger, Bradford; Mr. and Mrs. Kessler, Manchester; Miss Kessler, and Miss L. Kessler. The bride was attired in a white Ottoman broche and silk dress, trimmed with real lace and real orange blossoms. The bridesmaids, with the exception of the Misses Hutchison, wore dresses of crushed strawberry Ottoman silk and nun's cloth, with white straw hats, trimmed with lace and crushed strawberry aigrettes. The Misses Hutchison had dresses of electric-blue nun's cloth; Mrs. Wechmar wore a dress of electric-blue silk, trimmed with jet to match; Mrs. Averdieck had a dress of green satin with bonnet to match; and Mrs. Hutchison a dress of embroidered Tussore silk, trimmed with velvet.

The Robert Peel Connection

Born in 1857 in Chelford, Cheshire, the full title of R. P. Willock (who would live until the ripe old age of 83) was Reverend Robert Peel Willock and he did indeed have family connections with the Rt. Hon. Sir Robert Peel, who twice served as Prime Minster of the UK (1834-35, and 1841-46), and after whom, police bobbies are named.

In later years, Reverend R. P. Willock would father a son, also called Robert Peel Willock (1893-1973), who would fight in both World Wars, eventually rising to the position of Air Vice-Marshal. His son was also awarded the Companion of the Order of the Bath, and in retirement, served as the Civil Aviation Adviser to the UK High Commissioner in Australia.

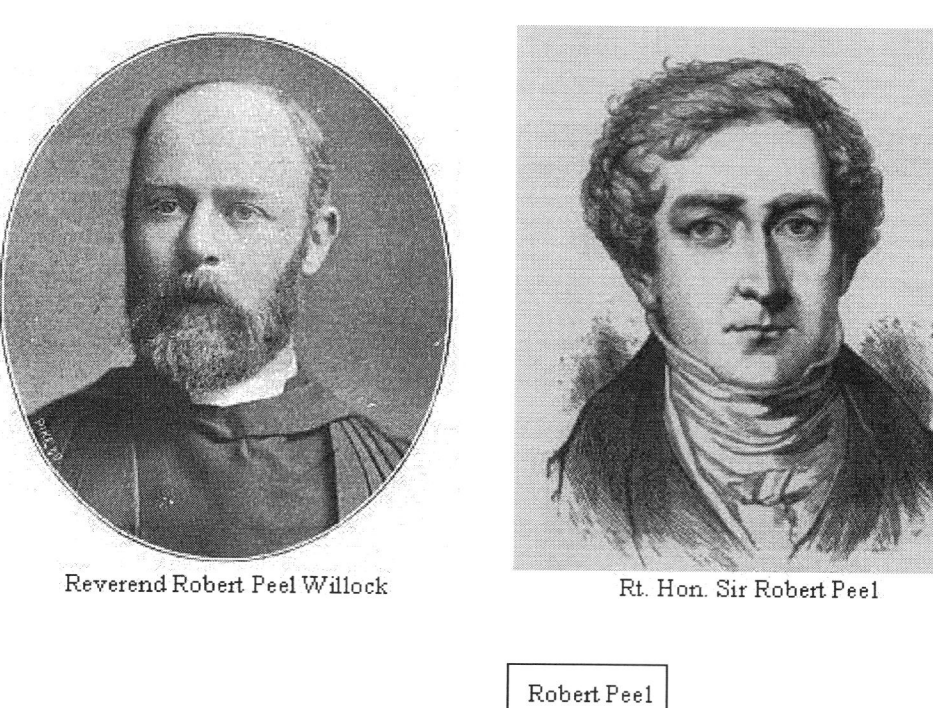

Reverend Robert Peel Willock

Rt. Hon. Sir Robert Peel

Simplified tree showing links between Reverend Robert Peel Willock and the Rt. Hon. Sir Robert Peel

Perhaps inspired by the presence of such illustrious companions, and with former player A. G. Steel having recently performed wonders down under for England, Whalley Range went on to enjoy an incredible season in 1883, losing just the once, and winning the vast majority of the others. The cricket in May continued with victory over Longsight in a low-scoring game (65 v 51), with Delius claiming a couple of stumpings. At the end of May, Cheetham Hill scored 227, with Delius taking three wickets and two catches. Then in June, Whalley Range had a perfect record of played 5, won 5, with wins overs South Manchester, Alderley Edge, Boughton Hall (Chester), Bowdon, and Kersal. In the game against South

Manchester, J. M. Cowie was the main star, taking seven wickets and two catches, to ensure victory by just 3 runs in a very tight game. The game against Alderley Edge was a low-scoring affair (73 v 57) allowing Whalley Range to enjoy some further batting practice, and in the second innings, A. M. Saunders, who'd scored a duck in his first attempt, promptly scored a remarkable unbeaten 90 out of a second innings total of 141-4. Then in the return game with Bowdon, against whom Delius had made his debut, came what proved to be his best ever performance for Whalley Range, claiming six wickets before top-scoring with an unbeaten 40 to help Whalley Range to victory :-

Bowdon v Whalley Range, at Bowdon, Saturday 23rd June 1883

Bowdon				Whalley Range			
J. P. Peacock	c Cowie	b Delius	10	G. A. H. Jones		b McKean	1
W. Mudd	st Lyon	b Gaddum	3	T. P. Bellhouse	c &	b Mudd	29
J. J. Hart		b Cowie	26	W. G. Mills	c Fairhurst	b Ch'berlain	33
J. McKean		b Delius	0	J. M. Cowie	c McKean	b Mudd	3
J. Fildes	c Kessler	b Delius	2	P. W. Kessler	c Ch'berlain	b Mudd	17
F. M. Jackson	c Mills	b Cowie	5	F. D. Gaddum		b McKean	14
R. C. Chamberlain	c Lyon	b Delius	21	F. Delius		not out	40
J. W. Gorton		b Cowie	7	C. S. Lyon	c Hart	b Peacock	15
W. A. Parker		not out	14	A. M. Saunders		b McKean	1
J. Fairhurst		b Delius	0	C. L. Graves		b Mudd	13
H. S. Jackson	c Bellhouse	b Delius	0	E. Woodforde	lbw	b McKean	7
Extras			6	Extras			7
Total			94	Total			180

June was capped off with a total of 202 in a big win over Kersal, with A. M. Saunders leading the way with 43 despite batting at number ten. Having experienced such a rewarding June, Whalley Range must have been in a mild state of shock after the first game of July with Cheetham Hill amassing a massive total of 302 against them, due in no small part to John Garsden Heap (their hired bat this season) who scored 120. With little time left to bat, Whalley Range replied with 35-3. Cheetham Hill at this time was sustained by the money and batting prowess of various family members of the brewers Joseph Holt, based near Strangeways off Cheetham Hill Road. Interestingly, another Manchester brewing family, the Hydes, lived in Whalley Range, but don't appear to have been involved with the club, apart from supplying the beer for many years (and a substantial loan in 2002!). A memorial to the son who died in World War I can be seen in St. Margaret's Church on Russell Road.

Winning ways were restored in the next game though, over Western (126 v 78) with Mills taking five wickets. With time still remaining, Western batted a second time, allowing Delius to take three wickets and three stumpings. All of the stumpings were off the bowling of Gaddum, who himself took six wickets in the second innings. For the next game, Whalley Range only had eight players, though even that fact shouldn't excuse them for their paltry effort of 22 against South Manchester, that resulted in their only loss of the season. Amazingly, Whalley Range went from scoring 22 one week, to scoring over 300 just seven days later, in a very one-sided affair against Mr. C. Malcolm Wood's XI :-

Whalley Range v Mr. C. Malcolm Wood's XI, at Whalley Range, Saturday 28th July 1883

Whalley Range				Mr. C. Malcolm Wood's XI			
T. P. Bellhouse	c Tomlinson	b Burrows	36	D. A. Bannerman		b Gaddum	1
J. W. Botsford		b Tomlinson	32	Tomlinson		b Gaddum	7
W. G. Mills	c Rawlinson	b Burrows	23	Barber		run out	11
J. M. Cowie	c Partridge	b Tomlinson	45	Grayshon	c T. Cowie	b Gaddum	0
P. W. Kessler	c Durrans	b Tomlinson	32	Partridge	lbw	b Gaddum	0
G. A. H. Jones	c Smith	b Burrows	83	Smith	c Bellhouse	b Gaddum	6
F. D. Gaddum		b Tomlinson	20	C. M. Wood	c Burton	b Gaddum	0
G. F. E. Burton		b Tomlinson	0	Durrans		not out	3
T. S. Cowie	c Bannerman	b Tomlinson	4	Wild		run out	3
C. H. Scott		not out	30	Burrows		not out	0
C. A. Sharp	c Grayshon	b Burrows	7	Rawlinson			
Extras			3	Extras			2
Total			315	Total		(for 8)	33

Most batsmen contributed, with G. A. H. Jones leading the way with 83. As alluded to previously, this was in effect the City Police team, and one suspects that Rawlinson who appeared at number eleven for the visitors, and thus didn't get a bat, was Captain E. C. B. Rawlinson, though neither title nor initials were in evidence to confirm this for definite.

It would be difficult to imagine that Whalley Range's season could possibly get any better, but thanks especially to Whalley Range's former Lancashire player, W. G. Mills, it's fair to say that August actually eclipsed the amazing months that had preceded it. At Alderley Edge on Saturday 4th August, Walter George Mills scored 105 out of a total of 218, before the opposition replied with 38-1 :-

Alderley Edge v Whalley Range, at Alderley Edge, Saturday 4th August 1883

Whalley Range

T. P. Bellhouse		b C. Welsh	1
G. A. H. Jones		b C. Welsh	3
W. G. Mills	c Stoehr	b C. Welsh	105
C. S. Lyon		b C. Welsh	2
J. M. Cowie		b W. Welsh	3
E. Woodforde		b C. Welsh	3
F. D. Gaddum	c Ashton	b V. Bellhouse	17
G. F. E. Burton		b C. Welsh	36
C. H. Scott		b Worthington	1
T. S. Cowie		not out	19
A. Railton	c W. Welsh	b Worthington	6
Extras			22
Total			218

Then just a fortnight later he re-wrote the record books with a remarkable knock of 165 in a Whalley Range total of 328, which left no time for Kersal to bat :-

Whalley Range v Kersal, at Whalley Range, Saturday 18th August 1883

Whalley Range

G. F. E. Burton		b Shelmerdine	24
T. P. Bellhouse	lbw	b Shelmerdine	10
W. G. Mills	c Lodge	b Kerr	165
J. M. Cowie	c Kerr	b Shelmerdine	50
G. A. H. Jones		b Solly	3
P. W. Kessler		b Sinclair	9
C. H. Scott		b Solly	6
E. Woodforde		b Openshaw	29
A. Railton		b Kerr	5
C. A. Sharp		not out	15
R. W. Sharp		b Sinclair	0
Extras			12
Total			328

Unsurprisingly, being in such scintillating form, W. G. Mills was representing the Manchester Club just a few days later, alongside F. D. Gaddum, with the latter capturing eight wickets, whilst "Salter" Mills, as he was affectionately known, claimed the other two, as Western were beaten by 14 runs. A few days later, they were lining up alongside each other for Whalley Range helping them beat Wavertree from Liverpool by 50 runs, a game in which C. H. Scott acquired the distinction of possibly being the first ever Whalley Range batsman to be given out "obstructing the field"!

Whalley Range were still riding on the crest of a wave for most of the 1884 season as well, a campaign that commenced with a routine win over Castleton with W. G. Mills taking seven wickets as the visitors managed just 53. The following week, the game with Bowdon was ruined by the weather, but this was followed by seven straight wins. In the first of these, Cheetham Hill, who had scored over 300 in their previous encounter with Whalley Range, managed just 30, with Mills claiming six wickets, though Whalley Range struggled in reply, only just surpassing their target with 35. This game also witnessed the first recorded instance of C. N. Stewart representing the club. Born on 19th August 1864, Charles Nigel Stewart was another player to represent the club (in addition to C. G. Hulton) who could claim to be descended from King Henry VII.

After a good win over South Manchester, Whalley Range then scored 268 against Boughton Hall from Chester, with six players reaching 30, the highest of which was 45 from C. H. Openshaw. Mills with six wickets, and Gaddum with four, then ensured a victory margin of 175 runs. A fine win over Manchester then ensued (186 v 104), where Mills was again the main star with 54 runs and five wickets. The other five wickets were claimed by Cowie, and when Manchester batted for a second time, Gaddum also claimed five wickets. The next victory was over Alderley Edge, with Gaddum (61 not out) and Bellhouse (47) prospering with the bat whilst Mills claimed another five-wicket haul. Bowdon were then soundly beaten thanks mainly to six wickets from Gaddum.

The seventh win in a row came with a thumping win over Western who were dismissed for just 40 with Mills adding another six wickets to his ever-burgeoning tally for the season. In reply Whalley Range scored 145 to win by over 100 runs. Following a few games lost to the weather, Whalley Range then suffered a 50-run defeat to Castleton with only wicket-keeper Charles Sturges Lyon (who'd previously represented the prestigious Manchester team) making double figures in a total of just 46. However, the game was noteworthy, since this was the earliest discovered scoresheet that contained the name of H. C. L. Tindall.

The Athletics Connection

Henry Charles Lenox Tindall was the first in a line of three Tindall brothers to represent Whalley Range, and was the son of Reverend Henry Woods Tindall. In later life, H. C. L. Tindall would also become a man of the cloth, but in between times, he would achieve huge success in his life, especially in the sporting world. He was born on February 4th 1863 at Margate in Kent, and would go on to become one of the greatest runners of his time, over all distances between 100 and 1000 yards. He won the AAA Championship quarter-mile in 1888 and the following year claimed both the quarter-mile and half-mile titles. He was also President of the Cambridge University Athletic Club in 1885, and not only did he play cricket for Whalley Range but in later years, 1893 to 1894, he would occasionally play first-class cricket for Kent.

Then on Saturday 9th August, Whalley Range amassed another formidable total, against Alderley Edge, smashing 345 at the College Road ground, an innings which deprived the visitors of any time to bat. It was a stupendous all-round effort by the Whalley Range players, with eight of the batsmen reaching at least 20, with the highest score being that of 73 from opener Thomas Percy Bellhouse, who obviously thought he had a point to prove, since there were at least a couple of Bellhouses playing for the opposition!

Whalley Range v Alderley Edge, at Whalley Range, Saturday 9th August 1884

Whalley Range

G. F. E. Burton	c &	b W. Welsh	49
T. P. Bellhouse	c Stanley	b W. Welsh	73
J. M. Cowie	c W. Welsh	b Crankshaw	25
P. W. Kessler		b C. Welsh	8
H. C. L. Tindall	hit wicket	b K. Bellhouse	32
H. F. B. Moore		b W. Welsh	42
G. A. H. Jones		b V. Bellhouse	21
W. Rogers		b W. Welsh	38
E. Woodforde	c Crankshaw	b W. Welsh	2
C. H. Openshaw		not out	23
C. N. Stewart		run out	0
Extras			32
Total			345

The next game in August saw Whalley Range score 210-6 to record a large victory over Kersal who'd earlier been bowled out for 78 with Mills taking six wickets. It was Mills who then top-scored in the batting, scoring 63 to complement 50 from opener W. Rogers. The following weekend, it was H. C. L. Tindall who was the bowler doing most of the damage, taking six Longsight wickets, though the game ended as a draw. Winning ways were soon restored at Chelford with Whalley Range amassing an impressive 202. The home side were listed as Chelford (with Nixon and Champion), presumably indicating some outside assistance, though Nixon proved to be one of H. C. L. Tindall's five victims as the home team were dismissed for just 57. In September, Mills then scored an unbeaten 74 in a drawn game with Western, whilst the season was rounded off in fine fashion by skittling Kersal for just 36 with Jones taking six wickets. With the game already won for Whalley Range, Kersal then batted again but fared little better, finishing on 22-7, with J. M. Cowie claiming five wickets.

The Earliest Whalley Range Cricket Team Photo

The following team photo from 1884 shows a lot of the notable players who graced Whalley Range during this period, including the fastest sprinter at the time, a boxing champion, and a couple of players who represented Lancashire :-

Whalley Range 1st XI 1884

H. F. B. Moore, C. H. Openshaw, W. G. Mills, H. C. L. Tindall, F. D. Gaddum, Turner (umpire)
J. W. Botsford, C. S. Lyon, P. W. Kessler (capt), J. M. Cowie, G. F. E. Burton, J. H. Beckett (hon treasurer 1869-99)
G. A. H. Jones, E. Woodforde, T. P. Bellhouse

Being such an important piece with regard to the history of the club, it is perhaps prudent to summarise the credentials of all of the players, and portray each of them in a bit more detail.

Harry Farr Bradley Moore was born on 18th May 1862 in Leominster, Herefordshire, to Susan and Henry Moore, though sadly he died young at the age of just 44 on 10th December 1906. He also played cricket for Knutsford, and rugby for Manchester. The 1901 Census lists his occupation as Bank Manager.

Charles Herbert Openshaw was born in 1850, and lived well into his seventies, dying on 21st April 1924. He was the cousin of William Edward Openshaw who played the occasional game for Lancashire. They both worked for the family firm of Charles Openshaw and Sons based in Bury that had been founded by their grandfather.

Walter George Mills was born on 2nd June 1852 in London, and was educated at Sheffield College. He died on 6th January 1902 in Chorlton-cum-Hardy, aged 49. He played six times for Lancashire between 1871 and 1877.

Henry Charles Lenox Tindall was born on 4th February 1863 in Kent, and died on 10th June 1940 in Sussex, aged 77. As well as being the fastest sprinter at one point, he also played cricket for Kent. His brother Sidney Maguire Tindall played for Lancashire, as well as Whalley Range. He also had a further brother who played for the club, namely Herbert Woods Tindall.

Frederick Ducange Gaddum was born on 28th June 1860 in Manchester, though died tragically young at the age of just 40 on 14th October 1900 in Wilmslow. A cotton merchant by trade, he played in 11 first-class matches, including one for Lancashire. His family established the Gaddum charity and the Gaddum Centre is today on Great Jackson Street, Hulme.

John William Botsford was born in December 1857 and died on 12th February 1939 in Monmouth, aged 81. He worked for the highly respected family jewellery business, Ollivant and Botsford Ltd. Three of his brothers also played for the club.

Charles Sturges Lyon was born on 22nd September 1854 to Sarah and Arthur Wentworth Lyon, and was educated at Repton. In 1892 he married Marion Armitage, though sadly she passed away the following year, following complications giving birth. A couple of years later, he married Hilda Mary Radcliffe who was a daughter of Joshua Walmsley Radcliffe, the Mayor of Oldham. Charles also played cricket for the prestigious Manchester Club. He passed away on 4th April 1929 in Kensington, aged 74.

Philip William Kessler was born on 15th October 1853 and died on 1st August 1932, aged 78. Other members of his family played for the club, including at least two of his brothers, namely Edward and George Albert Kessler.

John McRae Cowie was born in 1849 in Edinburgh and died on 26th September 1918. The 1881 census describes his occupation as a grey cloth salesman, whilst the 1911 census describes him as an insurance broker. He also had a younger brother who played for the club.

George Frederick Ellinthorpe Burton was born in Manchester in 1859. In 1887 he married Ellen Riggs, an Irish girl, though sadly their son, George Geoffrey Ellinthorpe Burton was killed in World War I in 1917. George Frederick Ellinthorpe Burton died on 22nd March 1937 in Bowdon, aged 77.

George Albert Hamilton Jones was born in 1854 in Devon and died on 22nd October 1936 in Llanfairfechan in North Wales, aged in his early eighties. In 1890 he married Sarah Ann Botsford, sister of team-mate John William Botsford.

Edward Woodforde was born in 1855 and died on 22nd April 1927 in Sussex, aged in his early seventies. He was born as Edward Ffooks though the family changed their surname to match that of his father's and brother's forename. As such, his name was often listed as E. F. Woodforde, where the middle initial served merely as a remnant of his original surname. He also played rugby for Lancashire, and his brother also played cricket for the club.

Thomas Percy Bellhouse was born in 1856 and died on 5th December 1902 in Brooklands. He also played cricket for the Manchester and Brooklands cricket clubs, but his biggest claim to fame was the fact that he was the inaugural ABA middleweight boxing champion.

Ernest Eden Steel   Sidney Maguire Tindall

1885 transpired into another successful season for Whalley Range with the arrival of new personnel who would take the club to even greater heights. Thus, following a rain-affected draw with Western, the first game in May witnessed the debuts of E. E. Steel and S. M. Tindall.

Ernest Eden Steel was born on 25th June 1864 in Liverpool. Back in 1877, his older brothers, A. G. Steel and F. L. Steel, had graced the club, before A. G. Steel had gone on to really excel at the game. This time, F. L. Steel had returned with E. E. Steel, a right-hand batsman and right-arm slow bowler, who'd already made his debut for Lancashire the previous season, and together they simply wreaked havoc with the opposing batting on many occasions during the coming seasons. Ernest Eden Steel would eventually go on to represent his county 40 times in total between 1884 and 1903.

Sidney Maguire Tindall was born on 18th February 1867, the brother of Henry Charles Lenox Tindall. Sidney would also represent Lancashire, making 42 appearances between 1894 and 1898. At one point, he was also regarded as one of the best hockey players in the country. Sidney, like his brother, was born in Margate, Kent, though strangely enough, Sydney would be where Sidney (actually spelt as Sydney in some references) would meet his maker. Having moved to Australia in 1911, he died on 19th September 1922 from a fractured skull which he sustained when falling from a moving tram.

For the debuts of E. E. Steel and S. M. Tindall, fittingly enough, the setting was Old Trafford, against a Manchester team that included E. Leese, J. G. Heap, E. B. Rowley, and W. E. Openshaw, who was opposing his cousin in this game. Despite such a wealth of talent in the Manchester side, they were consummately beaten by 132 runs, with E. E. Steel top-scoring with 59. Unfortunately S. M. Tindall was out for a golden duck in this game (as was F. L. Steel), both forming part of a hat-trick for J. G. Heap.

In the next game, the Steel brothers were simply stunning! Not content with opening the Whalley Range innings against Boughton Hall in Chester, they proceeded to take 19 wickets between themselves as the opposition were ruthlessly dispatched, managing just 24 in their first innings, and then even less in their next attempt, with the highest score by any batsman in either innings being just six. Frederick Liddell Steel claimed six in the first innings and a further three in the second, whilst younger brother Ernest Eden Steel with his slow deliveries captured four wickets in the first innings and six in the second, to help Whalley Range win by an innings and 58 runs. Ernest Eden Steel had also top-scored when Whalley Range batted, scoring 41.

Boughton Hall v Whalley Range, at Chester, Saturday 9th May 1885

Whalley Range

F. L. Steel		b Bretherton	4
E. E. Steel	c &	b Bretherton	41
T. P. Bellhouse		run out	24
C. H. Openshaw		run out	0
G. A. H. Jones	c Bretherton	b Cosens	6
C. S. Lyon		b Cosens	0
W. R. Richardson		b Bretherton	2
G. F. E. Burton	c E. S. Giles	b Bretherton	6
E. Woodforde		not out	10
J. W. Botsford		b Bretherton	0
C. N. Stewart		b Cosens	0
Extras			10
Total			103

Boughton Hall 1st innings				2nd innings		
J. Ravenscroft	c &	b F. L. Steel	3	b E. E. Steel		1
E. Hodkinson		b F. L. Steel	3	b F. L. Steel		5
E. S. Giles		b E. E. Steel	3	run out		0
C. T. Raynam		b F. L. Steel	6	b F. L. Steel		3
W. S. Ashton		b F. L. Steel	0	b F. L. Steel		1
A. Cosens	c Richardson	b E. E. Steel	3	b E. E. Steel		2
H. Hack		b F. L. Steel	0	b E. E. Steel		4
P. A. Sharman		b E. E. Steel	0	not out		5
J. Bretherton	st Lyon	b E. E. Steel	1	st Lyon	b E. E. Steel	0
A. Giles		b F. L. Steel	3	b E. E. Steel		0
T. A. Bellhouse		not out	0	b E. E. Steel		0
Extras			2	Extras		0
Total			24	Total		21

Bowdon were the next team to suffer the ignominy of failure in both innings, totalling just 41 and 44, with Cowie taking six wickets in the first, whilst E. E. Steel captured five in the second innings. At the start of June, Western were dismissed for just 62, with G. A. H. Jones and C. N. Stewart each taking five wickets, whilst the following week, Alderley Edge managed to go just one better with 63, as E. E. Steel ripped them apart with eight wickets.

Having had such an inauspicious start, being out first ball against Manchester, over the weeks that followed, S. M. Tindall found himself playing more for the 2nd XI than the 1st XI. Thus whilst E. E. Steel was bamboozling the Alderley Edge 1st XI, S. M. Tindall was also ensuring their 2nd XI suffered, scoring 101 out of a total of 213, whilst his brother H. W. Tindall provided valiant support with a knock of 37. Herbert Woods Tindall would go on to play for Lancashire 2nd XI in 1897 and 1898. A fortnight later, S. M. Tindall notched another hundred for the 2nd XI, this time scoring 109 out of 214-9, and as a result was recalled to the 1st XI the following week, where he scored 76 out of 181 as Bowdon were again beaten easily, by over 100 runs.

Over the rest of the season, Whalley Range lost as many games as they won, but their final record for this season (from the available records) was an impressive 10 wins and 4 defeats, with a further 2 games that ended in draws. T. P. Bellhouse in particular prospered during the final part of the season with fifties against Castleton and Alderley Edge, whilst H. F. B. Moore also scored 72 in a 119-run victory over Cheetham Hill who failed to cope with E. E. Steel who added another seven wickets to his season's tally, having also captured seven against Broughton in July, though this was in a losing cause.

1886 would provide some astonishing cricketing feats for Whalley Range, and for the Steel brothers in particular, who continued to wreak havoc with the opposing batting line-ups. The season actually started very quietly with a tame defeat to Manchester in a low-scoring game, followed by a draw against Castleton. There then followed some notable efforts in the rest of May and June, though nothing that was to match what was to come later in the season! The best results during this period were victories over Western thanks to 5 wickets and 52 from S. M. Tindall and an unbeaten 50 from W. G. Mills, and over Alderley Edge with H. W. Tindall scoring 64.

Having performed well against Yorkshire the previous season, E. E. Steel was drafted into the Roses match in mid-June, for what would appear to be his first match this season for either club or county. Admittedly, he didn't perform well on this particular occasion, and this would be just one of two appearances he would make for Lancs this season. However, Lancashire's loss would soon become Whalley Range's gain, with E. E. Steel joining his brother to play his first match for Whalley Range this season, in July. He took seven wickets in this game and top-scored with the bat, but it wasn't enough to prevent Broughton emerging victorious by 25 runs.

There then followed victory over Western on Saturday 10th July in what would transpire to be both a significant and poignant occasion. Making what would appear to be his one and only appearance for Whalley Range was E. H. Hardcastle. Edward Hoare Hardcastle was born on 6th March 1862 in Salford, and by the time he played for Whalley Range in this game, had already made a couple of appearances for Kent. He was the son of Conservative politician Edward Hardcastle, and was ordained in 1887 having studied at Trinity College, Cambridge. In 1924 he was appointed Archdeacon of Canterbury, a post he held until 1939, and in 1941 he had a book published called *"Memories of a Mediocrity, etc. With a Portrait"*. He passed away on 20th May 1945, aged 83. However this game against Western was more noteworthy because of the fact that it featured the last appearance of David Alexander Bannerman at the Whalley Range ground, prior to his tragic death at the swimming baths. Playing for the opposition, he made just 3 before G. A. H. Jones trapped him lbw.

There then followed a drawn game with Longsight, where the best performers for Whalley Range were again the Steel brothers, but they were clearly only just warming up for what they were to deliver over the remainder of the season, with the following scoresheet illustrating the start of a real purple patch.

Whalley Range v South Manchester, at Whalley Range, Saturday 31st July 1886

South Manchester				Whalley Range			
J. W. Hulse		b E. E. Steel	3	E. E. Steel		run out	146
F. H. Overman		b F. L. Steel	0	G. F. E. Burton		b Burd	88
W. O. Burd		b E. E. Steel	3	T. P. Bellhouse	c Whitley	b J. W. Hulse	9
J. McKie		b F. L. Steel	2	H. C. L. Tindall		not out	26
T. F. Waters		b E. E. Steel	6	P. W. Kessler		not out	10
R. S. Hulse		b F. L. Steel	9				
H. C. Arnold		b E. E. Steel	1				
H. C. Whitley		b F. L. Steel	1				
F. J. Overman	c Kessler	b E. E. Steel	6				
J. Heron		not out	0				
C. A. Sharp		b E. E. Steel	0				
Extras			4	Extras			14
Total			35	Total		(for 3)	293

As can be seen, the Steel brothers captured all ten wickets between them as South Manchester were simply blown away for just 35. To further rub salt into the wounds, Whalley Range responded with a mammoth 293-3, thanks mainly to a stupendous effort of 146 from E. E. Steel, ably supported by G. F. E. Burton who contributed 88 to a brilliant opening partnership.

Just two days later on the Monday, the Steel brothers would be tormenting the opposition again, with Huyton being the victims this time. E. E. Steel again opened the innings, and on the back of his 146 just two days earlier, smashed a superb 140. As well as both Steel brothers, the team this day, also featured all three of the Tindall brothers, and with further good knocks from H. C. L. and S. M., and 55 from P. W. Kessler, the Whalley Range total went sailing past the 300 mark, meaning that they had rattled up over 600 runs over an amazing Bank Holiday weekend!

Whalley Range v Huyton, at Whalley Range, Monday 2nd August 1886

Whalley Range				Huyton			
E. E. Steel	c W. Jackson	b P. Eccles	140	E. Jacques		b E. E. Steel	1
J. W. Botsford		b P. Eccles	5	H. Eccles	c Botsford	b F. L. Steel	1
H. C. Tindall		b H. Eccles	39	G. Jowett		b F. L. Steel	17
T. P. Bellhouse		b Fieldwick	3	E. Jackson		b F. L. Steel	13
P. W. Kessler	c J. Jackson	b Fieldwick	55	W. Gorst	c Bellhouse	b F. L. Steel	9
S. M. Tindall	c Jacques	b P. Eccles	47	C. Aldrich		b E. E. Steel	7
G. A. H. Jones	c E. Jackson	b Leventon	9	E. Fieldwick	c Bellhouse	b F. L. Steel	3
J. M. Cowie	c E. Jackson	b P. Eccles	1	A. P. Eccles	c H. C. Tindall	b E. E. Steel	0
H. W. Tindall	st Jacques	b P. Eccles	0	E. C. Leventon		b E. E. Steel	1
F. L. Steel	st Jacques	b P. Eccles	6	J. W. Jackson		b F. L. Steel	5
E. Woodforde		not out	3	E. Eccles		not out	1
Extras			4	Extras			2
Total			312	Total			60

The Steel brothers then spearheaded the bowling attack, again capturing all 10 wickets between them, as Huyton were dismissed for just 60. Not too surprisingly, there was time for Huyton to bat again, closing on 87-3. For the following three days, E. E. Steel would again be playing for Lancashire, against Derbyshire, though unfortunately for Cheetham Hill, he would be back playing for Whalley Range come the weekend. Again the Steel brothers were in a class of their own, capturing all 20 wickets. Amazingly though, it was a game that Whalley Range lost (by 5 runs based on 1st innings) as only W. Rogers made double-figures out of a total of 47, whilst five of the Whalley Range batsmen were out for a duck, including such big names as T. P. Bellhouse, W. G. Mills, and S. M. Tindall. As can be seen below, the Cheetham Hill line-up contained three members of the famous Holt family of brewers.

Whalley Range v Cheetham Hill, at Whalley Range, Saturday 7th August 1886

Cheetham Hill 1st innings				2nd innings		
J. Harper		b F. L. Steel	2		b E. E. Steel	5
W. Beeston		b F. L. Steel	1	c Cowie	b E. E. Steel	0
H. Holt		b F. L. Steel	6	c Kessler	b E. E. Steel	9
J. L. Bleackley	st Moore	b E. E. Steel	0		b F. L. Steel	4
P. E. Holt		b E. E. Steel	23	lbw	b F. L. Steel	1
W. J. Morgan	c Bellhouse	b E. E. Steel	2	c Rogers	b E. E. Steel	5
E. C. Holt		b F. L. Steel	4		b F. L. Steel	5
H. Perrin	c H. W. Tindall	b E. E. Steel	0	st Moore	b E. E. Steel	12
J. B. Southern	c H. W. Tindall	b E. E. Steel	10		b E. E. Steel	3
W. H. Walters		not out	0	c S. M. Tindall	b E. E. Steel	1
H. A. Swallow	c H. W. Tindall	b F. L. Steel	2		not out	7
Extras			3	Extras		0
Total			53	Total		52

Following a rain-affected draw away against Longsight (112 v 90-7), where apart from a run out, the Steel brothers again took all of the wickets to fall, Alderley Edge were the next team to visit Whalley Range and be simply torn apart by the relentless brothers, as they were thrashed by an innings and 143 runs! In their innings, Whalley Range made 195, of which F. L. Steel contributed the most, with 60. However, as can be seen again from the ensuing scoresheet, the two Steel brothers operating together, was a combination that was virtually unplayable at this level of cricket as Alderley Edge made just 25 in their first innings, and fared only marginally better at their second attempt, though they were a player short.

Whalley Range v Alderley Edge, at Whalley Range, Saturday 21st August 1886

Alderley Edge 1st innings

C. S. Welsh	st Moore	b E. E. Steel	2		b F. L. Steel	0
P. S. Worthington		b F. L. Steel	0		absent	0
W. W. Barlow	st Moore	b E. E. Steel	3	c Woodforde	b E. E. Steel	1
H. O. Lathbury	c Tindall	b E. E. Steel	9	c Tindall	b E. E. Steel	0
W. L. Welsh		b F. L. Steel	0		b E. E. Steel	7
V. Bellhouse	c Kessler	b E. E. Steel	4	c F. L. Steel	b E. E. Steel	5
C. Nelson		b E. E. Steel	0	st Kessler	b F. L. Steel	8
G. Bellhouse		b E. E. Steel	0	c Rogers	b E. E. Steel	4
C. Davis	c F. L. Steel	b E. E. Steel	6		b F. L. Steel	0
A. Sumner		not out	0		b F. L. Steel	0
W. A. Tonge	c Jones	b E. E. Steel	0		not out	0
Extras			1	Extras		2
Total			25	Total		27

In September, E. E. Steel continued to make hay, scoring his third century of the summer, 110 out of a total of 264-5 in reply to Castleton's 48, in which he'd added a further six wickets to his season's tally, and had a hand in all of the other four wickets as well. H. F. B. Moore was also amongst the runs with a knock of 73.

Whalley Range v Castleton, at Whalley Range, Saturday 11th September 1886

Castleton				Whalley Range			
A. M. Sawyer	c E. E. Steel	b G. A. H. Jones	3	E. E. Steel	c &	b H. Taylor	110
A. Molesworth	c S. Tindall	b E. E. Steel	3	H. C. L. Tindall	lbw	b F. Taylor	42
F. Taylor	c E. E. Steel	b G. A. H. Jones	23	S. M. Tindall		b Molesworth	7
W. Standring	c E. E. Steel	b G. A. H. Jones	0	W. Rogers		b Standring	9
E. L. Chadwick	c E. E. Steel	b G. A. H. Jones	7	H. F. B. Moore	c &	b Sawyer	73
H. Taylor	c H. Moore	b E. E. Steel	2	J. M. Cowie		not out	2
G. A. Watson	c H. Moore	b E. E. Steel	9	C. N. Stewart		not out	4
J. Thornton	c C. S. Lyon	b E. E. Steel	0				
A. Botsford		b E. E. Steel	0				
A. Patterson		not out	0				
J. E. Ducker	st H. Moore	b E. E. Steel	0				
Extras			1	Extras			17
Total			48	Total		(for 5)	264

E. E. Steel capped the season off in style with another five-wicket haul in the last game of the season, with W. G. Mills top-scoring with 62, to help beat a strong Broughton side by over 100 runs.

Batting Averages 1886

	Inns	n.o.	Runs	High	Ave
E. E. Steel	12	1	581	146	52.9
H. C. L. Tindall	4	1	151	44	50.1
W. Rogers	11	1	274	45	27.4
G. F. E. Burton	5	0	119	83	23.4
E. Kessler	3	0	66	40	22.0
F. L. Steel	12	3	164	60	20.4
P. W. Kessler	14	4	168	55	16.8
W. G. Mills	14	2	174	62	14.6
S. M. Tindall	14	1	178	52	13.9
H. F. B. Moore	12	0	149	73	12.5
E. Woodforde	6	2	48	34	12.0
T. P. Bellhouse	15	0	154	28	10.4
H. Thomson	7	1	42	25*	7.0
H. W. Tindall	14	1	88	35	6.1
J. M. Cowie	11	2	55	26*	6.1
G. A. H. Jones	15	1	72	16	5.2

Bowling Averages 1886

	Overs	Maidens	Runs	Wkts	Ave
E. E. Steel	280	60	439	70	6.19
G. A. H. Jones	119.2	40	226	28	8.2
F. L. Steel	151.4	64	249	30	8.9
W. Rogers	32	17	41	4	10.1
S. M. Tindall	66.2	23	131	12	10.11
W. G. Mills	84.3	25	185	16	11.9
E. H. Hardcastle	8	3	13	1	13.0
H. C. L. Tindall	9.2	1	33	4	8.1
J. M. Cowie	35	11	79	2	39.1
H. W. Tindall	27.1	9	42	0	42.0

After such a wondrous summer, one wonders whether it wasn't Ernest Eden Steel himself who ensured that the Whalley Range Cricket Club averages were made available for all to see for the first time, as he topped not only the batting averages but the bowling averages as well! Note that a few of the averages don't seem quite correct, but have been printed exactly as they appeared in the local papers (apart from correcting the name of H. Thornton to H. Thomson). In particular, the number of wickets for F. L. Steel seems shy of his real tally, since the preceding noteworthy scoresheets for this season alone, put his tally beyond the printed figure. Also the number of wickets for E. E. Steel this season, totals 81 in all of the reported games that were discovered, so maybe some of the innings where teams batted again did not count towards these figures. Having said that, it should be noted that the batting analysis for E. E. Steel correlates perfectly with the printed reports, and that includes an unbeaten 50 scored when Whalley Range batted a second time.

The Lowest Score in WRCC history!

After such an incredible year for Whalley Range, the 1887 season would prove even more remarkable, with some astonishing highs and lows! Whalley Range lost their traditional opener against Manchester at Old Trafford scoring just 37, though S. M. Tindall captured seven Manchester wickets in their reply of 123. S. M. Tindall was in fine form the following week in Chester, this time with the bat, which he carried for an unbeaten 59 out of a Whalley Range total of just 77, as all others around him contributed very little again, with Boughton Hall winning by replying with 84. Thus perhaps the scene was already being set for what happened next. Thus far, there'd been some Whalley Range performances where just one person had saved them from humiliation, so what would happen if all players failed to perform? Amazingly, this is exactly what happened just seven days later on May 14th when the Whalley Range 2nd XI team travelled to Chorlton-cum-Hardy. There could have been little excuse for what was to come next, even if it was their opponents' 1st XI they were playing, as the local papers seemed to imply, and the Whalley Range team were in fact a 2nd X as opposed to 2nd XI. Being one of the closest opposition grounds to reach, even if the team had walked to their destination, they would barely have broken sweat. As it was though, not one of the 10 Whalley Range batsmen managed to trouble the scorers, with only the gift of an extra saving them from the complete embarrassment of the worst total possible!

Chorlton-cum-Hardy v Whalley Range 2nd XI, at Chorlton-cum-Hardy, Saturday 14th May 1887

Whalley Range 2nd XI	1st inns		2nd inns
H. Thomson		0	2
A. Railton		0	not out 2
J. W. Botsford		0	9
Rev. R. P. Willock		0	11
R. W. Sharp		0	0
R. W. Hulton		0	0
F. J. Jackson	not out	0	3
S. J. Allen		0	10
S. R. Downing		0	5
C. A. Sharp		0	0
Extras		1	0
Total		1	42

Thankfully they responded better second time around (though they could hardly have done any worse one hopes!), but by then the damage had already been done, as they lost by an innings and six runs.

In late May and early June, Whalley Range 1st XI secured victories over Stockport, Huyton, and Bowdon, with the likes of J. M. Cowie, W. G. Mills, S. M. Tindall, and F. L. Steel, all performing well. However, soon after this, it would appear that the influential Western Club had managed to attract the services of E. E. Steel, thus depriving Whalley Range of one of their best ever players. As a result, Whalley Range seemed to be really languishing over the next month or so, with the next five games resulting in three defeats and two draws, and even in the drawn games, it would seem that they were saved by either time or the weather, conceding 339 against Cheetham Hill, in one of the drawn games. Thus it was quite a revelation, when on 23rd July, Whalley Range amassed a club-record total of 362, of which W. G. Mills made 114, whilst the middle and later order contributed significantly, most notable of which was 86 from H. W. Tindall. Bowdon then replied with 71-2 (or 69-2 according to a different report). Alan Railton and C. A. Sharp played in both historic matches (and one suspects there is a family connection here as well, since the maiden name of Charles Arthur Sharp's mother was Sarah Anne Railton). There were quite a few of the Sharp family who played for the club down the years with both Charles' older brother, Walter Ainsworth Sharp, and his younger brother, Reginald William Sharp, appearing for Whalley Range.

Whalley Range v Bowdon, at Whalley Range, Saturday 23rd July 1887

Whalley Range

S. M. Tindall		b McKean	11
E. Woodforde	c Wadsworth	b McKean	4
W. G. Mills	st Gibbon	b Wadsworth	114
J. M. Cowie		b Mudd	1
T. P. Bellhouse	c &	b McKean	7
F. Worthington		b Gibbon	9
H. W. Tindall	st Gibbon	b Wadsworth	86
P. W. Kessler		b Hampson	44
A. Railton	c Hall	b McKean	53
C. A. Sharp	c Terras	b Fletcher	5
T. S. Cowie		not out	15
Extras			13
Total			362

The following week, Whalley Range came back down to earth with a bang, scoring just 55 against Western, a team which now included E. E. Steel, who promptly captured five of his former team-mates' wickets, as Western won easily. Perhaps feeling guilty from such an act, he then appeared for Whalley Range, just two days later, in the Monday game with Huyton. Suddenly it was like he'd never been away, with the "Steel industry" soon back in full production, as all ten wickets again fell to the brothers. Ernest Eden Steel and Sidney Maguire Tindall then ensured a terrific start for Whalley Range's batting with Tindall going on to complete his century with a score of 115 out of a total of 295.

Whalley Range v Huyton, at Whalley Range, Monday 1st August 1887

Huyton				Whalley Range			
E. Jackson	c &	b F. L. Steel	6	E. E. Steel	c Gorst	b Dobell	83
P. Dobell		b F. L. Steel	2	S. M. Tindall		b Pilkington	115
E. Jacques		b F. L. Steel	8	T. P. Bellhouse	c Jacques	b A. Eccles	45
W. Gorst	c H. Tindall	b F. L. Steel	43	J. M. Cowie		b A. Eccles	10
A. Eccles		b E. E. Steel	44	F. L. Steel		b Pilkington	0
C. Pilkington		b F. L. Steel	5	H. Tindall		b A. Eccles	1
E. Fieldwick	c &	b F. L. Steel	32	G. F. E. Burton		not out	13
R. Moss	c &	b E. E. Steel	4	E. Woodforde	c Jacques	b A. Eccles	2
E. Eccles		b F. L. Steel	0	A. Railton		run out	0
R. Fieldwick		b F. L. Steel	0	G. A. H. Jones		b A. Eccles	4
E. Storey		not out	16	P. W. Kessler		b A. Eccles	4
Extras			16	Extras			18
Total			176	Total			295

The scoresheet didn't distinguish which of the H. Tindalls was playing, and sadly this was just a fleeting return from E. E. Steel, who was soon back playing for Western, where he was also joined by F. L. Steel. Thus, in the next game Whalley Range really suffered again. Earlier in the season, Whalley Range hadn't had time to bat at Cheetham Hill as the home side amassed a daunting 339. Amazingly, in the return game at Whalley Range, Cheetham Hill managed to inflict the same treatment again, this time occupying the crease all afternoon whilst amassing 320-9. Tough times indeed!

As it happens, E. E. Steel was dragged back into the Whalley Range team one further time this season against Liverpool, who were a formidable outfit at this time, which thus saw him going face-to-face against two of his brothers D. Q. Steel and A. G. Steel. Whalley Range batted first, with E. E. Steel opening the innings, but it was his brothers who soon did for him with the scorecard amazingly reading "E. E. Steel c D. Q. Steel b A. G. Steel 16". As it was though, it was Ernest Eden who had the last laugh, wreaking revenge by taking nine of the Liverpool wickets including A. G. Steel, with the only wicket to elude him being his other brother, D. Q. Steel, who was caught off the bowling of W. G. Mills. Liverpool were thus dismissed for just 110, to leave Whalley Range victors by 18 runs, after H. W. Tindall with 66 had top-scored in the home team's total of 128.

Whalley Range v Liverpool, at Whalley Range, Saturday 27th August 1887

Whalley Range

Batsman	Fielder	Bowler	Runs
E. E. Steel	c D. Q. Steel	b A. G. Steel	16
T. P. Bellhouse		b A. G. Steel	4
W. G. Mills	c Cornelius	b Nicholson	0
H. W. Tindall	st Kemble	b A. G. Steel	66
J. M. Cowie	c &	b A. G. Steel	3
H. F. B. Moore		b D. Q. Steel	6
C. N. Stewart		b D. Q. Steel	14
A. Railton		b Brancker	0
G. A. H. Jones	c Price	b A. G. Steel	3
E. Woodforde	c Price	b A. G. Steel	4
W. Lund		not out	1
Extras			11
Total			128

Liverpool

Batsman	Fielder	Bowler	Runs
D. Q. Steel	c Moore	b Mills	22
G. Nicholas	c &	b E. E. Steel	4
A. G. Steel		b E. E. Steel	3
A. Kemble	st Moore	b E. E. Steel	25
C. Brancker	c Moore	b E. E. Steel	31
Price	c Woodforde	b E. E. Steel	2
C. Cornelius	c Railton	b E. E. Steel	7
J. Arkle	c Jones	b E. E. Steel	13
H. Janison		not out	1
H. Richmond	c Stewart	b E. E. Steel	0
Edwards		b E. E. Steel	0
Extras			2
Total			110

Even though it was again just an ephemeral return from E. E. Steel, the victory over Liverpool seemed to inspire Whalley Range who then finished the season off in fine style as South Manchester were bowled out for a mere 36 with S. M. Tindall taking six wickets. Earlier, his brother H. W. Tindall had again top-scored, this time with 50 out of a total of 149. As with the previous year, the Whalley Range averages were published this season. Again there appear to be several obvious anomalies in the figures (there were no calculators back then!), but they certainly still provide clear evidence of who the main players were this season :-

Batting Averages 1887

	Inns	n.o.	Runs	High	Ave
E. E. Steel	3	0	115	83	38.1
S. M. Tindall	15	1	343	115	24.7
H. W. Tindall	16	1	329	86	21.1
W. G. Mills	9	0	159	114	17.6
H. C. L. Tindall	4	0	65	29	16.1
F. L. Steel	5	1	60	44	15.0
P. W. Kessler	10	0	125	44	12.5
J. M. Cowie	16	1	160	43	10.1
T. P. Bellhouse	16	1	160	45	10.1
A. Railton	11	1	102	53	10.2
W. R. Richardson	5	0	49	14	9.4
G. F. E. Burton	5	1	39	18	9.3
C. N. Stewart	4	1	29	14	9.2
R. P. Willock	4	0	35	18	8.3
H. F. B. Moore	11	0	73	25	6.7
G. A. H. Jones	13	3	67	12	6.7
E. Woodforde	10	2	34	6	4.2
James W. Botsford	6	0	20	10	3.2

Note that this season for the bowling it was the number of balls that was listed, rather than the number of overs, where at this point in the history of cricket, an over still comprised four balls, though this would be increased to five, two seasons hence. It wasn't until the turn of the century, that six balls in an over became the standard :-

Bowling Averages 1887

	Balls	Maidens	Runs	Wkts	Ave
F. L. Steel	388	23	162	18	9.7
E. E. Steel	377	17	173	18	9.1
G. A. H. Jones	709	55	255	23	11.3
S. M. Tindall	1035	43	521	42	12.2
W. G. Mills	767	48	307	23	13.8
J. M. Cowie	830	45	438	25	17.1
H. C. L. Tindall	87	4	59	3	19.2
H. W. Tindall	406	16	256	10	25.6

A name that made its one and only ever appearance in a Whalley Range line-up, in the last game of the 1887 season, was that of J. N. Forsyth. With so few people fitting the bill, one suspects that this is almost certainly James Nesfield Forsyth, who having been born in 1863, would have been in his early twenties. Like his father, he too became a sculptor, and acquired much recognition in the art world. He lived down south, which would explain his solitary appearance for the club, perhaps being up north for a short period, away on business.

During a lot of the 1888 season, rather than playing cricket, H. C. L. Tindall was understandably concentrating on, and excelling in the athletics world. Thus, together with Whalley Range no longer having the luxury of the services of the likes of E. E. Steel and F. L. Steel (though the latter did guest once this season), 1888 certainly wouldn't be as successful a season as the more recent ones, but it was nonetheless one of the most momentous seasons for Whalley Range as it transpired!

The traditional opener at Old Trafford saw Whalley Range beaten easily by the Manchester Club, though they bounced back well the following week to beat Western, only to then lose to "The Dingle" in Liverpool, in their next game. Whalley Range then found some form against Boughton Hall with H. W. Tindall scoring 79 out of a total of 182, which they followed up with victory over Bowdon, thanks to 51 from J. M. Cowie and an unbeaten 58 from W. G. Mills. The main highlight of the next game was 70 from S. M. Tindall in a drawn game with Broughton.

Twice in the previous season, Whalley Range had been forced to chase leather all afternoon without getting to bat, and the last day of June this season, proved to be the day when this would happen yet again, with Longsight closing on an impressive 320-7. In the return game with Western, F. L. Steel made his one and only appearance for Whalley Range this season, but it was his brother E. E. Steel who stole the show, taking five wickets to ensure victory for Western (169 v 130).

It wasn't until the back-end of August that Whalley Range won again, when Cowie took six wickets in an easy win over Alderley Edge. Whalley Range won their next game as well, thanks to 52 from W. C. Chapman (who represented the club between 1888 and 1893), and six wickets from H. W. Tindall. In fact this game featured all three of the Tindall brothers, with H. C. L. back from his successes in other sporting arenas. The ensuing game against South Manchester also featured all the Tindalls as Whalley Range turned their season round with a third successive win, thanks to 68 from S. M. Tindall and 45 from H. C. L. Tindall.

A. C. MacLaren – The Finest Batsman in the World

It had always been a widely accepted belief that Archibald Campbell MacLaren, who would score that amazing 424 against Somerset in 1895 for Lancashire (whom he also skippered for 12 years) and go on to not only play for England but captain them as well for several years (and in a record 22 Ashes matches), must have played for Whalley Range at some point in his career. We thus come to the momentous day of Saturday 15th September 1888, when Longsight were the visitors, and the final unearthing of a scoresheet that provided the incontrovertible proof that Archie MacLaren did indeed grace the College Road ground in Whalley Range and represent Whalley Range Cricket Club!

Whalley Range v Longsight, at Whalley Range, Saturday 15th September 1888

Longsight				Whalley Range			
W. Graham Hurst		b S. M. Tindall	65	S. M. Tindall		b Teggin	6
E. Rigby		b Jones	7	A. C. MacLaren		not out	14
A. Teggin		b J. MacLaren	8	J. A. MacLaren	c Higginb'm	b Shaw	3
T. Shaw	c Beeching	b Chapman	1	Rev. D. Dorrity		b Shaw	1
W. A. Hindley	c Railton	b Dorrity	40				
R. A. McFarlane		not out	87				
T. Higginbottom	c S. Tindall	b A. MacLaren	26				
W. White	c Railton	b A. MacLaren	0				
W. Cheetham	c Railton	b Jones	6				
W. Barraclough		b S. Tindall	11				
J. Taylor	c &	b Beeching	1				
Extras			12	Extras			3
Total			264	Total			27

Archibald Campbell MacLaren, pictured a few years hence, in his early twenties

Page 52

Since it is believed that all of the scoresheets from this season have been discovered, this is undoubtedly not only the debut appearance of Archie MacLaren but also that of his older brother, James Alexander MacLaren. Unfortunately, with Longsight accruing 264, there would have been precious little time to watch Archie bat that day. Even at such a tender age, Archie's reputation went before him. In Schools cricket he'd already scored centuries for both Elstree and Harrow, and been earmarked as a potential future county player. Thus, here on his debut for Whalley Range, despite being just 16 years old, we see him opening the innings for the 1st XI. For those who were fortunate enough to witness his batting that day, the enormous potential of the precocious youngster would undoubtedly have been very much in evidence, even in just the briefest of knocks. An upright stance, an attacking approach, which inspired Cardus to label him as "the noblest Roman of them all", MacLaren was for a time the finest batsman in the world.

Disappointingly, the 1889 season kicked off with both J. A. and A. C. MacLaren playing for the Manchester Club, though by the time they got to play Whalley Range in mid-May, even though A. C. had headed off to continue his education at Harrow, J. A. MacLaren was back playing for Whalley Range, though it was a game that Manchester won easily. However, it wouldn't be too long before J. A. MacLaren was finding his form for Whalley Range with a knock of 58 at Broughton in June. It was also a game that witnessed three members of the Butterworth family making their 1st XI debut for the club, with Joseph Francis Butterworth (senior) and his two sons, Charles Frederick Butterworth and Joseph Francis Butterworth (junior) all representing Whalley Range. A further son, Harry Clement Butterworth, would also start playing cricket for the club, a couple of seasons hence. Even though it was a game that Broughton won by 28 runs, C. F. Butterworth made an immediate impact for the club with a five-wicket haul on his debut.

The Astronomy Connection

Charles Frederick Butterworth was born on 29th November 1870, and at the time of making their debuts for the club, the family lived at Mayfield Mansions (now a block of flats), at 20 Alexander Road South, in Whalley Range. When C. F. Butterworth left school, he wanted to study chemistry, but his father who was a grey cloth salesman, wanted him to follow in his footsteps. Cotton is naturally grey before it is bleached white, hence the term "grey cloth salesman". Thus at the age of 15, he entered the cotton industry, though it would be in another line of work where he would gain much reward and recognition.

C. F. Butterworth suffered from chronic insomnia, so would often go for long bike rides around the countryside, during the night. He thus got to observe and develop a love for shooting stars and other wonders of the night sky, an interest that then turned to variable stars, a field of astronomy which he pioneered. Unlike our own sun, there are other stars whose luminosity fluctuate massively over days or even hours. Over his lifetime, he would get to observe over 100,000 variable stars, 70,000 from Britain and 36,000 from France – truly astronomical figures themselves!

By the time he was making his debut for Whalley Range, he had already become a founder member of the Societe Astronomique de France a couple of years earlier at the age of just 17. A few years later he moved to Waterloo Road in Poynton, where in 1897 he built his own observatory to house his Grubb refractor telescope. Sadly, the observatory is no longer extant, with just a bunch of nettles marking the spot where it used to be. In 1927, he retired to Port St. Mary in the Isle of Man, where he bought a house he named Beach Villa. It was here where he built another observatory, possibly constructed of materials from his previous observatory in Poynton.

In 1918, C. F. Butterworth had joined the Royal Astronomical Society, and a year later had become a Fellow of the Society. Over the years, he won many awards for his astronomical work. In

1927 he was awarded the first Abbott Silver Medal from Lyon University for his research into variable stars, and the following year was awarded the Palmes d'Officier de l'Academie by no less a person than the President of France, Edouard Herriot. In 1941 the British Astronomical Association awarded him the Walter Goodacre Gold Medal and Gift for his continuing work with variable stars, though he was unable to travel to London to receive this in person, due to the recent death of his wife, and his own ill-health.

His wife's illness had been a rather protracted affair and so C. F. Butterworth had employed a German woman called Erika Johanna Henrietta Fruhling to nurse his wife through her illness. However the onset of the Second World War saw Erika being interned in a women's camp though she was later released. With his wife now having passed away, and Erika not wishing to return to her native Germany, he tried to secure permission for Erika to become his housekeeper, but was unsuccessful because Port St. Mary was a protected area. Thus, Erika lived on the mainland for a short while, prior to C. F. Butterworth then marrying her, believing this would overcome any hurdles with regard to the authorities' concerns about Erika's allegiance. However, despite now being his wife, Erika was still refused permission to enter the protected area, and so when the couple returned back to Port St. Mary, Erika was not allowed back into their Beach Villa home, being turned away by an armed guard manning the nearby checkpoint. Most of his remaining life was thus spent living a short distance away in Colby at a friend's house, where he could be with his new wife, before he died in 1945.

During his life, he also found time for various other hobbies and interests. He played cricket for Whalley Range between 1889 and 1896, and at one point later in his life, he bought a yacht, which he sailed round Port St. Mary harbour. He was also a keen ornithologist and loved music. However, when the Second World War started, he was so incensed that "the Germans were at it again" that he took his beautiful Steinway Grand Piano out onto the lawn, took an axe to it, and set it ablaze with all of the German sheet music in his possession!

With regard to Whalley Range's continuing cricket season, W. C. Chapman scored 73 in a comfortable win over Boughton Hall the following weekend, with five wickets from G. A. H. Jones ensuring the opposition were all out for just 42. In mid-July when Bowdon were dismissed for just 27 in reply to the hosts' total of 132, it was Jones again doing most of the damage with a six-wicket haul. The next game in the calendar was the return fixture with Boughton Hall in Chester, and it produced an astonishing innings from H. W. Tindall as illustrated in the following scoresheet :-

Boughton Hall v Whalley Range, at Chester, Saturday 20th July 1889

Whalley Range

Rev. R. P. Willock		b Hack	7
E. V. Beeching		b Hack	2
J. A. MacLaren		b Hack	0
A. Railton		b Hack	0
T. P. Bellhouse		b Hack	3
H. W. Tindall	c Giles	b J. C. Thompson	106
G. A. H. Jones		b Hack	4
A. H. Hartwig		b Hack	8
E. Woodforde	st Sykes	b Hodkinson	2
H. Thomson		not out	10
D. Macfie		b Hack	0
Extras			1
Total			143

Whilst all around him, batsmen were being "hacked off", H. W. Tindall not only stood firm, but took the attack to the bowlers, scoring a whirlwind 106 in just 70 minutes, which included two sixes and 14 fours. Only one other batsman reached double-figures in the Whalley Range total of 143. However the game ended in a draw with the hosts replying with 113-7.

Declarations

Two years previously, there had been an amusing County Championship match between Notts and Surrey, where the Surrey batsmen had had to get themselves out in order to leave enough time for

them to bowl Notts out. It was a tactic that worked, but at the time it created a lot of controversy. Thus for the 1889 season, the cricket authorities had introduced the concept of declaring an innings, to prevent such a farcical situation from arising again. Another change to the game this season, was that overs would now comprise five balls, instead of four. In recent seasons, the strong Cheetham Hill side had twice made Whalley Range toil all afternoon without a bat. This season however, with the new rules in force, there could be no excuse for such ungentlemanly behaviour! As such, Saturday 3rd August 1889 would have been the first time that the crowd at College Road had witnessed a team declaring their innings closed. If the old rules had still been in place, then Whalley Range might have salvaged a draw, but as it was, Whalley Range were dismissed for just 56, after Cheetham Hill had declared their innings on 212-6.

Two days later on the August Bank Holiday Monday, J. A. MacLaren scored 61 against Huyton before the game was rained off, whilst the following weekend saw Whalley Range up against Western for whom F. L. Steel captured five wickets against his former team, to ensure victory for Western. The back-end of August also saw A. C. MacLaren returning to play for Manchester, and he was in superb form, hitting with great vigour, and scoring 75 out of an all-out total of just 116, an innings that was crucial in winning a very close game, since Leyland responded with 115. The following week, Archie was making his second ever appearance for Whalley Range, alongside his brother. Sadly, Archie wasn't able to repeat his form of seven days earlier. In fact none of the Whalley Range players seemed to find any form, and were dismissed for a mere 54, despite fielding such an illustrious looking line-up. Archie was dismissed by A. Whittles who finished with figures of 6-27 from his 14 overs. Sadly the scoresheet didn't distinguish which of the MacLarens took a catch and captured a wicket.

Whalley Range v South Manchester, at Whalley Range, Saturday 31st August 1889

Whalley Range				South Manchester			
E. V. Beeching	c Whittles	b Mason	2	C. W. Mason	c MacLaren	b Cowie	10
J. A. MacLaren	c Boddan	b Mason	1	A. Adderley		b Cowie	1
W. G. Mills		b Mason	5	J. W. Hulse		b S. M. Tindall	47
A. C. MacLaren	c Heron	b Whittles	1	A. Whittles	c Mills	b S. M. Tindall	13
S. M. Tindall		b Mason	8	J. Boddan	c Mills	b S. M. Tindall	3
J. M. Cowie	c Adderley	b Whittles	4	A. Briggs		b H. W. Tindall	14
H. W. Tindall	c Mason	b Whittles	5	R. Grogan		b H. W. Tindall	0
W. C. Chapman		b Whittles	4	F. H. Overman	c &	b H. W. Tindall	13
R. P. Willock	c Hulse	b Whittles	8	J. Heron		not out	1
D. Dorrity	c Adderley	b Whittles	7	A. Veevers		b MacLaren	0
R. W. Sharp		not out	6				
Extras			3	Extras			11
Total			54	Total			113

It wasn't long before Archie made his next appearance, with both him and his brother appearing against Brooklands. However, the MacLarens were completely eclipsed by another explosive innings from H. W. Tindall who scored 75 in the twinkling of an eye to sail past the Brooklands total and win the game for Whalley Range.

Whalley Range v Brooklands, at Whalley Range, Saturday 7th September 1889

Brooklands				Whalley Range			
J. A. Forsyth	c Mills	b Jones	3	J. A. MacLaren		b Howes	19
J. E. Hartley		b H. W. Tindall	17	S. M. Tindall	c Forsyth	b Howes	23
E. W. Critchley	c Willock	b H. W. Tindall	8	W. G. Mills	c Ireland	b Howes	1
H. D. Pagden		b Cowie	9	A. C. MacLaren	lbw	b Howes	15
H. F. Marsland		b Dorrity	20	J. M. Cowie		b Critchley	21
R. A. Howes	c &	b Mills	1	H. W. Tindall		not out	75
W. B. Steel		b Mills	2				
H. C. Edmondson		b Mills	29				
E. C. Mothersill	c Mills	b Jones	18				
P. Ireland		b Jones	9				
W. F. Forsyth		not out	4				
Extras			6	Extras			4
Total			126	Total		(for 5)	158

There was one further game for Whalley Range this season, away at Cheetham Hill, where Whalley Range returned the favour to their hosts of declaring, on 151-9, though why they should do this, and deprive C. F. Butterworth of a well-earned half-century is most perplexing. As it was, the number nine batsman finished with an unbeaten 49, with last-man T. Mason also unbeaten on 13. Making a guest appearance in the Whalley Range line-up was C. A. Holt, but this was another occurrence of a guest player contributing little to the Whalley Range cause, being out for a duck, bowled by E. C. Holt. Archie did not play in this game, though his brother did, in what was presumably the inaugural occurrence of a Whalley Range declaration. Cheetham Hill then replied with 111-4.

Making a name for himself at the nearby Hulme Grammar School during the 1889 season was a future Whalley Range player in the form of H. J. Amos. In all, Harold Joseph Amos bowled 133 overs for the school, with an amazing analysis of 67 wickets for just 130 runs! Thus not only was his bowling average less than 2, but he had an economy rate of less than 1 run per over. Having joined the school two years previously, he had quickly demonstrated his remarkable cricketing potential by capturing 9 wickets for just 1 run against Norman Road School who were bowled out for just 9, and when they were invited to bat again, H. J. Amos then claimed a hat-trick. In fact, he was a superb all-round sportsman, playing right-wing for the football team, as well as captaining the lacrosse team, and at athletics, won both the long jump and high jump in 1888.

The first noteworthy incident of the 1890 season was in mid-May when Whalley Range visited Longsight, a team that Whalley Range usually struggled against. On this occasion though, G. A. H. Jones tore them apart with figures of 13 overs, 7 maidens, 9-12, including a hat-trick, as the home team were shot out for just 25. In reply, Whalley Range secured an easy win scoring 73. The following week, there was another good win for Whalley Range, with W. G. Mills taking 6 wickets against Western.

However, the next five games produced four defeats and just one win when F. D. Gaddum's five wickets against Broughton proved to be the telling factor. The only other notable individual performance during this period was when H. W. Tindall scored 87 at Old Trafford against Manchester. At the start of July, F. D. Gaddum scored 52 in a drawn game with Dingle, but the best performance in July was saved until the end of the month against South Manchester at Withington, when J. A. MacLaren scored a brilliant 119 out of a partnership of 162 with J. F. Arnold, as Whalley Range coasted to an easy win :-

South Manchester v Whalley Range, at Withington, Saturday 26th July 1890

South Manchester				Whalley Range			
A. Whittles	c Gaddum	b Cowie	26	S.M. Tindall	c Overman	b Mason	8
F. H. Overman		b Cowie	1	T. P. Bellhouse	c Boddan	b Stevenson	6
A. Adderley	c Railton	b Cowie	4	J. M. Cowie	c Hulse	b Fairlie	22
H. Davies	c MacLaren	b Gaddum	3	J. A. MacLaren	c Overman	b Mason	119
J. Boddan		run out	16	J. F. Arnold		not out	40
C. W. Mason		b Gaddum	1				
J. W. Hulse	c J. Arnold	b Gaddum	8				
R. Grogan		b S. Tindall	9				
H. Stevenson	c J. Arnold	b Gaddum	4				
H. Furnival	hit wicket	b Gaddum	1				
S. M. Fairlie		not out	7				
Extras			8	Extras			3
Total			88	Total		(for 4)	198

During August, Whalley Range played six games, winning three and losing three, with F. D. Gaddum becoming the second bowler this season to claim 9 wickets in an innings, albeit in a losing cause against Western. However the most important aspect of this particular month in 1888 with regard to cricket and Whalley Range happened many miles away in Sussex on 14th August, where Archie MacLaren, despite being just 18 years old was already making his first-class debut for Lancashire, making 108 in just two and a quarter hours, out of a total of 248, to help his team win easily by an innings and 62 runs. It was a stunning debut, and one that heralded much praise from the plaudits.

At the back-end of August, Knutsford had been dismissed for just 39 with G. A. H. Jones and Reverend D. Dorrity each capturing five wickets, after Whalley Range had declared on 169-6. Then in early September, Lytham were removed for even less with W. G. Mills and H. W. Tindall also taking five apiece as the hosts were shot out for just 33. Perhaps the most notable game in September though, was the last game of the season, since it again featured A. C. MacLaren, who by now was clearly already destined to attain so much in the world of cricket, making his fourth and final appearance for Whalley Range.

Brooklands v Whalley Range, at Brooklands, Saturday 20th September 1890

Brooklands				Whalley Range			
H. Lomas		b Jones	18	J. F. Arnold	c Farrington	b Scott	0
H. D. Pagden		b Jones	56	A. C. MacLaren	c Pagden	b Scott	6
Scott		b Jowett	14	J. A. MacLaren		run out	34
A. Lyon		b Jones	0	G. A. Jowett	c Lyon	b Scott	0
R. Farrington		b Jones	0	H. W. Tindall	c Hartley	b Scott	10
G. Mothersill	c A. MacLaren	b Jowett	4	G. A. H. Jones	c Pagden	b Howes	0
E. Rome		b Jones	0	T. P. Bellhouse		not out	20
A. Lomas	lbw	b Jones	6	W. F. Forsyth		b Rome	3
C. Hartley	lbw	b A. MacLaren	24	W. Schiele		not out	4
H. Mothersill		not out	32				
H. A. Howes		b Jones	15				
Extras			26	Extras			2
Total			195	Total		(for 7)	79

Despite having scored a century for Lancashire just weeks earlier, Archie failed again with the bat for Whalley Range, but at least he signed off with a catch and a wicket. There were three guest players from Brooklands representing Whalley Range in this game, namely Jowett, Forsyth, and Schiele.

    The next time that Archie batted in earnest, was playing for Manchester in the season's opener at Old Trafford in April 1891. With Bolton already having been dismissed for just 40, Archie soon ensured the target was well and truly passed as he smashed a superb 133 before being run out. With others around him also cashing in, including an unbeaten 33 from J. A. MacLaren, Manchester rattled up a mammoth 460-6 for perhaps one of the biggest ever victory margins at this level of cricket. What a shame that Archie couldn't have produced such fireworks in his previous innings, against Brooklands!

    As it happened, whilst A. C. and J. A. were enjoying themselves at Old Trafford, Whalley Range were playing Brooklands again, and this time beat them thanks to six wickets from Gaddum. For most of May, Whalley Range performed very badly with the nadir being a total of just 29 against perpetual tormenters Cheetham Hill, where nobody could make double-figures, and 7 from H. C. Arnold would prove to be the top score. However at the end of May, two significant events occurred that more than compensated for the lacklustre performances of the preceding days of that month. On the 28th May, J. A. MacLaren made his first-class debut for Lancashire against Sussex at Old Trafford, or would have done if it hadn't rained all day. In fact the weather put paid to the following day as well, so it wasn't until 30th May that J. A. MacLaren got to bat. His younger brother Archie had also made his debut against Sussex, though unfortunately that was where the similarities ended. Whilst A. C. had made a wonderful century on debut, J. A. opened the innings and was run out for just 6.

    Whilst J. A. MacLaren was finally making his debut, just a few miles away at the College Road ground in Whalley Range, F. D. Gaddum would produce an astonishing bowling performance. He only bowled four overs, but it was enough to destroy South Manchester with figures of 9-5. South Manchester's innings which was over in just 20 minutes, lasted just seven overs, and only two of their batsmen managed to score!

Whalley Range v South Manchester, at Whalley Range, Saturday 30th May 1891

South Manchester

A. Whittles	c A. H. Hartwig	b F. D. Gaddum	12
A. Adderley	c A. H. Hartwig	b F. D. Gaddum	0
F. H. Overman	c H. W. Tindall	b F. D. Gaddum	0
R. Grogan	c H. W. Tindall	b F. D. Gaddum	0
H. Furnival	c J. F. Arnold	b H. C. Arnold	11
J. W. Hulse		b F. D. Gaddum	0
H. J. Adderley		b F. D. Gaddum	0
J. S. Harding	lbw	b F. D. Gaddum	0
G. Merritt		not out	0
F. Bowler		b F. D. Gaddum	0
C. Heywood	c W. C. Chapman	b F. D. Gaddum	0
Extras			0
Total			23

Certainly in the matches prior to the Second World War, these were the best bowling figures that were unearthed for Whalley Range, and came just a season after he'd taken 9 wickets in an innings against Western, though admittedly that was in a lot less dramatic fashion, and in a game that Whalley Range actually lost. He thus became the first and only bowler to capture 9 wickets in an innings on separate occasions, during the period up to the Second World War. Prior to F. D. Gaddum's performances, the only other occurrences of 9 wickets in an innings that came to light, were the 9-12 of G. A. H. Jones the previous season, E. E. Steel's 9 wickets against Liverpool in 1887, and J. M. Cowie's 9 wickets against the City Police in 1882, the earliest discovered 9-wicket haul for the club.

With J. A. MacLaren not making a big impression for Lancs on debut, he found himself opposing his former team-mates at the start of June, playing for Manchester, at Old Trafford. H. C. Arnold managed to get him out early, but it was a game that Whalley Range would lose by 47 runs. Playing in this game for Whalley Range were two members of the Bellhouse clan, with not just T. P. Bellhouse playing, but also E. W. Bellhouse making a rare appearance as well. Back in January 1889, Ernest Walter Bellhouse had made two appearances for Derby County in the first ever season of the Football League.

Later in June, Gaddum's fine season continued with him opening the innings against Alderley Edge and scoring an unbeaten 77, though it must be said he was overshadowed by H. W. Tindall who smashed a brilliant 104, out of a total of 239-8 before Whalley Range declared. In reply, Alderley Edge were bowled out for 186, with Gaddum capping off a fine day for him, taking four wickets. During the contest, he had been presented with a *"suitable testimonial"* to commemorate his recent exceptional performance against South Manchester.

Whalley Range v Alderley Edge, at Whalley Range, Saturday 20th June 1891

Whalley Range

T. P. Bellhouse	b W. H. Welsh	5
F. D. Gaddum	not out	77
H. W. Tindall	c & b W. Nelson	104
Rev. R. P. Willock	b W. Nelson	7
W. C. Chapman	c W. H. Welsh b V. Bellhouse	0
H. C. Arnold	b W. H. Welsh	1
Rev. D. Dorrity	b W. H. Welsh	3
A. H. Hartwig	c V. Bellhouse b W. H. Welsh	7
G. A. H. Jones	b V. Bellhouse	22
Extras		13
Total	(for 8 dec.)	239

Whalley Range seemed to do a fair amount of travelling in July. At the start of the month they played Dingle in Liverpool, and then the following week they were over a hundred miles away, playing Bilton Grange in Rugby. Gaddum had been educated in Rugby and so one imagines that it was because of his connections that this match was arranged. H. W. Tindall scored 69 in this game, but it wasn't enough to prevent Whalley Range suffering a second successive defeat on their travels.

Over the rest of the season, individual highlights included Gaddum taking another five-wicket haul (against Broughton), W. G. Mills scoring 69 to beat Brooklands, and J. M. Cowie scoring an unbeaten 51, his best score of the season, to ensure victory over Knutsford. However the main highlight was in mid-August when G. A. H. Jones captured 7-26 to remove Western for just 54 to secure an improbable victory after Whalley Range themselves had managed just 78.

The following tables show the averages for the 1891 season. Again it should be noted that a few of the averages don't seem quite correct, but have been printed exactly as they appeared in the local papers :-

Bowling Averages 1891

	Overs	Maidens	Runs	Wkts	Ave
F. D. Gaddum	181.2	39	422	38	11.4
H. C. Arnold	193.2	61	398	32	12.14
E. V. Beeching	51	14	132	10	13.2
J. M. Cowie	40.3	9	111	8	13.7
S. M. Tindall	132.1	27	317	23	13.18
G. A. H. Jones	197.1	59	516	32	16.4
H. W. Tindall	144.2	30	353	21	16.17

Batting Averages 1891

	Inns	n.o.	Runs	High	Ave
W. G. Mills	5	2	100	69	33.1
A. Thomson	3	1	55	37	27.1
F. D. Gaddum	14	3	229	77*	20.9
H. W. Tindall	13	0	260	104	20.0
S. M. Tindall	17	2	295	48	19.10
J. F. Arnold	13	2	217	42	19.8
J. M. Cowie	12	2	149	51*	14.9
G. A. H. Jones	13	2	155	27	14.1
E. W. Bellhouse	4	0	42	36	10.2
T. P. Bellhouse	11	0	89	35	8.1
H. C. Arnold	13	1	85	27	7.1
E. V. Beeching	11	2	62	27*	6.8
A. H. Hartwig	6	1	27	12*	5.2
W. C. Chapman	10	0	46	14	4.6
A. Botsford	4	0	19	8	4.3
R. P. Willock	3	0	13	7	4.1
E. Woodforde	4	0	16	10	4.0

For the 1892 season, a pre-season report in the Manchester Courier assessed the prospects of the forthcoming season for Whalley Range as follows :-

The strength of the Whalley Range team is well maintained and thanks to such names as W. G. Mills, T. P. Bellhouse, G. Jones, F. D. Gaddum, and the Tindalls they will be able to show a bold front. Mr. McRae Cowie, a veteran cricketer, has charge of the arrangements, which are quite as strong as heretofore.

As it happened, neither W. G. Mills nor T. P. Bellhouse would play for Whalley Range this season. W. G. Mills would spend most of his cricket playing for the Manchester team, where interestingly enough, he would sometimes be playing alongside a future Whalley Range player, A. G. Baker. As for T. P. Bellhouse, he would re-locate to Brooklands, and would end up playing cricket for them.

The loss of these players provided the opportunity for a few new faces, notably J. Escombe. Having taken three wickets in a rain-curtailed opening game in Liverpool against Dingle, he took five wickets in the second game, a feat matched by G. A. H. Jones, as Knutsford were comfortably beaten. The following game witnessed T. P. Bellhouse up against his former team-mates, where no mercy was shown by Jones who dismissed him for a duck, though the game ended in a draw, after Whalley Range had amassed 231-3 thanks to 90 from S. M. Tindall and 57 from J. M. Cowie. The following weekend saw J. F. Arnold notch an unbeaten 68 in a drawn game at Broughton.

Then, against Cheetham Hill, true to tradition, Whalley Range were simply blown away, managing just 33 as Pennington sliced through the team with nine wickets. The following game, in late May, pitted Whalley Range against former players J. A. MacLaren and W. G. Mills, and new recruit Escombe bagged them both, for just 0 and 3 respectively, though Whalley Range still ended up losing a game that they looked like winning for most of the match. At the start of June, S. M. Tindall made his debut for Lancs 2nd XI, where he would play alongside J. A. MacLaren.

June continued with F. D. Gaddum taking a side called Mr. Gaddum's XI, appropriately enough, to Bilton Grange in Rugby. Having travelled so far, it was a shame that the game was ruined by rain, though not before J. F. Arnold had scored 90. The side also included a lot of other Whalley Range players, and a former one, W. G. Mills, so it was essentially the Whalley Range team, and one that also included a one-off guest appearance by L. A. Orford. Back in 1883, Lewis Alfred Orford had been the Uppingham School cricket captain, and played in seven first-class matches for Cambridge University in the 1886 and 1887 seasons, playing against the likes of W. G. Grace.

More Notable Guests

The Whalley Range team was back in Rugby the following month in a 12-a-side game against F. D. Gaddum's former School, with the visitors emerging victorious by just 10 runs. Also representing Whalley Range this day was his cousin Frank Ernest Gaddum, who had also attended Rugby School (1881 to 1886) and prior to that, Bilton Grange School in Dunchurch, Rugby. In his final

year at Rugby School, Frank had played at Lord's when his school played against the MCC in a 2-day game, but the hosts won by an innings and 89 runs. However the more notable guest who represented Whalley Range in a one-off appearance on this day was D. H. Brownfield, and it was he who ensured victory for the visitors with an unbeaten 45.

Rugby School XII v Whalley Range XII, at Rugby, Saturday 16th July 1892

Whalley Range XII

R. W. Sharp		b Slater	3
S. M. Tindall		b Slater	10
J. M. Cowie		b Slater	6
D. H. Brownfield		not out	45
E. W. Bellhouse		b Slater	0
R. C. Farbridge		b Slater	0
F. D. Gaddum		b Dowson	1
F. E. Gaddum		b Slater	4
G. A. H. Jones		b Slater	0
Rev. D. Dorrity		b Slater	0
W. A. Arnold	c Lee	b Sample	8
A. H. Hartwig		b Sample	19
Extras			9
Total			105

D. H. Brownfield was a former Rugby School pupil who had also represented them at Lord's, including a game in 1874 against Marlborough College where he was up against A. G. Steel, interestingly enough. However, Douglas Howard Brownfield's main claim to fame was that he represented an England XI against the touring Australians in 1888. It wasn't a game that England prospered well in, losing by an innings and 135 runs, having been bowled out for just 28 in their first innings, with Charles Thomas Biass Turner taking 9-15 from 17.1 overs. The only wicket he didn't take was that of D. H. Brownfield who deprived him of the chance to claim all ten wickets by being run out. Thus, even though he may only have played for Whalley Range once as a guest, he was still the third player (thus far unearthed) to represent England, following in the footsteps of Allan Gibson Steel and Archibald Campbell MacLaren.

As can be seen from the previous scoresheet, E. W. Bellhouse made another fleeting appearance for the club in the game against Rugby School, though failed to trouble the scorers. Another name appearing in this scoresheet is that of R. C. Farbridge. This is Robert Cridland Farbridge who had played for Cheshire in 1889, and who in later life, would play cricket out in Shanghai, between 1897 and 1903. Between 1892 and 1900, several of his brothers would also represent the club, including Frank Holliday Farbridge, Edward Brisco Owen Farbridge, and a young Stanley Brisco Owen Farbridge, who in the coming years would be yet another Whalley Range player who'd opt for a profession in the church.

Speaking of the church, another notable name in the line-up against Rugby School was that of Rev. D. Dorrity. Reverend David Dorrity had made his first appearance for the club back in 1887. Between 1883 and 1887 he was the curate of Waterhead in Oldham, with responsibility for the St. Ambrose Mission Church, a role for which he had been specifically ordained in 1883. He later took on the prestigious role of being rector of St. Ann's Church in Manchester, a position he still held at the time of the outbreak of World War I. On the last Sunday before the war, he is recorded as telling his parishioners "fight if you must, not until you must".

A further interesting name in that previous scoresheet, is that of A. H. Hartwig. This is Alfred Hayman Hartwig Von Der Lahr, who though of German descent, was actually born in Stretford in the early 1860s, though certain future events (just previously referred to) would cause him to change his name to Alfred Hayman Russell in 1915, where Russell was his wife's maiden name. He went to Manchester Grammar School, before eventually becoming a director of a merchants' company called Jaffe and Co.

Reverend David Dorrity

The best batsman for Whalley Range in the 1892 season was undoubtedly J. F. Arnold, whose fine season continued with 74 in a comfortable win over Brooklands, followed in the next game by an unbeaten 50 in a drawn game against Western.

The Arnold Brothers

Born on 2nd March 1869 to Dumvilia and Alfred Robert Arnold, James Frederick Arnold was actually the youngest of four brothers who would play for the club in varying degrees, and who as elaborated on in the following chapter, would achieve the most in the cricketing world. The eldest brother was Willie Alfred Arnold who was born in 1861, and who would later become Reverend Willie Alfred Arnold, being ordained in 1895. Henry Charles Arnold was born in 1863, and like J. F. Arnold had first played for the club in 1890, but perhaps the brother who achieved the most in life was Alfred James Arnold who was born in 1866, since he would end up as Alfred James Arnold CBE. After being educated at Corpus Christi College, Cambridge, he then embarked on a long military career that would see him based in Africa for a lot of his life, where amongst many other notable achievements, he commanded the Royal Niger Constabulary from 1895 to 1899. He received many titles and awards throughout his career, crowned off with his CBE which he received on 1st January 1919, following his contributions to the First World War.

Sadly, their mother, Dumvilia, who'd been born in Dublin, the daughter of W. J. Taaffe, had died in 1874, aged just 39, though their father, who was a cotton goods merchant (a trade that some of his sons would also adopt initially) later re-married, to a young woman called Susannah from Kent.

As for the continuing 1892 cricket season, at the end of August came another potential mauling at the hands of Cheetham Hill, though having been reduced to 0-3, Whalley Range were rescued from any further humiliation by the weather. In September, having represented Manchester the previous week, opener S. M. Tindall scored a brilliant 105 out of a total of 161-3 against South Manchester at Withington, before Whalley Range declared, in a game presumably affected by the weather, since the hosts managed just 84-4 in reply.

South Manchester v Whalley Range, at Withington, Saturday 10th September 1892

Whalley Range

S. M. Tindall	c Smith	b Overman	105
R. C. Farbridge	c Adderley	b Stevenson	2
J. M. Cowie	c Hulse	b Whittles	9
J. F. Arnold		not out	41
Rev. D. Dorrity		not out	1
Extras			3
Total		(for 3 dec.)	161

As can be seen from the ensuing averages, S. M. Tindall's 105 transpired to be the highest score of the campaign (and thankfully the maths for the averages seem correct this time!).

There was one further game this season, with a match at Bowdon the following weekend, where opening the batting for Whalley Range was Ernest Butler Rowley, who would make his debut for Lancashire the following season. With Bowdon having posted 133-8 before declaring, Whalley Range then struggled in reply, but E. B. Rowley's 33 out of a total of 60-6 ensured the visitors of a draw.

Born on 15th January 1870 in Kersal, Ernest Butler Rowley would go on to represent his county 16 times in all, scoring four fifties, with a highest score of 65, and live until the ripe old age of 92. Aged in his mid-sixties, he would sire a son, Alexander Butler Rowley (not to be confused with his great-uncle of the same name!), who went on to play for Bramhall. As mentioned earlier, his father, Edmund Butler Rowley, had also represented Lancashire, playing 81 times between 1865 and 1880, whilst he had several uncles who were all involved with Lancashire cricket in the early days.

Ernest Butler Rowley

Batting Averages 1892

	Inns	n.o.	Runs	High	Ave
J. F. Arnold	15	5	372	74	37.20
W. A. Arnold	3	1	62	29	31.00
S. M. Tindall	17	1	344	105	21.50
F. D. Gaddum	10	2	159	38	19.87
Rev. D. Dorrity	12	3	157	33	17.44
H. W. Tindall	14	2	176	34	14.66
A. H. Hartwig	10	2	87	24	10.87
G. A. H. Jones	11	1	97	32	9.70
J. M. Cowie	15	0	141	57	9.40
R. C. Farbridge	13	1	107	34	8.91
C. J. Knowles	8	2	46	17	7.66
R. W. Sharp	10	1	67	33	7.44
H. C. Arnold	7	1	32	17	5.33
J. Escombe	5	0	23	18	4.60
A. Botsford	4	0	11	5	2.75

Bowling Averages 1892

	Overs	Maidens	Runs	Wkts	Ave
J. Escombe	78	21	161	20	8.05
F. D. Gaddum	155.3	34	329	26	12.65
S. M. Tindall	102.4	24	233	16	14.56
R. C. Farbridge	94	19	235	14	16.78
Rev. D. Dorrity	75.4	21	135	8	16.87
G. A. H. Jones	197.3	41	485	28	17.32
H. C. Arnold	92	29	203	11	18.45
J. M. Cowie	61	13	139	6	23.16
H. W. Tindall	44.2	8	90	3	30.00

Joining Forces (1892-1899)

On September 22nd 1892, the following report appeared in the local press under the heading "Proposed Manchester Cricket Association" about a meeting which had been held at 26 Barton Arcade, Manchester (the offices of Lancashire County Cricket Club) on Tuesday September 20th 1892 :-

A meeting of representatives of the principal clubs in the Manchester district was held at the County Cricket Club offices, Deansgate, on Tuesday evening, to consider a proposal for the formation of a District Cricket Association. Mr. James Horner, hon. sec. to the Cheshire Cricket Club, who had been the principal mover in the matter, pointed out the advantages that would be secured through an association in facilitating the arrangement of matches, and said that such an association would tend to improve the status of the game in the district, and at no distant date enable them to appoint neutral umpires. He deprecated the idea of Leagues, and was of the opinion that the present exorbitant terms offered to catch players were suicidal and would eventually cripple clubs. He complained, as also did other representatives present, of the poaching system of the League clubs and the heavy inducement offered to attract professionals. To counteract such a measure it would be necessary to form a powerful combination to be governed in a manner conducive to the best interests of cricket. Mr. N. C. Browning proposed, "That the clubs present form themselves into a body to be styled the Manchester Cricket Association". This was seconded by Mr. Duxbury and carried unanimously. It was resolved that a sub-committee, consisting of five representatives, be appointed to draw up rules, &c., and Mr. N. C. Browning moved, and Mr. J. B. Johnson seconded, the motion to appoint Messrs. Thornber, Duxbury, Horner, Swallow, and Walker. These gentlemen were asked to submit particulars to a future meeting, which will be held at an early date.

Thus, a short time later, the following article appeared in the Manchester Guardian on October 6th 1892, under the heading "Manchester and District Cricket Association" :-

A meeting of the newly-formed association was held on Tuesday evening at the County Cricket Office, Deansgate. Mr. Harry Thornber was in the chair, and there were also present Messrs. J. Leigh (Preston), W. E. Walker (Bolton), E. O. Swallow (Cheetham Hill), A. H. Nock (Broughton), H. Holroyd (Rusholme), C. H. Unsworth (Warrington), J. W. Clegg (Wigan), J. J. Mellor (Werneth), N. C. Browning (Sale), W. S. Gibbon (Bowdon), J. Horner (Stockport), J. M. Cowie (Whalley Range), J. B. Johnson (Longsight), and H. D. Rattray (Castleton). The sub-committee appointed to draw rules presented them to the meeting, and they were, with a few trifling amendments, unanimously adopted. The main object of the association stated in the rules was the fixing of a date convenient to the whole of the clubs, as soon as the county arrangements are completed, so as to arrange the whole of the club fixtures, and members of the association bind themselves not to arrange matches until such date except with clubs outside the present body. There was a very general opinion to discourage the help of Saturday afternoon professionals, as clubs so fortified often met others on an unequal basis, and in many cases it detracted from the friendly rivalry which the meeting of the clubs inspired. Eventually it was unanimously decided that clubs within the association must confine themselves to the services of professionals engaged on the ground only. The question of neutral umpires was also raised, but nothing was definitely settled, the clubs being divided in the matter, and the consideration of the proposal was left over. The qualification of membership is the playing of at least four clubs within the association, and clubs so eligible will have to be proposed and seconded and elected at a general meeting by a majority of at least two-thirds of those present. Mr. S. H. Swire, hon. secretary of the County Club, was elected chairman; Mr. James Horner, hon. secretary; Mr. Harry Thornber, hon. treasurer; and a committee was also elected, comprising the following: Messrs E. O. Swallow, W. E. Walker, J. Duxbury, and N. C. Browning.

We thus see the birth and early development of the Manchester & District Cricket Association to which Whalley Range Cricket Club would plead its allegiance over the next 120 years.

It is worth unpicking these notices. First, the clubs represented were very much the 'posh' clubs, and committed to the very Victorian notion of amateurism and the Corinthian spirit. They covered a fairly extensive geographical area, from Preston and Bowdon and from Warrington to Werneth. The deprecation of the 'Leagues' smacks of an antipathy to professionalism (*pace* rugby league/rugby union and the broken time disputes of the same era), and there is a touch of snobbery towards the working-class clubs in Leagues. Note also, though, the get-out clause, which allowed 'professionals engaged on the ground only', which allowed the groundsman to be paid for ground work: the fact that he might bat and bowl for the 1st XI on Saturday was purely incidental! Note also that the controversy about 'neutral' umpires was around 120 years ago, and was effectively 'parked'.

The effect on Whalley Range CC was profound: the club did not play for points, or enter the cup competitions introduced after the 1st World War, until the 1960s. The club did not engage professionals, and even in the last 20 years or so has done so intermittently and without true commitment. Until the 1970s, any groundsman was referred to by his surname only, and was a servant of the club, not an employee. On team pictures, the club's own umpire stands proudly alongside the players, but (in most cases) is referred to again simply by his surname.

John McRae Cowie

As can be seen from the preceding reports about the Manchester & District Cricket Association inaugural meetings, Whalley Range's representative was J. M. Cowie. As such, this seems an ideal time to pay tribute to one of the club's early stalwarts. As mentioned earlier, John McRae Cowie was born in 1849 in Edinburgh, to Alexander and Mary Cowie. His name had first appeared in the line-up for the team from Whalley Range back in 1874. However, in the seasons just prior to this, the coverage in the local press of the Athletic team, as they were known back then, was particularly minimalistic, and very few results came to light, let alone line-ups. Thus, it could well have been that J. M. Cowie had already represented the club for a few seasons previous to 1874, since the Cowie family were certainly living in the Manchester area according to the 1871 census. As it transpired, he would continue to play for the club until the end of the 1897 season, thus spanning a period of at least a quarter of a century.

J. M. Cowie had elder siblings in the form of Mary Watson Cowie and Alexander Samuel Watson Cowie, though no evidence has been unearthed of his older brother representing the club, unlike his younger brother Thomas Scott Cowie. As well as J. M. Cowie having both a mother and a sister called Mary, as of 10th June 1886, he would also have a wife called Mary, since on that date, he married Mary Ann(a) Butler in Pontefract. According to the various censuses, it appears that his early profession was working as a grey cloth salesman, before becoming an insurance broker. He would live into his late sixties, before passing away on 26th September 1918.

As for his cricketing career, he was a superb all-rounder, and by the end of his Whalley Range career in 1897, he would have scored at least eight fifties, and taken five wickets in an innings on no fewer than 38 occasions. Despite scoring a fair few fifties, of those that came to light, there was no evidence of him then going on to produce a really big innings, with the highest of those fifties, being an unbeaten 59. As for his bowling, his best was a nine-wicket haul against the City Police in August 1882 at the College Road ground, the earliest such discovered occurrence for the club. He also claimed a further two eight-wicket hauls, again including the earliest that was unearthed. This came in June 1874 when he ensured a narrow victory for the Athletic team as Heaton Norris Club & Ground were dismissed for 48 in reply to the home team's total of 65. One of the highlights of his cricketing days came in the twilight of his career in 1902, aged in his early fifties, at a time when he now represented Alderley Edge. At the start of the season, he was invited to play for a T. A. Higson's XI against a New Mills & District XVI. It was a game that his side won easily so he didn't get to bat, but he did get to field alongside Lancashire players in the form of Albert Ward, John Holland, and of course, Thomas Atkinson Higson. Also in his team was Derbyshire player Albert Edward Lawton, who would also later play for Lancashire.

For the 1893 season, there were 20 Whalley Range 1st XI games that made the local press, of which they won seven and lost just the once, in a midweek game to Huyton in May. The season started well for Whalley Range with a 49-run win over Brooklands with Reverend D. Dorrity capturing seven wickets. There followed several drawn games and the loss to Huyton, before another explosive effort from H. W. Tindall helped beat Knutsford. Coming in at number five, he dominated play so much, that J. M. Cowie batting at number four, finished with 35 not out, whilst Tindall smashed an incredible 115 out of 185-4 declared. This was the start of a real purple patch for Whalley Range which saw them win six games out of eleven (with the rest being drawn) from early June to late August.

Whalley Range v Knutsford, at Whalley Range, Saturday 10th June 1893

Whalley Range

J. F. Arnold	c Holbrook	b Gibbons	21
C. J. Knowles	c Monkhouse	b Caldicott	4
R. Ray		b Gibbons	4
J. M. Cowie		not out	35
H. W. Tindall	st Monkhouse	b Bolland	115
G. A. H. Jones		not out	0
Extras			6
Total		(for 4 dec.)	185

The Monkhouse who played for Knutsford was A. N. Monkhouse, later Literary Editor of The Manchester Guardian, under C. P. Scott: his son Paddy was Deputy Editor and his grand-daughter – Harriet Monkhouse – is a copy editor at Wisden. Walkers in Lyme Park will know of a bench dedicated to his memory up by the top wall. He also played against the touring Australians in 1880 for a Broughton XVIII team, where interestingly enough, upon his dismissal, the next man into bat, making a guest appearance for the Broughton team, was F. D. Gaddum, who had earlier captured the wickets of P. S. McDonnell and F. R. Spofforth when the Australians had batted.

July was welcomed in with the visit of a team from "The Dingle". The game ended in a draw, with the team from Liverpool having much the better of the game, in spite of five wickets from H. W. Tindall. Winning ways were restored the following weekend with victory over Western thanks mainly to 75 from opener J. Escombe. Two days later on Monday 10th July, H. C. L. Tindall, who'd returned south to become a reverend, made his first-class debut for Kent against Somerset at Taunton, though didn't manage to get a bat. Whalley Range then made it back-to-back wins, thanks to six wickets from F. D. Gaddum, as Alderley Edge were dismissed for just 46, after Whalley Range had made 93.

The Press Connection

Sir Thomas Sowler

A notable entry in the Whalley Range 2nd XI line-up this season was that of F. Sowler. Frank Sowler was born in 1873, and one of his achievements in later life was to be the Master of the Tanat Side Hunt from 1905 to 1908. However, the most important aspect about him was the fact that he was the son of Sir Thomas Sowler (1818-1891). On 1st January 1825, Sir Thomas Sowler's father (also called Thomas) had published the first ever edition of the Manchester Courier from his offices in St. Ann's Square. Sir Thomas and his brother John inherited the business following their father's death in 1857. The Manchester Courier had started life as a weekly newspaper, but from 1st January 1864 it became a daily newspaper, and when John passed away in 1871, Sir Thomas became its sole proprietor. Not long after the birth of his son Frank, Sir Thomas commenced the publication of a further newspaper, the Evening Mail, in 1874. Sir Thomas was also noted for being the Chairman of the Manchester Conservative Association, and of the Conservative Club. He was also the Director of several other bodies, including the Manchester Royal Exchange.

He received his knighthood on 1st January 1890, though passed away the following year. As for his son Frank, who played cricket for Whalley Range, he was a Captain in the Royal Field Artillery in the First World War, though later died from his wounds in July 1921, aged 48. He is buried in St. Mary's churchyard in Bowdon.

With regard to the continuation of Whalley Range's tremendous season in 1893, having competed against a former player the previous week, namely Brooklands' T. P. Bellhouse, the start of August saw Whalley Range up against Western for whom F. L. Steel was still playing. Steel did capture five wickets but not before Whalley Range had posted a commanding total of 173. In reply, Western capitulated completely with no player reaching double-figures in a sorry total of 36, as G. A. H. Jones with seven wickets tore them apart. An inspired Whalley Range team won the next two matches as well, against Broughton and Knutsford. The remaining games were all drawn, the highlight of which was 70 from J. A. MacLaren, in the return game against "The Dingle" in Liverpool. Not only was it the last game of the season, but it also marked J. A. MacLaren's last ever game for the club, since his undoubted talent meant that he'd be playing at a higher level for the remainder of his cricketing days.

From a team perspective, the 1894 season wouldn't be quite as rewarding as the previous season, with a few losses this time, but these were matched by the victory count, though similar to the previous season, most games ended in draws. Individually there was a lot of success, with H. W. Tindall scoring over 500 runs, J. F. Arnold scoring over 400 runs, S. M. Tindall scoring over 300 runs, whilst F. D. Gaddum captured 43 wickets to supplement the 289 runs he scored with the bat.

The season began with draws against Bowdon and Brooklands, followed by victory over Longsight. The Tindall brothers had performed well in these matches, and so in May, the prestigious Manchester team included two sets of brothers who'd played for Whalley Range, namely J. A. and A. C. MacLaren, and S. M. and H. W. Tindall. The start of June then witnessed an enthralling game at Alderley Edge. With the hosts having been dismissed for just 64 thanks to six wickets from F. D. Gaddum, one would have thought that with J. F. Arnold then scoring 37, he'd have done enough to be ultimately celebrating victory. However, it was not to be, as the next highest score by a Whalley Range batsman was a mere 6, as the visitors were dismissed just two runs adrift of the Alderley Edge total. Whalley Range gained revenge in the return game a fortnight later as Alderley Edge were again dismissed fairly cheaply, with G. A. H. Jones taking seven wickets. This time, another good knock from J. F. Arnold, of 52, was enough to see his team to an easy victory. Arnold's fine form was still very much in evidence at the end of June, as testified by the following scoresheet. Note that the rest of the batting line-up was not listed :-

Broughton v Whalley Range, at Broughton, Saturday 30th June 1894

Whalley Range

A. Botsford		b Hassell	9
J. F. Arnold		b Crummack	128
S. M. Tindall		b Windsor	22
J. M. Cowie	c Elwell	b Windsor	5
W. P. Kitcat		b Heap	18
H. W. Tindall	c Heap	b Payne	62
H. C. Arnold		not out	7
Extras			27
Total		(for 6 dec.)	278

J. F. Arnold's 128 was certainly the batting highlight of the season, coming against a strong Broughton side that included the likes of J. G. Heap, and who responded with 169-5 to ensure the game ended in a draw. It was performances like this that would eventually see James Frederick Arnold being added to the ever-growing list of Whalley Range players who'd go on to represent their county, a couple of seasons hence, making his debut for Lancashire at Old Trafford against no lesser team than the touring Australians, in late May 1896. In his team that day would be S. M. Tindall, and in fact, it was following the game just mentioned previously against Broughton, that S. M. Tindall made his debut for Lancashire, against Derbyshire on July 2nd 1894, playing alongside A. C. and J. A. MacLaren.

Speaking of Old Trafford, this was the venue for Whalley Range's next game in the 1894 season, where they were up against a Manchester team that included former players in the form of W. G. Mills and J. A. MacLaren, and as it happens, a future Whalley Range star in the form of A. G. Baker. Arthur George Baker was educated at the nearby Hulme Grammar School (now known as William Hulme's Grammar School) that had been founded in 1887, and was the first of a succession of "Old Hulmeians" who would go on to serve Whalley Range Cricket Club admirably over the next 100 years. However, in this game, he was playing for the opposition and really making his future team-mates suffer with an unbeaten knock of 82 in a massive Manchester total of 307-2 declared that was compiled in two and three-quarter hours. Whalley Range then responded valiantly with W. P. Kitcat top-scoring with an unbeaten 45 in a total of 188-5.

W. P. Kitcat, or Walter Parry de Winton Kitcat to give him his full name, was yet another Whalley Range player who was destined to become a reverend. Walter had been born in Berkshire in about 1874 to a large family that included an elder brother Charles de Winton Kitcat who would later represent Lancashire at hockey in 1892, playing alongside the likes of J. F. Arnold and H. W. Tindall. For Walter though, a life in the church beckoned, most of which would be spent in South Africa, following his emigration there in 1903. Apparently long after the car had been invented, he never learnt to drive, and instead chose to travel on his trusty horse, even on far-flung excursions which took him away from home for a week at a time. Walter died in 1959, with his final years having been spent at St. Bartholomew's Church in Grahamstown, a city in the Eastern Cape Province of South Africa.

Later in July, of the 1894 season, F. D. Gaddum was again making South Manchester suffer, the team that he'd previously taken 9-5 against. In reply to Whalley Range's 130, South Manchester managed to hang on for a draw though, closing on 34-8, with Gaddum adding another six wickets to his season's tally. For the rest of the season S. M. Tindall would intersperse his Whalley Range appearances with those for Lancashire, generally playing for his club team on the Saturday, whilst representing his county during the week. However in spite of a knock of 57 in a defeat against Brooklands, it was his brother H. W. Tindall who was proving to be the biggest star for Whalley Range this season. In early August, he took seven wickets in an innings against Huyton (though Whalley Range were easily beaten and had time to bat again), and welcomed in September with a score of 53 against Broughton. In mid-September a further knock of 72 against Cheadle Hulme, ensured that the milestone of 500 runs for the season was surpassed, as mentioned earlier. Looking back, it does seem amazing that in spite of H. W. Tindall's heroics and explosive batting for Whalley Range over the years, unlike his two older brothers, he never managed to play county cricket at 1st XI level, with the best he ever managed being to represent Lancashire 2nd XI a couple of times towards the end of the 1890s. However, from the players representing the Cricket Club during this period, despite the passing of the era of the Steel brothers, the MacLaren brothers and the like, the Whalley Range club were still clearly bathing in the midst of a "Golden Age", with players such as Gaddum, and the Arnolds and the Tindalls.

Another highlight during the season was at Knutsford in late August. Having batted first and scored 146-5 before declaring, Whalley Range routed their hosts for just 21, with each of G. A. H. Jones and F. D. Gaddum capturing a five-wicket haul. Whalley Range's final record for this season was Played 21, Won 5, Lost 4, with the other 12 games being drawn. In all, Whalley Range scored 2679 runs during the season for the loss of 161 wickets, whilst conceding 2636 runs for 168 wickets. The averages for 1894 were as follows, with the first table for the batting averages showing those who played at least eight innings, whilst the second table is for those who played between four and seven innings :-

Batting Averages 1894

	Inns	n.o.	Runs	High	Ave
H. W. Tindall	19	2	513	72	30.17
F. D. Gaddum	17	6	289	41	26.27
J. F. Arnold	19	1	415	128	23.05
S. M. Tindall	16	0	301	57	18.81
Rev. D. Dorrity	11	1	157	38	15.70
F. E. Hildyard	8	2	82	35	13.66
A. Botsford	13	2	129	25	11.72
J. M. Cowie	16	2	157	23	11.21
G. A. H. Jones	14	0	101	33	7.21
H. C. Butterworth	10	2	57	14	5.70
H. C. Arnold	10	1	38	9	4.22

	Inns	n.o.	Runs	High	Ave
C. W. Botsford	4	1	38	25	12.66
R. W. Sharp	4	2	24	15	12.00
W. R. Deakin	4	0	16	6	4.00
H. T. Mawson	5	3	4	4	2.00

Bowling Averages 1894

	Overs	Maidens	Runs	Wkts	Ave
H. C. Arnold	96	26	215	20	10.75
F. D. Gaddum	207.2	45	463	43	10.76
H. W. Tindall	120.1	20	324	27	12.00
H. C. Butterworth	163	32	431	27	15.96
G. A. H. Jones	260.2	86	549	34	16.14
J. M. Cowie	59	11	174	9	19.33
S. M. Tindall	67	17	191	8	23.87
Rev. D. Dorrity	49	12	125	3	41.66

The following photo is of the Lancashire team from a game in August 1894, featuring former Whalley Range player A. C. MacLaren, and at the time, current Whalley Range player S. M. Tindall, wearing his Whalley Range blazer, seated next to each other in the middle row :-

Lancashire 1894
A. W. Mold, A. G. Paul, Lunt (scorer), G. R. Baker, A. P. Smith
A. Ward, S. M. Tindall, A. C. MacLaren (captain), G. R. Bardswell, F. H. Sugg
J. Briggs, C. Smith, A. Tinsley

As can be seen from this season's batting averages, one of the new names for Whalley Range this season was F. E. Hildyard. Francis Edward Hildyard was born on 31st August 1859 into a family of considerable renown, having connections with the Plantagenet dynasty and having no fewer than ten knights amongst his forefathers. He also had a younger brother, Lyonel D'Arcy Hildyard, who played cricket for Somerset between 1882 and 1883, and for Lancashire between 1884 and 1885.

The Manchester United Connection

Also featured in the 1894 averages is W. R. Deakin, where all of the available evidence would suggest this is William Rothschild Deakin, who went on to become Chairman of Manchester United Football Club from 1909 until his death in November 1919. He was also the Managing Director of the Manchester Brewery Company, where the Club President of Manchester United, John Henry Davies, was one of his work associates. Deakin had first played for Whalley Range in 1893, having previously played for Rusholme. Deakin also played hockey for Didsbury, lining up alongside the likes of J. F. Arnold, R. W. Sharp, H. W. Tindall, and S. M. Tindall.

Though not featured in the averages, W. N. Fletcher, who usually played for Western at this time, was someone else who played for the club during 1894, if only for the last game of the season, against Cheadle Hulme. Fletcher was another who enjoyed playing hockey, and during the following winter, he too played alongside J. F. Arnold and the Tindall brothers, representing not just Lancashire at hockey (with games sometimes played at Didsbury), but with all four of them also representing the North (of England) against the South.

The 1895 season started in late April with a win over Bowdon thanks mainly to 61 from J. F. Arnold. Whalley Range then made it two wins out of two with victory over Brooklands, where the star of the show was undoubtedly H. W. Tindall who captured seven wickets, and top-scored with 34. As it happened, for most of the rest of the season, the Tindalls and the Arnolds would ply their trade elsewhere, and their absence was really felt, as these two early wins would prove to represent all but one of Whalley Range's successes this season. Of the remaining 21 games, 10 were drawn, 10 were lost, and only one more game was won. But Whalley Range's loss would certainly prove to be Manchester's gain as both J. F. Arnold and H. W. Tindall hit centuries for them, with the former scoring 763 runs throughout the year, whilst the latter also surpassed 500 runs. Thus, even though Whalley Range would be enduring one of their poorer seasons, some of their former players would really be thriving, most noteworthy of which would be the incredible exploits of A. C. MacLaren.

Indications of the tough season ahead, came in Whalley Range's next two games, where they were thrashed by both Cheetham Hill and Western. Cheetham Hill posted a moderate 122 but then bowled Whalley Range out for just 34 with nobody making double-figures. Asked to follow on, Whalley Range were 34-4 in their second innings at the close of play. The following weekend at Eccles, Western made 223-6 before declaring and then bowling out Whalley Range for just 59. At least Whalley Range saw out May with a victory, though as alluded to earlier, it would prove to be their last success of the season. Having bowled out visitors Knutsford for 108, it was Rev. D. Dorrity who guided the hosts home with an unbeaten 46.

In the defeat against Cheetham Hill, a notable name on the scoresheet in his one and only appearance for Whalley Range was that of J. Bythell. Unfortunately no middle initial was given in the paper, but it seems a strong possibility that this is John Charles Bythell since he certainly had connections with Whalley Range players, having played alongside the likes of the Tindall brothers and J. F. Arnold when playing for Lancashire at hockey. He also enjoyed playing tennis, which may explain his very rare ventures out onto a cricket field. He was born in Bombay (now Mumbai) in 1869, the son of John Kenworthy Bythell. Having been a partner in the firm of Gaddum, Bythell and Co., his father then joined the Board of Directors of the Manchester Ship Canal Company in 1887, before becoming Chairman in 1894. John Kenworthy Bythell was also a Justice of the Peace in both Bombay and Manchester.

During June, Whalley Range's record was three draws and three defeats, with the only highlights being E. A. Mayall and J. M. Cowie both claiming five-wicket hauls along the way, whilst the low-point was conceding 268-6 to Cheadle Hulme in a heavy defeat. However, there was a further highlight in the 2nd XI game at Alderley Edge on Saturday 15th June, with Charles Edward Dunderdale scoring an unbeaten 102, out of a total of 185-8 declared. In spite of another five-wicket haul for G. A. H. Jones, July started with another heavy defeat, with former Whalley Range player W. G. Mills scoring 96, as Whalley Range were thumped by Manchester at Old Trafford. Also playing for the hosts was A. G. Baker, though the following Saturday on July 13th he would make his debut for Whalley Range. Two days later, on Monday July 15th, A. C. MacLaren began his monumental innings against Somerset, which he concluded the following day, having smashed the Somerset bowlers all round Taunton, on the way to his record-breaking innings of 424.

Whalley Range's season continued with a succession of draws, with their best performance coming at home against Western with G. A. H. Jones scoring an unbeaten 68 out of a total of 186-5 before the weather forced the game to be abandoned. In August, Whalley Range suffered three defeats in a row against South Manchester, Castleton, and then Knutsford, though J. M. Cowie took five wickets against Castleton, and F. D. Gaddum captured six wickets against Knutsford. A difficult season for Whalley Range then concluded with draws against Cheetham Hill and Longsight, in games that were presumably affected by the weather.

Not the first time this season when they travelled away, the game at Knutsford involved Whalley Range having to make up their full complement of eleven players with a little assistance from their hosts. As such, brothers Theodore Llewellyn Fennell and William Whately Fennell found themselves in the Whalley Range line-up. For W. W. Fennell, this was another for whom a profession in the church beckoned, whilst T. L. Fennell became a physician, working down in Kent. However, on this particular occasion in late August of 1895, neither of the brothers did much to help Whalley Range's cause, with both being out for ducks!

For the 1896 season, Whalley Range would again be without their main stars for most of the season, with inevitable consequences. Whalley Range managed just two victories all season, with the likes of J. F. Arnold and the Tindall brothers making just three guest appearances for Whalley Range, when they were up against sterner opposition, in the forms of Manchester and Huyton (twice). The game against Manchester was a real cliff-hanger. With H. W. Tindall taking six wickets against the team that he normally played for this season, Manchester were dismissed for 171. Thus when Whalley Range had reached 170-7 in reply, thanks to 55 from S. M. Tindall and 31 from J. F. Arnold, only one result seemed to be on the cards. However, Whalley Range lost their last three wickets without adding to the total, to lose by just one run! The previous weekend at Old Trafford, J. F. Arnold had actually starred in an unbroken opening partnership of 274 for Manchester against Longsight, with his share being 116, whilst Ernest Butler Rowley had contributed 130 at the other end.

The highlight of Whalley Range's season was undoubtedly the first of two encounters with Huyton, both games of which were played on a Monday. Thus on May 25th 1896, Whalley Range entertained Huyton, and disposed of their formidable visitors for just 121. In reply, the hosts got off to a bad start losing opener J. F. Arnold for a duck, before the next three wickets all fell cheaply as well. At this point, H. W. Tindall coming in at number six, joined his brother S. M. Tindall, who had stood firm since the start, and together they turned the game around, easily overhauling Huyton's target, with H. W. Tindall going on to complete his century. This was his fourth recorded century for the club that has been unearthed, and even though the final digit is not very clear in the press, it would appear to have been 108, whilst his brother scored 77, to help Whalley Range to victory by well over 100 runs.

Whalley Range v Huyton, at Whalley Range, Monday 25th May 1896
Whalley Range

J. F. Arnold		b Fieldwick	0
S. M. Tindall	lbw	b H. Eccles	77
Rev. D. Dorrity		b E. Eccles	12
A. G. Baker		b H. Eccles	11
J. M. Cowie	lbw	b E. Eccles	0
H. W. Tindall	stumped	b T. Eccles	108
F. D. Gaddum	lbw	b T. Eccles	6
A. Botsford		not out	5
G. A. H. Jones		b T. Eccles	3
A. N. Other	c H. Eccles	b Fieldwick	7
E. A. Mayall	c Henery	b T. Eccles	0
Extras			19
Total			248

A. G. Baker, with a succession of unbeaten scores, would undoubtedly have topped the batting averages this season (of those who played regularly). In the first half of the season he scored 46 not out against Knutsford, an unbeaten 52 against Western, and also carried his bat with an unbeaten 50 against Longsight, though none of these performances would help Whalley Range attain victory. That only other triumph this season, came in mid-May when Alderley Edge were the visitors and Reverend D. Dorrity helped send them packing for 78 with a seven-wicket haul. In their innings, Whalley Range scored 104-9, with Harry Temple Mawson (of whom more anon) top-scoring with 44. A fortnight later, H. T. Mawson was in fine form again, scoring an unbeaten 71 in a drawn game with South Manchester, and in early July, he also scored 45 against Longsight, though this game marked the start of a run of seven successive defeats for Whalley Range. In amongst this losing streak, there was a game billed as F. D. Gaddum's XI versus T. P. Bellhouse's XI that ended in a draw, with the former team basically being represented by Whalley Range players.

Some of these defeats, especially in August, were of sizeable proportions. On Saturday 1st August, Bowdon won by over 100 runs, though A. G. Baker with an unbeaten 28, again carried his bat in a meagre total of 61. Worse was to come just two days later, when Whalley Range lost by over 200 runs to Huyton, who were clearly intent on revenge after their defeat earlier in the season. Thus, even with the Tindall brothers and J. F. Arnold drafted back in for this Bank Holiday Monday game, a strong Huyton outfit still amassed a mammoth 334. In reply, Whalley Range were dismissed for 128. The following Saturday, the Tindall brothers, J. F. Arnold, and W. G. Mills as it happens, were back playing for Manchester. Meanwhile Whalley Range were enduring another defeat by over 100 runs, against Western who scored 222-3 before declaring, and then bowling out Whalley Range for 108. If only Whalley Range could have called on the services of their "guest" players, and S. M. Tindall in particular, who smashed 152 for Manchester that day, since it seems like this run of heavy defeats was enough to convince F. D. Gaddum to hang up his boots, as this game against Western would appear to be the last time that his name graced a Whalley Range scoresheet.

Whalley Range's woeful run continued by being bowled out for just 41 against Alderley Edge. In the days when games were always decided by run margins, Alderley Edge responded with 148-8, in spite of five wickets from Edward Arthur Mayall, to win by over 100 runs. Then at South Manchester, the home team replied with 228-9 to Whalley Range's 119. As such, this was the fifth time in a row that Whalley Range had been defeated by over 100 runs in August 1896. Most of the few games that remained this season were badly affected by the weather, which perhaps could be viewed as some sort of blessing by the Whalley Range team!

The Argentina Connection

As mentioned previously, Harry Temple Mawson had first played for the club back in 1893, whilst one of his several older sisters, Alice Temple Mawson, had married Joseph Arthur Railton in 1890. During the 1896 season, H. T. Mawson had first begun to make his mark, generally opening the innings in the games where J. F. Arnold and the Tindall brothers were absent, making several notable scores, the highest of which was his unbeaten 71 against South Manchester. By trade, he was in the engineering profession, and it would appear that Harry travelled a bit, since he emigrated to Argentina at one point (on the ship Desire having embarked at Liverpool), and at the time of his death in 1936, aged 63, he was then living in America. Whilst in Argentina, he regularly played for the South (of Argentina) in the annual games against the North between 1906 and 1919, generally as opener. However, one of the more notable games was where he batted at number six, contributing 52 to a total of 453, scored from 115 overs. In this game, played in early February 1913, he played alongside some notable team-mates, including Charles Trevor Mold who played for Argentina at rugby union, and Harry Herbert Lorenz Kortlang, who though born in Australia, represented New Zealand at cricket. In 62 first-class innings, Kortlang averaged 49.77, including six centuries, the highest of which was an unbeaten 214. Such was the company that Harry Temple Mawson now found himself amongst!

The 1897 season then seemed to have started off really well with H. C. Butterworth taking nine wickets against Cheetham Hill, as the visitors were dismissed for 132. However, Whalley Range's proclivity to lose matches by over 100 runs was still very much in evidence, even from such an improbable situation, as they succumbed to just 29 all out!

Harry Clement Butterworth was at least the fourth member of the Butterworth family to play for Whalley Range, following in the footsteps of his older brothers Charles Frederick and Joseph Francis, and his father, who was also called Joseph Francis Butterworth. As mentioned earlier, his brother Charles Frederick Butterworth went on to become an eminent astronomer. Certainly with regard to cricket though, H. C. Butterworth was the brother who figured most prominently for Whalley Range. He was born on 9th May 1875, and had first played for the 2nd XI in 1891, when he was still short of his 16th birthday. Towards the end of the 1893 season, he scored 63 in a 2nd XI game, and perhaps on the back of this performance, spent a lot of the 1894 season playing for the 1st XI, finishing fourth in the bowling averages with 27 wickets. Most of the following season was also spent playing for the 1st XI, though without too much success. As such, some of the 1896 season, saw him back playing for the 2nd XI, where at least he was in the company of his brother Charles.

Thus it wasn't until 1897 that H. C. Butterworth really announced himself with that stunning bowling performance against Cheetham Hill, even if Whalley Range did end up losing heavily. Harry would continue playing for the club up until 1904, claiming many more sizeable wicket-hauls along the way, before re-appearing on the scene for the 1911, 1913 and 1914 seasons. Apparently after WWI, Harry became very much the black sheep of the family. Doubtless emotionally scarred from the effects of war, Harry then lost his wife to the 'Flu Epidemic shortly after the cessation of hostilities. His four children were then taken in by various relatives. One of his children, Clive, died believing that his father had simply abandoned them, for no better reason than being unwilling or too scared to raise a family on his own. However, the sad truth that later transpired, was that he'd begun an affair with a friend of the family, was subsequently declared unfit to be a parent, and was hounded out of town, as they say.

In mid-May, Whalley Range encountered a Brooklands team that included a future Lancashire player in the form of Charles Robert Hartley, and once the young American had completed his century, Brooklands declared on 262-3. Against such a strong team, it was perhaps inevitable that Whalley Range ended up adding to their recent burgeoning tally of defeats by over 100 runs.

Over the next few games, Whalley Range's winless streak continued, with the worst result being a heavy defeat to a Chorlton-cum-Hardy side that featured F. Howard, a future Whalley Range player. In this game, no Whalley Range player reached double-figures in their total of 57, an ignominy that befell very few of the opposition batsmen, as they reached 170-7 in reply, of which F. Howard made 29. Whilst Whalley Range were suffering yet another defeat by over 100 runs, S. M. Tindall was simultaneously playing well for Lancs in guiding them to a tight victory.

Whalley Range watched by over 2000 spectators!

In spite of Whalley Range's recent run of bad form, apparently over 2000 spectators came to watch their match on Saturday 26th June 1897! Admittedly the weather was glorious, and it was at Old Trafford against the prestigious Manchester side, but looking back now, it does seem amazing that the Whalley Range team used to play in front of such a large crowd. As it happened, even with the visitors' team reinforced with the temporary welcoming back of J. F. Arnold and H. W. Tindall, it was another heavy defeat for Whalley Range, replying with 111 to the 263 posted by Manchester.

July kicked off with an improved performance against Kersal, with A. G. Baker scoring an unbeaten 83 out of a total of 150-3 declared. However, in spite of H. C. Butterworth bagging another five-wicket haul, Kersal earnt a draw, finishing on 98-6. July then got even better against Monton, with H. J. Amos, another product of Hulme Grammar School as mentioned previously, wrapping up the opposition innings for 83 with figures of 5-11. Whalley Range then cruised to 120, to register their first victory for over a year. The next four games all ended in defeat, despite the occasional fine individual performance (J. M. Cowie 57 not out against South Manchester, and H. J. Amos 6 wickets against Huyton). The heaviest of these defeats was to the Brooklands team that the Tindall brothers now played for, and H. W. Tindall was in no mood to go easy on his former team-mates, scoring a fifty and taking a five-wicket haul as Brooklands amassed 206-6 before declaring, and then dismissed Whalley Range for just 69.

Whalley Range 2nd XI v Western 2nd XI, at Whalley Range, Saturday 7th August 1897
Whalley Range 2nd XI

N. Varbetian		3
Rev. G. Dale	not out	103
J. E. Daniel		69
J. M. Dale		17
F. Sowler		3
Extras		24
Total	(for 4 dec)	219

The arrival of August brought better times for Whalley Range. As can be seen above, in a 2nd XI game against Western, Rev. G. Dale scored an unbeaten 103, whilst in the corresponding 1st XI game, Whalley Range gained a creditable draw against a strong Western side, thanks mainly to an unbeaten 54 from C. W. Botsford, before dismissing Alderley Edge for just 35 in the next game. H. C. Butterworth, who had taken a five-wicket haul in the previous game, added a further six wickets in this game, and a stumping.

In fact, there were three stumpings in the innings, all by different Whalley Range wicket-keepers! Whalley Range replied with 126 to complete a comprehensive victory. Perhaps J. M. Cowie felt some degree of compunction for inflicting such a resounding victory over the opposition, since after a long and distinguished career representing Whalley Range, the following season would see him bolstering the Alderley Edge line-up. The rest of the games in the 1897 season then seem to have been affected by the weather, with those matches that did start ending in a draw.

The Tragic Case of A. L. A. Bull

Someone who first appeared for the Whalley Range 2nd XI team during the 1897 season was Archibald Louis Alfred Bull. He was born in about 1879 to Elizabeth and Henry Charles Bull, and had at least eight older siblings. The 1881 census lists the family dwelling as St. James Vicarage in Wigan, where the father was indeed the vicar. According to the census, there were also three servants employed at the Vicarage, so ones assumes that even though A. L. A. Bull had so many older brothers and sisters, his childhood wouldn't have been too uncomfortable, with the Bulls appearing to be a fairly prosperous family. He also appeared for Whalley Range 2nd XI the following season in 1898, but ultimately his life was to end in tragic circumstances. The following report from the Manchester Guardian on 6th March 1917 entitled "*An Altrincham Suicide*" and subtitled "*A Victim of the Drug Habit*" did state his age as 30, though he would actually have been in his late thirties when he decided to take his own life :-

> *An inquest was held at Altrincham yesterday on Archibald Louis Alfred Bull, aged 30, a salesman in the employ of Messrs. Ashton Brothers and Co. Limited, Manchester and Hyde, who lived at 91 New Street, Altrincham, and who committed suicide on Thursday by cutting his throat with a razor.*
>
> *According to the evidence Bull had been in bad health for two or three years and had taken drugs for sleeplessness and melancholia. Two or three months ago he lost money through gambling in cotton futures, and made a confession of this to Mr. Mark Winder, one of the heads of the firm by whom he was employed. Mr. Winder spoke to him severely about it, and he promised not to do it again. Mr. Winder asked him how he was going to pay his debts, and he said that he expected some money from his father's estate. During the last week or so he had been more depressed.*
>
> *On Tuesday last he went to his work as usual, but on Wednesday complained of feeling ill and was sent home, Mr. Winder at the same time telephoning to Dr. Luckman. A male nurse was also called to the house, and slept in the same bedroom. On Thursday, Bull was very much dejected, but seemed to improve later. He asked the attendant to go an errand, and Mrs. Probert, the lady with whom he had lodged for twelve years, came into the room and stayed with him. Suddenly he left the room, saying he was going to wash his hands. Shortly afterwards Mrs. Probert heard a gurgling noise, and when she went upstairs she saw him before the mirror cutting his throat with a razor. She rushed at him and had a very severe struggle with him, during which her hand was cut. The attendant then came back, rushed upstairs, and closed with the unfortunate man. After another desperate struggle, in which the razor was broken, Bull sank to the floor. The nurse ran for a doctor, but on his arrival the man was dead.*
>
> *The Coroner, in summing up, said it was a very sad case of a promising career cut short. His employers had given him the highest of characters, and it was satisfactory to know that he had not used any of the firm's money in his gambling, but they all knew that drugs and drink only ended in one way. It was a great pity that he had been addicted to the taking of drugs. The Coroner specially commended the bravery of Mrs. Probert. The jury returned a verdict of suicide during temporary insanity, and expressed their agreement with the Coroner's remarks as to Mrs. Probert's bravery.*

The 1898 season marked an important point in the history of the Whalley Range Cricket Club, with the first appearances of a number of players who'd contribute enormously to the club over the ensuing decades. As it happened though, with Whalley Range cricket still not having really recovered from the recent departure of so many significant players, the season started inauspiciously against Chorlton-cum-Hardy with Whalley Range being bowled out for just 42 in reply to the visitors' total of 108 in which H.

J. Amos had captured five wickets. However in the Whalley Range line-up for the corresponding 2nd XI fixture, a game in which N. Varbetian (a name of Syrian/Armenian extraction) scored 52, were the names of H. R. Classen and C. S. Baker.

Harry Rudolph Classen

Harry Rudolph Classen, or "Dolph", as he was more commonly known, was born on March 18th 1877 in Bradford to a German father and an Irish mother. In 1873, his father, Anthony Quirinus Rudolphus Classen, who was a foreign correspondent, had married Emma E. Boyd, in Belfast. Having attended Hulme Grammar School, Dolph then became a cotton merchant, an occupation that saw him visiting such far-flung places as Brazil, Argentina, and Uruguay.

Amongst Dolph's several siblings was a younger brother called Ernest who would also represent the Whalley Range club over the coming years, whilst Dolph's son Geoffrey would also play cricket for the club after the War.

Dolph would go on to be associated with Whalley Range cricket for the entire first half of the twentieth century, for many years as 1st XI captain (1914-1936), and in later years, as the President of the club (1937-1956). Dolph was a superb all-rounder, scoring countless fifties for the club and at least three centuries, and in the last full season before the First World War, he captured at least five 5-wicket hauls throughout the summer including a 7-wicket haul at Buxton. Famously, at least in Whalley Range cricketing circles, one of Dolph's centuries was scored at the grand old age of 58 against Bowdon in 1935. It was also at Bowdon, in the same fixture two years later, that Dolph played his last game for the 1st XI. As described in more detail later in this book, the Bowdon players marked the occasion by presenting him with a signed bat. Since Dolph continued to play 2nd XI cricket for a while, one suspects that he made full use of such a generous gift.

In 1903, he would marry Euphemie Blanche Leroy, sister of Ferdinand Raymond Leroy, who would go on to be another stalwart for the club. They would have an only child who, as mentioned above, would represent the club, though tragically Geoffrey was to die far too young.

After such tremendous devotion to the club, the gateway to the current ground in Kingsbrook Road was named in his honour, following his death in 1956. There is also a plaque in the clubhouse (see picture below), celebrating his dedication to the club, which indicates he joined the club in 1897, though admittedly it wasn't until the following season that we see his name appearing in any scoresheets.

H. R. CLASSEN
IN AFFECTIONATE AND EVERLASTING
MEMORY OF
"DOLPH"
PRESIDENT OF THIS CLUB
1937 – 1956
AND A MEMBER FOR 59 YEARS
1897 – 1956

Charles Shaw Baker

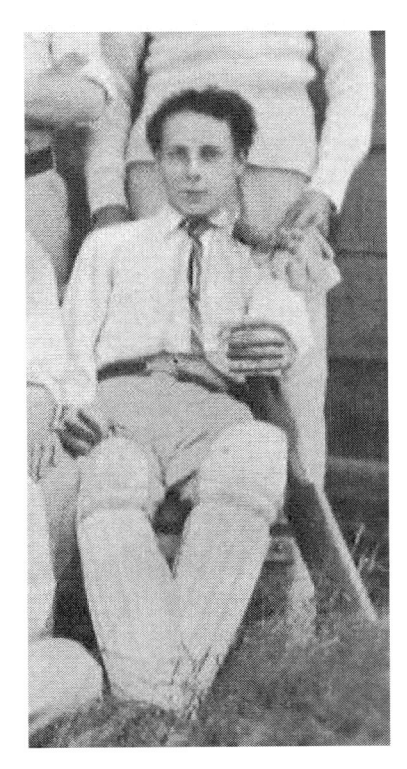

Charles Shaw Baker was born on 5th January 1883 in Moss Side, the younger brother of Arthur George Baker, both of whom attended Hulme Grammar School. The associated photo snippet is taken from the School 1st XI cricket team photo from 1897. Together the "Fabulous Baker Boys" (though admittedly the older brother was now well into his twenties!) would go on to perform brilliantly over the coming years, until eventually C. S. Baker honed his talents so much, that first-class county cricket beckoned in 1905.

Before this though, he played regularly for Whalley Range between 1898 and 1902 with a fifty in a 2nd XI game against Knutsford early in the 1898 season seeing him rise quickly to the 1st XI despite being so young. The following season, aged just 16, he scored his first century for the club, against Alderley Edge, and over the coming seasons, would score at least a further two centuries, against Owens College and Castleton. The left-handed Baker also became a very good bowler, claiming several five-wicket hauls with his leg-breaks.

In 1903, he started playing for Warwickshire 2nd XI, though did make one guest appearance for Whalley Range late in the season. Two years later, he made his first-class debut for Warwickshire on 8th May 1905 against Somerset, and celebrated the occasion with a fifty in the second innings. He would go on to play over 200 games for his adopted county, scoring close to 10,000 runs, a figure which he would undoubtedly have sailed past, but for the intervention of the First World War. He also scored 10 centuries, the highest of which was an unbeaten 155, scored in 285 minutes and including 18 fours, against close rivals Worcestershire at New Road in Worcester, in mid-May 1910. During this time he did make one further guest appearance for Whalley Range in 1906, as highlighted later in the book.

After the War, he played a few more games for Warwickshire, before moving further down south and playing Minor Counties cricket for Cornwall between 1925 and 1931, where he made an immediate impact with a couple of centuries in his first season for them. He would compile a further four centuries for Cornwall, including consecutive scores of 145 and 106 not out, in the 1929 season. C. S. Baker would end his days in Cornwall, living to the grand old age of 93.

Thus, on Saturday 21st May 1898, whilst the 15-year old left-hander C. S. Baker was scoring 50 for the 2nd XI, Dolph Classen was making his debut for the Whalley Range 1st XI, contributing 30 to a total of 101-2 declared. On a rainy day, Knutsford responded with 49-4. After his fifty for the 2nd XI, C. S. Baker made his first appearance in the 1st XI line-up the following week against Western, playing alongside his elder brother. Against such strong opposition, the young C. S. Baker performed well on his debut, taking a couple of wickets in the Western total of 201. Whalley Range then gained a creditable draw thanks to 51 from opener A. Botsford, and an unbeaten 32 from A. G. Baker.

The following weekend witnessed the Whalley Range team making one of their regular jaunts to Old Trafford, though having made just 70, Manchester coasted to victory, finishing on 157-4. Former Whalley Range favourite J. F. Arnold opened the innings for Manchester, but H. C. Butterworth bowled him out for a duck.

Towards the end of June, Whalley Range registered one of their rare victories in this rain-affected season, with a 100-run thrashing of a depleted Kersal team, for whom a few Whalley Range players appeared as guests. Having declared on 141-8, Kersal were then sent flying for just 41, with all of H. J. Amos, H. C. Butterworth, and G. A. H. Jones, amongst the wickets.

Another player enjoying what would appear to his debut season for the club was A. F. Walley. Archibald Frederick Walley was born in about 1881, and worked as a solicitor in the city centre. He played more or less continuously for the club up until the 1901 season before playing again in the 1905 season. However, he would die young, passing away in 1908.

The Book Connection

John Edward Gunby Hadath

The game on Saturday 2nd July 1898 then featured another in this season's list of notable debutants with the first recorded instance of J. E. G. Hadath playing for the club, though he was out for a golden duck! Born in 1871 in Lincolnshire, John Edward Gunby Hadath went on to become the author of more than 100 books for boys involving English public school life and wartime adventure, using the names Gunby Hadath and John Mowbray. Opinion appears to be divided as to whether Florence Gunby Hadath was another pseudonym that he used, with most people appearing to believe that this was also his work. However, the person who seems to be the foremost authority on the works of Hadath, a guy called Dick Chandler, is firmly of the belief that the books listed with Florence Gunby Hadath as the author, were indeed the works of his wife, Florence. One of his tales, 'Fortune Lane' was filmed by Elstree Independent Films in 1947. He also wrote a number of songs.

He played in two remarkable cricket matches in 1911 and 1912 at Lord's that pitted the Authors against the Publishers, where his team-mates included P. G. Wodehouse and Arthur Conan Doyle! As for his earlier cricketing exploits in the north-west, having represented Longsight in 1897, he then played for Whalley Range for the next two seasons, with some notable batting success, scoring at least a couple of fifties in his second and last season for the club. Gunby was a Francophile who maintained a chalet near Mont Blanc at St. Gervais les Bains, and was made an honorary citizen of St. Gervais in recognition of his efforts to publicise the spa town in England.

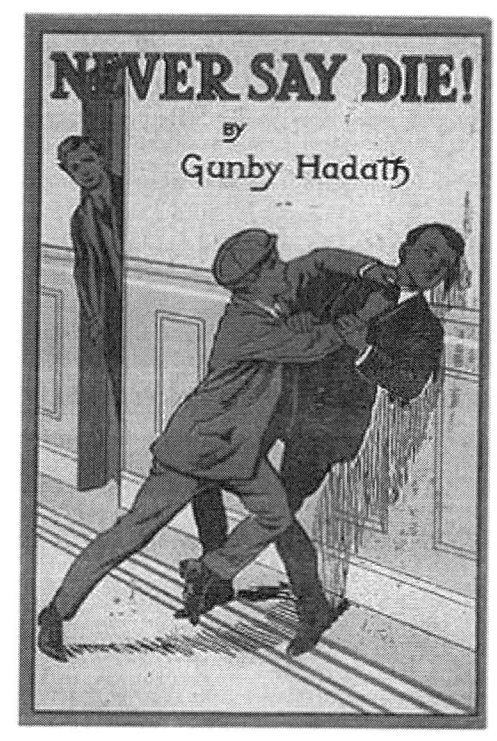

Just a couple of the many books written by John Edward Gunby Hadath

Following a draw, in which A. G. Baker scored 82 against South Manchester, Whalley Range won again in mid-July, in the return game against Chorlton-cum-Hardy. Batting first, Whalley Range posted 139, with S. A. Russell contributing the most with 37. The Chorlton-cum-Hardy line-up still included F. Howard, but with H. J. Amos taking four wickets and J. M. Dale taking three wickets, Whalley Range managed to emerge winners by 34 runs. Interestingly, number 11 in the Whalley Range batting line-up was F. R. Leroy, though he did fail to trouble the scorers on this occasion.

Ferdinand Raymond Leroy

Ferdinand Raymond Leroy would be another player who would be associated with the club for many years to come, as indicated in the ensuing picture of a plaque in the clubhouse. Ferdie was a fine all-round sportsman, since as well as playing cricket for Whalley Range for 40 years, he also represented Lancashire for over a decade at hockey, captaining them at one point, and was president of the Lancashire County Hockey Association in 1920 to 1921. Ferdie was born in 1880 to a family of French descent with the name originally spelt as Le Roy. Despite their French heritage, the family home was one with a Spanish title, namely Buena Vista on Alexandra Road South.

As previously mentioned, his elder sister, Euphemie Blanche Leroy, would marry Harry Rudolph Classen in 1903. Similar to Classen's plaque, it indicates he joined the club in 1897, though again, it wasn't until the following season that we see his name appearing in any scoresheets.

Ferdie was also the first ever Club Chairman, when the position came into being prior to the start of the 1937 season, though sadly it was a role that he would fulfil for less than a year, with his untimely passing towards the end of the year. His father, Jules Joseph Leroy, served as the Club President from 1914 to 1929.

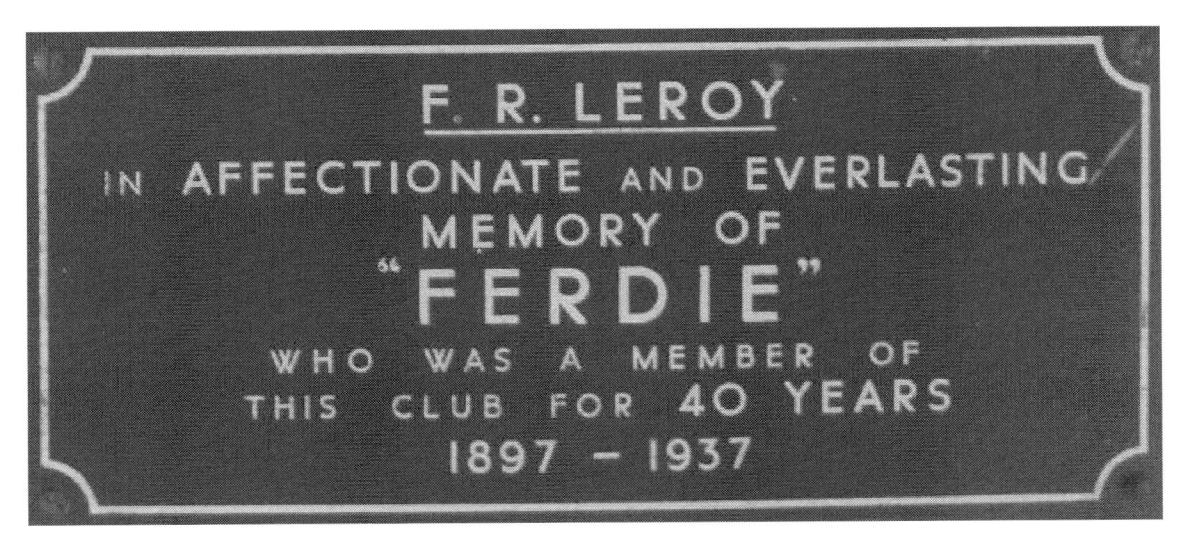

For the remainder of the 1898 season, Whalley Range were up against some stern opposition. At the start of August, they bumped up against a Western team that comprised both F. L. and E. E. Steel, though at 32-5, Whalley Range were rescued by the weather. Then in September, Whalley Range were easily beaten by a Brooklands team that included T. P. Bellhouse and C. R. Hartley.

Following the completion of the 1898 season, an article appeared in the local press on 4th November, about a proposed electricity sub-station, to be situated on the edge of the cricket ground, and from this article, it would appear that Whalley Range's recent poor form had become the source of some amusement. In the article, Mr. W. Becker, representing the company that wished to install the "transforming sub-station" was reported as stating that he did not think any great damage would be done to cricket by the utilisation of the cricket ground for such a purpose, as the cricket club never seemed to win a match anyway! The sub-station is still there, on Clarendon Road.

Perhaps it was this article that provided the necessary incentive for Whalley Range to try and rekindle the sort of success they'd enjoyed in the not-too-distant past, since the 1899 season would see a rejuvenated Whalley Range Cricket Club again achieving some notable successes, with of course the rapidly emerging talent of C. S. Baker, proving to be a significant factor in this regard. Of the sixteen 1st XI games that made the local press this season, even though most games were drawn, only one was lost, whilst there were four resounding victories.

For the 1899 season, F. Howard had changed his allegiance from Chorlton-cum-Hardy to Whalley Range, and would serve his new club admirably for many years into the future. Howard thus featured in an early season encounter with Monton, a game in which H. C. Butterworth took six wickets, though the game ended in a tame draw, having presumably been affected by the weather. Also featured in the line-up for this game was K. T. S. Dockray.

Kenneth Titus Smalley Dockray

Kenneth Titus Smalley Dockray was born in Manchester on 7th January 1875 to William and Hannah Dockray, and in 1895 gained admission to Trinity College, Cambridge, where he gained first class honours in Moral Science, though strangely enough someone referred to him as not having a first-class mind despite his first-class degree. Clearly undeterred by such comments, he later became President of the Manchester Reform Club, associated with the Liberal Party, and a gentlemen's club situated in Spring Gardens. The building itself was completed in 1871, though it is now a restaurant and bar.

Even though his playing days for Whalley Range would appear to have come to an end with the onset of the First World War, K. T. S. Dockray would still be associated with the club well over sixty years later, right up until his passing away in 1966, at the ripe old age of 91. He would also serve as the Club's Honorary Treasurer for the best part of thirty years from 1900 to 1929, and following this was the Club President up until 1937.

With regard to his playing days, the most notable moments of his career, were playing alongside his younger brother, Francis Smalley Dockray, during the 1906 season for the 2nd XI, and then four seasons later, he was a member of the tour party that travelled round North Yorkshire in 1910.

The weather seems to have ensured that all of the early fixtures in the 1899 season were either drawn or abandoned. Thus it wasn't until the start of June, that Whalley Range recorded their first win, but when it came, it was a very emphatic affair over F. Howard's former team, Chorlton. Howard himself scored only seven with the bat against his former team-mates but with 47 from J. E. G. Hadath, Whalley Range posted a respectable 154. In reply, no Chorlton player reached double-figures, with fast bowler H. J. Amos inflicting the most damage with a five-wicket haul. At the same time as Whalley Range were beating Chorlton, former player J. F. Arnold was scoring 124 for Manchester against Oldham.

The number of former Hulme Grammar School pupils starting to come through the ranks indicates a really significant shift in the social make-up of the club. Previously, it had been very upper-middle class, with the sons of the wealthy playing after learning the game at the great public schools and universities. Now, the local grammar school, catering for the well-to-do local middle-class, was the engine of growth, and indeed for nearly 100 years, the school was the club's breeding ground for emerging talent. Even in 2014, one midweek match saw two Old Hulmeians open the batting for the club.

The tennis section, which was officially re-embraced in 1912, also attracted the local girls of their social class, many of whom will have gone to Whalley Range High School for Girls, and many a successful marriage began at the club around this time.

Thus, we see the likes of Old Hulmeians, H. B. L. Muth and S. W. Saxelby starting playing for the club, mainly for the 2nd XI, but with the odd game for the 1st XI too. Hermann Bernhard Lionel Muth, to give him his full glorious title (though in later years he seems to have dropped the 'h' and simply gone by the name of Bernard Muth) was born on 18th January 1877. His father, Otto Muth, was German, and he had married a local woman, Harriet Emma Caldwell, the previous summer. Bernard Muth was one of the original 64 pupils of the Hulme Grammar School when it first opened on 26th January 1887. In 1907, he would marry Elsie Radford, and they would reside on Dudley Road in Whalley Range, not far from the College Road ground. Bernard Muth would live until the ripe old age of 88.

Born in 1876, Sydney Walter Saxelby would work for the family business of sugar and produce brokers at Hanging Ditch in Manchester. He would marry Ellen Mabel Horsfall on 9th September 1915 at Christ Church, West Didsbury, and he too would be another who would live into his eighties. Of the Old Hulmeians though, it was C. S. Baker, at the tender young age of 16, who was still clearly the pick of the crop, as he demonstrated in the next game with 100 against Alderley Edge :-

Whalley Range v Alderley Edge, at Whalley Range, Saturday 10th June 1899

Whalley Range				Alderley Edge			
C. S. Baker		b W. Mills	100	A. Sheldon		b Butterworth	4
H. C. Butterworth		b W. Symonds	2	W. Mills		b Butterworth	13
J. E. G. Hadath		b C. Symonds	79	G. Ross		b G. P. Joy	12
A. G. Baker	c Foster	b C. Symonds	6	J. Walsh		b G. P. Joy	0
N. Varbetian		not out	0	C. Symonds	c H. J. Amos	b G. P. Joy	19
Rev. W. H. Ashton		not out	5	W. Symonds	c A. G. Baker	b G. P. Joy	28
				W. Walsh		b G. P. Joy	0
				S. Ross	c Walley	b G. P. Joy	0
				R. Foster	c Ashton	b G. P. Joy	2
				W. White	c G. P. Joy	b H. J. Amos	0
				F. G. Hill		not out	0
Extras			34	Extras			6
Total		(for 4 dec.)	226	Total			84

With solid support from J. E. G. Hadath, Whalley Range rattled up 226-4 before declaring. With G. P. Joy then taking seven wickets and a catch, Alderley Edge made just 84, as Whalley Range wrapped up another comfortable victory. There was no such comfort in the next game though, as Manchester amassed an enormous 303-6 against them at Old Trafford. In the end though, Whalley Range salvaged a draw, thanks to an unbeaten 54 from G. P. Joy, in a total of 128-7. Having made such a big impact, following up his seven wickets in one game with an unbeaten fifty in the next, George Percy Joy then seems to have disappeared off the cricketing radar, as these were the only two times that his name appeared in the local press. Since he hailed from London and went on to become a medical practitioner working in London, one assumes that some of his medical training brought him up north for a short period.

The next few games were all drawn, though Whalley Range prospered well with the bat, with C. S. Baker scoring 78 out of 184-5 against South Manchester, whilst his older brother, and captain, A. G. Baker scored an unbeaten 64 against Chorlton-cum-Hardy, followed up the following weekend with an unbeaten 67 against Worsley.

Two days later on the August Bank Holiday Monday, Whalley Range rediscovered the winning formula with a superb win at Timperley. With the hosts having scored a commendable 161, Whalley Range easily overhauled this, finishing on 260-4, with significant contributions from several players. Leading the way was Reverend D. Dorrity (who'd missed the start of the season, having been abroad in delicate health) with an unbeaten 75, whilst another man of the cloth, Reverend W. H. Ashton scored an unbeaten 61. Prior to this, the Baker Boys had opened the innings together, and got the innings off to a solid start with A. G. scoring 54, whilst C. S. fell just short of his fifty, on 47. A. G. Baker then notched his fourth successive fifty in the next game, scoring 60 in an easy win over Alderley Edge. Whalley Range's only reported loss of the season came the next weekend in a low-scoring encounter at Monton, where the hosts replied with 83, with H. C. Butterworth claiming another six wickets, after Whalley Range had posted just 64.

The start of September witnessed an incredible innings from H. W. Tindall, though unfortunately it was against his former team-mates. Obviously relishing playing at the Whalley Range ground again, he opened the innings and blasted an unbeaten 126 out of a total of 166-5 declared! The Brooklands team that day was a strong one, also including T. P. Bellhouse and C. R. Hartley, but Whalley Range managed to salvage a draw, hanging on with 139-9, as the home team's fine season continued. The following week, Whalley Range played Brooklands again, and again earnt a draw, with the Baker Boys combining (A.G. taking the catch off C. S.'s bowling) to remove H. W. Tindall before he could wreak the same amount of havoc this time!

Dawn of a New Century (1900-1910)

Sadly the arrival of the new century witnessed the departure of two former Whalley Range players, with James MacLaren (father of Archie and James Alexander MacLaren) passing away prior to the start of the 1900 cricket season, whilst F. D. Gaddum died following the end of the cricket season, the tragic circumstances of which are detailed later.

Pictured here is the oldest surviving club handbook, dating back to the 1900 season. It illustrates that the club did just provide for cricket at this moment in time, with tennis not being re-introduced until 1912. The handbook lists W. G. Thompson as the President, K. T. S. Dockray as the Treasurer, with A. F. Walley and H. J. Amos as Secretaries. Numerous vice-presidents were also listed, including the likes of Henry Worrall, Percy Henry Marriott, and most notably, Sir John William Maclure, 1st Baronet, who was the MP for Stretford, a constituency that included Whalley Range at the time. However, it should be noted that for most of the more prominent names of vice-presidents that adorned the club handbooks over this and the coming seasons, the listing itself was probably as far as their association with the club went.

Whalley Range lost their first game of the season to Monton, followed by a draw against Brooklands, both in April. The first game in May brought Whalley Range's first win of the 1900s, and what a superb win it was. Thanks mainly to the Baker brothers (C. S. 57, A. G. 40), Whalley Range declared on 111-8, before Chorlton were dismissed for just 33, with H. C. Butterworth capturing seven wickets, the first of several big hauls he would claim this season. In late May against Worsley, C. S. Baker scored another fifty (53), and with Reverend W. H. Ashton also scoring an unbeaten 62, Whalley Range cruised to an emphatic win. In the next game, C. S. Baker scored another fifty, though as can be seen from the scoresheet, it was his older brother who stole the show, against Kersal.

Kersal v Whalley Range, at Kersal, Saturday 2nd June 1900

Kersal				Whalley Range			
L. Cox		b H. J. Amos	13	A. G. Baker	c Broughton	b J. Farrar	121
J. G. L. Farrar		run out	5	C. S. Baker	c Grave	b J. Farrar	65
H. L. Farrar		b H. J. Amos	1	I. Melling		b Cox	16
W. Grave		b H. J. Amos	0	Rev. W. H. Ashton	c Cox	b Pulling	1
C. W. Pulling		b H. J. Amos	15	H. C. Butterworth		b Cox	1
H. N. Barlow		b H. J. Amos	46	H. B. L. Muth		not out	14
G. C. Sheldon	c Clay	b H. J. Amos	0	H. J. Amos		not out	28
R. E. Cox	c Ashton	b Butterworth	7				
J. Broughton		b Butterworth	3				
R. E. Stephenson		b H. J. Amos	3				
J. Parkinson		not out	4				
Extras			5	Extras			21
Total			102	Total		(for 5)	267

It wasn't just a great day for the Baker Boys, but for the Old Hulmeians in general, with H. J. Amos taking seven of the Kersal wickets, as Whalley Range again enjoyed a comprehensive victory. C. S. Baker would presumably have made another fifty in the next game, but with so little time to bat against Ashton-under-Lyne, he scored an unbeaten 46 out of 65-1 in reply to the visitors' total of 156-2 declared.

Then came a bad day at the office for Whalley Range when Warrington came to town, since despite boasting their usual array of talent, Whalley Range were skittled for a mere 32. When Warrington batted, H. C. Butterworth did capture five wickets, but by then the game had already been lost. However, the seven wickets he took in the next match were very much in a "live" situation, as Alderley Edge batting first were sent packing for just 45. Another excellent innings from the irrepressible C. S. Baker, with a fine 81, ensured Whalley Range emerged victorious again.

Not content with 12 wickets in his previous two outings, H. C. Butterworth added a further seven against South Manchester who managed just 67, to facilitate another easy win for Whalley Range, as C. S. Baker guided them home with an unbeaten 30. Unusually for the time, Whalley Range then seemed to have concluded their innings on 68-3, though it could have been that time or the weather became a factor.

At the start of July, Whalley Range lost badly to Blackley (152 v 72), but this was followed immediately by a couple of resounding victories. The first of these was against Bollington where H. C. Butterworth added a further six wickets to his season's tally, and the second was against Kersal, who were dismissed for just 60, with H. J. Amos capturing seven wickets. Having scored a century against them earlier in the season, A. G. Baker made Kersal suffer again with 57, whilst Reverend W. H. Ashton top-scored with an unbeaten 65, as Whalley Range finished on 201-4.

In the previous game with Blackley, the opposition had batted first and scored 152, a feat they managed to repeat precisely in the return encounter. On that previous occasion, Whalley Range had surrendered tamely. This time, the Baker Boys made sure there was to be no repeat performance, batting solidly to finish on 91-0, with A. G. finishing on 41, whilst C. S. scored 44. The start of August saw a heavy defeat to Manchester at Old Trafford. Perhaps still suffering from the effects of this, Whalley Range surprisingly lost the following weekend as well, to Chorlton-cum-Hardy, in spite of another five-wicket haul from H. C. Butterworth. Winning ways were restored in amazing style in the next game. Having posted 135, Whalley Range routed Alderley Edge for just 40, with H. J. Amos taking a superb 8-11 that included a hat-trick. With time still remaining, the opposition batted again, but fared little better, finishing on 22-5 second time round, with C. S. Baker now demonstrating he was proficient with the ball as well, taking four wickets.

Having displayed his blossoming bowling talents the previous weekend, C. S. Baker captured five wickets against the mighty Brooklands team that included the likes of T. P. Bellhouse and H. W. Tindall. With Brooklands having been dismissed for just 89, Whalley Range managed to administer some rare revenge over the former Whalley Range players, though without a valuable 33 from C. S. Baker, would undoubtedly have fallen short of their target, as Whalley Range finished on 106-9, with only Reverend D. Dorrity (23) and H. B. L. Muth (17) also reaching double figures.

The first game of September saw H. C. Butterworth add another six wickets to his season's tally though the game against Worsley ended in a draw. The following weekend, a former Whalley Range player was in astonishing form for Western against Kersal. Not satisfied with scoring a century against their bowlers, E. E. Steel then destroyed their batting with remarkable figures of 9-7. However, on this particular day, Whalley Range were in no need of their former star, since they had their own bowling star this season in the form of H. C. Butterworth, who grabbed another six wickets as South Manchester were dismissed for just 37 in reply to Whalley Range's 95. True to form, H. C. Butterworth capped the season off with another five-wicket haul the following weekend as Longsight were bowled out for 107. A very fine season for Whalley Range came to a close with E. A. Smith scoring 47 and C. S. Baker an unbeaten 43, to ensure that the Longsight total was easily surpassed.

Thus despite figures of 8-11 against Alderley Edge for H. J. Amos, there was little doubt who the main bowling star this season was, with H. C. Butterworth claiming at least 83 wickets throughout the season, including three 7-wicket hauls, four 6-wicket hauls, and a further two 5-wicket hauls.

As alluded to above, former Whalley Range player E. E. Steel was having an incredible season in 1900 for Western, and would finish the season with an amazing tally of 140 wickets to add to 1241 runs he plundered with the bat.

Even though F. D. Gaddum had finished playing for Whalley Range four years previously, the events of October 14th 1900 would have come as a massive shock to all of those associated with the club. Apart from cricket, another of F. D. Gaddum's passions was cycling, owning no fewer than five bicycles. However whilst cycling down a steep hill on a Sunday afternoon in Wilmslow, a fracture in the bicycle at the junction of the front forks caused the front wheel to become detached with horrendous consequences. He never regained consciousness from his terrible injuries and sadly passed away that night. Aged just 40, it was a tragic end to the life of one of the club's favourite sons.

1901 welcomed in the Edwardian Age and what would appear to be Whalley Range's first ever proper full tour, with a jaunt to the north-east of the country for a few days at the end of May. At a time, when living conditions for most people were far from ideal, this was a good indicator of the affluence that was associated with the players who represented the club at this time.

The handbook for this season indicated that the 1st XI captain was still A. G. Baker, whilst the 2nd XI captain was listed as F. R. Leroy with H. R. Classen as his deputy. Interestingly, the club colours were also mentioned, and were reported to be chocolate, blue, and white.

For some reason, Whalley Range's main bowling star of the previous season was missing for all of the first-half of the season, with H. C. Butterworth not making his first appearance until the end of June, whilst Reverend D. Dorrity was now playing for the Manchester club. Among the early games of the season, the most notable performances were in the return game against Castleton where Reverend W. H. Ashton captured six wickets, before C. S. Baker ensured a draw with an innings of 59. In the first game of the season, also against Castleton, C. S. Baker had also ensured a draw with a score of 42.

Monkey Business

In mid-May, for the game against Manchester at Old Trafford, Whalley Range were up against A. N. "Monkey" Hornby, a nickname he acquired at school due to his small stature and boundless energy. It was a sobriquet that remained with him through later life. Albert Neilson Hornby was a true Lancashire legend, and was one of the early stars of the county club, which he represented for over 30 years up until 1899, scoring over 10,000 runs. He was the Lancashire captain for 17 seasons, and also excelled at rugby, achieving the rare distinction of captaining his country at both cricket and rugby. His disciplinarian approach to captaincy led to him also being referred to as "The Boss". Thus, the Whalley Range players were certainly in exalted company that day, though H. J. Amos was clearly not too overawed by the great man, bowling him out for just 11, but the visitors did go on to lose by 100 runs.

A. N. Hornby

In a midweek game against Owens College (i.e. Manchester University), opener A. G. Baker scored 53 out of a total of 179-7 declared, though the visitors replied with 119-4 to ensure a draw. Thus, Whalley Range's first win of the Edwardian Age didn't come until Saturday 25th May when Chorlton made the short trip to the Whalley Range ground, and were quickly disposed of for just 69. The home team made 144-7 with Reverend W. H. Ashton making 60.

The Whalley Range Touring Tradition Starts

Just a few days later, a party from Whalley Range made their way to the north-east of the country, and on Tuesday 28th May began what was presumably the club's first ever full tour, and it started well with a 29-run victory over North-Eastern Counties Schools, thanks mainly to five wickets from H. J. Amos. The following day, despite 57 from A. G. Baker and 49 from his younger sibling, Chester-le-Street managed to overhaul the tourists' tally of 135. On a more positive note, H. J. Amos took his tour tally into double-figures with another five-wicket haul. On the Thursday, Whalley Range were up against Barnard Castle, though the game was presumably affected by the weather, ending in a tame draw. The tour was concluded with victory over Durham University with Whalley Range replying with 124 after the hosts had managed to post just 73 with C. S. Baker claiming six wickets. Apart from Amos and the Baker brothers, other players who made the trip included F. Clay, J. B. Gow, F. Howard, T. Howard, F. R. Leroy, I. Melling, H. K. Oldfield, S. W. Saxelby, A. F. Walley, and J. L. Winchester.

The Whalley Range players were back playing on home turf the following day on the Saturday, though rain brought an early end to their game with Cheadle Hulme, with the visitors unable to bat. Following a draw against Blackley, Whalley Range travelled to Timperley and earned a comfortable win thanks to the Baker brothers, with C. S. taking six wickets, whilst A. G. scored an unbeaten 73. Strangely enough, for the return game with Cheadle Hulme, the tables were completely turned, and it was Whalley Range who were deprived of getting a bat by the weather. The end of June witnessed A. G. Baker scoring an unbeaten 59 in a drawn midweek game with Cheetham Hill, followed by the return of H. C. Butterworth for the home game with Monton, though he couldn't prevent the visitors from gaining an easy win.

Whilst the 1st XI were losing against Monton, amazingly Whalley Range 2nd XI were annihilating Fulshaw 1st XI. Batting first, the visitors made 140 before dismissing their hosts for just 13, with just nine runs coming off the bat. Sadly the bowling analysis was not provided, so it wasn't possible to determine who the bowlers were, causing all the damage.

The following photo dates from around this period, showing six of the Whalley Range team taking some time out to relax, including three of those who featured on the 1901 tour :-

H. R. Classen, F. R. Leroy, C. B. Kelly, H. J. Amos, F. Clay, and H. C. Butterworth

The first game of July was a midweek draw against Owens College. The next game, on Saturday 6th July 1901, was a significant one in the history of the club, since it witnessed the first definitive recorded appearance in the Whalley Range 1st XI of one of the Buckland clan, various members of which played for the club into the 1970s.

George Frederick Buckland – The Club's First Olympian

George Frederick Buckland was born on 13th April 1883 in Didsbury. Back in 1878, someone called Buckland had played one game for the Athletic club, but no initials were given, though it is likely that this would have been his father, James Edward Buckland, who can be seen pictured in the 1928 2nd XI team photo. George had two younger brothers, Herbert and Ron, who would also play for the Whalley Range team.

However, it was in a different sporting arena that the Buckland brothers would achieve so much success, since all were fine lacrosse players, none more so than G. F. Buckland who in 1908 would represent Great Britain at the Olympics, thus becoming the club's first Olympian!

Like many of his Whalley Range team-mates at this time, G. F. Buckland was educated at the nearby Hulme Grammar School, and starred for them at lacrosse, as he also later did for the Old Hulmeians, i.e. the team comprised of former Hulme Grammar School pupils. A later chapter in this book is dedicated to the exploits of the Old Hulmeians, which further elaborates on the amazing successes of the likes of the Buckland brothers and other former school associates.

As it happened though, on G. F. Buckland's debut, Whalley Range were bowled out for a mere 68 of which G. F. contributed just 4, before Worsley secured an easy win. Whalley Range experienced better fortunes during the rest of July, having much the better of a drawn game with South Manchester, where A. G. Baker scored 71 out of 191-3 declared, before H. J. Amos took 5 wickets as the opposition hung on for a draw on 111-9. The end of July brought an 81-run win over Chorlton-cum-Hardy, thanks mainly to six wickets from Reverend W. H. Ashton.

Winning ways continued at the start of August, with W. P. Bradshaw having the amazing figures of 5-0 to quickly wrap up the Earlestown innings for 76, before Reverend W. H. Ashton scored an unbeaten 60 out of 184-8. William Platt Bradshaw was born on 8th February 1882, and was another who attended Hulme Grammar School, as evidenced in the School Cricket 1st XI 1897 team photo in the Old Hulmeians chapter. He had several siblings, including an elder sister called Mary Lucy Bradshaw who would later marry a fellow club cricketer, namely J. B. Gow, who had featured in Whalley Range's first ever tour earlier this season. W. P. Bradshaw had first played for the club in 1898 and would represent the club up to and including the 1903 season. Later in life, he emigrated to Paraguay, which is where he started a family with young Rosa Becchi. It would appear that he came from a very prosperous family, since his grandfather, who was also called William Platt Bradshaw (1794-1874), lived at Burnage Lodge in Levenshulme, and he married Catherine Ann Allot (1806-1883) who was also descended from very well-to-do stock. John Biggart Gow, to give him his full name, was born on 11th March 1868 in Victoria, Australia, and would represent Whalley Range between 1900 and 1911.

On the Bank Holiday Monday, A. G. Baker played a starring role against Mr. R. Ballantyne's XI, capturing seven wickets, before guiding his team to victory by opening the innings and scoring 89 out of a total of 165. In the next game, C. B. Kelly scored an unbeaten 86 against Brooklands to ensure a draw. Cuthbert Bede Kelly was born in about 1882 to Constantine and Emma Kelly, and had an older brother, Francis James Kelly, who had also played for the club in the 1899 and 1900 seasons. Similar to J. B. Gow, C. B. Kelly would represent Whalley Range between 1900 and 1911.

There then followed a rain-shortened game against South Manchester where C. S. Baker captured all four wickets that were to fall before the weather put paid to cricket for the day. C. S. Baker's fine bowling form continued into the next game where he took eight wickets as Longsight were bowled out for 110. However, the Whalley Range batting line-up completely capitulated, with three of the first four batsmen out for ducks, with two more to follow. It was only thanks to F. Clay, who top-scored with 14 coming in at number eleven, that a modicum of respect was added to the Whalley Range total which finally closed on 49. Whalley Range made it successive defeats the following week, as only C. S. Baker with 45 managed to get on top of the Blackley bowlers. The season finished well for Whalley Range though, with A. G. Baker scoring 93 out of 205-4 in an easy win over Buxton, before his younger brother scored 45 in the last game of the season, where Whalley Range had much the better of a drawn game with the visitors Cheetham.

Following portions of the playing pitch being re-laid prior to the season, there was some remarkable cricket involving Whalley Range in 1902, most notably in the very last game of the season. The batting throughout the season was again dominated by the Fabulous Baker Boys with all but two of the fifties being credited to them. The season got off to a great start at Knutsford in April with the hosts being removed for just 40, with Reverend Ashton claiming five wickets. Captain A. G. Baker then ensured a resounding victory scoring an unbeaten 55 out of a total of 113-2. He scored another unbeaten fifty (52 not out) in the next game a fortnight later, after the weather had ensured no play was possible the previous weekend. In fact the captain carried his bat, out of a total of 111 against Worsley, who desperately clung on to a draw at the end, finishing on 81-9. Amazingly, A. G. Baker then scored another unbeaten fifty on the following Wednesday at Cheetham Hill, opening the innings and contributing a steady 54 out of a total of 174-9 before he declared. But for the declaration one suspects he would almost certainly have achieved the notable distinction of carrying his bat through successive innings. The hosts then responded with 102-2.

This day, Wednesday 14th May 1902, also witnessed the passing away of Reverend Henry Woods Tindall, who'd spent the past 20 years as rector of St. Edmund's Church in Whalley Range. As father of three of the best cricket players that Whalley Range had ever produced, it was a sad day for all those concerned with Whalley Range, both from a cricketing and a social point of view.

For the 1st XI game on Saturday 17th May, no report appeared in the local press, but a note in the handbook suggests they overcame Timperley. As for the 2nd XI, there can be no such doubt as to the result, as they dismissed Timperley 2nd XI for a mere 5, with just two batsmen managing to trouble the scorers! Unfortunately, the scoresheet did not provide any analysis of the bowling :-

Timperley 2nd XI v Whalley Range 2nd XI, at Timperley, Saturday 17th May 1902

Whalley Range 2nd XI			Timperley 2nd XI		
Buckland		15	E. Latham		0
Cummins		18	A. Law		4
Lomax		47	Fitton		1
Leroy		3	Nicholson		0
Rowbottom		0	James		0
Hiller		7	Edwards		0
H. K. Oldfield		5	H. D. Law		0
Saxelby		13	Coppock		0
Gilliat		0	Turton		0
L. Oldfield		0	W. Latham		0
Mountain	not out	1	Swift	not out	0
Extras		5	Extras		0
Total		114	Total		5

With regard to the top-scorer for Whalley Range 2nd XI, this is Harry Douglas Lomax, who was born in 1877, and traded as "H. D. Lomax and Co." and as "The Ardwick Hemming Company" in the bedding industry, until his passing away in September 1925, aged 48.

For the 1st XI's next game, on the Monday, West Derby were the visitors to the College Road ground, for what would appear to be their one and only time. It also appeared that perhaps some of their players got lost en route from Liverpool, since there was a fair few guest players from Whalley Range making up their team. Based on first innings, it was a match that the hosts lost by just 2 runs. However taking into account the second innings, it was a match where Whalley Range won easily, dismissing West Derby for just 22 second time round, with both C. S. Baker and H. J. Amos claiming five-wicket hauls.

The following weekend saw the 1st XI easily beat Urmston thanks to a fine 55 from A. G. Baker, and a superb tally of eight wickets from Reverend W. H. Ashton. However, next came a trip to Old Trafford to compete against a very strong Manchester team that again comprised A. N. Hornby and also T. A. Higson, the latter of whom scored an unbeaten century for the hosts out of a total of 243-8 declared, and then took five Whalley Range wickets as the visitors were dismissed for just 71, with only the Baker brothers making double-figures. The remaining game in May saw Whalley Range comfortably beat South Manchester, thanks to a five-wicket haul from H. J. Amos.

June kicked off with a superb midweek game against Owens College at The Firs in Fallowfield. Opening the innings, A. G. Baker racked up another fifty, though his 55 was overshadowed by the innings of his younger sibling who just managed to get his century before rain forced the game to be abandoned, with the total on 207-3. As can be seen from the scoresheet below, there were quite a few guest players for Whalley Range, in the form of H. Ashworth, Parker, W. H. Wilson, and J. Miller.

Owens College v Whalley Range, at Fallowfield, Wednesday 4th June 1902

Whalley Range

A. G. Baker	c Miller	b Harrison		55
H. Ashworth	c Moore	b Lees		0
Parker	c &	b Greenwell		18
C. S. Baker		not out		100
E. C. Allen		not out		9
J. A. Cummins				-
W. H. Wilson				-
J. Miller				-
F. R. Leroy				-
S. W. Saxelby				-
K. T. S. Dockray				-
Extras				25
Total			(for 3)	207

The rain was still prevalent at the weekend, meaning there was no play at Bollington, whilst the following weekend brought a narrow defeat at Chorlton-cum-Hardy, despite the visitors looking favourites to win for most of the game. The weather again proved to be the decisive factor the following weekend with rain preventing Whalley Range from completing victory over Urmston.

Thankfully for the rest of the month, there was a big improvement in the weather, thus allowing Whalley Range to register two comfortable victories. In the first of these, H. C. Butterworth claimed six wickets as Macclesfield were dismissed for just 67 in a midweek encounter, whilst the last game of the month saw Whalley Range easily beat Kersal. Batting first, Whalley Range declared on 227-5, thanks to 51 from C. S. Baker and another fine unbeaten knock from his elder brother who boosted his season's tally by 79 runs. Kersal were then dismissed for 102, with H. J. Amos the chief destroyer with a seven-wicket haul.

July started with the Baker brothers still in fine form, with A. G. Baker scoring 47 in the return game with Kersal, whilst the following weekend, C. S. Baker scored 53 against Castleton. Meanwhile, the 2nd XI were also performing well, with the following scoresheet showing a fine century from S. R. Oddy, who scored exactly 100 out of 222-6 in reply to the hosts' total of 99. Stephen Roberts Oddy also enjoyed lacrosse, and went on to captain the Old Hulmeians to some incredible successes before then becoming the team's chairman, in the years leading up to the First World War. In later years, his son, George Vernon Oddy, would represent the club at tennis.

Kersal 2nd XI v Whalley Range 2nd XI, at Kersal, Saturday 5th July 1902

Whalley Range 2nd XI

E. C. Allen		0
J. Hesketh		2
C. B. Kelly		8
S. R. Oddy		100
F. R. Leroy		50
J. T. Canton	not out	16
S. W. Saxelby		28
Extras		18
Total	(for 6)	222

Also featured in the above scoresheet is John Talbot Canton, the son of Rev. William John Canton who was the vicar of St. Margaret's Church in Whalley Range. John's older brother William Bashall Hick Canton also played for the club at this time. In 1919, John would marry Louisa Grace Worrall, the daughter of Henry Worrall. She was named after her mother, though as mentioned earlier, her mother would later have an affair with a local vicar, resulting in her parents getting divorced. The Canton family became very wealthy, buying land around Brantingham Road, some of which is now used as the playing fields of the local school. A memorial to the Canton family can be seen in St. Margaret's Church.

In a midweek game in mid-July, J. A. Cummins broke the sequence of Baker fifties for the 1st XI with a knock of 58 out of a total of 136 at Cheetham Hill, though the hosts won very easily, replying with 252-5. Just seven days after scoring a fifty against Castleton, C. S. Baker was inflicting further misery on their bowlers, as he registered his second century of the season in the return game, and what a brilliant hundred it was. Despite batting at number four, C. S. Baker scored 127 out of a final total of 188-5 declared, where for most of the time, he was partnered by his older sibling who scored 34. In reply, Castleton scored 161-4 :-

Castleton v Whalley Range, at Castleton, Saturday 19th July 1902

Whalley Range

J. L. Winchester		b Robinson	1
J. A. Cummins		b Petrie	15
G. F. Buckland	c Robinson	b Thorneycroft	5
C. S. Baker		b Bowen	127
A. G. Baker	c Taylor	b Bowen	34
F. Howard		not out	0
Extras			6
Total		(for 5 dec)	188

C. S. Baker then took five wickets against South Manchester before rain ruined proceedings. The start of August witnessed a 12-a-side game against Timperley, with the extra man probably to accommodate the beneficiary in the Timperley side, since the proceeds of this match were *"devoted to the benefits of T. Hobson, the Timperley groundsman"*, according to the local press, though the Whalley Range team's generosity didn't extend to the game itself, replying with 165 to the hosts' 115.

Following a routine win over Chorlton-cum-Hardy, where A. G. Baker scored another unbeaten fifty (53 not out), the ensuing game with St. Helens was a very strange affair. This was possibly the first ever meeting between the two, and was one where Whalley Range seemed in total control as six of the opposition scored ducks in a total of just 50, as H. C. Butterworth wreaked havoc with seven wickets. However in reply, Whalley Range managed just 22, where H. R. Classen with just 6 found himself the top-scorer. The following weekend, G. F. Buckland scored 52 in a drawn game with Bollington.

For the rest of the season, Whalley Range didn't fare too well in general. Against Knutsford they managed just 48 in reply to the opposition's 111, followed by an effort of 88 in reply to Worsley's total of 168-9 declared. The losing sequence was broken with a draw against Longsight with both Baker brothers scoring yet more fifties (C. S. Baker 50, A. G. Baker 58 not out). The final game of the season was then pretty late into the year, being played on Saturday 20th September, and perhaps most of the Whalley Range players were left wishing the season hadn't gone on quite so long, since none of them seemed able to cope with G. E. Radford of Cheadle Hulme, who captured all ten of the Whalley Range wickets to finish with the remarkable figures of 10-20. His tenth and final wicket was claimed when he caught eleventh man F. Clay for a duck off his own bowling. G. E. Radford also guided his team to victory with an unbeaten 25 out of 69-6, as perhaps a tendency was beginning to develop where teams batting second, sometimes closed their innings once their target was reached.

Sadly 1902 would see the passing away of two former prominent Whalley Range players, W. G. Mills and T. P. Bellhouse. Mills, who'd represented Lancashire, and once scored 165 for Whalley Range, died at the start of the year, aged 49, whilst Bellhouse, one-time ABA middleweight boxing champion, passed away towards the end of the year.

Now aged 20, C. S. Baker would begin to make his mark in the Warwickshire 2nd XI in the 1903 season whilst playing as a professional for Leamington, though he did make one guest appearance for Whalley Range late in the season. Another source states that C. S. Baker also played football for Aston Villa at one point. Another absentee this season was H. J. Amos, with Cheetham Hill now benefiting from his immense talents. The first game of the new season thus saw one or two new faces in the Whalley Range 1st XI line-up, and perhaps came a little too early in the year (mid-April) for most of these players, since they seemed very ill-prepared for this opening game, being bowled out for a miserly 17. In fact, this was the lowest ever score unearthed for the 1st XI team in the period covered by this volume. Longsight responded with 84 to win the game easily, though A. G. Baker did end his day on a high, claiming seven wickets.

Longsight v Whalley Range, at Longsight, Saturday 18th April 1903

Whalley Range

A. G. Baker	hit wicket	b Turner	3
W. B. H. Canton		b Whittaker	0
H. B. L. Muth	c Tester	b Whittaker	4
Rev. W. H. Ashton	c Issott	b Whittaker	0
W. P. Bradshaw		b Whittaker	0
G. F. Buckland	c Turner	b Whittaker	2
J. A. Cummins		b Turner	1
S. W. Saxelby		not out	3
S. R. Oddy		b Whittaker	4
F. R. Leroy	c Tester	b Turner	0
J. Stephenson		b Turner	0
Extras			0
Total			17

The following weekend, Whalley Range's season had barely improved, with another resounding defeat, this time at Sale. Only J. L. Winchester, with 29, contributed anything of note, as Whalley Range were routed again, this time for 49. Thus far in two innings, after John Lee Winchester's "monumental" (in the context of his colleague's scores!) 29, astonishingly the next highest individual score was a mere 5.

By May, at Macclesfield, Whalley Range's season had turned around to some extent, as the hosts were dismissed for just 22 with Reverend W. H. Ashton taking five wickets, to set up an easy win. A fortnight later H. C. Butterworth captured six wickets in a losing cause against Worsley, whilst the last game in May then saw the Whalley Range team up against a former player, J. A. MacLaren, who was now playing for Bowdon, and helping them to a comfortable win in this particular game. On Monday 1st June 1903, at Whalley Range, the home team rattled up an impressive 228-7 before declaring against

Chorlton-cum-Hardy. Both J. L. Winchester (53) and W. P. Bradshaw (50 not out) achieved what would appear to be maiden fifties for the club, whilst all of H. B. L. Muth, F. Casebourne, and Reverend W. H. Ashton scored thirties, with the latter capturing seven wickets to ensure victory for the home side by over 100 runs. Not a bad way to spend a pleasant Monday afternoon, though for A. G. Baker, who didn't play in this game having presumably had more immediate and important things to concern him, the week had much more to offer. The following day on Tuesday 2nd June, fifty miles away in Leeds, Arthur George Baker married Lilian Maud Sugden.

It wouldn't be long before there would be another marriage in the team. In between times, Whalley Range won a couple of games (against Longsight and Urmston), lost a couple of couple of games (against Cheetham Hill and South Manchester) and drew the other. During these games, Reverend W. H. Ashton prospered well with the bat, especially in the win over Urmston where he scored 86, whilst F. Casebourne took five wickets in the defeat to Cheetham Hill. Perhaps the most significant game though, was the drawn one, since this featured what was probably H. R. Classen's first fifty for the club, scoring 56 against Chorlton-cum-Hardy, and it was H. R. Classen who would be the next Whalley Range player to tie the knot.

On Thursday 2nd July, a month after A. G. Baker's wedding, Harry Rudolph Classen was married to Euphemie Blanche Leroy, the sister of Ferdinand Raymond Leroy. As mentioned previously, the Leroys were of French descent, and with Classen, though born in Bradford, of German descent, this was very much a cosmopolitan affair! In fact, the number of German names at the club (Kessler, Gaddum etc.) and Varbetian (Armenian), Leroy and others shows what a cosmopolitan area it has always been.

Mentioned in the previous few paragraphs, F. Casebourne is almost certainly Frederick Casebourne who had previously played once for Glamorgan at Cardiff Arms Park, though admittedly this was long before Glamorgan acquired first-class status. After a draw with Owens College, Whalley Range then beat Urmston replying with 79 to the visitors' tally of 77 in a very tight game, after H. C. Butterworth had captured six wickets.

Following his marriage, perhaps A. G. Baker now had other priorities in life, since his cricketing form certainly deserted him for most of the season. Having performed so brilliantly the previous season, at one point this season in mid-July, whilst the 1st XI were entertaining Blackpool, A. G. Baker appeared for the 2nd XI, and scored a duck. In the last game in July, E. C. (Ernest Cecil) Allen scored 50 in a defeat against St. Helens. The following week in the return game at St. Helens, the home team amassed 182-6 before declaring, though with a superb return to form, it was A. G. Baker who captured all of the six wickets to fall. Whalley Range had little time to reply before the rain curtailed their innings.

The Bank Holiday Monday game then produced an astonishing performance from one of the Whalley Range batsmen. Castleton batted first and posted 154 with A. G. Baker again in fine form with the ball, taking five wickets. In his previous three recorded innings, opener D. M. Peacock had barely troubled the scorers, failing to make double-figures on all three occasions. As it happens, his next innings wasn't in double-figures either, though only in the best way possible, as in a sensational turnaround in form, his innings of 157 would have been enough to overhaul the visitors total on his own! With Reverend W. H. Ashton also contributing 67, Whalley Range closed on an impressive 271-4.

Whalley Range v Castleton, at Whalley Range, Monday 3rd August 1903

Whalley Range

D. M. Peacock		b E. Jones	157
C. B. Kelly	c Bowen	b Thorneycroft	2
F. Casebourne	lbw	b E. Jones	16
Rev. W. H. Ashton		b Petrie	67
E. C. Allen		not out	9
F. Howard		not out	6
Extras			14
Total		(for 4)	271

Douglas Mason Peacock was born in 1882, and was thus in his early twenties when he produced this remarkable knock. Despite being such a huge talent, it appears his Whalley Range career was a rather short one, spanning the seasons 1902 to 1905. Perhaps it was soon after this that he crossed the Welsh border, since the 1911 Census would indicate that he was then living in Caernarvonshire. He was the son of Mary and John Pender Peacock, and he would have the pleasure of playing alongside his father, who would make an appearance for Whalley Range the following season against Manchester Clifford in June, at no lesser ground than Old Trafford – not a bad place to make your one and only appearance!

C. S. Baker's one and only game for Whalley Range this season, at Timperley on Saturday 5th September, was a very significant one. As expected, upon his return, he opened the innings, though was out relatively cheaply, and the team would eventually lose easily. However, in reply to Timperley's 145-9 declared, it was the other opener who made the game an important one in the history of the club, since opening the innings with C. S. Baker was H. Buckland.

Herbert Buckland, or Bert as he was affectionately known, was the second of the Buckland brothers to play for Whalley Range 1st XI, following in the footsteps of G. F. Buckland who was in the side that day to witness his brother's 1st XI debut. Like his brothers, Herbert was a superb lacrosse player, and over the coming years would become a very useful cricketer too, though in this particular game, he was out for a duck. For A. G. Baker, the season finished well, at least with the ball, taking five wickets in the defeat at Timperley, before taking six wickets in the last game of the season in a drawn game at Withington, against South Manchester.

For the 1904 season, the President of the club was now Henry Worrall, with W. G. Thompson having stepped down, whilst there was further change with Arthur Cecil Elderton taking over the role of Honorary Secretary from Isaac Melling. In the first game of the season, Whalley Range were up against former player H. J. Amos, who took two early wickets dismissing both openers, Classen and Howard. However, thanks to 52 from Reverend W. H. Ashton, and an unbeaten 77 from C. A. Wicks on debut, Whalley Range recovered superbly to post 197-5 declared. Being a schoolteacher at Hulme Grammar School, one wonders whether Mr. Wicks had an extra incentive in ensuring that former pupil H. J. Amos didn't get the better of him! In the end, Cheetham Hill managed to escape with a draw from this game and then beat Whalley Range the very next weekend, though H. J. Amos didn't play against his former team on this occasion.

The Malaysia and Ceylon Connection

Charles Alfred Wicks was born on 10th March 1877 in Bethnal Green in London, to Edward Wicks and Louisa Fleming. He studied at Caius College, Cambridge, before working as a teacher in the Malaysian state of Penang. Whilst working in Penang, he represented the state cricket team against Singapore in 1901. By January 1904, he was back in England and teaching at Hulme Grammar School. However in 1908, he was bitten by the travel bug again, and thus emigrated to Ceylon (now Sri Lanka), having been appointed Science Master at the Royal College in Colombo. He continued to play cricket in the Subcontinent, and in 1909, we see him representing a cricket team referred to as "Europeans (Ceylon)" that toured India in December that year. On his departure from Hulme Grammar School, the staff and pupils wished him well in his new teaching post, by presenting him with a watch.

Following this defeat, Whalley Range went on a fine run through the middle of the season, losing just the once, on the Whit-Monday to Timperley. Against Knutsford, C. A. Wicks showed he was a fine bowler as well as a superb batsman, taking six wickets, whilst H. C. Butterworth again displayed his bowling prowess with several more five and six-wicket hauls. During this period, the highlight from a batting perspective was in mid-June when Whalley Range amassed 225-3 before declaring against Urmston, with all of D. M. Peacock, C. E. Barnes, and A. G. Baker making worthy contributions. However the most noteworthy contribution was from Reverend W. H. Ashton (more of whom anon) who scored an unbeaten 90, though in the end, Urmston claimed a draw, finishing on 135-8. Whalley Range were in fine batting form the following week as well, scoring 168-3 before declaring against Chorlton-cum-Hardy. The main scorers on this occasion were J. L. Winchester, with an unbeaten 79 against his former team, whilst C. E. Barnes scored 48, though again Whalley Range had to settle for a draw. Having just missed out on his fifty in this game, a fortnight later, C. E. Barnes made 51 to salvage a draw against Didsbury.

Next came two emphatic wins in mid-July, over Rusholme and then Castleton. Having scored an unbeaten 104 out of 166-2 and taken 6-18 for his school against West Didsbury during the week, C. A. Wicks continued his fine form with 44 against Rusholme, before C. B. Kelly, coming in at number nine, scored 64, to boost the total to 227. Wicks then took five wickets as Rusholme were dismissed for 72. In reply to Castleton's 119, Whalley Range scored 232-9 thanks to 61 from C. A. Wicks and 80 from C. E. Barnes. The following day, on Sunday 24th July, S. R. Oddy, who was the 2nd XI vice-captain at this time, married Nora Birdsall.

C. A. Wicks was then missing from all of the five matches in August, as he too tied the knot, marrying Florence Vaughan Field, an Essex girl, on Wednesday 3rd August at Leytonstone. His absence was clearly felt, as Whalley Range lost four of those five matches during the month. On the Bank Holiday Monday, they lost to Bowdon, despite another five-wicket haul from H. C. Butterworth and a superb unbeaten 58 from G. F. Buckland, coming in at number eight. A draw against Earlestown was the only saving grace amongst further defeats to South Manchester, Manchester Clifford, and Knutsford, though H. C. Butterworth did take eight wickets in a losing cause in this latter game, a game in which Whalley Range scored 75 for the second game in a row. However the biggest coincidence of the season was saved for the last game of the season, or certainly the last game that was reported on by the local press this season. In the first game of the season, C. A. Wicks had scored an unbeaten 77 on his debut for the club. For the game on Saturday 10th September, back in the team following his honeymoon, C. A. Wicks again opened the innings, and whilst wickets were falling all around him, he alone remained steadfast against the Earlestown attack. In the end, he finally ran out of partners, carrying his bat for another unbeaten 77 strangely enough. Not a bad way for him to start and end the season from a personal perspective, though this game resulted in another big defeat, with Earlestown replying with 238-4 to Whalley Range's 147.

Drink is the Curse of the Working Classes!

As evident in the previous paragraphs, Rev. W. H. Ashton was beginning to make a bit of an impact during the early part of the century, with several notable performances with both bat and ball. William Henry Ashton was born in Wigan on 10th June 1872 to James Thomas Ashton and Jane Ashton (nee Melling). He was educated at Wigan Grammar School before attending St. John's College, Cambridge, where he acquired his B.A. in 1894, and his M.A. in 1899. In 1895 he became the curate of St. John's, Oldham, before transferring to St. Margaret's, Whalley Range in early 1898, the same year that he would start playing cricket for Whalley Range. On 27th April 1899, he married Ada Helen Jane Gibson, at Parbold, near Southport, and in 1902, he became the rector of St. John's Church, Old Trafford – strangely enough, the third time that he'd been associated with an establishment that bore the name of St. John's. In later life, he worked at Broughton Rectory, before moving to Herefordshire in the late 1920s, where initially he was incumbent at the parish church in Burrington in the north of the county, and in 1938 was installed as the Prebendary of Moreton Parva at Hereford Cathedral. The cathedral, which is now a Grade I listed building, dates back to 1079, with its most famous treasure being the *Mappa Mundi*, a mediaeval map of the world dating from the 13th century.

With regard to his cricket, he would continue playing for Whalley Range until 1909, though he did take a sabbatical for the whole of the 1907 season for some reason, before re-appearing again in mid-July 1908. Of the scoresheets that have come to light, he scored 10 fifties for the club, and also captured 10 five-wicket hauls. He saved his best performances for the games against Urmston, with his best bowling, an eight-wicket haul, and his two highest scores, 86 and 90 not out, all coming in successive seasons against Urmston.

Ever since cricket began, the recreational game has been associated with strong drink. Indeed the earliest teams were often associated with pubs and taverns. However, being a man of the cloth, Rev. W. H. Ashton, took it upon himself to be honorary secretary of the Manchester Diocesan Church of England Temperance Society, and would write several letters to the Manchester Guardian on the subject. One such letter, which was published on 18th November 1908, refers to Mr. Dorrity, who undoubtedly is Rev. David Dorrity who also used to play for Whalley Range :-

> *To the Editor of the Manchester Guardian.*
> *Sir, – Mr. Price-Heywood informs us that Mr. Dorrity's sensible suggestions are based upon an economic fallacy, and brings forward the old Socialist theory, long exploded, that if the working man stopped drinking his wages would drop. Carried to its logical conclusion, Mr. Price-Heywood's argument comes to this, that the more a working man spends in wasteful luxury the higher his wages will be, and, presumably, the more satisfactory his condition.*
> *In turn, we reply that it has frequently been pointed out that all this is based upon a fallacy – viz., the assumption that if a man does not spend money on alcoholic liquor his total requirements will be less, his standard of living will be a cheaper one, and his ability to command a reasonable wage will be diminished. Whereas the precise opposite is the fact. The temperate man does not spend less than the heavy drinker; he only lays out what he has more wisely. He does not lay up his money in a napkin or bury it in the earth; he*

uses it for food, clothing, furniture, books, and sensible recreation. His standard of living rises, and he ceases to be content with the evil conditions under which he lived before. But he is not the man to be content with a low wage; he is the stamp of man who keeps wages up and renders good wages possible. It is the man who spends half his wages on drink who is the curse of the labour market, the man who has no reserve to fall back upon and cannot stick out for a better wage nor resist a reduction, and who has to be kept by his fellow-men when a strike occurs.

The expenditure of £100,000,000 by the working classes on a luxury is a great national extravagance, and is bound to produce poverty. A tithe of that amount turned into profitable channels, and away from this unproductive trade, would go far to remedy our social evils and distresses. It is well for the working man to hear some home-truths sometimes, and we say that until he reforms his drinking habits little can be done. What is the use of taking money from the pockets of the capitalist land-owner if you are going to put it in the hands of the capitalist brewer? Ever since Isaiah's day we have had the two great problems before us – the land and the drink. The two "woes" are with us still – "Woe unto them that join house to house, that lay field to field, till there be no place." "Woe unto them that rise up early in the morning that they may follow strong drink, and continue until night."

Let social reformers apply their brains and their energies to both these evils, and not to one alone, or the last state will be no better than the first. – Yours, &c.,

W. H. ASHTON.
St. John's, Old Trafford.

One wonders whether he was quite so censorious about the middle-classes drinking, and playing against Cheetham Hill, a club afloat on the profits of Joseph Holt's! The other thing to note is that the Manchester Guardian was the house-journal of the North West, and though clearly a Liberal newspaper, it was read by anyone who was anyone, and the Reverend's views would have been known to the great majority of his team-mates and opponents.

For the 1905 season, C. S. Baker would make his 1st XI debut for Warwickshire and establish himself in the team for the rest of the pre-War years. During his first season for Warwickshire he scored his first century for them, with a knock of 102 against Cambridge University at the Fenner's ground in Cambridge, in mid-May.

Whilst his brother was embarking on a successful first-class career, A. G. Baker continued to play for Whalley Range, though for this season in particular, it appeared that he wasn't quite the force he used to be. Furthermore, the role of 1st XI captain which he had valiantly fulfilled for the last few seasons, was now in the hands of F. Clay, according to the handbook. Instead, for the 1905 season, Whalley Range were heavily reliant on the more recent Hulme Grammar School acquisitions in the form of C. A. Wicks, whose bowling was again very much to the fore, and the likes of the Buckland brothers. Also, J. L. Winchester, who had performed well recently, was now playing for Brooklands, whilst it would appear that H. C. Butterworth, who had bowled brilliantly over the last decade or more, was also no longer playing for Whalley Range, though he would re-appear again a few seasons hence, when Whalley Range were in desperate need of him.

After a wet start, the season eventually kicked off in fine style with South Manchester being dismissed for just 24 with C. A. Wicks taking six wickets, though Whalley Range weren't totally convincing in their reply of 46. Reverend W. H. Ashton was the bowler doing the most damage in the next game with five wickets, though it was a game that Whalley Range eventually lost. The following weekend, S. W. Saxelby was denied his fifty against Chorlton-cum-Hardy, being marooned on 49 not out, when he ran out of partners.

The start of June witnessed some more superb bowling from C. A. Wicks. Against Chorlton-cum-Hardy, his figures of 6-31 were the deciding factor in assuring victory for Whalley Range, but as it happened, he was merely warming up for the following weekend, when he took 9-31 against Knutsford, with his contribution again crucial in gaining victory for his team. As can be seen in the ensuing scoresheet, F. Clay is not playing for the 1st XI at this point, and in fact, after appearing in the first three games of the season, didn't re-appear until late in the season. Thus one wonders whether he was away on business, or perhaps injured for a while, in which case it could well have been that A. G. Baker re-assumed the captaincy during this period, despite his own indifferent form.

Knutsford v Whalley Range, at Knutsford, Saturday 10th June 1905

Knutsford				Whalley Range			
F. C. Rivaz		b Wicks	1	C. B. Kelly		b Bowen	11
G. Harlow		b Wicks	15	H. R. Classen	c G. Beb'ton	b Bowen	0
H. Todd	c Kelly	b Wicks	8	H. Buckland		b Bowen	8
G. Bebbington		b Wicks	2	Rev. W. H. Ashton		b Bowen	21
J. Simpson	c Jackson	b Wicks	1	C. A. Wicks		b F. Rivaz	1
J. D. Crawford		b Wicks	11	G. F. Buckland		b Bowen	21
W. H. Daniel		b Ashton	0	A. G. Baker	c G. A. Beb'ton	b Simpson	17
C. F. Rivaz		b Wicks	14	F. Jackson		b Bowen	20
G. A. Bebbington		b Wicks	0	F. Casebourne		run out	0
E. C. Bowen		not out	9	J. A. Cummins		not out	4
B. Bebbington	c &	b Wicks	0	H. K. Oldfield		b Bowen	0
Extras			14	Extras			4
Total			75	Total			107

On the following Monday, Whalley Range travelled all the way to Llandudno in North Wales. Batting first, most batsmen made the 80-mile journey worthwhile, with nine of them in double-figures in a total of 191. In reply, Llandudno made 88-8. Two days later, in a busy Whit-week, Whalley Range were playing at Bramhall, where in spite of five wickets from C. A. Wicks, the hosts posted exactly 200. Wicks's fine day continued, as his unbeaten 37 helped salvage a draw in a response of 131-7. The end of June saw Whalley Range unlucky to lose to Urmston despite a valiant effort of 70 from C. B. Kelly. With Urmston having posted 214, with the help of Kelly's innings Whalley Range were just four runs shy of this total when the last wicket fell.

C. A. Wicks was in the wickets again at the start of July, taking 7-22 against Didsbury, before F. Howard steered Whalley Range to victory with a knock of 45. In fact, July overall was a superb month for Wicks, scoring 44 with the bat to help beat Earlestown, before taking another seven-wicket haul against Knutsford, following on from his nine-wicket haul against them in the previous meeting. He then took five wickets against Manchester Clifford, though Whalley Range did lose both of these last two games. Wicks was still in fine form at the start of August, taking a further six wickets to help thrash South Manchester, after G. F. Buckland had earlier scored an unbeaten 52.

For the game on Saturday 19th August against Rusholme, C. A. Wicks added another five wickets to his season's tally, though the most important aspect of this game was the fact that three of the Buckland brothers now appeared in the top five of the batting order, with Ronnie joining his brothers, though opening the innings he was out for a duck, and Whalley Range did go on to lose by 30 runs. In late August, Whalley Range lost again, this time to Urmston. Following this, it seems that the rest of the season simply got washed away, since there were no further reports on Whalley Range during September, though games against the likes of Didsbury, Earlestown, and Manchester Clifford were definitely scheduled.

How's This For A Ringer?

With C. S. Baker now firmly established in the Warwickshire 1st XI, it would have seemed fairly safe to assume that his playing days for Whalley Range were well and truly behind him. As it happened though, he would make one further appearance, helped to some extent by another former player, namely Archie MacLaren. On Thursday 10th May 1906, Warwickshire began what was scheduled to be a 3-day county game at Old Trafford. Batting first, Warwickshire made just 91 in 45.1 overs. Lancashire fared even worse, being bowled out for a mere 76 in 34.2 overs. In their second innings, Warwickshire made 113 in 44 overs. Then, on a pitch that had really troubled all the batsmen thus far, Archie MacLaren played a real captain's knock in guiding Lancashire to victory with an unbeaten 58 out of 129-2 in 44.5 overs, to wrap the game up within two days. Thus, being in the vicinity, on the Saturday, C. S. Baker was again playing alongside his brother at Rusholme, and as can be seen in the ensuing scoresheet, he certainly made his presence felt. With the hosts having batted first and made 85, C. S. Baker opened the innings for Whalley Range and made a fine 53, to help secure an easy victory. With C. A. Wicks scoring 41 to add to his six wickets, the final Whalley Range total was 188.

Rusholme v Whalley Range, at Rusholme, Saturday 12th May 1906

Rusholme			Whalley Range			
W. J. Jump	b H. Buckland	8	C. S. Baker		b Haslam	53
W. Hitchen	b Wicks	0	H. R. Classen	c Fowler	b Weir	15
H. A. Buckley	b Wicks	0	F. Howard	c Haslam	b Carrington	26
W. A. Carrington	b H. Buckland	9	C. A. Wicks	lbw	b Haslam	41
T. McGeoch	b Wicks	0	A. G. Baker		b Haslam	9
L. Haslam	b Wicks	9	S. W. Saxelby		b Jump	1
H. Royle	run out	25	F. Clay	c Jump	b Haslam	16
T. Clarke	b Wicks	7	H. Buckland	c &	b Haslam	10
H. Cottam	b G. F. Buckland	19	J. A. Cummins		b Haslam	3
T. Weir	b Wicks	3	H. B. L. Muth		b Haslam	0
P. R. Fowler	not out	1	G. F. Buckland		not out	3
Extras		4	Extras			11
Total		85	Total			188

C. S. Baker, circa mid-1900s

Rain seems to have badly affected the rest of May, before C. A. Wicks captured another five-wicket haul at the start of June in a losing cause against Longsight. Two days later on the Monday, Wicks was in fine form again, this time with the bat, scoring 82 out of a total of 285, to which Rev. W. H. Ashton also contributed 60. In fact, it was a fine all-round performance by Rev. W. H. Ashton, having earlier in the game, taken five wickets, as Rusholme were dismissed for 111.

Having struggled the previous season with the bat, perhaps invigorated by having played alongside his illustrious younger brother again, 1906 would see A. G. Baker really re-capture his form of old. In mid-June he scored 54 out of a total of 171-8 declared to help beat Macclesfield, and the following week scored an unbeaten 43 to help secure a draw against Knutsford. A fortnight later, in the return game with Knutsford, he made them suffer again with a superb 69 as Whalley Range coasted to an easy win, helped also by 43 from Ron Buckland. In between these Knutsford encounters, C. A. Wicks took eight wickets to help beat Urmston.

Thus, Whalley Range were on a bit of a roll, but in the next game they were really struggling against Timperley, until C. B. Kelly came in at number 11 (though admittedly he'd usually been an opener for much of the previous season) and smashed an amazing 43. Prior to this, the highest score had been 16 by the number nine batsman J. A. Cummins. Thus, when a total of below 50 seemed likely, suddenly Whalley Range had managed to post 116. As it happened, the late burst by Kelly was absolutely vital in ensuring victory as Timperley were all out for 109.

Whalley Range's fine form continued against Chorlton-cum-Hardy, having much the better of a drawn game, with G. F. Buckland scoring 59, and C. A. Wicks adding six wickets to the 57 he scored with the bat. The following week at Old Trafford, Whalley Range easily beat Manchester Clifford, with A. G. Baker scoring 67, and Reginald Sykes, another Old Hulmeian who lived at Alton Towers – on Withington Road (now flats), rather than in Staffordshire – taking five wickets. This season, it would seem that Whalley Range 2nd XI were also thriving, rattling up 262-8 against Heaton Moor with W. C. Smith making 78 and J. Kirkman 55, and followed this up in the next game with 214 against Longsight 2nd XI. Also appearing in the 2nd XI line-up this season was Ernest Classen, a younger brother of Dolph Classen. By 1910, Ernest would be teaching German (a post he forsook two years later to teach English) at the University of Manchester, of which he was a graduate, having married Lillie Vestergren on 20th December 1909, in Stockholm.

During the rest of the 1906 season, there were some further fine bowling performances. Against Didsbury, R. Sykes captured seven wickets to help dismiss the opposition for 72, though Whalley Range still lost, replying with just 51. However, the best performance of the whole season came in September from C. A. Wicks, who with his second eight-wicket haul of the season, helped bowl out Manchester Clifford for just 36. In reply, Whalley Range scored 138 to record an easy win. The season finished tamely the following week with a draw against Cheetham.

Just prior to the start of the 1907 cricket season, the Old Hulmeians lacrosse team had enjoyed some rather amazing success, as detailed in the later chapter about the Old Hulmeians. One of the main reasons for their success was the form of Wilfred Alston Hobbins, who in the forthcoming cricket season, would also play for Whalley Range, though admittedly only at the end of the season. Another Old Hulmeian who would represent Whalley Range in the forthcoming cricket season would be F. B. Turner.

Wilfred Alston Hobbins

Wilfred Alston Hobbins was born in Exeter in the early part of 1881, to Charles and Annie Hobbins. In 1888, the family moved north to the Manchester area. In September 1891, Wilfred started attending Hulme Grammar School, joining his two older brothers, Herbert Charles, and Alan Edward, who'd been pupils there since the family's move up north. By 1896, Herbert Charles Hobbins was beginning to make an impression with the Old Hulmeians lacrosse team. A couple of seasons later, it was Alan Edward Hobbins and Wilfred Alston Hobbins who were beginning to make their mark with the Old Hulmeians.

Alan Edward Hobbins left England for Shanghai in 1903, though sadly died of typhus fever in

the Far East on 1st February 1905. Another of Wilfred's brothers also died young, with Percy April Hobbins, aged just 25, passing away on Christmas Day 1911, by which time, his father Charles had also died.

In the meantime, Wilfred Alston Hobbins had continued to excel at lacrosse with the Old Hulmeians, and would play a big part in helping them win several titles before the war, latterly as captain. His successes were further rewarded by being selected to play for the England lacrosse team, where he played alongside fellow Old Hulmeian, George Frederick Buckland. On 14th July 1909, he would marry Susan Florence Fox, elder sister of fellow lacrosse players, Charles Henry and Gilbert Wheaton Fox.

By all accounts, 1907 transpired to be one of the wettest cricket seasons on record, with many games badly affected by the weather, if not completely cancelled in many cases. It looks like the wet wickets suited C. A. Wicks who claimed five-wicket hauls in each of the first two games that actually started, against Rusholme and Didsbury though both ended in curtailed drawn games. He took a further six wickets in the next game, against Macclesfield, and this time, thanks to 72 from A. G. Baker, who was now back as captain, Whalley Range were able to force a win.

Thus there wasn't a great deal to report on during certain parts of this season with most of late May and a lot of June washed out apparently, though C. A. Wicks did manage to claim another five-wicket haul against Urmston, before the rain came. At the end of June, there was further evidence of just how wet this season was, with the abundance of ducks parading on the Knutsford scoresheet – seven to be exact! Whalley Range had batted first and scored just 69 themselves, but on what were obviously very treacherous – and uncovered, of course – wickets, Knutsford were dismissed for just 24 with R. Sykes claiming six wickets and C. A. Wicks the other four.

The weather wasn't quite as bad in July, with H. Buckland scoring 54 out of 128 in Whalley Range's meeting with Sefton, though Sefton responded with 131-1, perhaps closing their innings once the target was reached, though in such a wet summer, it's just as plausible that the weather intervened at this point. Whalley Range then closed out July with wins over Timperley and Chorlton-cum-Hardy, though the first of these was an incredibly close affair. Chasing 100 for victory, it seems Whalley Range made precisely that, before immediately losing their last wicket. In this game C. A. Wicks took six wickets, and in the win over Chorlton he scored 55 to supplement the 50 made by A. G. Baker. At the start of August, Whalley Range then made it three wins in a row, easily beating South Manchester by 100 runs thanks to another fifty from C. A. Wicks, who scored 53, a score he repeated later in the month, in an undefeated innings in a drawn game with Urmston.

Next came the game in which it would appear that W. A. Hobbins made his 1st XI debut, at home against Manchester Clifford, and coming in as tenth batsman he remained undefeated on 12, though the game ended in a tame draw. According to notes in the handbook, Whalley Range ended the season with successive victories over Earlestown, though neither of these games made the local press.

The 1908 season would be quite a revelation for Whalley Range, though the better weather certainly played a factor in this regard. Over the last few seasons they hadn't done badly, though admittedly there wasn't anything too amazing either, certainly from a batting perspective. Perhaps inspired by the arrival of Frank Fairbank, a moustachioed Yorkshireman who had already represented his county at 2nd XI level, that was all about to change during the upcoming season.

The season started inauspiciously enough, with defeat at Urmston, though at least C. A. Wicks claimed six wickets in his final appearance for the club, prior to his emigration to Ceylon. This was at least his 24th five-wicket haul for the club, which considering his short time at the club (just over four seasons) was a superb record. Included amongst these figures were his best of 9-31 in 1905, and two further eight-wicket hauls the following season. In addition to this, he also scored at least eight fifties with a highest of 82 for the club.

R. Sykes then captured five wickets against Knutsford, before A. G. Baker showed he was running back into some decent form with the bat, scoring 52 against Bramhall, though it was a game that Whalley Range ultimately lost. Opener J. A. Cummins scored 84 in a commanding win against Poynton, though judging by the below-strength line-up, this was probably a 2nd XI game, though not labelled as such. It was at the start of June that the first signs began emerging that this might be a fairly magical season for Whalley Range, with a hard-fought victory over Timperley, thanks mainly to a five-wicket haul from Ron Buckland. On the following Monday, F. Fairbank captured seven wickets to help remove Rusholme for 156, before ensuring victory with 86, ably supported by J. A. Cummins who scored 59, and J. R. Schofield who also contributed 45 to a large total of 253-9.

Not since 1903 had there been a report of someone scoring a century for Whalley Range, so it seemed quite remarkable that two should then suddenly come along on the same day, and four in total during the season. As can be seen in the scoresheet below, on Saturday 20th June at Whalley Range, A. G. Baker scored an unbeaten 101 out of a declared total of 197-6, before F. Fairbank captured six wickets to ensure victory for Whalley Range as Rusholme were dismissed for 125.

Whalley Range v Rusholme, at Whalley Range, Saturday 20th June 1908

Whalley Range

F. Fairbank	c Hitchen	b Powell-Jones	1
F. Howard		b Screeton	0
A. G. Baker		not out	101
J. A. Cummins	lbw	b Screeton	19
H. Buckland		b Screeton	38
G. G. Howard		run out	6
R. Buckland	lbw	b Haslam	22
Extras			10
Total		(for 6 dec)	197

Meanwhile, at Rusholme, the hosts' 2nd XI team had declared on 177-6, presumably thinking that would be sufficient to ensure at least a draw. However, S. Nixon had other ideas and promptly scored an unbeaten 100, to guide Whalley Range 2nd XI to victory on 183-7.

Rusholme 2nd XI v Whalley Range 2nd XI, at Rusholme, Saturday 20th June 1908

Whalley Range 2nd XI

G. N. E. Gilliat		2
S. Nixon	not out	100
H. B. L. Muth		6
F. F. Dawson		30
C. Gates		7
F. R. Leroy		7
J. Hesketh		5
R. Pearson		0
S. Arden	not out	5
Extras		21
Total	(for 7)	183

As can be seen in the scoresheet above, opening the batting with S. Nixon was G. N. E. Gilliat. George Nicholas Earle Gilliat was born in 1882, attended Hulme Grammar School, and would represent Whalley Range from 1903 up until the First World War. One of his younger brothers, Algernon Earle Gilliat, had a distinguished career abroad, holding various important posts in India, and was Chancellor of the Exchequer for Burma. As for G. N. E. Gilliat, he was President of the Old Hulmeians Association on two separate occasions, 1935-36 and 1940-46, a position that his son, John Martyn Gilliat would also hold in later years (1997-98).

Amazingly, there was barely any time to wait before the next century for Whalley Range, with the team's rising new star, Frank Fairbank, scoring 102 against Sefton, at the start of July :-

Whalley Range v Sefton, at Whalley Range, Saturday 4th July 1908

Whalley Range

F. Fairbank	c Vickess	b Atherton	102
H. Buckland		b Withers	15
A. G. Baker	lbw	b Atherton	27
G. G. Howard	c &	b Boswell	8
J. A. Cummins	c Vickess	b Boswell	0
G. F. Buckland	lbw	b Edwards	52
F. Howard		not out	6
Extras			4
Total		(for 6 dec)	214

Sefton had earlier been dismissed for 127 with S. R. Oddy (whose younger brother, Norman Lee Oddy, was also now representing the club's 2nd XI team) taking six wickets. As well as F. Fairbank's hundred,

G. F. Buckland also contributed 52, as Whalley Range completed a superb win. Whalley Range were really in the midst of a purple patch at this point, with what would transpire to be a run of six wins in seven games, securing further victories over the likes of Didsbury and Urmston. The Didsbury game was a very tight affair. In reply to Whalley Range's 135, Didsbury got to within two runs of that total, though ultimately S. R. Oddy with six wickets proved decisive. The Urmston game wasn't quite so tight, with F. Fairbank (62 not out) and Reverend W. H. Ashton (32 not out) guiding Whalley Range home to an easy eight-wicket win.

Elephants and Crocodiles

George Guest Howard at school, 1905

A name appearing for Whalley Range this season, and appearing in each of the two previous 1st XI scoresheets, is that of G. G. Howard. George Guest Howard was born in about 1889 to Edwin and Hannah Howard. He attended Hulme Grammar School in 1904, before progressing to Liverpool University in 1905, where he won his first team colours for both football and cricket in 1910, before captaining the university cricket team in 1911. He first appeared on a Whalley Range scoresheet in 1906 and represented the club for at least four seasons. Having qualified as a veterinary surgeon at Liverpool University, he received an appointment with a timber firm in India to care for about 300 elephants. When war broke out in 1914 he resigned this post to join the army and served in France until 1919, and afterwards in Germany and Ireland. On demobilisation, he took a commission in the Indian Veterinary Service, and in 1922 married Eileen Marjorie Cox in Calcutta. The following year they had a son, Peter George Guest Howard. However on 21st January 1927, G. G. Howard was out crocodile shooting in a place called Angus in Bengal, in a boat along with his sister, his wife, and their young child, and on leaning forward to reach the child, his rifle, which had a faulty trigger, fell and went off. Tragically the bullet passed straight through George's heart, killing him instantly.

At the start of August 1908, there then followed a minor setback with defeat to South Manchester, but importantly H. Buckland was running into form with a score of 49, and the following week, became the fourth Whalley Range player this season to score a century. Herbert Buckland's 100 not out came out of a total of just 165-4, as he ensured a draw against Castleton who'd earlier posted 202.

Whalley Range v Castleton, at Whalley Range, Saturday 8th August 1908

Whalley Range

F. Fairbank	c Porritt	b Robinson	15
H. Buckland		not out	100
G. F. Buckland		b Robinson	11
Rev. W. H. Ashton		b Porritt	2
H. R. Classen	lbw	b Porritt	3
F. Howard		not out	32
Extras			2
Total		(for 4)	165

Following a draw against Bramhall, Whalley Range wrapped the season up rather fittingly with four wins out of four, assuming that the local press managed to capture all of their remaining games, with wins over Knutsford, Timperley, Poynton, and Didsbury. In the Poynton game, Whalley Range amassed 193-5 before declaring, and then dismissed Poynton for just 31. Thus, all in all, it was a fantastic season for Whalley Range, especially from June onwards, with ten victories compared to just two defeats, including some fine individual performances. Of course, for G. F. Buckland, the year would get even better, with his appearance at the 1908 Olympics.

It was unlikely that 1909 would be quite as remarkable as the previous season, though there was another century registered this season, with A. G. Baker notching another hundred for the club with 101 out of 201-5 declared against Macclesfield early on in the season, though the opposition managed a draw, replying with 140-6. Sadly, the full scoresheet wasn't given, with just the following details appearing in the local press :-

Whalley Range v Macclesfield, at Whalley Range, Saturday 8th May 1909

Whalley Range

A. G. Baker		101
F. Howard		19
H. Buckland		20
Rev. W. H. Ashton		8
R. Buckland		10
G. F. Buckland	not out	23
R. Sykes	not out	11
Extras		9
Total	(for 5 dec.)	201

Whalley Range's first reported win of the season came against Bramhall, who were dismissed for 130, with F. Fairbank taking five wickets and a catch. Whalley Range coasted to victory on 199-2, thanks to an unbeaten 65 from H. Buckland, 54 not out from R. Reynolds, and 44 from A. G. Baker. At the end of May, A. G. Baker was in fine form again, scoring 65 in a drawn game with Rusholme.

In June, G. F. Buckland was in good form with the bat, scoring 52 against Castleton (where F. Fairbank ensured victory with a five-wicket haul), and 56 against Earlestown, though Whalley Range lost this latter game in spite of S. R. Oddy taking an eight-wicket haul. July began with defeat to Sefton, before A. G. Baker prospered again against Macclesfield, this time scoring 66, to complement his century at the start of the season. Didsbury were then beaten thanks to H. K. Oldfield and F. Fairbank both capturing five-wicket hauls, before R. Reynolds notched another fifty this season with 57 in a drawn game with Urmston. F. Fairbank was in inspired form with the ball at the start of August capturing seven-wicket hauls in successive games, against Castleton and then Bramhall. In the first of these A. G. Baker scored 52 to salvage a draw, whilst in the latter, G. F. Buckland's 64 guaranteed a comfortable win.

Following a draw against Knutsford, there was a remarkable game at Timperley. With just G. F. Buckland making double-figures, Whalley Range were routed for 36. Timperley didn't fare too much better themselves, and despite six wickets from H. K. Oldfield, ensured victory with 54. As was often traditional at this time with such a low-scoring affair, play continued, and in their second innings, Whalley Range scored 69-4 before declaring. Timperley then won the game for a second time, in effect, replying with 71-3. No further games made the local press this season for Whalley Range.

Sport in the Whalley Range area seemed to be really thriving at this time. The Old Hulmeians lacrosse team, featuring the Buckland brothers, was continuing to reap huge rewards at the start of 1910, whilst the 1910 cricket season would prove to be another successful one for Whalley Range, for both the 2nd XI as well as for the 1st XI.

It seems fairly safe to assume that the season started off at the end of April with more than just a hint of rain in the air though, since Rusholme generously declared on 25-8. On what suspects must have been a bit of a sticky wicket, Whalley Range then struggled to victory, closing on 32-7. The next game was another low-scoring encounter which resulted in a narrow defeat against Didsbury. Then in Whalley Range's first reported encounter at Leigh, the visitors scored 117, before the hosts were simply blown away for just 35, with F. Fairbank in the kind of form which would shortly earn him a place in the Manchester team, taking 6-10. On the following Monday, F. Fairbank took another five wickets against South Manchester, before 60 from G. F. Buckland helped secure victory for Whalley Range. At the start of June, F. Fairbank again took five wickets, this time against Timperley, though ultimately it was in a losing cause. The following Saturday, A. G. Baker scored 50 in a drawn game with Castleton.

The Second Tour

In mid-June, the Whalley Range players, affluent as ever, embarked on a tour of North Yorkshire, along with a few guests. On Monday 13th June, their first hosts were Harrogate, and batting first, Whalley Range posted a respectable 196, with H. Buckland the top scorer with 80. Whalley Range were lucky to escape with a draw though, as Harrogate looked in a healthy position on 176-4, before time ran out. The following day on the Tuesday, Redcar Cricket Club & Ground were the hosts. The best players for Whalley Range on the day were a couple of the guest players who'd come along on the tour, namely Norman Fletcher and Rowlands, the former being an Old

Hulmeian who played for Chorlton, and who scored 53 out of the tourists' total of 165. In reply the hosts were dismissed for 83 with Rowlands taking 7-28. For the Wednesday game, the tourists had travelled 50 miles or so down the coast to Scarborough, where the hosts gave them a rude awakening by amassing 261 despite a five-wicket haul from F. Fairbank, who was now back in his home county. In reply, Whalley Range settled for a draw on 102-6. The next game for the tourists was a further 20 or so miles down the coast against Bridlington Cricket Club & Ground, where F. Fairbank had retained his fine form of the previous day. Having scored 52 out of a total of 165, he then ensured victory with another five-wicket haul as the hosts were dismissed for 140. The tour was wrapped up on Friday in York with a brilliant run-chase against the Yorkshire Gentlemen, a team which included a number of military chaps. With the hosts having posted 210, one suspects they were a bit surprised to see their total overhauled for the loss of just two wickets. The batsman doing most of the damage for the tourists was another guest, namely L. Oliver, who normally played for Ashton-under-Lyne, who blasted an unbeaten 105. With opener A. G. Baker also scoring an unbeaten 64, it was a superb way to conclude the tour :-

Yorkshire Gentlemen v Whalley Range, at York, Friday 17th June 1910

Whalley Range

F. Fairbank	c Robertson	b Tew	19
A. G. Baker		not out	64
H. Buckland	c Moss Blundell	b Tew	1
L. Oliver		not out	105
Extras			24
Total		(for 2)	213

Whalley Range on North Yorkshire Tour 1910
Garnett (umpire), H. Buckland, K. T. S. Dockray, G. F. Buckland, J. B. Gow, F. R. Leroy
S. R. Oddy, F. Fairbank, A. G. Baker, W. J. Mountain, J. A. Cummins
L. Oliver (Ashton-under-Lyne), R. Sykes, N. Fletcher (Chorlton-cum-Hardy)

There was very nearly two centuries in two days for Whalley Range with F. F. Dawson scoring 98 on the Saturday at home against Rusholme out of a total of 169-4. Earlier in the game, F. Fairbank added another six wickets to his season's tally as Rusholme were dismissed for 130. Frederick Francis Dawson was born on 11th July 1891 to Frank Talbot Dawson and Agnes Alyne Georgina Dawson (nee Hardwick). He was another who attended Hulme Grammar School, and at the school sports day in July 1907, had won the Cardwell Cup for the best under-16 athlete, winning all of the high jump, the 100 yards, and the quarter mile. The following weekend in a draw against Earlestown, F. Fairbank boosted his tally by a further eight wickets.

It wasn't too long though before there was another century by a Whalley Range batsman with A. G. Baker, continuing in his role as 1st XI captain, scoring an unbeaten 106 at Prestwich (see scoresheet below). Just a few seasons back, it looked as though he was really struggling with the bat and had even dropped down to the 2nd XI at one point. However, inspired presumably by his younger sibling's continuing success playing for Warwickshire, this was the third season in a row that A. G. Baker had scored a century for Whalley Range. In the end, he had the tail-enders to thank, for managing to hang around long enough for him to complete his century, especially number eleven H. K. Oldfield whose unbeaten 16 was vital in this regard. Prestwich settled for a draw, replying with 108-6.

Prestwich v Whalley Range, at Prestwich, Saturday 9th July 1910

Whalley Range

Batsman	Fielding	Bowling	Runs
F. Fairbank	lbw	b Fearnley	12
F. Howard		b Fearnley	14
H. Buckland	st Walkden	b Fearnley	3
J. A. Cummins	c &	b H. Parker	1
A. G. Baker		not out	106
G. F. Buckland	st Walkden	b Fearnley	4
R. S. Watson		b H. Parker	1
C. B. Kelly		b H. Parker	4
R. Sykes	c Birchenall	b H. Parker	2
W. J. Mountain		b Kenyon	9
H. K. Oldfield		not out	16
Extras			12
Total		(for 9 dec)	184

Henry Keeler Oldfield had first appeared for the 1st XI in 1901, whilst his younger brother Leonard had represented the 2nd XI for a few seasons around this same time. Henry would continue to play cricket for the club up until the late 1920s, and can be seen in one of the 1927 2nd XI team photos.

Whalley Range's fine season continued the following week, with F. Fairbank taking 8-25 to help remove Didsbury for 107. Following on from his century in his previous innings, A. G. Baker guided the hosts to victory with 65 out of 143-9. W. J. Mountain captured six wickets in the next game, though it wasn't enough to prevent defeat at Urmston. Whalley Range returned to winning ways in fine style, rattling up 245-6 at home to South Manchester, thanks to 72 from F. Howard and 71 from H. Buckland, before W. J. Mountain was then amongst the wickets again, as he and F. Fairbank each claimed five.

Mountain at his Peak

Amazingly enough, W. J. Mountain claimed a further six wickets in each of the next two games, in the August Bank Holiday game with New Brighton (in Wallasey, Merseyside) and at Castleton, though similar to the last time he took six wickets, Whalley Range again found themselves on the losing side, even if it was by just four runs in the New Brighton game. Now in his late twenties, having been born in 1883, and educated at Hulme Grammar School, 1910 proved to be a very rewarding year for William John Mountain, since not only was he capturing a fair few wickets, but this year also saw the birth of his son, George Talbot Mountain, who would also grace the Whalley Range Club in later years. According to the 1911 Census, W. J. Mountain's occupation was a Rent Bailiff. He would live into his 90th year, passing away on 12th August 1972 at Carisbrooke, Gorton. During his life, he would also be associated with the Chorlton Liberal Club, the Carlton club, and the Manchester Pedestrian Club.

F. Howard then got Whalley Range's season back on track with a truly astonishing innings against South Manchester at Withington, where he opened the innings for Whalley Range and smashed an unbeaten 150, at which point Whalley Range declared on 243-2. Also in the runs was H. Buckland who scored a fine 66. South Manchester fought valiantly in reply, eventually securing a draw on 171-8.

South Manchester v Whalley Range, at Withington, Saturday 13th August 1910

Whalley Range

F. Fairbank	c Russell	b Cox	10
F. Howard		not out	150
H. Buckland	c Wedlake	b Cox	66
F. F. Dawson		not out	0
Extras			17
Total		(for 2 dec)	243

Whalley Range 1st XI, circa 1910
Brown (umpire), G. F. Buckland, R. Sykes, H. Buckland, C. M. Howard, Austin (umpire)
J. A. Cummins, F. Fairbank, A. G. Baker (capt), F. Howard, K. T. S. Dockray
S. R. Oddy, R. Buckland

The runs were flowing the following week at Whalley Range as well, with A. G. Baker scoring an unbeaten 58, and G. F. Buckland 51 in a drawn game against Knutsford. Meanwhile the 2nd XI at Knutsford dismissed the hosts' 2nd XI for just 25 to win by 100 runs. Whalley Range 2nd XI were actually enjoying an even more successful season than the 1st XI in 1910, and would end the season with an amazing tally of 19 wins from 26 games, with 5 defeats and 2 draws. Then for the second game in succession for Whalley Range, both A. G. Baker and G. F. Buckland scored fifties, with A. G. Baker scoring 51 and G. F. Buckland scoring precisely 50. Interestingly enough, in light of subsequent events, in between these two previous games, both F. Fairbank and A. G. Baker played for Sale alongside A. F. Stockton in a game at Ashton-under-Lyne in a benefit game for one of the home players. A couple of days later, both represented A. F. Stockton's XI in a game against Glossop, further substantiating an association with the Sale team. In September, Whalley Range lost to Stand, but then beat Warrington, to finish the season with a record of Played 28, Won 11, Lost 6, and Drawn 11. The individual averages for the 1910 season were as follows :-

Batting Averages 1910

	Inns	n.o.	Runs	High	Ave
A. G. Baker	23	6	644	106*	37.88
F. Howard	13	2	410	150*	37.27
F. F. Dawson	8	2	142	98	23.66
H. Buckland	27	3	464	80	19.33
G. F. Buckland	21	3	327	60	18.16
F. Fairbank	22	1	344	52	16.38
J. A. Cummins	19	2	184	42	10.82
R. Buckland	10	1	94	23	10.44
R. Sykes	11	1	101	27	10.10
C. B. Kelly	11	2	88	27*	9.65
H. K. Oldfield	8	2	57	16*	9.50

Bowling Averages 1910

	Overs	Maidens	Runs	Wkts	Ave
F. Fairbank	318	47	1134	87	13.03
W. J. Mountain	129	14	458	33	13.87
S. R. Oddy	96	13	340	22	15.36
H. Buckland	57	12	205	11	18.63
H. K. Oldfield	115	13	413	21	19.76

As can be seen, there were some brilliant individual performances throughout the season, with five players scoring over 300 runs, with A. G. Baker topping the list with 644 runs. The bowling of Frank Fairbank was also quite remarkable, bowling over 300 overs and capturing 87 wickets. Thus, as can be seen, Whalley Range were really experiencing another purple patch in their history, with a highly successful, enjoyable and rewarding season that had also seen them on a tour of North Yorkshire. Unfortunately though, moves were afoot that would mean that was all about to change, as Whalley Range's world was shortly to come crashing down all around them!

On The Move (1911-1922)

After such a rewarding and enjoyable season in 1910, it seems especially cruel that Whalley Range's world then suffered a heart-wrenching blow, as highlighted in the following report from the Manchester Guardian on 30th March 1911 :-

All interested in local cricket will regret to hear that the Whalley Range Club have had to give up their pleasant ground in College Road, which they have held for over fifty years, in consequence of building operations. So far the club have been unable to find another suitable ground, but it is hoped they will soon succeed. The ground has many interesting associations, many famous county cricketers having been regular players there in their younger days, and on Saturday afternoons the matches there were watched with great interest. The club's difficulty as regards the first eleven fixtures for this season has been got over by arranging to play all matches away, but it was impossible to do this with the second eleven matches, and these have had to be cancelled.

This really was terrible news for the club. By all accounts, the ground had been a lovely place to play cricket, and had certainly been conducive to producing some fine innings over the past few decades. Suddenly though, the hallowed turf where the likes of the MacLaren, Steel, Tindall, and Arnold brothers, and latterly the Baker brothers had trodden, would soon be no more.

With nowhere to call home, together with a reduced fixture list, and the uncertainty of the future of Whalley Range Cricket Club, perhaps it wasn't too surprising that the better players decided it was time to move on. The two best players from the previous season had undoubtedly been F. Fairbank with 87 wickets, and A. G. Baker with 644 runs. Whether it was almost inevitable or not, the loss of these two star players was another dagger in the heart of the club. Baker joined the Sale team, who now also boasted C. R. Hartley amongst their ranks, whilst Fairbank initially joined Ashton-under-Lyne, where he played alongside L. Oliver who'd been a guest on Whalley Range's 1910 tour to North Yorkshire. However, it wouldn't be too long before Fairbank was reunited with A. G. Baker, at the Sale club, renewing acquaintances that had been seen developing the previous season. Furthermore, with the 2nd XI being without any fixtures, after such a brilliant season, there were presumably many other players who were forced to fulfil their cricketing aspirations elsewhere.

Not only did Whalley Range lose their best players, but the loss of their ground also meant they lost their membership of the Manchester & District Cricket Association. Admittedly, the Association's Centenary Booklet, published in 1992, lists Whalley Range's first membership stint lasting from 1892 to 1909, but there would appear to be little reason why Whalley Range would have ceased membership in 1909, whereas the loss of their ground would definitely have resulted in the loss of their affiliation. The area that used to be occupied by the cricket ground is today home to the people who live on Burford Drive and the surrounding houses, though one wonders if the current residents are fully appreciative of the sporting history of the ground that lies beneath them.

In spite of the uncertain times, Whalley Range had a convincing victory at Didsbury early on in the season with opener H. R. Classen scoring half of the team's total with 55. Six wickets for W. J. Mountain was usually a bad omen for Whalley Range, but on this particular occasion, his haul ensured an easy victory with Didsbury all out for just 58. This could easily have been followed by another win the following week at Buxton, but the hosts hung on for a draw with eight wickets down, after H. Buckland with an unbeaten 67, and Austen Bradbury, another Old Hulmeian, had scored 41 in a total of 159-4 declared. After poor showings against Timperley and South Manchester, winning ways were restored against Castleton.

Following a thumping at Knutsford, the next time that some of the Whalley Range players made an appearance was under the guise of F. Leroy's XI, but they too were soundly beaten at Mobberley. Interestingly enough, the next game against Didsbury featured H. C. Butterworth, probably coming out of retirement to help Whalley Range in these troubled times. Over the years he had taken well over 300 wickets for the club, including as previously mentioned, a superb tally of over 80 wickets in the 1900 season. This particular game ended in a draw, with Whalley Range replying with 129-7 after Didsbury had posted 184.

The next Whalley Range game reported in the local press was of a game played on Saturday 29th July against Urmston. It was a game that Whalley Range lost, but interestingly enough though, the game was played at Whalley Range according to the Manchester Guardian. This is presumably Whalley

Range's first game at what would become their new home for the next few years, namely Hough End Playing Fields (roughly on the present site of Broughton Park Rugby Club), which was rented at a cost of £60 per annum from Lord Egerton. It is worth noting that the opening batsmen for Whalley Range on this occasion were F. Howard and H. R. Classen, since it would be this same pair who would perform the same role when Whalley Range played their first game at their next home (the current ground) more than a decade later.

Admittedly, none of the remaining games of the season were played at home according to the local press, which perhaps adds an element of doubt as to whether the Manchester Guardian had been slightly premature in announcing Whalley Range's new home venue. Of course, most fixtures for the rest of the season would already have been scheduled to be away games, so this may have been some sort of trial game, to assess the viability of the venue, prior to a more definite arrangement the following season. What is definite though, is that Hough End Playing Fields would represent Whalley Range Cricket Club's home turf certainly from the start of the following season, if it hadn't already during the back-end of the 1911 season.

Of these remaining four games, Whalley Range won two and lost two, beating Rusholme and South Manchester, before losing to Timperley and Stockport. In the two games they won, they reached 200 both times, with F. R. Leroy taking five wickets against Rusholme, whilst W. J. Mountain did the same against South Manchester, with the victory secured with 72 from F. Howard and 52 from H. Buckland. In the two games that they lost, they conceded over 200 runs both times, and on neither occasion, made three-figures themselves. Thus, a fairly troubled season for Whalley Range concluded rather fittingly. At least for the following season, they would start off knowing they'd have somewhere they could call home.

During the 1911 season, the recent exodus of some of the more notable players had not only prompted the re-emergence of some old faces, but had also allowed for the appearance of some new ones, most notable of which was that of the teenage S. E. Woollam, even if it was for only the one game this season (perhaps just as a guest, since the ensuing plaque lists his membership as commencing in 1912).

Samuel Edward Woollam

Samuel Edward Woollam was born in 1892 to Samuel and Annie Woollam, and at the time of his debut in 1911, the family home was on Manley Road in Whalley Range. Eddie, as he was known, was educated at Manchester Grammar School, and even though he may have only played just the once in his debut season, he would go on to become not just an incredibly loyal servant of the Whalley Range Club, but someone who also contributed much to sport in general in the local area.

In the end, he would be associated with the cricket club for over half a century, including many years as 2nd XI captain, and a period where he also served as the President of the Whalley Range club.

However, it was in the world of football that he left an indelible mark, with a long and rewarding association with the Lancashire & Cheshire Amateur Football League. Soon after the League had been formed, Eddie was a player with South West Manchester in 1910. For the 1911-12 season, he was invited on to the committee, taking up the role of honorary treasurer in 1912, before becoming vice-chairman in 1922. Three years later, he would become the League chairman, a position he maintained for a further 38 years! In recognition of such devoted service to the League, he then served as President for three years from 1959, extending his association with the League beyond half a century. With regard to his playing career, he played in the League for well over a decade, and during the First World War played for his battalion and brigade teams. He represented his county and the League and on his retirement in 1923 became a referee, achieving county and FA recognition. He continued refereeing for a long period, indeed until the point when his application to continue as a referee was returned on the grounds that he was too old!

As a player he was awarded badges by the Lancashire & Cheshire Amateur League and the Lancashire FA. He also served on the Lancashire FA amateur committee from whom he was awarded a gold badge on completion of 21 years service, though he continued on the committee for several years after this as well. He served throughout the First World War and was promoted to the rank of major, though in football spheres, he was usually known as "the chief" because of his dominant personality. Thus, it is true that there were some in the game who viewed him as too much of a disciplinarian, but the net result was that the Lancashire & Cheshire Amateur Football League was one of the best run leagues in the country, and in his honour there is now the S. E. Woollam Aggregate Trophy.

Overall, the Woollams were quite an amazing family. In addition to all of Eddie's achievements, his father would serve as Lord Mayor of Manchester (1934-35), and his younger brother, J. P. V. "Jack" Woollam, who would also represent the Whalley Range club at both cricket and tennis, would become one of the best lacrosse players in the country and represent Great Britain at the 1928 Olympics.

The memorial service for S. E. Woollam was held at Manchester Cathedral on 8th April 1965 conducted by The Dean, not long after he'd conducted a service of thanksgiving at the same cathedral to celebrate the life of Sir Winston Churchill, on 31st January. The following plaque is on the clubhouse wall to commemorate Eddie's devotion to the Whalley Range club.

> S. E. WOOLLAM
> IN AFFECTIONATE AND EVERLASTING
> MEMORY OF
> "EDDIE"
> PRESIDENT OF THIS CLUB
> 1957 – 1961
> AND A MEMBER FOR 53 YEARS
> 1912 – 1965

The 1912 season set sail with the recent sinking of the Titanic still dominating the front pages. For Whalley Range, even though they now had somewhere to call home, there was no luring back of A. G. Baker and F. Fairbank, who continued to play for Sale. In fact this season they also appeared together playing Minor Counties Championship cricket for Cheshire, though admittedly A. G. Baker only appeared the once, unlike Fairbank who commanded a regular place in the team.

Also, having forfeited their membership of the Manchester & District Cricket Association, who had strict limits with regard to membership numbers, their position would already have been quickly taken, so there was no automatic and immediate regaining of their place. However, with all games still being of a friendly nature, even for those who were members of the Association, this wasn't such a big issue, and Whalley Range still boasted a fairly full fixture list for most of this season.

All in all, 1912 wasn't a bad season for Whalley Range with the victories marginally outnumbering the defeats, in the games that were reported on. The first of these wins was over Rusholme in early May, thanks to 56 from opener F. Howard, 48 from A. Bradbury, and an unbeaten 37 from W. H. Wood. However, towards the end of May, on the Whit Monday at Withington, South Manchester really put them to the sword with a total of 327, in spite of five wickets from F. R. Leroy. When Whalley Range batted, both G. F. Buckland (46), who was now the 1st XI captain, and H. Buckland (52) performed well, but they couldn't prevent a sizeable defeat, as South Manchester ran out winners by 162 runs. Also playing in this game, and making a rare appearance alongside his brother, was Ernest Classen, in what was probably his 1st XI debut, having played for the 2nd XI back in 1906.

In June, Whalley Range beat Tyldesley, who had also recently relinquished their membership of the Association, so it seems strange that all the time they were in the Association together they never played each other, yet almost as soon as both were no longer members, here they were meeting each other. Whalley Range followed this up with victory over Knutsford a week later, where the main star of the show was new recruit H. P. Shanks who captured four wickets and then guided his team to victory with an unbeaten 31. Shanks also took six wickets the following weekend, though these were in a losing cause against Castleton. Whalley Range's next victory came at the end of June against Knutsford thanks mainly to 43 from A. Bradbury. As with their previous victory, it appeared that Whalley Range closed their innings once the victory target had been achieved, though this was still by no means a policy that was always adopted at this time.

Henry Pearson Shanks, who had previously played for Urmston for the best part of two decades, would only represent Whalley Range for this and the coming season, before turning his attention to golf. In later years, he did play cricket again, representing Lytham St. Annes, where not only was he was secretary of the cricket club, but he was secretary of the yacht club as well. He also played cricket for the District Bank, the Lytham St. Annes branch of which he was now the manager.

In late July, H. Buckland scored an unbeaten 66 in a drawn game with Rusholme, which was followed seven days later with victory over Castleton thanks to 48 from opener Classen and a five-wicket haul from C. H. Kilminster. Kilminster was sometimes spelt as Kilmister in the local press, so there is a fascinating possibility that this is the same person that batted alongside C. A. Wicks out in Ceylon.

The following weekend saw A. Bradbury scoring 52 in a drawn game with South Manchester. From mid-August onwards, there was no further mention of Whalley Range cricket this season, though notes in the handbook suggest that the season ended in mid-September with victory over Didsbury. The handbook also shows that the 2nd XI team were back up and running this season with a full list of fixtures, under the captaincy of F. R. Leroy.

However, the most important information that the 1912 handbook provides, is that the club now catered for tennis once again. As detailed later in the chapter devoted to tennis, after an inaugural tournament in 1881, little evidence was found suggesting that tennis continued to be played at the club in the many years following this, with the surviving handbooks certainly indicating that at the turn of the century, the club was solely devoted to cricket. However, with a change of ground, and Hough End Playing Fields presumably being able to provide for tennis, where the College Road ground couldn't, the club once again became known as Whalley Range Cricket & Lawn Tennis Club (at least on the inside of the handbooks since it would be a couple of seasons before this was reflected on the cover!).

Just prior to the start of the 1913 cricket season, W. A. Hobbins, and all three Buckland brothers, George, Ron, and Herbert, were helping Lancashire beat Middlesex 22-11 at lacrosse in the County Championship final, having already starred in an amazing lacrosse season for the Old Hulmeians, that had seen them crowned as North of England league champions for the first time. The start of the cricket season was then a very wet affair, but once the season had started in earnest, for whatever reason, most games resulted in a definite result, as was the case with all of the first 14 games that were reported on. Of these Whalley Range won just five, with the first of these being against South Manchester, thanks to five wickets from H. K. Oldfield and three from H. C. Butterworth. Appearing in the line-up in this game for Whalley Range was Charles Henry Fox, better known for being the goalkeeper of the all-conquering Old Hulmeians lacrosse team. Successive defeats to Buxton, Cheetham, and Castleton ensued, though H. B. L. Muth had a good knock of 63 in this latter loss.

The local press then reported on a midweek cricket game between the Stockport lacrosse team and the Old Hulmeians lacrosse team, which of course featured many Whalley Range players, though the Old Hulmeians were soundly beaten. However, one suspects they weren't overly concerned, having recently got the better of Stockport where it mattered most, on the lacrosse field.

Towards the end of June at Earlestown, the home side rattled up 304-5 before declaring. In reply, despite the efforts of two of the Buckland brothers (George 45, Ron 40), Whalley Range lost by 140 runs. After such a heavy defeat, perhaps it was fortunate that the next weekend witnessed a practice game for the Whalley Range players, in a match billed as "Married v Single"!

The start of July witnessed a couple of wins on the bounce for Whalley Range, against Brooklands, and amazingly enough, against Earlestown, the team that had just recently thrashed them. In this latter game, R. Sykes was the main wicket-taker with five, though also amongst the wickets was Walter Henderson Mills, the son of Walter George Mills who had played for Lancashire and then Whalley Range. In reply to Earlestown's 172, Whalley Range cruised to victory, with two of the Buckland brothers again doing the bulk of the scoring, with Herbert scoring 84 whilst George scored an unbeaten 55. Whalley Range were then beaten by Bowdon, though W. H. Mills did take five wickets.

Next came successive victories over Rusholme and Castleton. In the first of these, H. R. Classen and H. K. Oldfield each captured four wickets. Opener G. F. Buckland then continued his fine batting form with a knock of 61, before R. Sykes guided them home with an unbeaten 49. Sykes performed well in the ensuing victory as well, taking four wickets, to complement a knock of 42 from H. Buckland and

59 from F. Howard, as Whalley Range won a close encounter by just nine runs. Meanwhile, the 2nd XI team, were also performing well, scoring 206-9 declared against Castleton 2nd XI, before dismissing the visitors for 136.

Following these victories, Whalley Range's season took somewhat of a nosedive with successive defeats to Timperley, Chorlton-cum-Hardy, and Buxton, before F. Howard scored 50 in a drawn game against Northwich at the end of August. Only one further game was reported on this season, which was a drawn game in late September against South Manchester.

For the 1914 season, Henry Worrall stepped down as President, and was replaced by Jules Joseph Leroy, the father of F. R. Leroy. The coming season would of course be one of the saddest on record, and couldn't have started much more poignantly as it happens, with Herbert Buckland scoring a superb unbeaten century to guide Whalley Range to victory in their first game of the season in mid-April against Northwich. After such a classy century, and following on from further successes in the lacrosse world, life must have seemed idyllic for Herbert Buckland, blissfully unaware of the horrors that were imminently to be unleashed on the world. Sadly, Herbert would be one of those who would pay the ultimate price in the atrocities of the First World War, as did Austen Bradbury, who shared a sizeable partnership with him in this game, on his way to a fifty.

Northwich v Whalley Range, at Northwich, Saturday 18th April 1914

Northwich				Whalley Range			
J. Brown		b H. B. L. Muth	17	H. R. Classen	lbw	b G. C. Hilditch	28
E. C. Hilditch	lbw	b H. B. L. Muth	1	A. Bradbury	c Doughty	b Lawton	56
A. H. Orme	c &	b H. B. L. Muth	24	H. Buckland		not out	103
R. Miller	lbw	b H. K. Oldfield	3	R. J. Bradbury		not out	3
Lawton		b H. K. Oldfield	42				
F. C. Hilditch		run out	1				
B. H. Doughty		b H. K. Oldfield	29				
G. C. Hilditch		b H. K. Oldfield	16				
H. Gidman		b H. K. Oldfield	0				
F. W. Bailey	c Fox	b H. B. L. Muth	2				
A. Jervis		not out	6				
Extras			31	Extras			8
Total			172	Total		(for 2)	198

Following a 66-run defeat to Didsbury in their second game of the season, Whalley Range recovered well the following weekend to beat Rusholme, with William Herbert Thornton taking four wickets, before Old Hulmeians, Ross James Bradbury (elder brother of Austen) with an unbeaten 52 and H. B. L. Muth with an unbeaten 41, guided Whalley Range to victory. Dolph Classen then captured successive five-wicket hauls against Chorlton and Timperley, though the former game was drawn, and the latter was lost. Meanwhile, James Arthur Barber, another of the successful Old Hulmeian lacrosse team scored 81 for the 2nd XI against Timperley 2nd XI.

During late May and June, Whalley Range endured six successive defeats. It was mainly the batting that failed with low totals such as 47 against Buxton, 61 against South Manchester, and 68 against Earlestown, with the only batting highlight during this period for the 1st XI being G. F. Buckland's 54 against Castleton. For the 2nd XI, J. A. Barber was continuing to prosper with scores such as 48 against Buxton 2nd XI and 69 against Hale 1st XI in a Wednesday game, which was enough to see him making his debut for the 1st XI come the weekend. During this barren run for the 1st XI, at least the bowlers had some notable successes with W. H. Thornton taking six wickets against South Manchester, and Classen taking six Earlestown wickets and five Brooklands wickets in successive games at the end of May. The losing sequence came to an end when they drew with Cheetham, not that Whalley Range fared too well in this game conceding 236-7, but the game did mark the 1st XI debut of H. T. Eke who would continue to represent the club for several years following the War. Herbert Thomas Eke actually emanated from Kent, being born to Edward and Sarah Ann Eke (nee Davies) in 1885.

In mid-July, G. F. Buckland then made 50 against Earlestown as Whalley Range finally recorded a further win this season. The following weekend, almost all cricket in the country was cancelled as the country was gripped by a portentous wintry spell. A few days later, on Tuesday 28th July 1914, the First World War began.

Cricket continued this season, at least for a short while. Whalley Range 2nd XI amassed a formidable 288 against Chorlton 2nd XI, and the following week, the 1st XI rattled up 239-3 before declaring against Buxton. All those who batted contributed well, with the scorecard reading as follows : H. R. Classen 32, G. F. Buckland 47, H. Buckland 53 not out, H. T. Eke 61, and R. Sykes 28 not out. Buxton were then dismissed for 179 as Whalley Range celebrated what would be their last victory before Great Britain became enveloped in the War along with the rest of Europe. In the one further game that was played this season, Whalley Range drew with Cheetham, at the end of August.

Cricket throughout the country did continue during 1915, though Whalley Range like most teams were severely depleted by those who were competing in a far nobler cause. Understandably, cricket didn't feature too highly in the list of priorities for the local press during these troubled times, and only two results surfaced for Whalley Range this season, of which only one featured the line-ups. In the second of these games, Whalley Range beat Northwich by 65 runs in late August, whilst the first of these was an away game against Castleton, the scoresheet of which was as follows :-

Castleton v Whalley Range, at Sparth Bottoms, Saturday 31st July 1915

Whalley Range				Castleton			
H. R. Classen	lbw	b Rickson	2	E. C. Cronshaw	c Buckland	b Classen	14
J. A. Barber		b Lewis	0	F. H. Rudd		b Thornton	7
R. Buckland		b Lewis	0	E. Rickson	c &	b Classen	7
W. H. Thornton	c sub	b Lewis	2	E. Clegg		run out	10
H. L. Palmer	lbw	b Lewis	4	B. W. Shaw	c Barber	b Classen	0
W. C. Smith	c Shaw	b Lewis	13	A. S. Lewis		b Classen	0
J. S. Ardern		b Rickson	15	G. Butterworth		b Thornton	11
E. C. Gregson	c Rickson	b Cliff	14	F. Taylor	c Walker	b Classen	2
J. P. V. Woollam	c P. Clegg	b Rickson	17	F. Bolton		b Classen	1
G. S. Walker		b Lewis	2	E. B. Burnett		not out	2
H. Burton		not out	2	P. Clegg		b Classen	0
Extras			16	Extras			4
Total			87	Total			58

It was a game that Whalley Range won, thanks mainly to Dolph Classen managing to capture seven wickets. Notable names in the Whalley Range line-up are J. P. V. Woollam and H. L. Palmer (more of whom later) making their earliest known appearances for the club. Also featured is G. S. Walker who sadly was another player who would lose his life in the First World War.

During the following season, the local papers certainly covered the games of teams who were in the Manchester & District Cricket Association. However, perhaps owing to the fact that Whalley Range were no longer members of this association, only one result featuring them, made the papers in 1916, which was a tight victory over close neighbours Chorlton by 134 to 128, in mid-August.

First World War Heroes

The ensuing picture (see next page) is of a tablet which adorns one of the walls of the Whalley Range clubhouse, paying tribute to all of the club members who lost their lives in either of the two World Wars. Sadly, as can be seen, there were ten club members in all, who perished during the First World War, and a further seven who lost their lives during the Second World War. Those who lost their lives during the First World War were A. Bradbury, H. Buckland, W. L. Holden, J. Nelson, H. E. Sanby, R. Sykes, G. S. Walker, J. H. Walker, W. L. P. Walton, and A. Worthington. There follows a brief description of each of these heroes, in recognition of the ultimate sacrifice that each of them made for their country.

Captain Austen Bradbury of the Tank Corps was killed in action at Hangard on 8th August 1918, aged just 25, whilst leading his section of the Tanks against the enemy lines, not long before the end of the War. He joined the Rifle Brigade in 1914, and soon obtained a commission in the Manchester Regiment, transferring afterwards into the Machine Gun Corps and the Tanks. He served in Salonica and in France. Born on 5th September 1892 to Arthur Wellesley and Rebekah Jane Bradbury, Austen excelled at sport, and prior to admirably representing Whalley Range at cricket, he had been Hulme Grammar School captain at both football and cricket, and was also awarded the Gaskell Cup for being the best all-round athlete at the School sports. It was this same resolve and determination that he took with him onto the battlefield, where he was awarded the Military Cross for gallantry and devotion to duty.

WHALLEY RANGE CRICKET & LAWN TENNIS CLUB.

THIS TABLET IS DEDICATED TO THE PROUD MEMORY OF THE MEMBERS OF THIS CLUB WHO LOST THEIR LIVES IN THE TWO WORLD WARS.

1914—1918

A. BRADBURY	J. NELSON	G. S. WALKER
H. BUCKLAND	H. S. SANBY	J. H. WALKER
W. L. HOLDEN	R. SYKES	W. L. P. WALTON
	A. WORTHINGTON	

1939—1945

J. HARGREAVES	G. H. ISHERWOOD	J. C. SCAMMELL
R. HAWLEY	P. S. PRESTON	J. E. L. WOOLLAM
	F. CLARKE	

Memorial tablet adorning the clubhouse wall

Herbert "Bert" Buckland at the start of the war, enlisted in the 20th Royal Fusiliers, the Public Schools Battalion, and on 14th November 1915, the Battalion proceeded to France and saw action on the Western Front. Bert was promoted to Lance Corporal during his time with the Battalion, but sadly he was killed in action on 20th July 1916, aged 30, at High Wood along with five fellow Old Hulmeians that day. He was buried at Bouzincourt Ridge Cemetery in Albert, France.

William Leak Holden was born on 26th September 1898 to John William and Annie Florence Holden, and attended Hulme Grammar School between 1908 and 1915, where he excelled at sport, and just as A. Bradbury had a few years earlier, was awarded the Gaskell Cup for athletics. Also in his last summer at the School, he played for the 1st XI cricket team alongside the likes of J. P. V. Woollam and G. S. Walker, and was described in the Hulmeian magazine as a *"strong forcing batsman"* and a *"useful change bowler"*. Second Lieutenant William Leak Holden went missing on 4th January 1917, whilst in action in France, after just a few days at the front. He was just 18 years of age. Sadly, his parents did not receive notification of his death, the exact details of which were never known, until August.

Sergeant Harold Ernest Sanby was born in about 1884 in Northumberland, a grandson of William Worthington, of Whalley Range. He was one of the buyers employed by Messrs. T. H. Rigby and Co. Limited, Manchester, and joined the forces, along with thirty other employees of the firm, in August 1914. He was part of the 9th Battalion Rifle Brigade (Prince Consort's Own), but was killed in action in Flanders on 9th August 1915. At one point, his education took him to the Bourne College in Quinton, Birmingham, where his name was proudly emblazoned on their memorial tablet. When the college shut down in 1928, the tablet was removed to a nearby chapel, but was destroyed when the chapel was demolished in the 1960s. Sadly the Whalley Range club's tablet has his middle initial incorrect.

John Nelson was living with his parents, Phyllis and John Allen Nelson, on Clarendon Road, Whalley Range, when he enlisted with the Royal Garrison Artillery in December 1915. He was killed in action in France, on 28th November 1917, aged just 21, and was buried at The Huts Cemetery in Belgium.

Corporal Reginald Sykes of the Rifle Brigade was killed in action on 15th September 1916, just twelve days after his 28th birthday, and less than a year after his wife Dorothy had given birth to their son. Reginald had been a supreme sportsman. Not only had he starred for Whalley Range at cricket, but he'd also excelled for Old Hulmeians Football Club, and the Manchester Rugby Club, having played at half-back for Lancashire on several occasions.

George Stanley Walker was killed less than a month before the end of hostilities, on 23rd October 1918 whilst, in the words of his commanding officer *"leading his men gallantly in an attack on a village"* in France. Having been born on 15th September 1898, to Arthur William and Rebecca Walker, Second Lieutenant George Stanley Walker was barely 20 years of age, when he was killed. He was buried at Pommereuil British Cemetery in France.

John Haslam Walker was born on 30th March 1887, and attended Hulme Grammar School between 1898 and 1905. In his last three years at the School, he was captain of the lacrosse team, and would go on to play for Lancashire, as well as playing a large part in the success of the Old Hulmeians team. He also played for the School 1st XI at cricket where in his last season his batting was described in the Hulmeian magazine as *"wonderfully improved"*. Similar to two others in this section, he was another who won the Gaskell Cup, for being the best all-round athlete on School sports day. Soon after the outbreak of war, John joined the 1/6th Manchesters, a Territorial battalion, and proceeded to Egypt in September 1914. He was promoted to Sergeant and served in Gallipoli from May 1915. In January 1917 John obtained a commission and, as a second lieutenant, was attached to the 16th Battalion Sussex (Yeomanry) Regiment and proceeded once more to Egypt. He was wounded in action on 6th November 1917 at Sheira and sadly died of his wounds on 22nd November at Nasrieh Hospital, Cairo.

Lieutenant William Lees Percival Walton, 217th Company, Machine Gun Corps (Infantry), was killed in action on 30th November 1917, having married Hilda Stanley earlier in the year. Born in 1893 to Emma and John Albert Walton, he was aged just 24 when he was killed. The stone cross War Memorial in Northenden bears his name, as does the memorial in St. Wilfrid's Church in Northenden.

Arthur Worthington was killed on the same day as his brother, Cecil, on 20th July 1916 at High Wood (Bois de Fourcaux) in France. He was a Private with the 20th Battalion, Royal Fusiliers (City of London Regiment). Arthur's body was never found, and he is commemorated on the nearby Thiepval Memorial, on the Somme front.

In 1917, as the First World War raged on, Hough End Playing Fields was appropriated for use as an airfield, and all club assets were sold off. As such, the following advert appeared in the local press in late October this year, where the H. R. C. referred to, is in fact Dolph Classen :-

For Sale, 87 6-foot Wooden Posts, 5in. x 3in., and about 260 yards Wire, forming fence round cricket ground: one 33ft. Flagpole, 2 Small Sheds, 12ft. x 10ft. x 7ft., and 10ft. x 5ft. 6in. x 5ft.: may be seen on Whalley Range Cricket Ground, Alexandra Road South: must be removed immediately. Send offers to H. R. C., 8 Range Road, Alexandra Park.

Size of Grounds

From the sale of 260 yds of boundary fencing, we can work out the size of the ground as being about 83 yds across, and about 1.25 acres. The current playing surface is nearly three times the size: about 130 yds across, or nearly 4 acres. The total area purchased in 1923 was about six acres, including tennis courts, club house, car park etc. We don't know the shape of the first ground on College Road, and we suspect it shrank over time, especially after Beech Hurst House was built, and the electricity sub-station in the 1900s. We know the site was bounded by College Road, the College wall and Burford Avenue: at its greatest extent it was smaller than the current ground, but much larger than the Hough End ground. The tennis courts might have been included in that space too.

Manchester's First Airport

During the last few months of the war, Alexandra Park Aerodrome, as the airfield then became known, was used for the assembly and test flying of warplanes. The terms of Lord Egerton's lease stated that all flying activities would cease five years after the end of the war, and so its use as an air terminal was short-lived, closing down in 1924, though during this period after the war (with Ringway not being in existence until the late 1930s) Alexandra Park Aerodrome (or Didsbury Aerodrome as it was also known) was viewed as the most important passenger airport in the area, with regular flights to London, Blackpool, and Dublin.

With the war having finally ended in November 1918, even though most other local cricket clubs were back up and running for the 1919 season, with the loss of Hough End Playing Fields, Whalley Range were once again homeless, and as such, the club was very much in abeyance, until such time as a new ground could be acquired. The likes of H. R. Classen and F. R. Leroy were thus forced to continue their cricketing careers for the nearby Chorlton-cum-Hardy club for the next few years, as did F. Howard for a short time, before moving on to Brooklands.

In 1920, the Manchester & District Cricket Association decided to spice things up by finally introducing a competitive spirit to their games. This season, 1st XI teams were invited to compete for the Stockton Trophy, whilst the following year, the Burrows Trophy began to be competed for by 2nd XI teams. It wasn't compulsory to compete for the trophies though, with some teams preferring to continue to treat the games as friendlies, a practice which persisted at Whalley Range CC until 1962. The Stockton Trophy was presented to the league by Edwin Stockton who played for the Sale club between 1890 and 1918. He also became President of the Manchester & District Cricket Association from 1920 up until the outbreak of the Second World War. He was Honorary Treasurer of Lancashire County Cricket Club from 1918 to 1924 and President from 1925 to 1926. Knighted in 1921, Sir Edwin Forsyth Stockton was also a Member of Parliament for the Exchange Division of Manchester. Fittingly enough (and certainly very much a case of keeping it in the family!), the first award of the Stockton Trophy in 1920 went to Sale, which meant that Edwin Stockton got to present the Stockton Trophy to his younger brother Albert Stockton, who just happened to be captain of Sale at the time. Sadly, this original Stockton Trophy was lost in the Cheadle Hulme pavilion fire in 1946, and so a replacement was obtained and inscribed as the previous one. The final league table for the 1920 season was as follows :-

Manchester & District Cricket Association, Final Table 1920

	Won	Lost	Drew	Percentage
Sale	13	2	4	68.42
Chorlton-cum-Hardy	10	3	3	62.50
Earlestown	7	2	3	58.33
South Manchester	7	5	3	46.66
Broughton	7	3	6	43.70
Bolton	3	4	0	42.85
Worsley	4	5	1	40.00
Stockport	6	4	6	37.50
Urmston	6	8	2	37.50
Winnington Park	3	5	2	33.33
Blackley	4	6	3	30.76
Cheetham Hill	4	7	4	26.66
Flixton	2	9	1	16.66
Cheadle Hulme	2	7	4	15.38
Heaton Mersey	1	5	2	12.50
Bramhall	1	5	4	10.00
Didsbury	1	5	8	07.13

The calculation for percentage was based simply on the number of wins from number of games played. Note that for the Winnington Park percentage to be correct, this would need to imply there was one less loss or draw, or perhaps the figure should really have been 30%. Even allowing for the slight discrepancy with the Winnington Park record, the total number of wins (81) doesn't equal the total number of losses (85), presumably implying that for games involving competitive teams versus non-competitive teams, the results counted towards the table for the competitive teams. The non-competitive teams this season, of which there were eight out of the twenty-five Association members, were Bollington, Bowdon, Bury, Castleton, Leigh, Macclesfield, Warrington, and Wigan.

Sadly, 1920 would witness the passing away of H. W. Tindall at the age of 54. In his day, he had been one of the most dynamic batsmen ever to represent the club, scoring at least four centuries, and countless other fifties.

Before Whalley Range became homeless for the second time, the number of Old Hulmeians who were playing for the club was increasing to the point where it would appear that they probably outnumbered the members of the club who hadn't attended the nearby Hulme Grammar School. As such, there was a very strong bond between the Old Hulmeians and the Whalley Range Club, and of course, a great sense of camaraderie amongst all of the players, undoubtedly strengthened by their resolve to overcome the traumatic horrors of recent times. It was this strength of character, together with the steely determination and fortitude of the likes of H. R. Classen and F. R. Leroy, that ultimately ensured the club's survival, since with the club very much in hibernation at this point, this could easily have become a slumber from which there was no awakening. Thus, in the early 1920s, the joint forces of the Old Hulmeians and the Whalley Range Club came together to purchase the ground that still serves as the club's home to this day, on Kingsbrook Road.

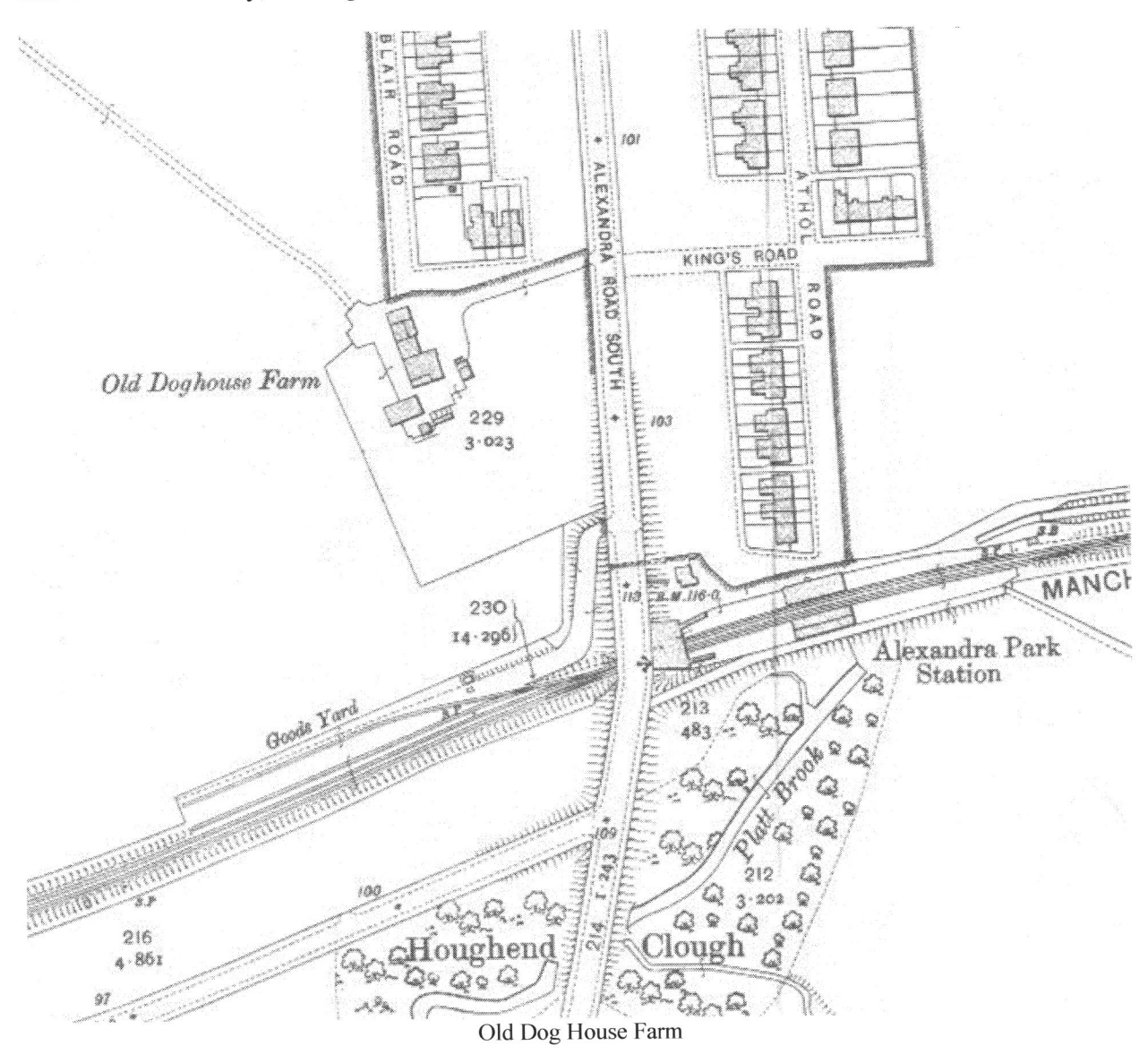

Old Dog House Farm

As can be seen from the above map from 1907, the farmland area associated with Old Dog House Farm (comprising six acres on the western side), which was to become their new ground, wasn't too distant from the home they'd rented at Hough End, just before the war. Though not present at the time of this map, what had previously been known as Old Doghouse Lane had now become Kings Road (today

Kingsbrook Road), running perpendicular to Blair Road, just to the north of the farmhouse. A track ran from the farm to Hough End Hall, along which the hunting dogs (hence the "Dog House" part of the name) travelled to meet up for hunts. The track crossed where the cricket square is today, and its ditches can still be seen on the outfield. The Whalley Range club purchased their three acres in 1921, though it wasn't until the following year that the Old Hulmeians managed to accumulate enough capital to purchase the remaining half of the land.

Sadly, by this time, one of the more noteworthy Old Hulmeians had passed away. Arthur George Baker, the older half of the Fabulous Baker Boys, died after a long illness on 28th March 1922, aged 47. At his peak, he was certainly one of the best cricketers to represent the Whalley Range Cricket Club, scoring centuries in three successive seasons at one point. He was also a fine footballer, and not a bad musician either apparently, being adept both as a violin player and an organist. As already mentioned in a previous chapter, 1922 also witnessed the passing of another prominent past player who had contributed so much to the fortunes of Whalley Range, with Sidney Maguire Tindall dying in Sydney, Australia on 19th September, aged 55, when he fractured his skull when falling from a moving tram. Like A. G. Baker, he too scored at least four centuries for the club.

Having finalised the acquisition of the land, the area then needed a fair bit of renovation to transform it into somewhere that was ideal for the likes of cricket and lacrosse. Thus, Whalley Range cricket wasn't quite up and running in 1922, and the only time that we see most of them playing together this season was under the guise of Mr. Classen's XI in a game against Hulme Grammar School, played in mid-May at the school. Dolph's former school were bowled out for just 59, of which his son Geoffrey contributed eight. Geoffrey was Dolph and Blanche's only child and sadly he would go on to die far too young, aged just 23, on 9th February 1929, after an attack of influenza developed into pneumonia and proved fatal within just six days.

Also playing for the school that day was Winston Williamson, a star in the making, who would represent Whalley Range admirably in the future. In reply, Mr. Classen's XI scored 85-4 before closing their innings and allowing the School to bat a second time, with H. T. Eke and R. Buckland scoring most of the runs. Dolph's team also included the likes of G. F. Buckland, F. Howard, R. E. Howard, Mountain, and Pennington. In their second innings, the School scored 94-7.

Thus it wouldn't be until the 1923 season that Whalley Range cricket again began in earnest. With the former pupils from Hulme Grammar School having played a vital role in the survival of the Whalley Range club, the next chapter pays tribute to the Old Hulmeians.

The Old Hulmeians Connection

Hulme Grammar School pictured in 1911

The previous chapters bear testament to the inextricable links between the Whalley Range club and the Old Hulmeians, culminating in the joint-purchase of the Old Dog House ground in the early 1920s, where the Whalley Range club is still based. As such, this book would not be complete without an appreciation of the early history of the Old Hulmeians.

The name Old Hulmeians refers to the former pupils of the nearby William Hulme's Grammar School on Springbridge Road, an institution first established on 26th January 1887, as Hulme Grammar School, before adopting its current lengthier title in 1939. The William Hulme after whom the school was named lived from 1631 to 1691, and was the founder of the William Hulme Charity

Almost as soon as the school was founded, sports including cricket, lacrosse and football were being played, leading two years downstream to the formation of a Games Club, the first committee meeting of which was held on 1st April 1889. Notable amongst those first representatives was A. G. Baker who was elected to be the school cricket captain, and H. J. Amos who was elected vice-captain. Later on that year, another conspicuous name appearing was that of a young H. R. Classen. As evidenced elsewhere in this book, these were people who would go on to feature significantly for the Whalley Range club over the coming years.

Second in the cricket batting averages for 1889 was A. G. Baker with 189 runs at an average of 11.1, and a top score of 42. Amazingly, H. J. Amos topped the bowling averages with an average of just 1.9 with a season's analysis of 133 overs, 62 maidens, 67 wickets for 130 runs! As well as playing for the School's first team at cricket, H. J. Amos, A. G. Baker and H. R. Classen, also played for the School's first team at football.

In 1890, in The Hulmeian (the School magazine), we see the first mention of "Old Hulmeians", referring to the former pupils of the school, the number of which was inevitably growing with the passage of time. The start of the relevant report read as follows :-

The idea of forming an Old Hulmeians' Cricket and Football Club had long been present in the minds of the School Staff, but owing to the small number of those who had left the School in earlier years of its existence, the formation was postponed to a favourable opportunity. Fortune has favoured the scheme and the Club is now fairly started.

Thus the Old Hulmeians Football Club was started in October 1890, followed in early 1891 by the formation of the Old Hulmeians Cricket Club. An account in The Hulmeian in 1891 reported that the Old Hulmeians cricketers had obtained a cricket ground close to Chorlton Railway Station (where the new Metro station is now). Their very first game was played on 25th April 1891 and was against Chorlton Juniors CC who were dismissed for just 8 in their first innings, and 18 in the second innings. Old Hulmeians in their only innings scored 47 to register a very easy victory. Another of their victories this season was against their former school, though they were consummately beaten in a return game later in the season, as we can see below, with only the first four batsmen managing to trouble the scorers. For the School, A. T. Ward-Jones had the exceptional figures of 8 overs, 6 maidens, 6 wickets for 3 runs, with all of his wickets being clean bowled, whilst G. Youatt took 3-17 from his 8 overs.

Hulme Grammar School v Old Hulmeians, Saturday 11th July 1891

Hulme Grammar School				Old Hulmeians		
E. Shorrocks		b Baker	2	E. Rowe	b Youatt	8
L. Norbury		b Baker	5	E. E. Wright	b Ward-Jones	1
P. M. Bennett		b Baker	1	A. G. Baker	b Ward-Jones	8
R. B. Spencer		b Rowe	1	P. Williams	b Ward-Jones	3
H. R. Classen	c Shorrocks	b Rowe	9	S. Payne	b Youatt	0
H. Ford		b Rowe	1	O. Hague	b Youatt	0
G. Youatt	c Wright	b Baker	2	T. Hart	b Ward-Jones	0
L. Barrett		b Baker	7	Adshead	b Ward-Jones	0
S. W. Saxelby		not out	9	F. Shorrocks	run out	0
A. T. Ward-Jones	c &	b Rowe	7	G. Farquharson	not out	0
H. F. Clarke		b Baker	0	C. P. Williams	b Ward-Jones	0
Extras			7	Extras		9
Total			51	Total		29

The Old Hulmeians final record for that first season was listed as played 15, won 7, lost 6, and 2 draws, though one of these drawn games was in fact a tie against Chorlton Juniors CC, with both sides scoring 72 in the return game. As can be seen from the scoresheet above, A. G. Baker was now playing for the Old Hulmeians, and he topped the bowling averages with 50 wickets at an average of 4.46. He was also the Old Hulmeians football captain this year, and for the ensuing 1891-1892 season, though the football season started off in October with heavy defeats to St. Bede's College (1-6), and St. James' AFC (0-12), and by the end of the season, just two out of thirteen games had resulted in victories.

Prior to the 1892 cricket season, there was talk of disbanding the Old Hulmeians cricket team, though the acquisition of a new ground seemed to provide fresh impetus, as reported in The Hulmeian :-

> *...but we are glad to inform our readers that a field has been engaged for twelve months for both cricket and football. It is situated close to the Princess Road gate of Alexandra Park, and a more desirable field, so far as central position is concerned, could not have been obtained.*

Sharing the same ground, the Old Hulmeians Football and Cricket Clubs amalgamated and actually fielded two teams in the coming seasons for both cricket and football.

In complete contrast to the previous season, the 1892-1893 football season kicked off with a 7-0 win over Northenden, followed by a 5-0 victory over Eccles 'A', and a 9-1 thrashing of Manchester Wanderers. Suddenly, the Old Hulmeians were a football force to be reckoned with, which was further emphasised by an 11-0 drubbing of their former School. It was presumably because of such results that the football team decided it was time to take a step up in class, and so they joined the Lancashire Amateur League for the 1893-1894 season, and the ever-improving team actually finished as league runners-up the following season, with a record of Played 20, Won 14, Lost 4, Drawn 2, Goals For 77, Goals Against 45.

A meeting of the Old Hulmeians Games Committee on March 28th 1893 included discussions about forming a lacrosse club, as did a meeting on March 30th 1894, though it wasn't until the following year that the Lacrosse Club was finally formed at a meeting on May 16th 1895. However, in spite of the advent of the lacrosse team and the success of the football team, 1895 also saw the demise of the cricket team which was disbanded due to problems with ground availability and financial issues. Old Hulmeians' loss was very much the gain of some local clubs, with Whalley Range in particular benefiting from an influx of players.

Even though there was now no 'official' Old Hulmeians cricket team, the traditional cricket encounter between past and present pupils of the School was to continue for many years to come, though apparently on occasions, these matches suffered some times from a lack of Old Boy players who were now playing for their various clubs on Saturdays.

For the 1895-1896 season, the Old Hulmeians acquired the use of a large field in Wilbraham Road *"on which there is ample room for both Football and Lacrosse"* it was reported, and one suspects that nobody who witnessed those first few lacrosse games on that field, could possibly have imagined the amazing success that this team would go on to achieve. Captained this season by P. M. (Percy Mayson) Bennett, with E. B. Rowe as vice-captain, their first game was a friendly against Newton Heath on September 28th though they their opponents emerged 8-4 winners in very hot weather.

For their first season, the Old Hulmeians Lacrosse team had joined the Fourth Division of the North of England Lacrosse League, and so their next match was a league encounter with Christ Church on October 12th and what a game it turned out to be, with the Old Hulmeians running out comfortable winners by the commanding score of 9-0. In fact, they went on to win all three of their first league encounters, before suffering their first ever league defeat against Didsbury Park who just got the better of them 7-5, in a well-contested and exciting game. At the end of their first season, their league record was Played 12, Won 8, Lost 4, Goals Scored 60, Goals Conceded 30, a record which left them placed a meritable third out of seven in their first ever season.

As for the Old Hulmeians football team, captained by A. G. Baker with H. R. Classen as vice-captain, the 1895-1896 season proved to be very successful with a record of Played 19, Won 13, Lost 5, Drawn 1, Goals Scored 60, and Goals Conceded 40.

Hulme Grammar School lacrosse team 1897
(Winners of the North of England Schools Challenge Flags)
W. O. Brelsford, C. S. Baker, H. W. L. P. Ilderton, W. J. Dearden, C. S. Chalmers, B. Robinson
O. S. Flinn, P. J. Jefferis (capt), C. H. Hawkins, E. C. Allen
G. F. Buckland, A. Merchant

Meanwhile, Hulme Grammar School themselves were making a big impression in lacrosse, winning the North of England Schools Challenge Flags competition in 1893, 1894 (winning 26-0 in the final!), 1896, and as shown in the above photo, successfully defended their title in 1897 as well. The team comprised some young players who would feature prominently for both Old Hulmeians and Whalley Range in the coming years, most notably C. S. Baker who played in goal, and G. F. Buckland who played in the cover point position.

As for the Old Hulmeians lacrosse team in the 1896-1897 season, they managed to improve on their previous season's performance, losing just twice in the league, both by a two-goal margin, to St. Helen's and Ashton(-under-Lyne), and thus finished second in the league, with 16 points from a possible 20, missing out on top spot solely on goal-average. However, this was still sufficient to gain promotion.

The most significant name in the line-up this season was that of James Henry Buckland, the eldest brother in a family whose name would become synonymous with the sport of lacrosse. His younger brother, George Frederick, who as just mentioned, was playing for the school at this time, would go on to play for England and appear in the Olympics, whilst his two other younger brothers, like himself, would also excel at the sport. Their father, James Edward Buckland, can be seen in the Whalley Range 2nd XI team photo from 1928. Another notable name in the line-up was that of Herbert Charles Hobbins, who would also have a younger brother who would go on to represent his country at lacrosse.

For the 1896-1897 football season, A. G. Baker was again captain, whilst E. Shorrocks took over as vice-captain, and then possibly captain as well for most of the season, since A. G. Baker suffered a serious knee injury in the very first game. The team also contained such familiar names as S. W. Saxelby, H. R. Classen, and H. J. Amos.

Hulme Grammar School 1st XI Cricket Team 1897
W. Payne (Professional), P. F. S. Tyrer, W. P. Bradshaw, F. E. Green, C. H. Hawkins, W. A. Hobbins
A. E. A. Searle (capt), R. E. van der Veen (vice-capt), A. K. Wilkins, C. S. Baker
P. J. Jefferis, H. P. Brown

The photo above shows Hulme Grammar School's 1st XI for the 1897 season, with some familiar names again being featured, including future Whalley Range players in the form of W. P. Bradshaw, W. A. Hobbins, and C. S. Baker. Note also W. Payne described as 'professional'!

By the summer of 1897, it looks like H. R. Classen had wandered further afield, and according to the July 1897 edition of The Hulmeian had gone to Para in Brazil. The same edition also reported that A. G. Baker had been *'scoring in fine style for the Manchester Club of late'*, making an unbeaten 108 against Urmston and an unbeaten 154 against Chorlton-cum-Hardy. Also mentioned was the fact that on Saturdays, he played cricket for Whalley Range, as did another Old Boy, H. J. Amos. It looks like H. R. Classen's Brazilian excursion wasn't too extensive since he represented Old Hulmeians in the second half of the 1897-1898 football season, for which H. J. Amos was the vice-captain.

In 1898, Hulme Grammar School, captained by G. F. Buckland, captured their third successive North of England Flags, an achievement which meant they got to keep the flags for good. However, it must be said that there wasn't a great deal of competition this time, with just one other school vying for the title, namely Woodlands School who beat them 5-4. Thankfully the title wouldn't be decided by just the one game, and Hulme Grammar School responded well in levelling the series with an 11-5 victory. The final game was played on March 26th at Didsbury Cricket Ground, with Hulme Grammar School again running out easy winners, 11-3. The victorious team is shown below, apart from E. C. Allen who replaced W. R. McChlery in the final game :-

Hulme Grammar School lacrosse team 1898
(Winners of the North of England Schools Challenge Flags)
W. R. McChlery, E. Derbyshire, W. Stubbs, E. R. Wood, W. J. Dearden, H. Hough
J. Norquoy, G. F. Buckland (capt), E. T. Wihl, C. S. Chalmers
A. E. Chalmers, R. A. Phibbs

Old Hulmeians lacrosse team, having been promoted the previous season, found themselves in the Third Division for the 1897-1898 season, and kicked off their league season in fine style, with a 13-1 thumping of Bolton, before eventually finishing in third place out of seven.

The July 1898 edition of The Hulmeian reported that all of the following Old Hulmeians were now playing cricket for Whalley Range: A. G. Baker, C. S. Baker, H. R. Classen, S. W. Saxelby, H. J. Amos, and H. B. L. Muth, with A. G. Baker and H. R. Classen in particular, performing especially well.

From here on in, over the ensuing years, the Old Hulmeians continued to enjoy their football, though without any noteworthy success. The lacrosse team on the other hand, were really beginning to make their mark, and though they wouldn't have known it at the time, some of them were continuing on a monumental and wonderful journey that would eventually reap incredible rewards. As such, together with the fact that this was also the team that would later provide the main connections to the Whalley Range club, it is mostly the achievements of the lacrosse team that the remainder of this chapter concentrates on.

Having just missed out on promotion the previous season, Old Hulmeians lacrosse team made sure there was no mistake in the 1898-1899 season with a record in all matches (competitive or otherwise) of Played 24, Won 22, Lost 1, Drawn 1, with 223 goals scored to 68 conceded. This amazing record meant that not only did they finish top of the Third Division, but they also captured the Lancashire Junior Cup, where having thrashed Rochdale 'A' in the second round, they then beat Heaton Mersey 'A' in the semi-final, to set up a final against Albert Park 'A' from Didsbury. The final was played at the South Manchester ground in Fallowfield, and at half-time the score was only 1-0 to the Old Hulmeians, but they eventually ran out 5-2 winners. The following report of the Lancashire Junior Cup final appeared in the Manchester Guardian :-

For the winners Goodier, in goal, was excellent. He stopped several very hot ones at close quarters, and played well outside too. Buckland was very cool, repeatedly breaking up dangerous rushes, and always making good use of the ball. The same may be said of Merchant, who was very prominent all through. On the attack the brothers Hobbins, especially W., were exceedingly dangerous, whilst Van der Veen, although well looked after by Southward, showed first-class capabilities. On the whole the Old Hulmeians thoroughly deserved their victory, as they were more energetic and smarter on the ball, and worked unselfishly together in couples in the true Canadian style.

As alluded to above, Goodier in goal was a significant factor this season, and it is worth noting that the one game they lost this season, against Prestwich, Goodier was absent from the team. Finishing top of the Third Division didn't guarantee automatic promotion to the Second Division, with a "qualification match" having to be played against the team that finished bottom of the Second Division. That team was Birch, who were promptly thrashed 7-1, thus ensuring promotion for the Old Hulmeians.

Thus, the 1899-1900 season saw the Old Hulmeians lacrosse team in the Second Division, though life in these new echelons didn't start too promisingly with just one victory from their first six league matches. However, they finished their season in style, cementing second place by virtue of winning all of their last three games. The next three seasons saw the Old Hulmeians making further valiant efforts to claim the Second Division title, though on all three occasions had to settle for third place.

However, in 1903-1904, under the inspirational leadership of J. H. Buckland, they were to have their best season thus far, incredibly winning all of their first 17 league matches, before they succumbed to the narrowest of defeats to Rochdale in the final league game of the season, but by then they were already assured of the Second Division title.

Finishing top of the Second Division did not warrant automatic qualification for the First Division and so a play-off match ensued against Offerton, the team that had finished bottom of the First Division. Amazingly, this was a game that Old Hulmeians completely dominated, eventually running out 19-3 winners, to claim their place in the heady heights of the First Division. The season was then completed in fine style by beating Rochdale 11-5 in the semi-final of the Junior Flags competition of the North of England Association, followed by a 16-1 mauling of Monton in the final.

Now in the First Division, the 1904-1905 season was always going to be tough, but was made desperately more so, by the loss of their captain for the last few seasons, J. H. Buckland, who had gone to Egypt on business. As such, five of their first seven matches in the top division resulted in defeats, but when they did win, they won handsomely, beating Offerton 20-1 in the very first game, before beating Cheetham 18-7 in their sixth game. However after Christmas, the Old Hulmeians won five in a row to catapult themselves up the table, finally finishing fourth.

The 1905-1906 season started off with a couple of defeats (to Stockport, and South Manchester), but this was followed by six successive victories. In the second half of the season, the Old Hulmeians again won considerably more games than they lost, eventually settling for third in the league, their best ever finish, with only South Manchester and Stockport finishing above them. In spite of J. H. Buckland's emigration the previous year, the team this season, again comprised three Buckland brothers with all of George Frederick, Herbert ("Bert"), and the youngest, Ronald, playing alongside each other.

For the 1906-1907 season, both the lacrosse and football teams had swelled sufficiently in numbers to allow a third team to be submitted in both sports. However, it seems like the lacrosse team was a bit short of some of their better players, especially for the first few games, with several away on business. For the past few seasons, Percy Joseph Jefferis had been one of the better players, often being selected to represent the county, and so when he sailed off for a nine-month spell in China, his fellow team members were sorry to see him go, but then absolutely devastated when they heard of his sudden death at sea, just a week later.

Such a loss took an inevitable toll on the team in the first part of the season, with six of the first nine games resulting in defeat. However, the return of W. A. Hobbins and H. Shorrocks, seemed to inspire the team, and with the youngster S. D. Harrison showing real potential, the season was abruptly turned around, though with such a bad start to the season, a top two league position was always beyond them. In the Flags competition, they beat Eccles 15-11 in the first round, and then beat Heaton Mersey 15-8 in the semi-final, to set up a final with last year's winners, South Manchester. It was an incredibly tight final that had to be decided in extra time, with Old Hulmeians winning 10-7, to claim the North of England Senior Flags.

Champions of England

Having won the North of England Senior Flags, the Old Hulmeians then played Surbiton, the Southern champions, and thrashed them 12-0 to claim the Iroquois Cup, and with it, the title of Champions of England. It truly was an amazing story, with the Lacrosse team in just 12 seasons since they first formed, rising from the Fourth Division to the point where they were Champions of England, and the only pool of players they could choose from, was restricted to Hulme Grammar School old boys. Captained this season by S. R. Oddy, who also played cricket for Whalley Range, the victorious team is shown below :-

Old Hulmeians lacrosse team
Winners of North of England Flags and Iroquois Cup 1907

R. G. Clarke, H. Shorrocks, A. Merchant, R. Buckland, T. F. Jefferis, C. H. Fox, W. N. Law, W. F. Merchant
S. D. Harrison, W. A. Hobbins, S. R. Oddy (capt), G. F. Buckland, H. Buckland
J. A. Barber, J. R. Clegg

Rather fittingly, the name of Jefferis is still conspicuously present in the photo, with Percy's brother, Thomas Frederick (though known as Fred), having filled the void that had been so tragically created.

Following their recent successes, the Old Hulmeians were able to field four teams, for the first time ever in their short existence, for the 1907-1908 season, with the first team remaining more or less unchanged from their previous campaign. The season started brilliantly with five consecutive league victories, but they then suffered successive defeats against both Stockport and South Manchester. Shortly after this, they were annihilated 17-2 by Eccles. This third defeat in the space of four games was a severe setback with regards to topping the league but from here on in, just one more defeat and a draw from their remaining eight league games, did ensure their best ever finish of second in the league.

With regards to the Flags, Old Hulmeians set off in defence of their title in fine style, thrashing Cheetham 20-1, in a match played at Fallowfield. Then in the semi-final played at Didsbury, they beat Stockport 9-8 in a brilliant encounter. The final was also at Didsbury, and again they managed to avenge one of the teams that had beaten them in the league, winning an epic encounter with South Manchester 10-7 to retain their title. Thus, they were again through to contest the Iroquois Cup, where they would meet Surbiton again. The match wasn't as one-sided as their previous encounter, but Old Hulmeians again emerged victorious (4-1) to be crowned Champions of England for the second year in succession. It was an achievement that also benefited the current pupils of Hulme Grammar School, since by way of celebration, the Headmaster added an extra day to the Easter holidays!

R. Buckland, H. Shorrocks, and A. Merchant, earned particular praise in the School magazine, and for G. F. Buckland, the year got even better, as he was selected to represent Great Britain at the 1908 Olympics. At one point South Africa were also going to send a team, but in the end it was just Canada, the country that had invented the game, that were Great Britain's only opponents. In a keenly contested game it was Canada who came out on top, winning 14-10, but at least the 12 British players were guaranteed an Olympic silver medal. Another Old Hulmeian, H. Shorrocks, was in the final squad of 18, though was not one of those who took to the field that day.

For the 1908-1909 season, S. R. Oddy was still captain, and G. F. Buckland was vice-captain, in what proved to be a fairly successful season. Early on in the season however, the Old Hulmeians lost to Stockport, which as it transpired, was the first of three occasions that this would happen, including in the first round of the flags competition, which meant they'd be unable to defend their prestigious title.

Champions of England for the Third Time

Amazingly, the 1909-1910 season would conclude with the Old Hulmeians winning the Iroquois Cup, and therefore being declared Champions of England, for the third time in four seasons :-

Old Hulmeians lacrosse team
Winners of North of England Flags and Iroquois Cup 1910
J. A. Barber, J. H. Walker, R. Buckland, C. H. Fox, A. Merchant, T. F. Jefferis, H. Shorrocks
S. D. Harrison, H. Buckland, G. F. Buckland (capt), W. A. Hobbins, J. R. Clegg

For this season, G. F. Buckland took over the captaincy of the first team, whilst W. A. Hobbins became the vice-captain, with S. R. Oddy now in charge of the second team. Apart from this, the team itself was much the same as the previous season, with the one notable addition being J. H. Walker. The season started off with a 25-4 walloping of Manchester University, and the goals continued to rain in with 131 goals being scored in total in just the first seven games, with the 20-goal barrier being reached on a further two occasions. Despite so many goals, these games did include a 9-11 defeat to the strong South Manchester team, who also beat them in the return match, and with a further loss to Stockport, the Old Hulmeians had to settle for third position in the league.

In the first round of the flags competition, Heaton Mersey were beaten 3-2 in a very tight game. The semi-final against Offerton was another close exciting affair, with Old Hulmeians again winning by the odd goal, 9-8. In the final they were up against South Manchester who had already beaten them twice. However, Old Hulmeians were surprisingly easy winners in the final, beating South Manchester 10-4. This again qualified them for the final of the Iroquois Cup, where Catford the Southern champions were mercilessly thrashed 20-6. Thus, as previously highlighted, Old Hulmeians were Champions of England for the third time in four years, a superb achievement which again earnt the pupils of Hulme Grammar School an extra days holiday. According to The Hulmeian, the return of S. D. Harrison for the second half of the season, playing at first home, was worthy of special mention, for his marvellous play.

This season, H. Shorrocks, and two of the Buckland brothers, George and Ronald, found places on the North team. Also, George Buckland, Shorrocks, and Walker were picked for Lancashire, with the first of these two also chosen to represent England against Wales at Cardiff on May 7th.

Having been so successful the previous season, it was little surprise that the 1910-1911 season kicked off with some thumping triumphs, beating University 17-1, Manchester Southern 17-3, Albert Park 12-3, and Offerton 14-1, in their first four league games. Then came a creditable 7-7 draw, away against the ever-strong Stockport, the oldest team in England. Rather than inspiring the team, this seemed if anything to have a slightly detrimental effect, with Heaton Mersey only just being beaten in the next game, followed by a surprise loss to Monton. Their first game in the New Year was against Stockport, and despite rattling up double figures themselves, they still succumbed to defeat 10-15. In fact the only point that Stockport dropped all season in the league was their draw against Old Hulmeians, as they eased to the league title. Old Hulmeians didn't give up without a fight though, and finishing the league season with four successive victories ensured they claimed the runners-up spot.

In the first round of the flags competition Old Hulmeians beat Albert Park 11-5, and then overcame Heaton Mersey in the semi-final 8-5, in a well-contested game. In the final they were up against league champions Stockport, and the much-anticipated final drew a large crowd who were not disappointed, witnessing what was described as one of the best games of lacrosse ever played. It was a final that ended 7-7, just like their first league encounter this season, but one where the Old Hulmeians felt slightly aggrieved having had what they believed were two perfectly good goals disallowed. The replay was a week later and again attracted a large crowd. However this time Old Hulmeians were without Hobbins who had starred the previous week, and then to make matters worse, lost Ron Buckland soon after the final started. Thus, deprived of one of the best attacks in the country, Old Hulmeians never really seemed to get going, and Stockport eventually ran out 6-1 winners.

With regard to the league, the 1911-1912 season was very much like the previous one, with most sides being beaten, with the one notable exception again being Stockport. To make matters worse though, this season they were knocked out in the first round of the flags competition.

League Champions

For the 1912-1913 season, Old Hulmeians started their campaign off in fine style, though as always, the true test wouldn't come until they confronted Stockport. This season for once, the Old Hulmeians got the better of Stockport, running out 14-8 winners, cementing their position at the top of the league, a position they were never to relinquish as they went on to claim their first ever league title, thus securing the North of England Lacrosse Shield. Their final league record was Played 18, Won 17, Lost 0, Drawn 1, Goals Scored 245, Goals Conceded 91. Unfortunately, the Old Hulmeians were unable to do the double, as they again lost in the first round of the flags competition, though apparently this was more the result of some deplorable refereeing decisions than anything else, which allowed South Manchester to emerge 7-6 victors. The team this season included the three Buckland brothers (who were all picked to represent Lancashire), A. F. Cooper, J. H. Walker, Hobbins, Shorrocks, Jefferis, and Merchant, amongst others.

In fact, 1913 was a pretty eventful year for the Old Hulmeians, since on January 8th the Old Hulmeians Association Games Club was dissolved, and in its place was born the Old Hulmeians Association. The aims of this new association were to involve even more past members of Hulme Grammar School by offering a more diverse range of events and occasions, including those that were non-sport related, though of course the continuing success of the Lacrosse section of the Association, commanded a lot of the attention.

The All-Conquering Old Hulmeians!

The 1913-1914 season would witness the Old Hulmeians reaching even greater heights, capping off an incredible season by winning all of the major titles. The victorious team was as follows :-

Old Hulmeians lacrosse team
Winners of North of England Shield, Flags, and Iroquois Cup 1914
A. Leggat (umpire), A. F. Cooper, C. H. Fox, R. Buckland, G. W. Fox, S. R. Oddy (chairman)
H. Buckland, G. F. Buckland, W. A. Hobbins, A. Merchant, H. Shorrocks
J. A. Barber, H. A. Linfoot, J. H. Walker

The season kicked off with four easy victories over Albert Park, Monton, Eccles, and Cheadle Hulme, though they then lost to South Manchester. However, there followed a long string of victories that included a 20-3 thrashing of Offerton, a 21-4 rout over Eccles, two victories over arch-rivals Stockport, and the avenging of their earlier defeat to South Manchester, beating them 12-11 in an epic battle. They lost the last league game of the season to Boardman, but by then, the title was theirs for the second time in their history. By this time, they were also through to the semi-final of the flags competition having beaten South Manchester 10-8. In a very tough draw, they then beat Stockport 10-6, to set up a final against Heaton Mersey, whom they then beat 9-6 to capture the North of England Flags for the fourth time.

Page 124

The Old Hulmeians thus qualified for the English Championship play-off, in which they annihilated the Southern champions, Lee, beating them 21-2 at Lord's Cricket Ground, to wrap up what was truly a sensational season, capturing all three of the major titles, the North of England Shield (league winners), the North of England Flags (cup winners), and the Iroquois Cup (English champions).

Quite prophetically, part of the report in The Hulmeian read as follows :-

> *In view of the above magnificent results the Old Hulmeians Association are naturally very proud in possessing such an excellent team, who for the next 12 months may be called the champions of England, and may hold this title for many years to come!*

As it happened, the Old Hulmeians did hold the title for many years to come, though only in the worst way imaginable. The intervention of the First World War not only deprived the great team of Old Hulmeians of almost certain further titles, but one that tragically took the lives of a third of the team. Thus the previous photo of the all-conquering lacrosse team of 1914 serves as a poignant reminder of how wonderful life seemed during the first half of that decade, when few could have foretold of the horrors ahead. The four players who paid the ultimate sacrifice for their country were Herbert Buckland, Albert Frederick Cooper, Alfred Merchant, and John Haslam Walker. Herbert Buckland had also starred for Whalley Range at cricket, starting off the last season before the War, with a wonderful century at Northwich, whilst Albert Frederick Cooper had occasionally played against him, representing Didsbury for the last few seasons.

The Great War

During the First World War, 670 Old Hulmeians fought for their country, of which 111 were killed in action. As well as four of the current lacrosse team being killed, former player Fred Jefferis also lost his life, in Gallipoli on August 7th 1915. Of the lacrosse players' deaths not already elaborated on earlier in this book, Lieutenant Alfred Merchant, of the Lancashire Fusiliers was reported wounded and missing on April 9th, though his official death date was given as April 10th 1918, aged 35, whilst Second-Lieutenant Albert Frederick Cooper, of the Middlesex Regiment, died of his wounds (believed to have been inflicted at Elzenwalle in Belgium) on May 9th 1918, aged 28. He was buried in Esquelbecq Military Cemetery, in France, close to the Belgian border.

In true Old Hulmeians character, many Old Hulmeians were dedicated to the cause of serving their country, with many receiving awards and recognition for their devotion, with both Wilfred Alston Hobbins and Harold Anyon Linfoot being awarded a D.S.O. The citation for Captain (Acting Lieut.-Col.) W. A. Hobbins, Lancashire Fusiliers, read as follows :-

> *By skilful leading, he brought his battalion into action at a most opportune time. He behaved with the utmost resource against counter-attacks, and rallied the remnants of the front line when, being unsupported, he was compelled to withdraw.*

The citation for Lieutenant (Acting Captain) H. A. Linfoot, M.C., Cheshire Regiment read as follows :-

> *He was acting second in command of his battalion, and followed the attack with the rear companies. On arriving at the first objective while fighting was still in progress, he rushed a dug-out containing four machine guns, capturing the guns and teams. He then moved along the line, under continuous shell-fire and sniping, organising the first objective and the further advance. Throughout the action he sent back full and accurate information, and his example and leadership were of the highest service.*

Further to this award, H. A. Linfoot was also later decorated by H.M. the King of Italy with the Medal for Valour. Others to receive distinctions during the war included S. D. Harrison and G. W. Fox. The citation for Lieutenant S. D. Harrison, Lancashire Fusiliers read as follows :-

When the enemy entered our front line in overwhelming numbers he collected a party of men, formed bombing blocks, and held up the enemy for over an hour, using a Lewis gun with great effect. He showed magnificent courage and coolness.

The citation for Lieutenant (A./Captain) Gilbert Wheaton Fox, Manchester Regiment read as follows :-

For conspicuous gallantry and devotion to duty while commanding his company, and later as adjutant to a force heavily engaged for several days. On one occasion when the enemy made successive attacks, and the troops on the right gave way, he reorganised his line, and brought enfilade fire to bear, thereby breaking up the attack. His personal example of great courage and disregard of danger gave the utmost confidence to very fatigued troops.

On November 11th 1918, the signing of the Armistice signalled the end of the First World War. However, it would be a while before life got back to normal, and it wasn't until July the following year that the first meeting after the war of the Old Hulmeians Association took place, with the main item on the agenda, being the proposal of a Memorial to those Old Boys who had fallen in the war. Thus, an Old Hulmeians War Memorial Fund was put in place, which over the coming years would eventually accrue enough money to join forces with the Whalley Range Club, in buying the land that is still the home of Whalley Range Cricket & Lawn Tennis Club.

The immediate post-war lacrosse team included the likes of H. A. Linfoot (captain), C. H. Fox, R. E. Howard, J. A. Barber, R. Buckland, and J. P. V. Woollam, with the latter in particular, going on to achieve many honours in the sport over the coming years, whilst also playing cricket for Whalley Range.

On June 13th 1921 at Hulme Grammar School, a bronze memorial tablet bearing the roll of honour of Old Hulmeians who fell in the war was unveiled by the Lord Mayor of Manchester (Alderman W. Kay), and the following piece, under the heading "The Old Hulmeians' War Memorial Grounds" later appeared in The Hulmeian, April 1922 edition :-

The scheme for providing playing fields as a War Memorial to Old Hulmeians is now approaching its fulfilment. Lack of funds had prevented the design being carried out in its original form but a plot of land at Alexandra Park lying between Woodlands Road and the Great Central Railway and containing just over 3 acres has been purchased from the Egerton Estates. Its position was marked by the group of half a dozen fine beeches which occupied the centre of the large field on the Chorlton side of the Dog House Farm and which it has unfortunately been necessary to fell. An adjoining plot has been purchased on behalf of the Whalley Range Cricket Club. Arrangements for joint use have been entered into under which the whole ground, including the pavilion belonging to the club, will be available for use by the Old Boys Lacrosse and Football sections during the winter months and in return the club will have the use of the whole during the summer. Only in this way has it been possible to provide adequate grounds for the two main branches of the Old Hulmeians Association.

About £2000 has so far been raised. It is estimated that to carry out the purchase and meet incidental expenses a further £300 will be required.

In 1923, the Old Hulmeians again won the North of England Lacrosse Flags, with some emphatic victories along the way, beating Old Mancunians 17-7 in the first round, and Offerton 22-0 in the second round. In the semi-final they beat Eccles 9-5, before beating old adversaries Stockport 6-4 in the final, on Saturday 24th March. Sadly though, Charles Henry Fox who was goalkeeper that day, and who had also played cricket for Whalley Range, passed away less than a month later on 14th April, after an operation. He was aged just 35.

Later that year, the Old Hulmeians War Memorial Ground was formally opened on the afternoon of November 10th, by Councillor J. H. Birley, Governor of Hulme Grammar School. The ceremony was held on the ground at the half-time interval of a lacrosse match, with Mr S. W. Saxelby, chairman of the War Memorial Committee, handing over the ground to Mr. Arthur Payne, president of the Old Hulmeians Association. It was further noted in The Hulmeian, that at this time, it was decided not to apply for a licence, in connection with the new ground (though that would soon be rectified!).

Thus, the fortunes and history of Old Hulmeians and Whalley Range Cricket & Lawn Tennis Club became inextricably entwined. The Old Hulmeians continued to play lacrosse at the ground up until the end of the 1993-1994 season, before moving to Brooklands, and renaming themselves as Brooklands Hulmeians Lacrosse Club (and perhaps there was a certain element of congruity to this, with Brooklands being named after Samuel Brooks, the guy who had initially established the Whalley Range area). Though they never quite rediscovered the amazing success they experienced just prior to the First World War, there were six further Iroquois Cup triumphs prior to their metamorphosis in 1994.

As alluded to earlier, the Iroquois Cup is played for between the North of England Champions and the South of England Champions. The full list of Old Hulmeians appearances in Iroquois Cup finals is as follows :-

Old Hulmeians' Iroquois Cup Final Appearances

Year	Winners	Score	Finalists
1907	OLD HULMEIANS	12-0	Surbiton
1908	OLD HULMEIANS	4-1	Surbiton
1910	OLD HULMEIANS	20-6	Catford
1914	OLD HULMEIANS	21-2	Lee
1932	OLD HULMEIANS	13-1	Oxford University
1949	OLD HULMEIANS	12-4	Cambridge University
1950	OLD HULMEIANS	18-4	Cambridge University
1956	Cambridge University	8-4	OLD HULMEIANS
1962	OLD HULMEIANS	10-5	Cambridge University
1964	OLD HULMEIANS	21-5	Lee
1968	OLD HULMEIANS	13-3	Lee
1976	Hampstead	20-8	OLD HULMEIANS

A New Beginning (1923-1929)

Whalley Range Cricket and Lawn Tennis Club
Opening of the New Ground
28TH April 1923.
Whalley Range V Chorlton-C-Hardy.

Opening Batsmen for Whalley Range
H.R.Classen. F.Howard.

As can be seen from the montage on the left, Saturday 28th April 1923 was a truly momentous day in the annals of the Whalley Range club, since this marked the inaugural game at the new ground. In the background of the top picture is Shakespeare House, on Kingsbrook Road.

Perhaps fittingly enough, the opening game was against Chorlton-cum-Hardy, since whilst the Whalley Range club had lain dormant over the past few seasons, it was at Chorlton that Leroy, Classen, and Pennington *et al* had been able to continue their cricketing endeavours.

However, less appropriate for the occasion was the weather, with April unfortunately living up to its reputation. Thus it was the showers that ultimately had the last say on this historic day.

Just as they had over a decade earlier, when Whalley Range had last christened a new ground, it was Classen and Howard who opened the innings for the home team. Both players got a start, though neither they nor anyone who followed, managed to go on and produce a really telling innings. In the end, Dolph Classen's 28 proved to be the top score in a Whalley Range total of 104.

When Chorlton-cum-Hardy batted, C. B. Ackroyd quickly gained the notable distinction of becoming the first Whalley Range player to claim a wicket at the new ground when he had S. Radford trapped lbw. He then took the next wicket to fall as well, when he caught H. Henshaw off his own bowling. Unfortunately this proved to be last delivery of the day, with rain preventing any further play.

It had been a long time since the previous home game, and in that intervening period, the club could so easily have perished altogether. So despite the inclement weather, and after many years in the wilderness, this day really did signal the dawning of a new era. The scorecard was as follows :-

Whalley Range v Chorlton-cum-Hardy, at Whalley Range, Saturday 28th April 1923

Whalley Range				Chorlton-cum-Hardy			
H. R. Classen	c Higgins	b Clapham	28	H. C. Gill		not out	18
F. Howard		b Clapham	16	S. Radford	lbw	b Ackroyd	1
R. Buckland		b Clapham	11	H. Henshaw	c &	b Ackroyd	15
J. P. V. Woollam	c &	b MacBean	0				
H. Pennington	c Clapham	b MacBean	19				
H. T. Eke		b Clapham	1				
A. Carter		not out	11				
C. B. Ackroyd	c Radford	b Clapham	9				
W. H. Thornton		b Clapham	0				
J. B. Winson	c Gill	b Henshaw	0				
W. W. Land	st Alexander	b Henshaw	4				
Extras			5	Extras			0
Total			104	Total		(for 2)	34

Cyril Brewood Ackroyd, who took Whalley Range's first wicket at the new ground, was born in November 1902 to Annie and John Orme Ackroyd, and was educated at Hulme Grammar School. At one point during the coming season he did open the batting in a game but without much success, and for most of the second half of this campaign and the ensuing 1924 season (which was his last for the club), he generally appeared for the 2nd XI.

At least Whalley Range had managed to get a bat in this opening game on the new ground, since that was more than they achieved the following Saturday at Cheetham Hill, when having disposed of their hosts for exactly 100, rain prevented Whalley Range from even starting their innings.

The following weekend witnessed Whalley Range's first win of the new era with a hard-fought victory in a low-scoring encounter (77-50) at Buxton, with all of H. R. Classen, H. T. Eke, and W. H. Thornton each taking three wickets. The end of May saw a brilliant individual performance from A. W. Wrigley, who coming in at number 9, top-scored with 41, and then took seven wickets and a catch as Brooklands were dismissed for 121, to leave Whalley Range victorious by just over 50 runs.

Whalley Range's superb season continued as they rattled up 232 at home against Bowdon, with openers Dolph Classen (45) and Jack Woollam (51) laying down a good foundation before S. R. Gresham added a fine 72, though Bowdon hung on for a draw with the last pair at the wicket. Against the same opposition the following weekend, Whalley Range having posted 194, were not to be denied this time, bowling Bowdon out for 117. Following a five-wicket win against Hulme Grammar School, J. A. Darbyshire captured five wickets against Knutsford though not for the first time this season, Whalley Range found themselves one wicket away from victory when time ran out. W. H. Thornton then took six wickets in a comfortable win over Cheetham Hill at the end of June, before taking a further five at the start of July in a drawn game at Castleton.

In what was already turning out to be a fine season, things got even better with a real purple patch that saw them win all of their next six games. The first of these was an easy win over Hulme Grammar School, in spite of fielding a slightly weakened team, with the new and temporary opening pair of Trevor Dennis and L. E. Angel both scoring fifties. Being headmaster of Hulme Grammar School, Trevor Dennis was actually playing against his pupils, who may have been somewhat reluctant to get him out too quickly, for fear of reprisals! Also, as with the earlier season's encounter, Dolph Classen was playing against his son Geoffrey, whilst future club stalwart Winston Williamson was also still representing the School.

The following weekend, the visitors to Whalley Range were Cheadle Hulme, and as can be seen from the ensuing scorecard, what a tremendous occasion it turned out to be! Batting first, Cheadle Hulme started

Trevor Dennis, Hulme Grammar School Headmaster

well, though the wickets fell quickly towards the end, with A. W. Wrigley claiming a hat-trick in figures of 6-17. One suspects that this was the first hat-trick performed at the new ground, and it was also a match that witnessed the first century at the new ground, and how beautifully poetic it was that Dolph Classen claimed that accolade, scoring an unbeaten 104. Thankfully these were still times when the passing of the required target didn't necessarily herald the end of the game, otherwise Dolph would clearly have been denied his hundred! Another interesting thing to note about the ensuing scorecard is that J. N. Gresham (who was playing for Chorlton-cum-Hardy at the start of the season) was apparently caught by one of his own men! Assuming this wasn't a printing error, it would appear that Jack Woollam was acting as a substitute fielder for the opposition. These were obviously still days when the game was played in the most gentlemanly of manners, with players deputising for the opposing team, and batsmen being given the opportunity of reaching personal milestones even when the result of the game had long since been determined. James Neville Gresham (born 1897 in Brentford) was the slightly older brother of Samuel Rowland Gresham (born 1898) who also played for Whalley Range this season.

Whalley Range v Cheadle Hulme, at Whalley Range, Saturday 21st July 1923

Cheadle Hulme

Dr. H. Wilson	c Pennington	b Darbyshire	29
D. Marsden		b Wrigley	26
P. Sutton	c Wrigley	b Darbyshire	2
H. P. Baynes		run out	8
W. A. Howard	c Darbyshire	b Wrigley	11
H. T. Seward	c Howard	b Wrigley	17
A. Clayton	c Mountain	b Wrigley	0
J. L. Summerfield		b Thornton	1
J. L. Douglas		b Wrigley	0
Taylor		b Wrigley	0
E. Ashington		not out	0
Extras			18
Total			112

Whalley Range

H. R. Classen		not out	104
J. P. V. Woollam	c &	b Taylor	4
R. Buckland	c &	b Taylor	27
F. Howard		b Taylor	7
J. N. Gresham	c Woollam	b Taylor	6
W. H. Wood		b Taylor	2
Extras			9
Total		(for 5)	159

Whalley Range were then in devastating form for the next few matches, thanks mainly to the bowling of W. J. Mountain. Against Brooklands, he took 6-32 as the visitors were dismissed for just 57 to help Whalley Range win by 95 runs, and then followed this up with 7-50 against Knutsford who were bowled out for 89. Whalley Range responded with 197-8 thanks to 62 from H. R. Classen and an unbeaten 51 from Ron Buckland. The next result that featured in the papers was one where Castleton were dismissed for a mere 29. Sadly the details of the game weren't printed, though one suspects this was probably W. J. Mountain again causing havoc, since a fortnight later it was he who was still in amazing form, taking 7-9 as Urmston were skittled for just 36.

At this point in the season, with just one game to go, of the 18 known games this season (i.e. those that had made the local press), Whalley Range's remarkable campaign had comprised 12 wins, 6 draws, and no defeats, and in two of the drawn games, they had been just one wicket away from victory. They had started the season hosting Chorlton-cum-Hardy, and they would also end the season up against the same opposition. Similar to the opening game, nobody in the Whalley Range line-up was able to make a really significant contribution, and the visitors were eventually all out for 98. When Chorlton batted, Whalley Range were unable to remove their opener H. C. Gill, and it was he who carried his side to victory, whilst Whalley Range captured eight wickets at the other end to nearly register another win.

Crime and Punishment

Despite defeat in this last game of the season, Whalley Range could hardly have wished for a more successful first season since their re-forming – certainly not with regard to on-field matters anyway. However, with regard to other off-field issues, the wheels were not running quite as smoothly. With the purchase of the new ground, finances were a bit stretched, and so the club decided to run a sweepstake in order to bring in some much needed revenue. The sweepstake was in connection with the Manchester November Handicap, and 250 books of tickets were prepared and sent to sports clubs up and down the country. In its day, this horse race was a very prestigious event, and was the highlight of the final fixture of the British flat racing season which, as tradition dictated, was held in Manchester. The race had first been staged in 1876 at New Barns, but when this closed down in

1902, the season's finale was transferred to the Castle Irwell course, until it too closed down in 1963. Since then, the equivalent race is now held at Doncaster though no longer commands the same amount of prestige as it did in times gone by.

At the time however, there were strict laws with regard to the operation of sweepstakes and lotteries, and Whalley Range Cricket & Lawn Tennis Club were deemed to be in breach of these. Thus on 12th October 1923, three members of the Whalley Range Sweepstakes Committee were summoned to appear before the magistrate. At the same time, Chorlton-cum-Hardy Conservative Club were also up in court on a similar charge, and together these two cases attracted a great deal of interest. As such, William Theodore Barnes (chairman of the Whalley Range Sweepstakes Committee), George Greenup (secretary), and William Gilbert Swain (also on the Sweepstakes Committee) found themselves up in front of not only the magistrate but a crowded court as well. Apparently, the case was pretty clear-cut, with a witness from Birmingham stating that he received *"without application for them, a book of tickets and a notice to put up in the pavilion at his club"*. As such, each defendant was fined £10, a not inconsiderable sum of money back in the 1920s. One final thing to note about this whole affair is that the Manchester November Handicap never actually got run in the end in 1923. One assumes that this was presumably because of inclement weather – or perhaps it was cancelled because of the associated scandal created by the Whalley Range Cricket & Lawn Tennis Club?! Either way, it is therefore unlikely that the club made any profit from this venture, and what with the fines, presumably ended up as a financial disaster, at a time when they could ill-afford such setbacks!

There was further activity in the close season with Whalley Range applying to re-join the Manchester & District Cricket Association at a meeting held in December 1923. However, both Cheadle and Newton Heath were also vying for the one space available. In the end, it was Whalley Range who got the vote, and Cheadle would have to wait another three years before being admitted when the permitted membership of the Association was increased from 30 to 35, whilst it wasn't until after the Second World War that Newton Heath finally joined the party, and then for only a few seasons. Even though in 1920, the Manchester & District Cricket Association had introduced the Stockton Trophy to compete for, Whalley Range decided still to regard their games as friendlies, and chose not to compete for points, believing that such practice removed the "gentlemanly element" from the game. It was only in 1962, when member teams were forced to compete for points, that Whalley Range were finally (and reluctantly) obliged to regard their games as competitive.

Having enjoyed such a superb season the previous year, the 1924 season began rather inauspiciously with a rained-off game against Chorlton in April, followed by defeat away against Cheetham Hill at the start of May, a game in which the visitors totalled just 44. With the weather in May not proving to be especially conducive to cricket, the next three encounters were also low-scoring affairs. In the first of these, Buxton were dismissed for just 63 with Dolph Classen taking six wickets, whilst W. H. Thornton claimed the other four. Whalley Range were struggling at 13-3 in reply when rain brought a premature conclusion to the contest. The following weekend, Whalley Range again struggled with the bat, scoring just 81. However this proved more than sufficient as South Manchester managed just 47, with J. A. Darbyshire taking 5-31 whilst W. H. Thornton claimed successive four-wicket hauls with figures of 4-11. Then, away at Brooklands, W. J. Mountain took 4-8 as the hosts were removed for just 51, though the game was again ruined by the rain, with Whalley Range's reply barely having started.

Judging by the scores in the ensuing games, it would seem that the weather improved quite drastically, with Whalley Range enjoying the luxury of being able to declare at Bowdon, having posted 156-8, thanks mainly to an unbeaten 58 from W. H. Thornton. The hosts were then skittled for just 74 with A. B. Crawford capturing 7-24. The following weekend, Knutsford also got themselves into a position where they were able to declare, having scored 167-8. However, the visitors were presumably a little stunned to see this overhauled for the loss of just five wickets thanks to a classy 69 from Classen. Classen was in fine form the following weekend as well, scoring 64 out of a total of 178, before Broughton were dismissed for just 60 with W. H. Thornton taking 6-16. Thus, at this point in the season, there is little doubt that if Whalley Range had been competing for points, they would have been amongst those challenging for the top few places.

In late June, Whalley Range's traditional encounter at Hulme Grammar School saw J. B. Winson score 50 in a total of 142. John Barrie Winson had played in the first game at the new ground in 1923 against Chorlton, and would subsequently spend most of the rest of his cricketing days at Chorlton, where in the late 1930s, he played alongside his younger brother Sydney. He also represented the Manchester club at one point. Playing for the School that day were Geoffrey Classen, who took four wickets, and future Whalley Range players, Winston Williamson and Kenneth Rains. A month later, Williamson scored 133 in a school game against King Edward's School, and followed this up with five wickets, to wrap up victory by 190 runs. A name appearing on the Whalley Range 1st XI scoresheet for the first time, in this game against Hulme Grammar School was that of A. J. Leggat.

Alexander James Leggat

Alexander James Leggat was born in 1905, and was the son of Alexander Leggat, the umpire who appears in the 1914 Old Hulmeians lacrosse team photo. After a few seasons (1924 to 1929) with Whalley Range, A. J. Leggat would then represent the Manchester Cricket Club, before later going on to become president of Lancashire County Cricket Club in 1991/92, when he was well into his eighties.

Alick, as he was known, also served on the LCCC committee from 1961 to 1987, taking on the role of Treasurer for many of those years.

One of the most interesting facts about Alick is that he enjoyed a close relationship with the famous artist, L. S. Lowry. Lowry didn't drive, and instead relied on friends such as Alick, to act as chauffeurs for him. Often, Lowry expected his friends to provide this service, free of charge, though it must be said that Alick was another who was also careful with his financial outgoings apparently!

As it happens, Alick was an avid collector of Lowry's work, and indeed advised him about technical details of some of the paintings that related to cricket. Shortly after Alick had passed away, two original oil paintings by L. S. Lowry that were part of Alick's collection, "Lancashire League Cricket Match" and "Crowd Around A Cricket Sight Board", sold together for £677,250 at Christie's auction house in London, on 19th November 2004.

Alick evolved into a very classy batsman in his time at Whalley Range, and in his penultimate season for them, scored a superb unbeaten hundred against Hulme Grammar School. When he died in early 2004, he was just short of another hundred, aged 98.

On July 12th 1924, Whalley Range hosted the mighty Manchester team for the first time since before the war, and they performed admirably, scoring 158. Opener J. P. V. Woollam carried his bat for 53, whilst J. A. Darbyshire coming in as last man contributed 26. However, their illustrious opponents reached their target for the loss of just three wickets, with a team that comprised no fewer than three players who'd be playing for Lancashire the following season, namely Tom Halliday, Frank Sibbles, and Roy McNairy, whilst another, Albert Woolley, would make his first-team county debut two seasons hence. During the rest of July, Whalley Range won three out of three, starting with an emphatic win over Cheadle Hulme, where H. L. Palmer top-scored with 53, before A. B. Crawford returned figures of 7-47. Then despite Winston Williamson scoring 73 for Hulme Grammar School, Whalley Range won by three wickets, thanks mainly to 49 from A. B. Crawford. July was concluded with South Manchester being routed for just 64 with W. H. Thornton claiming half of the wickets, before Whalley Range replied with 154. August started with defeat to Brooklands in spite of a six-wicket haul for W. H. Thornton. The only other two further results that surfaced during the rest of the season were drawn games against Knutsford and Bowdon, where in both games Whalley Range were eight wickets down and well adrift of their target at the close of play. Even though they were not reported on, from this season's handbook, we also know that midweek evening games were starting to take place, as early as the 1924 season.

The first game of the 1925 season saw Whalley Range suffer a bad loss to Chorlton in late April, being dismissed for just 50. The second game of the season witnessed them desperately clinging on to a draw against Cheetham Hill in early May, a month which also saw victory over South Manchester, and what would have been an almost certain victory over Brooklands but for the intervention of the weather. However, the best individual performance in May came at the end of the month at Bowdon, where the young Hulme Grammar schoolboy Winston Williamson captured 7-44 on what would appear to be his debut. Such was his reputation that he had also opened the innings for Whalley Range, though having failed with the bat, scoring just 2, he certainly made up for this with his bowling. However it was not enough to ensure victory as Bowdon replied with 131 to Whalley Range's 111. Also appearing in the 1st XI team line-up for the first time this day, was Archibald Gordon Campbell, another product of Hulme Grammar School. He was the younger brother of Charles Douglas Campbell who'd made his club debut the previous season.

June kicked off with an 8-wicket defeat to Cheadle Hulme on the Monday. Whalley Range also played the following day as well, faring slightly better, by hanging on for a draw at Broughton. The following Saturday brought a reversal in fortune, with a fine win over Knutsford where Whalley Range amassed 192-8 before declaring, with opener H. R. Classen scoring 62, before T. Dennis coming in at number five, scored 50. The following weekend, Whalley Range made 157 against Broughton, though this was easily overhauled by Broughton for the loss of just three wickets. Following a midweek win over Hulme Grammar School, Whalley Range were back to losing ways at the weekend, though admittedly it was a very close affair. Heaton Mersey had posted 173, but thanks to 48 from H. L. Palmer, Whalley Range got to within one run of the hosts' total before agonisingly losing their final wicket. However, the month was seen out with a fine win over Cheetham Hill thanks to five wickets from W. H. Thornton.

Superstars Fall to Earth

After an indifferent previous month, July proved to be a sensational month for Whalley Range, with three wins and a draw, and even in this drawn game, Whalley Range posted 198-8, with H. T. Eke top-scoring with 61. It was the next game though that defined Whalley Range's month, and perhaps their season as a whole, with victory over a Manchester team that included at least seven current or future cricketers who would represent Lancashire! Most notable of these players were Frank Sibbles who would make over 300 appearances for his county, taking over 900 wickets; Frank Booth who would take over 450 wickets for Lancashire in 140 matches, and Bill Farrimond who not only represented his county on 134 occasions but also played for England, being a fine wicket-keeper as well as a talented batsman. The Manchester team also boasted a future Lancashire County Cricket Club chairman and president, in the form of Dr. J. B. Holmes, who owned a doctor's practice in Chorlton. John Bowling Holmes, whilst clearly destined to excel at cricket with such an appellation, was also a director of Manchester City Football Club for a quarter of a century. He was also a vice-president of the Whalley Range club in 1937 and 1938.

Thus it was a great win for Whalley Range against such a team, since not only did they win, but they won at a canter. Manchester batted first and were bowled out for just 95, with W. W. Land taking at least six wickets. The proviso "at least" is given, since Booth's dismissal was reported as "lbw b Booth", which even for someone as athletic as him would have taken some manoeuvring! Whalley Range then got off to a solid start through opener Classen who scored 31, and Jack Woollam who scored 30 coming in at number three. However, it was then a superb knock of 67 from F. Furnival that took Whalley Range's final total to a commanding 172. William Walker Land was born at the turn of the century, and would go on to be chairman and then president of the club in the 1960s. He would continue to live well into his late eighties, and following his passing away, the club kindly received a sum of money from his estate.

Whilst Whalley Range were beating Manchester, Kenneth Rains, a future Whalley Range player, was scoring an unbeaten 119 for Hulme Grammar School against King Edward VII School at Lytham, a game in which W. Williamson took six wickets to complete a consummate win. Next for Whalley Range, came a victory at Cheadle Hulme where the star of the show was W. H. Thornton who captured 8-32. Whalley Range's superb July form continued with a comprehensive win at South Manchester where, batting first, Whalley Range racked up 242-7 before declaring. The main contributor was opener Classen who scored 71, before W. Williamson (45 not out) and W. H. Thornton (40 not out) provided a late boost. A. J. Reeve then captured six wickets as the hosts were dismissed for 120.

Alfred Joseph Reeve, who is pictured in the ensuing 1st XI team photo and several others as well, was born in 1903, and went on to become a Bank Inspector. He played in all of the Whalley Range seasons between the wars, and in his twenties was a superb bowler, capturing five-wicket hauls on at least 20 occasions. In his thirties, it was mainly his batting that was to the fore, scoring fifties in each of the 1937 and 1938 seasons. Sadly, he was to die, after much suffering, aged just 44.

For the rest of the season, Whalley Range continued in similar successful vein, winning four of the five games that were reported on, whilst the other game against Castleton at Rochdale was abandoned before Whalley Range batted. In the first of these wins, Knutsford were removed for just 71 with A. J. Reeve taking 7-34. With openers Classen and Howard scoring 61 and 45 respectively, one suspects that the winning target was passed without the loss of a wicket, though Whalley Range finally finished on 178-4. Reeve was in the wickets again the following weekend, capturing a further five as Heaton Mersey were shot out for 66. Jack Woollam with 44 and H. Pennington with 38 then ensured a comfortable win. Following the abandoned game at Rochdale, Whalley Range posted 91 against Buxton, thanks mainly to 39 from A. D. Thomson coming in at number eight. In the end, these proved vital late runs, as Whalley Range won by just seven runs, with A. J. Reeve again capturing five wickets. A fortnight later at Hardy Lane, in the last game of the season, Chorlton-cum-Hardy posted 123. Amazingly, A. D. Thomson again top-scored coming in at number eight, and his 29 runs again proved crucial, with Whalley Range finishing on 125-8, to claim an improbable two-wicket win. The following photo is from this game :-

Whalley Range 1st XI 1925
W. Williamson, F. Furnival, J. R. Palmer, A. J. Reeve, H. Pennington, A. D. Thomson
H. L. Palmer, W. H. Thornton, H. R. Classen, H. T. Eke, F. Howard

Whalley Range 2nd XI 1925
N. A. Barber, W. W. Land, G. F. Henson, H. K. Oldfield, G. Greenup, J. W. Greenup
A. G. Campbell, A. Carter, F. R. Leroy (capt), S. E. Woollam, G. Russel-Fisher, F. R. Stubbs

The 2nd XI team from this season is featured above, and includes a few new faces. Amongst these is Graham Russel-Fisher who was born in 1905 and played many seasons for the club, and was an honorary life member of the club at the time of his passing, aged in his eighties. Notably, another of those pictured above who would become an honorary life member, is Norman Alexander Barber who was born in 1906, and made his debut for the Whalley Range club in 1923. He was the son of James Arthur Barber who also played cricket for the club at this time, and like his father, he too would play lacrosse for both Old Hulmeians and Lancashire. During the Second World War, N. A. Barber was held as a Japanese POW in Singapore, and after the war, spent a lot of time in the Territorial Army, eventually rising to the position of Honorary Colonel, where his endeavours also saw him being rewarded with the MBE. Another significant name in the line-up above, is that of G. F. Henson.

George Frederick Henson OBE

George Frederick Henson was born in 1894 to Annie and Edward Henry Henson. His father, who went to the Wesleyan School on Chapel Street in Beeston, Nottinghamshire, became a schoolteacher. By the time of his birth, the family had moved to the Manchester area. He first played for Whalley Range in 1924 and played in every season thereafter up until the Second World War, and even after it, and appears in the 1947 2nd XI team photo that is hanging in the clubhouse. He married Mary "Molly" Walton on 24th October 1931, and lived on Roxton Road in Heaton Chapel. G. F. Henson's biggest claim to fame though, was that he became President of the Grenadier Guards Comrades Association in Manchester, and won an OBE in the 1954 New Year Honours. He passed away on 23rd November 1972, aged 78.

Whalley Range kicked off the 1926 season at home against Chorlton. This time, the rain didn't prevent a definite conclusion to the game, with Whalley Range winning the contest by 26 runs thanks to 52 from J. P. V. Woollam and five wickets from W. W. Land. However, it looks like rain accounted for the next couple of weekends, whilst the following Saturday, on May 15th 1926, it apparently snowed in some parts of the north-west! At Whalley Range though, the weather was sufficiently clement to allow the hosts to win a tight encounter against South Manchester with the visitors falling just six runs short of Whalley Range's 79. Coincidentally, the next game also saw both teams dismissed in the seventies, though this time it was Whalley Range falling just six runs short of the 77 posted by Brooklands, an innings in which W. H. Thornton claimed five wickets. On the following Monday, Whalley Range managed to escape with a draw with Cheadle Hulme, in a game presumably affected by the weather. Whalley Range played the following day as well, at Broughton, where a five-wicket haul from H. T. Eke managed to restrict the hosts to 153. In reply, Whalley Range scored 140-7 to secure another draw, with J. P. V. Woollam unbeaten on 75.

The first game in June witnessed Whalley Range rattling up 202-8 before declaring, with new recruit, 22-year-old H. P. Marrian, the main contributor with 53. Harry Platt Marrian was born in Stockport on 21st March 1904 and attended Rossall School in Fleetwood. A good all-round sportsman, having played rugby for Kersal and the newly-formed Didsbury Rugby Club, he'd also spent the past few seasons playing for Didsbury Cricket Club, for whom he'd scored an unbeaten century, the previous season. However, in this particular game, it was H. T. Eke who proceeded to steal the show, with figures of 9-78, as the visitors Knutsford were bowled out for 135. This was the first recorded instance of a Whalley Range player capturing nine wickets at the new ground. The bowler who captured the other wicket, and thus prevented Eke from claiming all ten, was A. J. Reeve, who captured the eighth wicket to fall, trapping E. Shaw lbw.

Whalley Range v Knutsford, at Whalley Range, Saturday 5th June 1926

Whalley Range				Knutsford			
H. R. Classen	c &	b Shaw	19	E. Sanderson	lbw	b H. T. Eke	5
F. Howard	lbw	b Flood	23	A. Dick	st Pilkington	b H. T. Eke	18
J. P. V. Woollam		b H. Moreton	16	F. C. Hilditch	c Furnival	b H. T. Eke	15
W. Williamson		b Dick	27	N. Flood	c &	b H. T. Eke	3
H. P. Marrian	lbw	b H. Moreton	53	E. Moreton		b H. T. Eke	6
A. Horrocks		b Flood	15	H. Moreton		b H. T. Eke	1
H. T. Eke		b Dick	8	C. A. Johnson		not out	64
F. Furnival		b Flood	19	W. Bancroft		b H. T. Eke	9
A. J. Reeve		not out	17	E. Shaw	lbw	b A. J. Reeve	1
S. Pilkington		not out	4	G. Beech		b H. T. Eke	0
				W. Wildgoose	c Furnival	b H. T. Eke	6
Extras			1	Extras			7
Total		(for 8 dec.)	202	Total			135

Following a draw with Broughton, and a surprising loss to Hulme Grammar School, the month of June witnessed Whalley Range's trip to Old Trafford to play Manchester. Clearly intent on meting out revenge for their mauling the previous season, the hosts rattled up 226-9 in spite of five wickets from A. Horrocks. Faced with such a daunting target, Whalley Range hung on valiantly for a draw, thanks mainly to a superb 77 from W. Williamson. At the end of June, H. R. Classen scored 50 in a drawn game with Cheetham Hill, and carried his fine form into the next game, against Castleton, where he captured five wickets and scored 60. However it wasn't enough to prevent defeat, in a game that saw the teenage Kenneth Rains making his first team debut. Kenneth Rains had started the season playing for the 2nd XI but his undoubted talent, which had seen him score an unbeaten century for Hulme Grammar School the previous season, soon saw him forcing his way into the 1st XI. Tubby Rains (as he was affectionately known!) was also a fine lacrosse player, as was Jack Woollam, and the two would often play alongside each other over the coming years, not just for the Old Hulmeians, but for Lancashire as well.

Following a trouncing by the Manchester club in July (still clearly intent on inflicting further retribution!), Whalley Range responded well in the next game, rattling up 229-5 declared, away at Cheadle Hulme, thanks to 56 from F. Howard, and 69 from J. P. V. Woollam, though the hosts replied with 189-5. Whalley Range won the following Saturday though, responding with 157-6 after South Manchester had declared on 129-8. The top-scorer was A. G. Campbell who scored 58, whilst the name of H. B. Brooks also appeared on the Whalley Range scoresheet for the first time in this game.

As had happened just a few weeks before, immediately following a thrashing, Whalley Range seemed to be galvanised into action. Thus, having conceded 256-9 on the Saturday against Brooklands, they amassed 250-9 on the August Bank Holiday Monday against Bowdon, thanks to a fine opening stand between H. R. Classen (57) and W. Williamson (91), followed by further good knocks from H. P. Marrian (46) and K. Rains (30). Victory by over 100 runs was then assured by W. W. Land who captured six wickets.

A tight exciting game away against Knutsford ensued with Whalley Range posting 91, but in spite of seven wickets from H. B. Brooks, the hosts just about scraped home, finally being all out for 93. The following Saturday, Whalley Range amassed 187-4 before declaring against Heaton Mersey. Young Winston Williamson was again in the runs, opening the innings and top-scoring with 62, before A. Horrocks captured five wickets in the visitors' innings of 143-6. The next game, away at Castleton, was fairly similar in that A. Horrocks again took five wickets, and Williamson again opened the innings and top-scored. However, this time he was the only Whalley Range player in double-figures with a mere 14, as the visitors were shot out for just 44, in reply to Castleton's 84. Williamson was top-scorer again the following Saturday, this time with a much more impressive 83, out of a total of 185-8 declared, to which Buxton replied with 102-8. Following this game, only one further match seemed to be reported on this season, a game in which Whalley Range desperately managed to hold out for a draw on 100-9, after Bowdon had clocked up 210-9 before declaring.

Whalley Range 1st XI 1927
A. Horrocks, W. Williamson, H. P. Marrian, A. J. Reeve, S. S. Kiernan, J. W. Greenup
J. P. V. Woollam, S. Pilkington, W. H. Thornton, H. R. Classen, H. T. Eke, W. J. Mountain

As was now becoming traditional, Whalley Range's curtain-raiser, at the start of the 1927 season, was at home against Chorlton, at the back-end of April, a game which Whalley Range won by three wickets, with H. T. Eke guiding them home with an unbeaten 37. It was Eke who was the star the following weekend as well, taking five wickets to help beat Cheetham Hill. It was then the turn of A. J. Reeve to star in the next game, though despite his seven wickets, Buxton emerged victorious by the small margin of seven runs. Whalley Range then produced a fine two-wicket win over South Manchester, who'd posted 169, thanks to 37 from opener H. R. Classen, an unbeaten 38 from W. Williamson, and 43 from H. B.

Brooks. The next game was pretty similar in a lot of ways. Whalley Range again won by two wickets, to make it four wins out of five, with opener Classen scoring another 37, whilst it was Williamson who again guided them home, this time with an unbeaten 57.

The next game was a midweek contest against Hulme Grammar School, a game in which the School team comprised four players who would represent Whalley Range in the future, namely T. L. Brierley, G. T. Mountain, W. B. Stansby, and E. G. Widdows. Batting first, the School amassed 151-8 before declaring, and then dismissed their hosts for 102. George Talbot Mountain (son of William John Mountain and Florence Carmona Mountain), Walter Bennett Stansby (son of Walter Buxton Stansby and Gertrude Bennett), and Ernest Geoffrey Widdows (known as Geoff, and son of Ernest and Elizabeth Widdows), would devote many years of service to the club over the coming years, but it would be Thomas Leslie Brierley who would go on to make the biggest impact in the world of cricket.

Thomas Leslie Brierley – The Canadian Connection

Thomas Leslie Brierley, who was born on 15th June 1910 in Southampton, would progress from representing Hulme Grammar School, to joining Whalley Range in 1928 and scoring an unbeaten century for them in 1929. For the 1931 season, he started off playing for Whalley Range, but by the end of it, he was playing first-class cricket for Glamorgan, having made his debut on 29th August at Swansea against Nottinghamshire. He continued to play for Glamorgan up until the Second World War, and then after the War, he returned back up North, and represented Lancashire. In all, he played 232 first-class matches, scoring over 6000 runs. Strangely enough, his highest score for Glamorgan was 116 against Lancashire in 1938, whilst his highest score for Lancashire was an unbeaten 116 against Glamorgan in 1947. After three seasons with Lancashire he emigrated to Canada, which was quite fitting since he was also an accomplished lacrosse player. In Canada, he quickly gained recognition as one of the leading cricket coaches, whilst continuing to also play his cricket, and even ended up commanding a place in the national side, which included being part of a Canadian touring side that visited the UK in 1954. Whilst playing for the Canadians, he faced such notable opponents as Ray Illingworth, Brian Close, Fred Trueman, and Pakistan's Hanif Mohammed.

In the next Saturday game, H. R. Classen was again out in the thirties opening the innings, this time with 36, whilst the top-scorer was F. Howard with an unbeaten 55 that ensured a comfortable draw against Stockport. The start of June welcomed a large win over Knutsford. Batting first, Whalley Range notched up 171-9. Once again, opener Classen got the innings off to a good start but was unable to convert that start into a fifty, being dismissed for 43. Someone who did reach his fifty was W. Williamson, and upon him reaching that milestone, Whalley Range declared their innings. Victory by over 100 runs was achieved thanks to a seven-wicket haul from A. J. Reeve.

During the ensuing "Whit Week" (when it seemed that virtually all employees enjoyed a week's holiday at this time), Whalley Range played no fewer than four midweek games. In the first of these, on the Monday, W. H. Thornton's five wickets helped dismiss Cheadle Hulme for 85. Winston Williamson, continuing in a supreme run of form, then guided Whalley Range to victory with an unbeaten 51. In the next midweek game, Stockport amassed 234-5 before declaring. However, it was that man Williamson again who ensured a draw, with another gritty unbeaten innings, this time with 49, out of a total of 129-8. The following day, the Whalley Range team travelled to Bury, where the hosts posted 170, with Williamson this time starring with the ball, taking five wickets. Whalley Range's reply got off to a brilliant start with openers F. Howard scoring 91, and H. R. Classen 68, before Williamson and A. Grey saw them home to a seven-wicket win. This was an amazing seventh time in a row that Williamson had preserved his wicket, with consecutive unbeaten scores of 38, 57, 9, 50, 51, 49, and 3. With so many games in such quick succession, perhaps it was no surprise, that the following day on the Friday, Williamson finally came a cropper, being out for just 2 against Heaton Mersey, though Whalley Range still managed to win by two wickets. In all, Williamson had scored 259 runs between dismissals. In the end, it was a former Whalley Range player, A. W. Wrigley, who finally managed to claim his wicket.

On the Saturday, in the return game against Knutsford, the home side again struggled to cope with A. J. Reeve who finished with 6-24, as the hosts made just 56. Certainly at this point in history, when chasing such a low score, the team batting second would often play out the rest of the afternoon, with Whalley Range thus closing on 206-8 to register another consummate win. As was also seemingly becoming traditional, opener H. R. Classen would see Whalley Range off to a solid start but be unable to complete his fifty, this time being just agonisingly one run short with a fine 49, but by this time the match had already been won. Also in the runs were Jack Woollam with 51, and H. B. Brooks with 48.

The middle of June witnessed Whalley Range back playing at Old Trafford in a midweek game, where clearly the illustrious setting inspired W. Williamson who contributed 81 to a total of 149, before being run out. In reply, Manchester finished on 129-2, presumably in a rain-affected game. Further inclement weather not only put paid to any cricket the following weekend, but also spoilt the viewing of the total solar eclipse on Wednesday 29th June that would otherwise have been visible in the UK. However, there was little to eclipse the batting of Williamson, who continued on his merry way, this time with an unbeaten 43 that ensured a draw against Castleton, at the start of July.

The following weekend, Whalley Range entertained the Manchester team, and having removed them for just 74, thanks to seven wickets from H. B. Brooks, it seemed like Whalley Range might complete another notable victory over their prestigious opponents, especially when opener F. Howard had got the innings off to a good start. However his dismissal for 26, then started a woeful collapse that left the number three batsman, Jack Woollam stranded on 16 not out, as Whalley Range amazingly collapsed to 62 all out.

For 1927 there would appear to be a couple of Whalley Range 2nd XI team photos for this season. In the first of these, Whalley Range's umpire is Holwell Walshe Spear, who is the father of the club's young umpire who appears later in one of the 2nd XI team photos from 1933, namely Harold Spear.

Whalley Range 2nd XI 1927
F. R. Stubbs, K. Rains, G. F. Henson, R. Buckland, A. G. Campbell, G. B. Chronnell, H. W. Spear
S. E. Woollam, A. D. Thomson, A. Pitt, F. R. Leroy (capt), J. Mawdesley, H. L. Palmer

A drawn game with South Manchester at Burton Road was the next reported game, with the top scorers being A. Horrocks with an unbeaten 41, and H. R. Classen with an unbeaten 33. The final game in July was another drawn affair. Yet again, opener Classen got a start, and when he was dismissed for 29, it was H. P. Marrian with 80, and W. Williamson with an unbeaten 31, that enabled the home team to close on 171-7 in reply to Brooklands' total of 197. In the remaining games in the season, Whalley Range lost to Heaton Mersey, and had further draws with Northwich, Buxton, Bowdon, and Chorlton, where the main highlight was A. J. Reeve taking five wickets against Northwich. There was also one further game against Bowdon at the start of August where it was unclear from the poor quality of the newspaper copy, whether Whalley Range had lost, or perhaps had managed to force a tie, before losing their last wicket. Throughout the season, the main star was undoubtedly Winston Williamson, who scored 533 runs in 22 games, and managed to average over 44, thanks to his inordinate amount of not outs.

Whalley Range 2nd XI 1927
H. E. Elderton, H. K. Oldfield, G. B. Chronnell, A. J. Reeve, A. S. Trafford, F. Furnival, F. R. Stubbs, J. Mawdesley
A. D. Thomson, F. R. Leroy (capt), S. E. Woollam

The other 2nd XI photo from 1927 features Henry Edward Elderton whose uncle, Arthur Cecil Elderton, had also represented the club around the turn of the century and as mentioned earlier, had become the club's Honorary Secretary in 1904 immediately prior to Classen's extensive tenure of the role.

Prior to the start of the 1928 season, both Jack Woollam and Kenneth Rains represented Lancashire at lacrosse, and also helped Old Hulmeians to become Northern Lacrosse League champions. As for Whalley Range's 1928 cricket season, what a glorious summer it turned out to be. Of the 23 matches that were reported on, Whalley Range were victorious on 13 occasions, whilst there were only two defeats, both to the formidable Manchester team. A lot of the success, including a fair few centuries as it happened, was down to Old Hulmeians with a continuing influx of superb young talent from the nearby Hulme Grammar School, augmenting those who were already well established at the club.

On Saturday 21st April, the traditional opening game of the season saw Whalley Range hosting Chorlton, who rattled up 140-6 before declaring. As they had five years earlier, Classen and Howard opened the innings for Whalley Range, though it was then more like the previous season for Classen, as after making a good start, he was out for 31. Thankfully though, as the season wore on, there would be times when Classen would be able to convert these good starts into something a lot more substantial. In this opening game, the other opener Howard also did well, contributing 39 to Whalley Range's reply of 98-5, as the match ended in a tame draw.

The following Saturday at Cheetham Hill, the hosts were dismissed for just 45 with H. T. Eke doing most of the damage with figures of 6-28, whilst A. J. Reeve claimed 4-17. Whalley Range, with a hint of the good times ahead for this season, responded with 221, with opener H. R. Classen finally able to convert a promising beginning into a fifty. When he was finally out for 60, the match was already well and truly won.

On Saturday 12th May, the runs were really flowing for both Whalley Range 1st and 2nd XIs. At home, the 1st XI were indebted to a superb opening partnership between H. R. Classen and W. Williamson. Classen was finally out for a brilliant 115, and upon Williamson also completing his century, Whalley Range declared their innings on 259-2. On what was clearly a superb day for batting, South Manchester ensured a draw, replying with 188-5

Whalley Range v South Manchester, at Whalley Range, Saturday 12th May 1928

Whalley Range

H. R. Classen	c Watson	b Wright	115
W. Williamson		not out	100
J. P. V. Woollam	c Smith	b Hargreaves	31
A. Horrocks		not out	4
Extras			9
Total		(for 2 dec)	259

Meanwhile, in the corresponding 2nd XI fixture, South Manchester amassed 284-6 before declaring. The delayed declaration would then appear to have been quite prudent, with over 500 runs being scored in the afternoon, as Whalley Range responded with 242-8. The future Lancashire player, T. L. Brierley was in the team, but it was the future Lancashire president, A. J. Leggat, who was the main scorer with 84 before being run out.

During the ensuing week, in a game reported on Thursday 17th May, Whalley Range hosted Hulme Grammar School, who were dismissed for 143, with H. Smith capturing seven wickets. Smith then scored 66 as well to complete a fine afternoon. However, the main batting star was A. J. Leggat, who following his fine innings on the Saturday for the 2nd XI, was back in the 1st XI line-up for this midweek game. It was an opportunity he certainly made the most of, opening the innings, and scoring a superb unbeaten 112, as Whalley Range racked up another impressive total.

Whalley Range v Hulme Grammar School, at Whalley Range, Wednesday 16th May 1928

Whalley Range

H. R. Classen		run out	4
A. J. Leggat		not out	112
A. Horrocks	c Astin	b Ratcliffe	0
H. Smith	c Stansby	b Ratcliffe	66
H. T. Eke		b Farrell	13
K. Rains	c Wilkinson	b Richards	19
J. A. Barber	c Hodgkinson	b Stansby	8
S. S. Kiernan		not out	9
Extras			12
Total		(for 6)	243

After a draw against Stockport, Whalley Range continued on their winning ways with a couple of midweek victories. The first of these was against Cheadle Hulme at Whalley Range, where five wickets from A. J. Reeve helped remove the visitors for 96, before Jack Woollam steered the home team to 170-7 with an unbeaten 54. The other midweek game this week was against Heaton Mersey at Heaton Moor. Playing for Heaton Mersey was A. W. Wrigley, the former Whalley Range player, but W. Williamson accounted for him in his seven-wicket haul, as the hosts were dismissed for just 68 in reply to Whalley Range's 107. It was sweet revenge for Williamson, since it was Wrigley who'd ended his superb run of unbeaten innings the previous season. The other three wickets were taken by A. S. Trafford, with all three being assisted by a stumping from wicket-keeper S. Pilkington. Alan Shaw Trafford was born on 2nd January 1905 and can be seen in the previous 1927 2nd XI team photo. At one point he was in business with his father, Albert William Trafford, as cotton goods merchants in Manchester. He played for Whalley Range between 1923 and 1928, with his best recorded performance being a five-wicket haul against Hulme Grammar School in 1926.

At the weekend, Whalley Range's superb form continued as they amassed 252-5 before declaring against Knutsford. Classen was again in excellent form opening the innings, coming close to another hundred, before finally being out for 93 after chipping one back to the bowler. Jack Woollam was also in the runs, contributing 66. Knutsford were dismissed for 108 thanks to five wickets from A. J. Reeve.

The rest of June wasn't quite as prosperous for Whalley Range with three successive draws, followed by defeat at Old Trafford to Manchester, where Halliday scored 114 for the home team. The highlight of these draws was an unbeaten 66 by Ron Buckland away at Northwich. July started with another defeat in the return game with Manchester, where the only people to shine were Classen who scored 41 at the top of the order, whilst H. B. Brooks claimed five of the eight wickets to fall.

Next came an extraordinary game where Whalley Range seemed to be heading towards a slightly below par total against Cheadle Hulme. However Kenneth Rains, batting at number nine, scored an unbeaten 59, ably supported by the number ten batsman, A. Pitt, who scored an unbeaten 27, thus allowing the visitors the luxury of being able to declare at 193-8. Cheadle Hulme seemed destined for a heavy defeat, with A. J. Reeve destroying their top order with six wickets. However, when their number ten batsman, E. J. Cutler, came to the crease, he promptly smashed an unbeaten 54, though Cheadle Hulme were finally all out for 127. Whalley Range made it back-to-back wins the following Saturday, replying with 209-5, after South Manchester had posted 128, with A. Horrocks claiming seven wickets. Top scorers for Whalley Range were Jack Woollam with 57, and W. Williamson with 52. The last game in July saw Whalley Range up against a former player, with J. N. Gresham now playing for Brooklands, though the game ended in a draw, with Whalley Range having little time to bat.

Conspicuous by his absence in the first three games in August, was Jack Woollam, who had slightly more important matters to deal with, over in Amsterdam!

John Philip Victor Woollam – The Club's Second Olympian

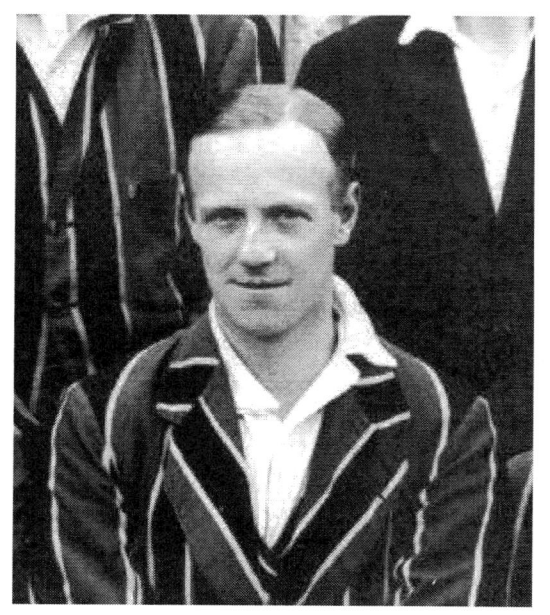

John Philip Victor Woollam was born around the turn of the century, the younger brother of Eddie Woollam. Jack, as he was known, would be associated with the Whalley Range club for the best part of 50 years. He was a superb batsman, scoring countless fifties for the club, though (certainly in the period up until WWII) the coveted century seems to have eluded him, with his best being a score of 97 against Stockport in 1930. Having been vice-captain under Dolph Classen, he replaced him as captain when he stepped down in 1937, and continued in the role until 1950. Two years later, he took on the role of Club Chairman, a position he then relinquished to become the Club President in 1961, succeeding his brother Eddie, a role he fulfilled until 1964.

However, it was on the lacrosse field that Jack really excelled, being hailed as one of the best lacrosse players in the country, in his day. He was a member of the successful post-WWI Old Hulmeians team who were champions of England, and also represented Lancashire, and at one point was captain of the North of England team. The pinnacle of his career though, was when he was part of the Great Britain squad that competed in a lacrosse demonstration event at the 1928 Olympics in Amsterdam. In Great Britain's first match on 6th August, they beat USA 7-6, though the following day, were beaten 9-5 by Canada. With USA having beaten Canada in the opening game, honours were shared in the tournament, with all three teams having won one and lost one.

In business life, J. P. V. Woollam, M. I. Chem. E, worked for Simon Carves Ltd, and during the 1950s was joint managing director of their Australian section, rising to become Deputy Chairman in 1960.

In spite of Jack Woollam's absence for a few games, Whalley Range finished the season strongly, winning six of the remaining seven games that were reported on, and drawing the other. Thus, there is little doubt that had Whalley Range been competing for points this season, they would clearly have been serious contenders for the Stockton Trophy, since their only two defeats this season were to Manchester, who since 1918, were no longer members of the Manchester & District Cricket Association. Thus it would appear that in all of their contests with Association members, they either won (as was the case in most games) or they drew.

In these remaining games, Northwich were disposed of for 101, with A. J. Reeve the main destroyer with six wickets. Whalley Range responded with 201-4, thanks to 49 from T. L. Brierley and an unbeaten 57 from W. Williamson. Two days later on the August Bank Holiday Monday, Bowdon were dismissed for 120, before openers H. R. Classen and F. Howard, who both scored 31, set Whalley Range well on their way to their final winning total of 177.

On the following Saturday, Whalley Range were struggling at home against Heaton Mersey until the last-wicket pairing of number ten batsman, A. J. Reeve, and number eleven batsman A. S. Trafford came together. Thanks to 20 from Reeve, and an unbeaten 25 from Trafford, Whalley Range finally managed to post a moderate 111. As it happened, those late runs proved absolutely vital, as Whalley Range won by just five runs in the end, with Trafford enjoying further success with four wickets.

Whalley Range 1st XI, 1928
T. L. Brierley, K. Rains, H. B. Brooks, W. Williamson, A. J. Leggat
A. J. Reeve, A. Horrocks, F. Howard, H. R. Classen (capt), S. Pilkington, J. P. V. Woollam

Whalley Range were next up against Castleton, the team that would claim the Stockton Trophy this season, and they displayed their pedigree to the champions-elect, rattling up 178-9 before declaring, with A. J. Leggat the main contributor with 76. Also back in the side for Whalley Range for the first time since his Olympics exploits was Jack Woollam, so one assumes that the home players would have been exhilarated and inspired by the sight of an Olympics medal. As it transpired though, Whalley Range didn't quite have enough time to force victory, with Castleton finishing on 87-5. In the final three games that were reported on this season, Whalley Range easily beat Buxton, Bowdon, and Chorlton. In the first of these, H. B. Brooks was the main star, opening the innings and scoring 51, whilst in the ensuing game, A. J. Reeve captured seven wickets, before H. R. Classen with 33 and T. L. Brierley with an unbeaten 34 ensured victory for the home team.

Thomas Leslie Brierley, the future Glamorgan and Lancashire player, can be seen in the previous team photo of the Whalley Range 1st XI team from this season, and what a brilliant team it was, with most of the batsmen scoring centuries for the club at some point in their careers.

The ensuing photo of the Whalley Range 2nd XI team from 1928 features John William Greenup, now in his seventies, who is present in a few of the team photos from this period. He was a vice-president of the club from 1924 until 1937, and also served on the committee from 1925 to 1932. Also present in the photo, is his son, George Greenup, who was involved in the Sweepstakes scandal back in 1923, and who also appeared in the 1925 2nd XI team photo alongside his father :-

Whalley Range 2nd XI 1928
S. S. Kiernan, C. D. Campbell, G. B. Chronnell, R. Buckland,
H. L. Palmer, G. T. Mountain, G. Greenup, F. R. Stubbs
J. E. Buckland, A. D. Thomson, S. E. Woollam, A. Pitt, F. R. Leroy (c), H. T. Eke, W. J. Mountain, J. W. Greenup

As well as featuring Ron Buckland, the photo also shows his elderly father, James Edward Buckland, who in his cricketing prime, had played for Longsight and then Didsbury. He was another who was a vice-president of the club, a position he would hold from 1905 up until his passing away in 1934, at the grand old age of 87. Though not present in the photo above, someone else who was still appearing for them this season was N. A. Barber, and following the close of the cricket season, he represented Lancashire at lacrosse, playing alongside Jack Woollam, whilst a future Whalley Range star, Raymond Nichols Ainsworth, represented Lancashire Juniors.

Crimes and Misdemeanours

Something else that made the news during the close season was the theft of a wheelbarrow from the Whalley Range club! Michael Richardson, aged 42, had apparently been on a stealing spree, looking for Christmas presents, and as well as the wheelbarrow, he stole clothes from a shop, a garden roller (not an easy thing to steal!) from the Carlton Bowling Club in Whalley Range, and also committed robberies from a doctor in Moss Side. For these offences, he was jailed for nine months, and one assumes, Whalley Range got their wheelbarrow back!

As mentioned previously, the start of 1929 saw the sad passing away of Dolph Classen's only son, Geoffrey, who had played for Whalley Range 2nd XI during recent seasons.

Whalley Range 1st XI 1929
F. B. Proctor, J. P. V. Woollam, H. B. Brooks, A. J. Reeve, T. L. Brierley
W. Williamson, S. Pilkington, H. T. Eke, H. R. Classen (capt), F. Howard, A. Horrocks

As tradition now dictated, Whalley Range kicked off the new season at home against Chorlton, on Saturday 20th April, a game which ended in a draw, with H. B. Brooks (34) and W. Williamson (45) the main contributors with the bat for the home team. Whalley Range then went on a superb run of four wins out of five, as they carried on with the kind of form that had brought them so much success during the previous season. The first of these wins was against Cheetham Hill, who were dismissed for 90. In reply, despite five players getting ducks, Whalley Range accumulated 116, with H. B. Brooks (29) and H. T. Eke (25) the top scorers. The next weekend, Buxton were all out for 92, with A. J. Reeve claiming five wickets, allowing the visitors to cruise home by five wickets. Following a draw in a less competitive midweek clash against the nearby Hulme Grammar School, South Manchester were the next team to be disposed of, short of three figures, as they were bowled out for 83. In reply, thanks mainly to 68 from Jack Woollam, Whalley Range amassed a winning total of 153. Whalley Range's fine run continued with victory at Brooklands, where the main stars were H. T. Eke with five wickets, and W. Williamson with an unbeaten 62.

During this period, the 2nd XI were also performing well, with a comfortable win at Hulme Grammar School with A. D. Thomson capturing six wickets, whilst in another game they disposed of Buxton 2nd XI for just 20, with G. B. Chronnell taking five wickets, to help the hosts win by 68 runs. Born in 1904 to Robert and Mary Chronnell, Gerald Bernard Chronnell went on to become a dentist, with his practice being on Withington Road, Whalley Range. In 1932, he married Helena Mary O'Neill, and continued playing for Whalley Range up until the outbreak of the Second World War, though shortly after this, he died suddenly on 8th July 1940, aged just 36. He can be seen in both of the 1927 and the 1928 2nd XI team photos.

The next game for the 1st XI was a Bank Holiday Monday encounter with visitors Cheadle Hulme who clocked up a respectable 184. Whalley Range fought valiantly to overhaul their total, but in the end had to settle for a draw, with just one wicket intact, on 162-9. Opener H. R. Classen scored 32, but the crucial role in preserving their unbeaten start to the season was a defiant unbeaten 42 from A. J. Leggat. Winning ways were restored at the weekend, at Knutsford's expense, who were removed for 111, before the home team really showed their prowess, rattling up 174-3, with J. P. V. Woollam again top-scoring, this time with a fine 88. Again, if Whalley Range had been competing for points this season, they would surely have been very close to the top of the pile, if not at the very summit itself.

Strength in Depth

With Whalley Range now enjoying so much success, there were occasions this season when Whalley Range boasted not just three, but sometimes four separate teams on a Saturday. For whatever reason, there was a definite aversion to referring to a team as a 3rd XI (and certainly not 4th XI), and so on Saturday 1st June 1929, Whalley Range fielded four teams, with the 1st XI naturally being listed as such, whilst all of the other three teams were listed as Whalley Range 2nd XI. On this day, the 1st XI played Stockport 1st XI, whilst the various 2nd XI teams played Stockport 2nd XI, Arley 2nd XI, and Dunham Massey. It could be argued that the "real" 2nd XI was that team which competed in the corresponding fixture to the 1st XI, i.e. those that played Stockport 2nd XI, since this would come under the jurisdiction of the Association. However, one suspects that another reason for referring to all three teams as 2nd XIs was that there was a fairly even sprinkling of talent across all three teams, to obviate any embarrassment that might possibly have arisen by having all the weakest players in the same team. Sometimes during the season though, especially when there were three teams listed, a team was listed as Whalley Range 'A', in addition to the usual 1st XI and 2nd XI teams, though as highlighted above, never ever referred to as a 3rd XI, at this point, other than for midweek evening games.

In the game against Stockport, the opposition rattled up 228-9 before declaring, with H. T. Eke claiming five wickets. Whalley Range responded well, with H. R. Classen scoring 75 and W. Williamson 52, though at the end, were hanging on for a draw, on 198-9. Following a further draw at Knutsford, Whalley Range travelled to Northwich and removed them for just 66. However, with only A. J. Leggat managing to get into double-figures, the visitors were finally all out, still two runs shy of the hosts' total. Whalley Range then drew with Cheetham Hill, before winning ways were restored against Castleton, the reigning Stockton Trophy champions. As can be seen, the newspaper copy is not clear enough to determine precisely what happened, but Whalley Range definitely won, rattling up over 200 for the loss of just three wickets, with the diminutive 19 year-old T. L. Brierley scoring an unbeaten century (probably 110 not out), whilst A. J. Leggat scored an unbeaten fifty.

Eddie Paynter

July started with a draw against a Manchester team that included the legendary Eddie Paynter opening the innings and scoring a fifty. Eddie was a remarkable cricketer who went on to score over 20,000 runs in first-class cricket, mainly for Lancashire, including a score of 322 against Sussex in 1937 in just five hours. He also made 20 appearances for England at an incredible average of just under 60, scoring four centuries, the highest of which was 243 against South Africa at Durban during the 1938-1939 tour. He was also a superb fielder, which was all the more amazing, since in his younger days, he had lost the ends of the first and second fingers of his right hand in a brick press, whilst working at the same brickworks where his father laboured. Less than a fortnight after scoring fifty in this game against Whalley Range, Eddie scored a century in each innings for Lancs 2nd XI against Notts 2nd XI.

The next game witnessed victory over Cheadle Hulme with A. J. Reeve taking six wickets, and H. B. Brooks scoring 48 not out. In the corresponding 2nd XI fixture, A. Pitt coming in at number seven, scored an unbeaten 105, out of a total of 223-7 declared. The opposition were removed for 173, to leave the 2nd XI victorious by exactly 50 runs.

Whalley Range 2nd XI v Cheadle Hulme 2nd XI, at Whalley Range, Saturday 13th July 1929

Whalley Range 2nd XI

G. T. Mountain	c Barton	b Wilson	0
H. T. Eke		b Tallantire	11
R. Astin		b Wilson	0
F. B. Proctor		b Tallantire	15
S. S. Kiernan		b Knight	33
E. Barnes	st Hardy	b Buckland	0
A. Pitt		not out	105
F. R. Leroy		b Peak	48
E. G. Widdows		not out	7
Extras			4
Total		(for 7 dec.)	223

A. Pitt first played for Whalley Range before the First World War and was still playing for them at the time of the outbreak of the Second World War. In fact the 1938 season would also see him playing alongside D. Pitt for the 2nd XI, and in the weekday game against Wythenshawe, they actually opened the batting together. A. Pitt can be seen in one of the 1927 2nd XI photos and also the 1928 2nd XI photo.

In a midweek game at Old Trafford, Whalley Range 1st XI earned another creditable draw against Manchester, thanks to 43 from Jack Woollam, an unbeaten 43 from W. Williamson, and 35 from A. J. Leggat. On the Saturday there was a close exciting game with South Manchester who'd batted first and posted 196. Thanks to opener H. R. Classen, who scored 65, the target seemed eminently achievable, though at the close, they were tantalisingly just six runs adrift, with two wickets in hand.

The last weekend in July witnessed some superb performance against Brooklands, by both the 1st and 2nd XIs. In the 1st XI encounter at Whalley Range, eight wickets from H. B. Brooks limited the visitors to 138. When Whalley Range batted, the runs simply flowed, with opener H. R. Classen again top-scoring with a fine 73. With A. J. Leggat also contributing 69, Whalley Range eased to an impressively large total of 291-7. Meanwhile at Brooklands, the runs were also coming easily, with Brooklands 2nd XI amassing precisely 250. Amazingly though, this was a target that Whalley Range chased down with just a couple of wickets to spare, in a thrilling finish. Openers G. T. Mountain with 47 and Frederick Burdett Proctor (another former Hulme Grammar School pupil) with 32 ensured there was a solid start, before G. B. Chronnell carried on the good work with 39. In the end though, it was a real captain's innings of 52 not out, from F. R. Leroy that guided the ship home, finishing on 257-8 for a quite remarkable win.

August started well for W. Williamson, who scored an unbeaten 69 in a drawn game with Northwich, though on the following Monday, Whalley Range were soundly beaten by Bowdon, in a game that started at 12 noon. Then, on the ensuing Saturday, five wickets from H. R. Classen ensured victory over Heaton Mersey, whilst the next game, against Castleton, was severely curtailed because of rain. The following weekend witnessed a comfortable win over Buxton, with opener Classen (40), W. Williamson (47 not out) and A. Horrocks (27 not out) all amongst the runs. It looks like Buxton were a player short for this game, since their eleventh man was S. S. Kiernan, the Whalley Range player. As ever, Whalley Range went about their business in the most gentlemanly of manners in these days, and lending a player to the opposition certainly seemed the correct etiquette if they were short. In fact, the 1929 season seemed to be pretty gentlemanly in general with just fourteen teams (i.e. fewer than half of the Association members) opting to compete for the Stockton Trophy, which this season was won by Macclesfield, who were clearly a strong outfit, as this was their fifth triumph already.

The Thornton Family

Saturday 17th August 1929 appears to have been a rainy day with very little play managed in the 1st XI game against Castleton at Sparth Bottoms. Also scheduled for the same day at Poynton was a game against a Whalley Range team captained by F. R. Leroy. Being a somewhat overcast day, it is not definite that the game went ahead, but this fixture does represent the first recorded instance

that was unearthed that has all of W. H. Thornton, W. S. Thornton, and J. T. Thornton in the same line-up. William Herbert Thornton was born in 1882 and had graced the Whalley Range 1st XI since before the First World War. Now in the twilight of his career, he tended to represent the 2nd XI these days, thus providing him with the opportunity to play alongside his two up-and-coming sons. The elder of them was John Talbot Thornton, who was born in 1908, whilst William Sydney Thornton, was born the following year. Both sons continued to be members of the Whalley Range club for many years to come.

William Sydney Thornton, or Bill as he was known, passed away in 1984, and in recognition of his considerable devotion to the club, one of the benches outside the clubhouse bears a plaque in his memory. Bill became Cricket Secretary at least as early as 1943, a role he continued to fulfil until 1952. He was also the Honorary Secretary for the 1946 season, and was a member of various committees up until 1958. He was made a vice-president in 1964, and an honorary life member in 1972, as was his brother.

Commemorative plaque for Bill Thornton on clubhouse bench

In the last game of August, H. T. Eke captured five wickets in a drawn game against Bowdon, whilst the following week, in the traditional season finale for the 1st XI at Chorlton-cum-Hardy, it was the turn of A. Horrocks to capture five wickets as the hosts were dismissed for just 65. Whalley Range then responded with 167-7, with W. Williamson scoring 42 and H. B. Brooks scoring 37. In the corresponding 2nd XI game at Whalley Range, H. L. Palmer scored 62. There was one further game for the 2nd XI this season, with former Hulme Grammar schoolboy E. G. Widdows scoring 61 against Ashley, as they narrowly missed out on securing victory, replying with 155-7 to Ashley's 157 all out.

Doctor in the House

Making his debut for Whalley Range during the 1929 season was Dr. P. B. Mumford, who would become renowned and respected in his field. Percival Brooke Mumford was born on 7th April 1896. His father, Alfred Alexander Mumford, was a physician, and his mother, Edith Emily Mumford, was the daughter of Charles Read, who was also a physician. Thus it was little surprise that Percival would also find his way into the medical profession. He was educated at Manchester Grammar School, and Manchester University, where he qualified in 1920 with distinctions in pathology, surgery, gynaecology, and obstetrics. He gained his MRCP (Membership of the Royal College of Physicians), a postgraduate medical diploma, in 1922, and his MD in 1925.

He held many and various simultaneous posts throughout his career. At the Manchester and Salford Skin Hospital, he progressed to become consultant dermatologist in 1931, a position he held for the next 30 years. He was honorary dermatologist at Warrington Infirmary from 1929 to 1938, and the Park Hospital, Davyhulme, from 1929 to 1939. He was visiting pathologist at the Cheshire County Mental Hospital, Macclesfield, from 1921 to 1933; honorary dermatologist at the Manchester Royal Infirmary from 1931 to 1961; a clinical instructor in venereal diseases from 1932 to 1954; and lecturer in dermatology at Manchester University from 1936 to 1961.

His services to the community and to dermatology in the north of England were unique. His name became a household word amongst patients, general practitioners, solicitors, trades unions and insurance companies, making him the first choice in medico-legal aspects of his speciality. Thus it is no surprise to see him referred to as the *"doyen of dermatologists in Manchester"*.

During the First World War, he saw service on the French and Italian Fronts, though during this period, he was thrown from his horse and fractured his skull. It was an incident that left him with permanent partial deafness in his left ear. In 1918, he married Kathleen Vera Neill, daughter of John Neill, who was a printer in Whalley Range. They had three children, a son and two daughters, who all followed their father's footsteps into the medical profession. Apart from cricket (where he represented Whalley Range in the 1929 and 1930 seasons), Dr. P. B. Mumford also played golf and lacrosse. He died in the Christie Hospital, Manchester on 10th June 1972, aged 76.

On the Way to a Century (1930-1945)

There is little doubt that Whalley Range were a force to be reckoned with at this time, due to a very strong line-up, and the new decade heralded further successes for the team. Of the 22 1st XI matches that would be reported on in the 1930 season, there were 10 victories, 11 draws, and just the one defeat. The 2nd XI teams (of which there again appeared to be several, since this was another season where Whalley Range seemed to have a surfeit of players and teams) would prove more than useful as well, with some incredible performances, especially during the month of June.

At the start of the cricket season, Raymond Nichols Ainsworth (born 1909) should have been captaining the Manchester University cricket team, but being a fine all-round sportsman (having already represented Lancashire at junior lacrosse level), he was abroad in America, playing lacrosse for what was essentially an England touring team. Also in the squad were his younger brother, Geoffrey Nichols Ainsworth, and Kenneth Rains. By the end of the cricket season, R. N. Ainsworth would have scored an unbeaten century for Whalley Range 2nd XI, and made his way effortlessly into the 1st XI. Over the ensuing seasons, he would go on to become one of Whalley Range's leading players, especially with regard to the number of centuries scored.

After a few drawn matches, Whalley Range's first reported victory of the season, was against Knutsford, with H. T. Eke starring with both bat and ball, top-scoring with 48 out of a total of 170-6, before taking six wickets, as the visitors were bowled out for just 57. On the following Wednesday, Whalley Range entertained Hulme Grammar School, presumably as ever on the look-out for future players from this hotbed of talent. The School batted first and made 105 with F. B. Proctor taking five wickets. Opener Rains then scored 49 against his old school, and A. Horrocks made 53. The result was listed as a seven-wicket win for Whalley Range, though they carried on batting to be 189 all out.

On the last day of May, Jack Woollam came desperately close to getting a century against Stockport, scoring 97 before being bowled. With W. Williamson also scoring an unbeaten 51, Whalley Range declared on 209-5, though Stockport responded well with 173-5. Jack Woollam was in the runs again the following Saturday, with an unbeaten 73 out of a total of 168-3, after Knutsford had been bowled out for 101. Throughout the coming "Whit Week" there were various games for the 1st and 2nd XIs. On the Monday, Whalley Range entertained Cheadle Hulme, and thanks to yet another undefeated effort from Williamson, 66 not out, the home side posted 208-6. However they were unable to force victory, with the visitors finishing on 132-8. Meanwhile, over in Ashley, Whalley Range 2nd XI were rattling up a phenomenal 277-2. The man doing all the damage was opener H. L. Palmer who finished unbeaten on an amazing 152. Also in the runs were George Talbot Mountain who scored 46 and George Frederick Henson who scored an unbeaten 42. In reply, Ashley succumbed to 102 all out, to leave Whalley Range 2nd XI victorious by over 150 runs.

Hubert Leslie Palmer MBE

Hubert Leslie Palmer was born in 1897 to James Osborn Palmer and Jane Yeoman Palmer (nee Warren) in Bedfordshire. In 1913, the family moved to Whalley Range, and so H. L. Palmer and his younger brother, John Raymond Palmer (born 1902), enrolled at Hulme Grammar School. At the school, H. L. Palmer excelled at sport, winning various events at the annual sports day in May 1914, namely, throwing the cricket ball, broad jump, 100 yards, and also featured in a dead heat in the hurdle race, to thus earn himself the Gaskell Cup.

Thus it was no surprise that he would also become a fine cricketer. His name first appears on a Whalley Range scoresheet in 1915, with his older brother, Sydney James Palmer, having made his debut for the club, the previous season. His younger brother, J. R. Palmer, would also start playing for the club as soon as it had re-

formed after the War. It was because of his efforts during the First World War, that H. L. Palmer was awarded the MBE in 1917, having enlisted with the Lancashire Fusiliers the previous year.

In 1922 he married Dorothy Marsh, and continued to play cricket for Whalley Range up until the end of the 1933 season, when it seems that work commitments caused him to relocate to Formby, to take up the role of Sales Manager for William P. Hartley Ltd., preserve manufacturers, of Aintree. Just prior to this, he partnered Ernest Pyecroft as Wholesale Egg and Produce Dealers in a business based on Stockport Road in Ardwick. He continued to play cricket prior to the Second World War, representing Formby Cricket Club, and also became a member of Formby Golf Club.

His house on College Avenue in Formby overlooked the Liverpool to Southport railway line, and countless times over more than twenty years, he travelled the route that involved using the self-operated Wicks Lane level crossing, to traverse the railway line. In the early evening of Saturday 16th October 1954, H. L. Palmer was returning from enjoying a local rugby match. Sadly, in the gathering gloom, with dusk and heavy rain falling, his car was struck by a Liverpool-bound train, killing him instantly. It really was a tragic ending to someone who'd contributed so much in life, especially as he'd served with such distinction through both of the World Wars.

Ashley v Whalley Range 2nd XI, at Ashley, Monday 9th June 1930

Whalley Range 2nd XI

H. L. Palmer		not out	152
A. D. Thomson	lbw	b Worthington	16
G. T. Mountain	lbw	b Worthington	46
G. F. Henson		not out	42
Extras			21
Total		(for 2 dec)	277

Two days after scoring this monumental unbeaten 152, H. L. Palmer was dismissed for just 7, but Eddie Woollam notched 62 to ensure that the 200-barrier was surpassed again, with the 2nd XI declaring on 203-7, though Stockport 2nd XI earnt a draw replying with 152-8. The following day, another of the teams labelled as Whalley Range 2nd XI were also amongst the runs, scoring 205-6 against Wythenshawe, with G. H. (George Herbert) Isherwood the top-scorer with 55. The opposition were then bowled out for 108. During the rest of Whit Week, the 1st XI were scheduled to play four games on consecutive days, though the game on the Wednesday against Stockport appears to have gone unreported. The following day's game at Bury was drawn, where H. T. Eke was the top-scorer with 62, whilst Friday 13th proved anything but unlucky to A. J. Reeve, whose six wickets helped Whalley Range beat Heaton Mersey by 70 runs.

On the Whit-Saturday, Whalley Range travelled to Northwich for their next game, and removed the hosts for 92, with A. J. Reeve claiming a further seven wickets. Winston Williamson then saw the visitors home with an unbeaten 52, batting at number four, in an all-out total of 118, as his propensity for keeping his wicket intact continued unabated. During the following week, H. L. Palmer captained the 2nd XI (or at least one of the teams designated as such) against Willaston School, ensuring a draw with a fine knock of 57 not out, as the runs continued to flow for him in June.

Whilst the 1st XI were drawing at Cheetham Hill the following Saturday, one of the 2nd XI teams was playing Manchester University at Fallowfield, where Whalley Range posted 132 before R. N. Ainsworth very nearly led his university team to victory, scoring an unbeaten 33 in their reply of 126-8. One suspects it was at this game that the seeds were sown with regard to Ainsworth being persuaded that Whalley Range was where his future cricketing career lay. Also, being a keen lacrosse player, he would have been well aware of the strong lacrosse connection that existed at the club, maintained by the likes of Woollam, Rains, and Brierley.

The end of June was seen out with a fine win over Castleton who were bowled out for 117, with A. Horrocks capturing five wickets. Opener Classen then scored 77 before being out "hit wicket" in a winning total of 162-4. Whalley Range's fine season continued with another creditable draw against a strong Manchester team that not only included former Whalley Range player, A. J. Leggat, but also Harry Makepeace. Though now in the twilight of his career, Makepeace would score over 25,000 runs for Lancashire, and was also one of a rare breed who represented England at both football and cricket. He also appeared in two successive F. A. Cup finals for Everton, beating Newcastle United in 1906, before losing out to Sheffield Wednesday at the final hurdle the following year.

Someone who started appearing for Whalley Range this season was a certain G. B. Brookes :-

Gordon Bertram Brookes – The Fabulous Baker Boy

Having boasted the Fabulous Baker Boys, Arthur George and Charles Shaw Baker, in their side a few decades earlier, the Whalley Range club could now lay claim to a "real" Fabulous Baker Boy!

Gordon Bertram Brookes was born on 13th July 1911, and would go on to team up with W. J. Barton to create a company called, slightly confusingly, W. J. Brookes, on Skerton Road, parallel to Seymour Grove. Gordon controlled the wholesale side of the business, whilst W. J. controlled the retail side. The business they were involved in was baking, and it was their company that created the Mother's Pride brand of bread in the mid-1930s, which went on to become the best-selling white bread in the UK at one point.

As such, G. B. Brookes soon became a very wealthy man, and apparently after the Second World War at the end of every cricket season, he would just write a cheque for whatever the club's financial shortfall was! Gordon would also go on to become president of the Whalley Range club between 1972 and 1975, and in his final year in office, he presented both a Ladies and a Gents Ladder Trophy to the club, to be competed for by the club's tennis members. He lived until the age of 75, passing away on 8th August 1986.

Saturday 12th July was a busy and rewarding day for the various Whalley Range outfits, with five players scoring at least 70. At Cheadle Hulme, the 1st XI disposed of their hosts for 95, before then rattling up 239-6 thanks to 76 from H. T. Eke, and 72 from T. L. Brierley. In the corresponding 2nd XI fixture at Whalley Range, former Hulme Grammar schoolboy Eric Barnes scored 78 against Cheadle Hulme 2nd XI. Another Whalley Range 2nd XI team played Oughtrington Park, where G. T. Mountain scored 83 to help his team win, whilst in a further team labelled as Whalley Range 2nd XI, Ralph Astin scored an unbeaten 80 against Wythenshawe, on what would appear to be a glorious day for batting!

Following a draw at Withington against South Manchester, four wickets from Classen helped Whalley Range secure a narrow win at home against Brooklands on Saturday 26th July. Having played against Whalley Range earlier in the season for Manchester University, the name of R. N. Ainsworth appeared in the Whalley Range line-up for the corresponding 2nd XI fixture at Brooklands. Coming in at number five, Ainsworth scored an incredible unbeaten 114 out of a total of 264-6, on what is believed to be his debut appearance for the club! Brooklands had batted first and been dismissed for 90, so these were still days when the surpassing of the opposition's total did not necessarily herald the end of the day's proceedings :-

Brooklands 2nd XI v Whalley Range 2nd XI, at Brooklands, Saturday 26th July 1930

Whalley Range 2nd XI

T. M. Tillotson	c Grimshaw	b Hall	31
S. R. Banks		c & b Clarke	26
C. D. Campbell		b Hall	5
G. F. Henson		run out	21
R. N. Ainsworth		not out	114
E. G. Widdows	c Hall	b Clarke	3
G. F. Hodgkinson		c & b Roscoe	4
S. E. Woollam		not out	38
Extras			22
Total		(for 6)	264

Not surprisingly, R. N. Ainsworth would find himself promoted to the 1st XI the following weekend, for the game against Northwich. As it happened though, it was another player who'd been promoted, Ralph Astin, who stole the show in this game, opening the innings and scoring an unbeaten 72 out of a total of 157-5. Northwich were struggling at 13-3 in reply when they were rescued by the weather.

Following a drawn game in the traditional August Bank Holiday Monday all-day clash (i.e. 12 noon start) at Bowdon, Whalley Range suffered their only reported defeat of the season, when they were dismissed for just 91 by Heaton Mersey, though at least one of the 2nd XI teams was simultaneously doing really well, with G. T. Mountain taking eight wickets and a catch to dismiss Arley for just 36. The 1st XI quickly rediscovered their winning form though, beating Castleton the following Saturday with H. T. Eke claiming five wickets, whilst Kenneth Rains was scoring 86 in the corresponding 2nd XI game. This was followed by victory over Buxton who scored just 64, before Jack Woollam scored 72 out of a total of 143-5. The final game in August produced a draw against Bowdon. Whalley Range's last game of the season was supposed to be against Chorlton at Hardy Lane on Saturday 6th September. However a very wet day and no cricket, provided the ideal opportunity for the following team photo to be captured :-

Whalley Range 1st XI 1930
A. Horrocks, R. N. Ainsworth, A. J. Reeve, H. L. Palmer, R. Astin
S. Pilkington, F. Howard, H. R. Classen (capt), H. T. Eke, J. P. V. Woollam, W. Williamson

As can be seen in the photo, some of the new recruits to the 1st XI line-up are bereft of their Whalley Range blazers! Thus even though Whalley Range's season may have ended on somewhat of a damp note, there was no denying it had been another rewarding and enjoyable campaign for the Whalley Range cricketers.

The ensuing team photo is purportedly of the Whalley Range 2nd XI for the 1931 season. Amazingly it features T. L. Brierley, who would be playing for Glamorgan by the end of the season. However, if truth be known, the photo is more than likely taken from the home game against Chorlton that was played towards the end of the previous season, judging by the correlation between the line-up for that match and the players in the photo. If this was the case, this photo was taken on the same day as the 1930 1st XI photo shown above. Either way, it still illustrates just how good the Whalley Range 1st XI must have been at this time, if an imminent first-class cricketer couldn't always command a place in the team!

Whalley Range 2nd XI 1931 (or maybe 1930?)
J. J. Butler, F. B. Proctor, T. L. Brierley, W. B. Stansby, K. Rains, G. H. Isherwood, N. E. Hawley
F. R. Stubbs, G. Greenup, S. E. Woollam, F. R. Leroy (capt), G. T. Mountain, W. J. Mountain, J. W. Greenup

Some of the early part of the 1931 season would appear to have fallen victim to the weather. The first properly completed fixture seems to have been when Whalley Range beat South Manchester by the narrow margin of six runs, with opener H. B. Brooks contributing 56 out of a total of 119. In the next game, A. Horrocks took five wickets, before opener Ralph Astin with an unbeaten 43 ensured a draw against Brooklands. In the corresponding 2nd XI game, A. Pitt scored an unbeaten 52, for which he was rewarded with promotion to the 1st XI for the following game. This was against Stockport, a game in which Kenneth Rains scored 74 before the home side declared on 154-9. However, rain prevented the visitors from even starting their innings. On the Monday, Whalley Range drew with Cheadle Hulme, before losing a couple of days later to Stockport in a further game during Whit Week.

Then came an extraordinary day on Saturday 30th May. At Whalley Range, Knutsford were the visitors, and were dismissed for a mere 60, to which Whalley Range replied with 122-9. However, all the real excitement was in the corresponding 2nd XI fixture at Knutsford, where Whalley Range 2nd XI batted first and posted 165-8 thanks to a solid start from Eddie Woollam and W. S. Thornton. However, when Knutsford 2nd XI batted, apart from the two openers, who made 4 and 1, nobody else managed a single run between them! A. S. Bell was the main hero with five quick wickets, whilst former Hulme Grammar schoolboy, Leonard Lawton Cooper, captured three, with the other two being run outs :-

Knutsford 2nd XI v Whalley Range 2nd XI, at Knutsford, Saturday 30th May 1931

Whalley Range 2nd XI				Knutsford 2nd XI			
S. E. Woollam		b Allsop	34	W. Allsop		run out	4
W. S. Thornton	lbw	b Eaton	30	W. Moreton		b Cooper	1
P. Hodgkinson	c &	b Eaton	19	S. Newton	c Woollam	b Bell	0
F. B. Proctor	st Brooks	b Barker	35	A. Hulme	c Hilton	b Cooper	0
T. M. Tillotson		b Eaton	7	K. Barker		b Bell	0
J. R. Palmer	c Thomas	b Barker	14	H. Eaton	lbw	b Bell	0
F. R. Stubbs	st Brooks	b Barker	8	F. Brooks		b Bell	0
K. B. Hilton	c Eaton	b Barker	3	B. Paton	c Tillotson	b Bell	0
W. S. Grimshaw		not out	0	F. Thomas		not out	0
L. L. Cooper		not out	5	D. Howell		run out	0
A. S. Bell			-	B. Wright	c Stubbs	b Cooper	0
Extras			10	Extras			1
Total		(for 8)	165	Total			6

The first game in June was a midweek affair against Manchester at Old Trafford, but with only two players in double-figures, Whalley Range managed only 90. However in reply, Manchester only just made it over the finishing line, closing on 99-9. Whalley Range then beat Northwich, with A. Horrocks taking five wickets. Batting at number four, W. Williamson finished with an unbeaten 38, though the contributions of number eight batsman W. S. Thornton with 23, and 26 from G. H. Isherwood coming in at number ten, proved vital.

Draws against both Castleton and Manchester ensued, where in the first of these two games, H. T. Eke captured six wickets, whilst in the latter game, Whalley Range were up against a former team-mate, A. J. Leggat. Following victory against Cheadle Hulme, Whalley Range lost to both South Manchester and Brooklands, where in the latter of these games, Whalley Range were again up against former team-mate J. N. Gresham.

August began with victories over Northwich and Bowdon, with A. Horrocks capturing seven wickets in the latter game. This Bank Holiday Monday game at Bowdon, commencing at midday as always, would also appear to be T. L. Brierley's last appearance for the club, before crossing the Welsh border. In the corresponding 2nd XI game, Whalley Range amassed an impressive 271-8 declared before bowling out the opposition for 101. On the same day, in light of recent routs over Ashley (even with under-strength teams), a further Whalley Range team that turned out this particular day, must have been especially weak, since they found themselves on the wrong end of a hiding! Ashley rattled up 278-9 before declaring, and then dismissed the Whalley Range team for 118.

Rain accounted for most of the rest of the games in August. However at the end of the month, on Saturday 29th August, the weather was fine enough for Whalley Range to register a comfortable win over Bowdon, with W. Williamson now exhibiting his bowling skills with a six-wicket haul. However, more significantly on this day, over in Swansea, Thomas Leslie Brierley was making his first-class debut for Glamorgan against Nottinghamshire. Under the heading *"Manchester Man in Welsh Side"*, the Guardian reported that *"Glamorgan are giving a trial to T. Brierley, a wicket-keeper from Manchester."* Brierley didn't make the best of starts, scoring 4 and 2 on his debut, though admittedly he was up against the ferociously fast Harold Larwood at the peak of his career, who clean bowled him in his second innings. However, he did keep wicket and caught both openers in Nottinghamshire's one and only innings.

Interestingly, an article entitled *"When I Was in Manchester"* written by Archie MacLaren, the best ever cricketer to play for Whalley Range, appeared in the Manchester Guardian on 30th December 1931. It was a lengthy piece of which the most salient aspects were his connections to the likes of the Bannerman, Carver, Rickards, and Hulton families, and his appraisal of the Steel brothers who graced the Whalley Range team in the 1870s and 1880s. As alluded to earlier, at the time when Archie played for Whalley Range, he lived at Sunnyside, close by the ground on College Road. The previous occupants of the house had been the Carver family, whilst just a few doors down at The Cedars, lived the Hultons. The Rickards family also lived nearby, at Carlton Lodge on Dudley Road :-

> *The Manchester of my boyhood consisted of Whalley Range and its inhabitants, a goodly number of which were my father's and mother's relations and connections, such as Grandma Carver, Fred Carver her son and his family, Henton Carver another son, Dr. Daniel Leach, who married my father's sister, the David Bannermans, the Rickards family, the Railtons, the Radfords, the Richardsons, and the Campbell Hultons. The head of the last family, and from whom I get my second name, kindly acted as my godfather. He was a very keen cricketer and later became a member of the Marylebone Cricket Club Committee. Many times my father and godfather accompanied me on a Sunday morning, when we would walk to the county cricket ground, Old Trafford, through delightful country, long since shorn of its beauty by the builders and have a quiet practice in front of the pavilion rails....*
>
> *...A. G. Steel was a very great Lancashire and England player, and I am sure I never saw a better slow bowler of the right-handers throughout my career. His batting was beautiful to watch, scoring all round the wicket, if his cutting was possibly the most telling factor...*
>
> *...E. E. Steel, the youngest of the Steel family, was an exceedingly clever slow bowler and good batsman, who would have more than held his own in Test cricket to-day...*

Just as the 1932 cricket season was beginning, the Old Hulmeians (featuring Whalley Range cricketers, N. A. Barber, K. Rains, A. R. Merchant, and J. P. V. Woollam) were again being crowned lacrosse champions of England! They won the Iroquois Cup, thrashing Oxford University, the reigning holders, by the impressive score-line of 13-1, at New Beckenham. The following is an extract from a report that featured in the Guardian on Monday 2nd May 1932 :-

> *The Old Hulmeians played so well as a team that it is perhaps invidious to pick out individuals, but Barber was often prominent, and Rains at second home and Merchant at first were good. Rains in particular gave a polished display, and his crosse handling, instinct for position, and shooting were those of the great player. Merchant is a fine opportunist at first home, if not the polished artist that Frank Poole, for instance, used to be. There was quite a fair attendance, and the Manchester team did not lack supporters. Their goals were scored by K. Rains (5), A. R. Merchant (3), M. D. Pearson (2), J. P. V. Woollam, R. E. Howard, and N. A. Barber.*

With regard to the cricket, the first reported game in May saw Whalley Range draw with South Manchester thanks to an unbeaten 44 from W. Williamson, after H. T. Eke had taken five of the visitors' wickets. Then came a strange game away at Brooklands, who were dismissed for just 59 with A. J. Reeve capturing six wickets. When Whalley Range batted, only one batsman managed to make double-figures. However, thanks mainly to 25 from opener H. L. Palmer, and the fact that they were chasing such a modest target, Whalley Range somehow forged a win, being all out for 64. The end of May witnessed defeat to Stockport. In fact this season, Whalley Range would lose a lot more games than they were used to, compared to recent seasons, though there would certainly be some fine individual performances along the way, especially from R. N. Ainsworth.

At the start of June, Whalley Range drew with Knutsford thanks to an unbeaten 59 from Classen, before the midweek visit of Hulme Grammar School allowed Whalley Range to record what would be their last victory for several games, with H. T. Eke capturing five wickets as the School were dismissed for just 65, before G. Greenup top-scored with 50 in the home team's reply of 215. This was followed by a draw against Northwich where Williamson was again displaying his proclivity to keep his wicket intact with an unbeaten 72.

Having lost very heavily to Whalley Range's first team three days earlier, Hulme Grammar School then played Whalley Range's second team, perhaps in the hope of better fortune! However, G. Greenup was again in the Whalley Range line-up, and he followed up his 50, with a score of 81 out of a total of 165. Without such a potent bowling attack to face though, the School this time strolled to victory, finally finishing on 193-7. Next came Whalley Range's annual trip to Old Trafford, where they scored a respectable 184-8 before declaring. The top scorers were opener H. L. Palmer with 38 and W. Williamson with 37. In reply, Manchester scored 151-3, thanks to fifties from Charles Hallows and Richard Pollard. Hallows who was now coming towards the end of his career, would end up with over 20,000 runs for Lancashire, including two double-hundreds.

The recent educational theme continued for the 2nd XI with a trip to Fallowfield to meet Manchester University. Whalley Range batted first with R. N. Ainsworth opening the batting, but he was soon heading back to the pavilion after getting a duck against his former colleagues, much to their amusement, one suspects! The visitors eventually posted 128 thanks mainly to 41 from G. B. Brookes, though the University encountered little trouble in overhauling this, losing just three wickets in the process. June concluded for the 1st XI with a draw against Castleton, with Jack Woollam scoring 49 not out. The next game, at home against Manchester, also featured a Whalley Range player scoring an unbeaten 49, with W. Williamson this time being the batsman to narrowly miss out on a fifty, at the close of play. Earlier, A. J. Reeve had claimed five Manchester wickets.

On Saturday 9th July, Whalley Range again had four teams in operation with the only team that didn't win this day, being the 1st XI who were soundly beaten by Cheadle Hulme in spite of a five-wicket haul from A. Horrocks. The top-scorer for the 1st XI was W. S. Thornton who scored an unbeaten 28 coming in at number ten. Meanwhile, the "real" 2nd XI won the corresponding fixture, a further 2nd XI beat Rostherne, and the final team, labelled as Whalley Range 'A', beat Wythenshawe. Considering there was also a midweek team, it shows just how popular cricket in the Whalley Range area was at this time.

Despite Whalley Range being fairly well beaten by South Manchester in the next game, R. N. Ainsworth showed for the first time that he could bowl as well as bat, capturing four wickets, a feat matched by A. J. Reeve. It had thus been a while since the 1st XI had last tasted victory, and when they were struggling again with the bat, against Brooklands, one suspects that most were again expecting defeat. However, G. H. Isherwood, coming in at number eight, top-scored with an effort of 29 to boost the total to 137. Thanks to another five-wicket haul from A. Horrocks, Whalley Range registered a hard-earned victory by the margin of 23 runs. Having regained the winning formula, Whalley Range really made the opposition suffer in the next game, dismissing Northwich for a mere 40, before rattling up an impressive 207-6, with opener R. N. Ainsworth scoring 116.

Whalley Range v Northwich, at Whalley Range, Saturday 30th July 1932

Whalley Range

R. N. Ainsworth		b Carlon		116
H. L. Palmer		lbw b Miller		2
J. P. V. Woollam	c Birchall	b Whalley		10
E. G. Widdows		not out		11
K. Rains	c Maddock	b Wilkinson		8
W. S. Thornton	c Carlon	b Alcock		40
S. Pilkington		lbw b Birchall		8
Extras				12
Total			(for 6)	207

After losing against Heaton Mersey, Whalley Range travelled to Castleton in Rochdale, where the events of the day uncannily mirrored those of a fortnight earlier. Back then, R. N. Ainsworth had opened the innings and scored 116 out of 207-6. In this game, R. N. Ainsworth opened the innings and scored 116 out of 207-6, for a quite amazing repeat performance! In fact, bearing in mind that apart from these two centuries, Ainsworth's next highest recorded score during the season in eleven other innings would only be 21, this indeed was a rather strange occurrence.

Castleton v Whalley Range, at Sparth Bottoms, Saturday 13th August 1932

Whalley Range

R. N. Ainsworth	c Holt	b Belmont		116
H. L. Palmer		b Clegg		55
E. G. Widdows		run out		1
W. S. Thornton		b Lewis		12
N. E. Hawley		b Lewis		0
W. B. Stansby	c Roberts	b Belmont		11
G. Greenup		not out		4
H. R. Classen		not out		5
Extras				3
Total			(for 6)	207

In reply, in spite of five wickets from N. E. (Norman Edgar) Hawley, Castleton salvaged a draw with 152-7. Whalley Range then lost to Buxton and drew with Bowdon, with Williamson again showing his reluctance to lose his wicket, scoring an unbeaten 46 against Buxton, and an unbeaten 34 against Bowdon. With the home game against Chorlton no longer being the traditional season's curtain-raiser, Jack Woollam scored an unbeaten 67 in a nine-wicket thrashing of the lads from Hardy Lane, before the season finished with another victory, this time against Bury, with A. Horrocks bagging another five-wicket haul.

Following an indifferent 1932 season, Whalley Range had a much more successful season in 1933, with one person in particular, being instrumental in the improvement. Thus, at the start of the season, the talk may well have been about the "Bodyline" tour that had recently caused so much controversy Down Under, but by the end of the season, the conversation would undoubtedly have moved on to the brilliant season that W. Williamson was experiencing. At one point, prior to his three failures in the last three innings of the season, he had scored 577 runs at an average of over 70, once again repeating the feat of scoring over 200 runs between dismissals at one point, as his ability to keep his wicket intact was again very much in evidence. It was a superb batting display by Williamson, the likes of which probably hadn't been seen at Whalley Range since the legendary E. E. Steel. Though not as dynamic a player as Steel, for sheer consistency and seeming immovability once he was settled at the wicket, perhaps this season of Williamson's ranked even higher than Steel's stunning 1886 season.

At the back end of April, W. Williamson actually failed with the bat, scoring just 6 at home against Cheetham Hill, but then starred with the ball, taking five crucial wickets, as Whalley Range won a very tight game by just two runs. The next game, against Buxton, was rained off before it had barely started. Then came the first signs of Williamson's fine batting season to come. Like the previous weekend, the weather played its part, but with Whalley Range batting first, they managed to accumulate

134-8 before the match was abandoned. Coming in at number four, as he always did whenever he played this season, Williamson notched up an unbeaten 62. The next game was also drawn, though only just, as Whalley Range hung on grimly, with just one wicket intact, still nearly 100 runs adrift of the total posted by Brooklands. The final game in May, against Stockport, was also drawn, to complete a clean sweep of four draws in the month. Williamson with an unbeaten 44 was the top-scorer.

The following photo is of one of the 2nd XI teams for this season, captained by S. E. Woollam, and as can be seen, includes W. E. F. Stockton. William Edwin Forsyth Stockton was a member of the prestigious Stockton family, with his uncle being Sir Edwin Forsyth Stockton, after whom the Stockton Trophy is named, whilst his father was Albert Forsyth Stockton, who as Sale captain was the first to receive the Stockton Trophy. He represented Whalley Range for just this and the following season, and lived to the grand old age of 98, passing away recently on 18th October 2012.

Whalley Range 2nd XI 1933
E. Stanley, F. B. Proctor, G. B. Chronnell, W. B. Stansby, W. E. F. Stockton, H. Spear
H. B. Brooks, G. F. Henson, S. E. Woollam (capt), T. M. Tillotson, G. H. Isherwood
K. B. Hilton, G. Russel-Fisher

Also featured in the line-up above are further products from the local grammar school, in the form of Kenneth Boyd Hilton and Tom Mackenzie Tillotson. Someone who features in not only the above photo, but also the 1928 and 1929 1st XI team photos is Harold Buckley Brooks, who was born in 1901 to Buckley and Anna Maria Brooks. His earliest recorded appearance for the club is in 1925, with his 1st XI debut coming the following summer, a season which would see him capture a seven-wicket haul away at Knutsford. He claimed a further seven-wicket haul the following season against no less an outfit than the mighty Manchester team. During the winter, he married Mabel Stanley at St. Werburgh's Church in Chorlton-cum-Hardy on 8th December 1927. As can be seen from the two earlier photos especially, he was a tall athletic man, attributes which helped him become a fine all-rounder, with him scoring at least three fifties for the 1st XI. His best performance though was when he captured eight wickets against Brooklands in July 1929. He continued playing for the club until 1935, though sadly he would die fairly young, aged just 45, on 29th October 1946.

June commenced with a superb win at Knutsford where the home team managed just 69, with W. S. Thornton wreaking havoc with eight wickets. It was then left to the irrepressible Williamson to safely see his side home with an unbeaten 68 out of a total of 147-5. On the Monday, Horrocks claimed six wickets as Cheadle Hulme made just 84. However, when Whalley Range batted, everyone (including Williamson!) fell cheaply, as the home side were surprisingly routed for just 70. As it happened, it proved to be only a temporary setback, with no further reversals during the first half of the season. Williamson made another fifty the following Saturday as well, in the return game with Knutsford, scoring an unbeaten 53 out of a declared total of 167-3, before a five-wicket haul from A. Horrocks saw the visitors dismissed for 72. Whalley Range then produced a fine win over Northwich. Just prior to the start of the cricket season, R. N. Ainsworth was playing alongside J. P. V. Woollam, representing Lancashire at lacrosse. On this day though, his batting skills were very much to the fore, opening the innings, and scoring an unbeaten 72 out of 128-2, in reply to the 102 of Northwich. The final game in June eventually fell victim to the weather, though not before Ralph Astin had scored 41, at Cheetham Hill.

Astin carried that form into July, scoring 57 as Whalley Range just about hung on for a draw against Castleton. This was followed by a trip to Old Trafford against Manchester, though this was another game that was ruined by the weather with the home team being deprived of getting a bat, whilst Whalley Range managed 106-6 in the play available, with J. P. V. Woollam scoring 37. Whalley Range's next recorded game was a fortnight later when they totalled 204 against South Manchester. Openers H. L. Palmer and R. N. Ainsworth led the way with scores of 59 and 40, respectively. The visitors were assured of an easy win thanks to a seven-wicket haul from W. S. Thornton.

Whalley Range 2nd XI 1933
L. Skinner, G. Greenup, J. A. Darbyshire, J. A. Bertenshaw, W. J. Mountain, J. J. Butler
W. W. Land, F. R. Leroy (capt), A. Pitt
N. E. Hawley, H. Pickering, B. C. K. Ballinger

The photo above shows another of the 2nd XI teams from this season, captained by F. R. Leroy. Notable amongst the line-up is a teenage B. C. K. Ballinger. Brian Charles Keene Ballinger, who was actually born in Lincolnshire in about 1916, was a product of the nearby Hulme Grammar School, and would go on to represent the club for over 30 years, including a period where he was 1st XI captain, before his untimely passing in 1968, aged in his early fifties. Brian was also a superb goalkeeper for the Old

Hulmeians lacrosse team and was part of the team that won the Iroquois Cup after the war, and also represented Cheshire. Another new face in the line-up, is that of James Alec Bertenshaw (though known as Alec) who not only also played for the Whalley Range football team, but combined this with the role of being the football club's honorary secretary at one point prior to the War. Bearing in mind that Enid Grace Pickering was one of the tennis ladies who helped win the club's ladies' doubles trophy in 1938 and 1939, there is certainly a possibility that she is related to H. Pickering who also features in the previous team photo.

Following victory over Brooklands, W. Williamson scored 70 in a superb two-wicket win over Northwich for the 1st XI. The traditional Bank Holiday Monday game with Bowdon witnessed Whalley Range's second defeat of the season, in spite of 54 from Jack Woollam and an unbeaten 40 from G. H. Isherwood. In reply though, Bowdon got off to a great start with both openers reaching fifty, with J. D. Worthington going on to score 133 before being stumped by G. H. Isherwood off the bowling of Classen. Bowdon's final total was an impressive 252-7. Whalley Range conceded over 200 in the next game as well, as visitors Heaton Mersey rattled up 217, but Williamson's unbeaten 76 ensured Whalley Range a draw. Next, as the ensuing scoresheet shows, came a trip to Castleton in Rochdale, which saw Williamson acquire the century that he'd been destined to score all season, with a terrific unbeaten 109 out of a total of 233-7 declared, on the same ground that Ainsworth had scored a century the previous season. In reply, Castleton were dismissed for 128. Again, if Whalley Range had been competing for points this season, they would undoubtedly have been among the main challengers for the Stockton Trophy with their record of eight wins, eight draws, and just two defeats at this point.

Castleton v Whalley Range, at Sparth Bottoms, Saturday 19th August 1933

Whalley Range

R. N. Ainsworth	c Belmont	b Raby	11
H. B. Brooks	st Wild	b Heywood	1
J. P. V. Woollam		b Raby	0
W. Williamson		not out	109
R. Astin	c Wild	b Heywood	17
G. H. Isherwood	c Raby	b Nuttall	20
E. G. Widdows		b Raby	30
H. R. Classen	c Nuttall	b Belmont	13
A. J. Reeve		not out	12
Extras			20
Total		(for 7)	233

In the last three games of the season, Williamson's form deserted him, as did Whalley Range's as a result. Thus, defeat ensued to Buxton, which was followed by Bowdon rattling up 230-5 against them, though 55 from G. B. Brookes managed to stave off defeat. However, the following Saturday, in what would appear to have been the last game of the season, saw a heavy defeat to Chorlton-cum-Hardy who responded with 214-8, after the visitors had posted 120. Thus, even though the season had ended rather disappointingly, overall it was another successful and rewarding campaign for Whalley Range, and for Winston Williamson in particular.

After such a superb season the previous year, 1934 wouldn't quite live up to expectations, with six defeats, though most of these came in a bad patch around the time of July, when Whalley Range suffered the ignominy of five successive losses. At least the weather seemed very clement this season, with few if any matches cancelled because of rain, and again it seems that Whalley Range had enough resources to field four teams on various Saturdays.

The season kicked off on Saturday 21st April at Chorlton-cum-Hardy, where Whalley Range managed a draw, when seemingly set for victory. In the interbellum period, Whalley Range always commenced their season with a game against their local rivals, and during the 1920s always finished the season against them. During most of the 1930s, games against Bury in late September became the season's finale, though being so late in the year, were rarely reported on, though one assumes they may often have fallen victim to the weather anyway.

The first defeat of the season came in early May at home against Buxton, though E. G. Widdows with five wickets, ensured the result was very much in the balance until the end, with the visitors finishing on 175-9, in reply to the 167 posted by their hosts. In a midweek game against Hulme Grammar School, a below-strength Whalley Range 1st XI team responded with 144-4 to the visitors' total of 138, with R. N. Ainsworth guiding the home team to victory with a fine unbeaten 65.

In the next game, Jack Woollam scored a fine 61, as Whalley Range chased down South Manchester's 150 for the loss of just four wickets, and then made it successive fifties, with an unbeaten 56 in a drawn game at Brooklands. Two days later on the Bank Holiday Monday, Whalley Range won easily, with Cheadle Hulme skittled for just 54 with A. D. Thomson taking five wickets. The good form in May continued, with T. M. Tillotson scoring an unbeaten 58 out of a total of 173-7 against Heaton Mersey, though the home side clung on for a draw with 109-9. The month concluded with a good win over Knutsford, with G. Rothwell's five wickets helping remove the visitors for 77, before A. J. Reeve top-scored with an unbeaten 38 out of a total of 120.

June began with a comfortable win over Knutsford, whom they'd played the previous Saturday, with W. Williamson scoring 52 out of 180, whilst G. Rothwell's six wickets helped dismiss the hosts for 116. The next game was drawn against Stockport, with new recruit A. Rhodes scoring an unbeaten 42. Then came Whalley Range's annual midweek trip to Old Trafford, where the visitors posted a respectable 162, with opener H. R. Classen top-scoring with 35. The bowler taking most wickets for Manchester was Albert Edward Nutter who would go on to play 70 matches for Lancashire over the coming seasons. Another interestingly named player in this game was the Whalley Range last batsman, who was listed as N. O. Good! (though in defiance of his presumably fictitious name, he did actually fare okay, finishing with an unbeaten 9). Manchester replied with 124-2 to claim a draw.

The next game, in mid-June, saw Whalley Range making hay at Northwich, scoring 210-7 before declaring. The top scorer was W. Williamson, who batting in his traditional number four slot, fell just short of another century for the club, with 94. In reply, the hosts struggled against W. S. Thornton, who ended up with eight wickets as they were bowled out for 96. Williamson's superb form continued into the following weekend, where his unbeaten 81 formed the backbone of Whalley Range's total of 183-5 declared, though the visitors Cheetham Hill earned a draw, finishing on 114-5.

Whilst the 1st XI were making hay at Northwich, the 2nd XI were entertaining Hulme Grammar School, in what was very much a contest between past and present pupils. The hosts totalled just 127 with only Alan Roy Merchant with 24 and S. E. Woollam with 26, being able to contribute anything of note. The schoolboy inflicting most of the damage was a certain R. Mark who finished with figures of 5-41. The School then passed their visitors' total for the loss of just five wickets.

Sir Robert Mark GBE QPM

Sir Robert Mark pictured in later life

In later years (in 1942 according to one source), Robert Mark would be another Hulme Grammar schoolboy who would enrol with the **Whalley Range** club, and continue playing tennis for the club into the 1950s, along with his wife, Kathleen Mary Leahy, whom he'd married in 1941. His wife won the club's mixed doubles handicap event in 1955 partnering C. K. Sarkis.

Robert was born on 13th March 1917 in Chorlton-cum-Hardy, the youngest of five children, and after leaving Hulme Grammar School in 1935, Robert initially worked as a carpet salesman. Needing something more stimulating, he joined Manchester City Police in 1937, much to the dismay of his father, who protested that it was only one step better than going to prison! He joined Special Branch, the following year.

His rise through the ranks eventually saw him become Commissioner of the Metropolitan Police from 1972 to 1977, during which time he was knighted in 1973, and was awarded the GBE (Knight Grand Cross of the Order of the British Empire) in 1977, to add to the QPM (Queen's Police Medal), that he'd been awarded in 1965. During his time as Commissioner, he was frequently on the television screen, featuring in a series of adverts, endorsing a well-known make of tyre, with the catchphrase *"I'm convinced they're a major contribution to road safety"*!

Robert also excelled at lacrosse, and was a member of the Old Hulmeians team that won the Iroquois Cup in 1949 when they beat Cambridge University 12-4 in the final, and a year later, when they beat the same opposition 18-4. He also represented Lancashire.

In retirement he held several directorships and wrote his memoirs *"In the Office of Constable"*. Sadly, Sir Robert Mark passed away recently, on 30th September 2010, aged 93.

Returning to Whalley Range 1st XI's cricket season, there then came a really bad patch with five successive defeats. Considering they'd only lost one game prior to this during the season, it was a perplexing turnaround in form. The rut started by being bowled out for just 76 against Castleton, before the visitors replied with 168. Admittedly, the next defeat was against a strong Manchester team, though opener R. N. Ainsworth prospered well, scoring 59. The next defeat was a game that Whalley Range looked destined to win for most of the time, before a late collapse saw them lose at Cheadle Hulme. The hosts had posted 150 with E. G. Widdows claiming seven wickets, but with the visitors getting off to a solid start through openers Ainsworth (71) and Rhodes (27), ably supported by the next two batsmen, Jack Woollam and Winston Williamson, victory looked inevitable. However, after all of the first four batsmen had made double-figures, sadly this was not something achieved by any that followed, with the next highest score being just 6, and in the end, Whalley Range lost by just four runs. Whalley Range lost heavily in the next game, away to South Manchester, before making it five defeats in a row, at home against Brooklands.

When the losing sequence was finally ended, it really was quelled in some style, with Ainsworth scoring yet another century for the club, in a total of 172-6 declared, before Northwich were bowled out for a mere 52.

Whalley Range v Northwich, at Whalley Range, Saturday 4th August 1934

Whalley Range

R. N. Ainsworth	c Taylor	b Wych	105
G. T. Mountain	c Riley	b Robinson	23
E. G. Widdows		b Whalley	0
W. Williamson		b Whalley	9
A. J. Reeve	c Holland	b Taylor	7
G. Rothwell	c Robinson	b Taylor	4
G. Greenup		not out	15
Extras			9
Total		(for 6 dec)	172

In the next weekend's game, Whalley Range were just one wicket away from victory over Heaton Mersey, when time ran out. It was a game in which H. R. Classen relished being opener again, top-scoring with 60. Further victories ensued against Castleton, with W. Williamson scoring 62 and A. Horrocks taking six wickets, and against Buxton who were bowled out for just 67. In a drawn game with Bowdon, Whalley Range rattled up 178-7 with E. G. Widdows scoring an unbeaten 54, whilst Classen, again as opener, scored 31 for the second game in a row. At home against Chorlton, the visitors batted first and amassed 187-7 before declaring. In reply, Whalley Range nearly pulled off a fine win, finishing on 181-6, with A. Rhodes the top-scorer with 41. The final game of the season was supposed to be at home against Bury in late September, though it was a game that went unreported.

Like the previous season, 1935 was another year of strange fortunes. Early in the season, from the back-end of April through May, there were four defeats with the Whalley Range batting line-up misfiring quite badly, apart from a comfortable win over the local Hulme Grammar School. However a remarkable game against Stockport at the end of May seemed to galvanise Whalley Range's season quite drastically. Thereafter, throughout the rest of the campaign, there were eleven wins, three draws, and just the one defeat, and a very narrow one at that.

Whalley Range's season was supposed to start on Saturday 20th April at Hardy Lane in Chorlton, though it seems likely that the game did not get played, since no reports appeared in the local press, and it was a rainy weekend. Thus, in all probability, Whalley Range's season kicked off in earnest the following Saturday at Cheetham Hill. However, they were sent packing for just 53, a total that was easily overhauled by the hosts. Whalley Range then lost at home to Buxton, before entertaining Hulme Grammar School, who were shot out for 85, with A. D. Thomson taking 5-26. The home team responded with 182-8, with the runs spread around most of the batsmen. It was only a temporary relief from their bad start to the season though, as they followed this up with defeat against South Manchester, albeit by just three runs in a tight affair, despite the efforts of opener R. N. Ainsworth who scored 52. The next game was at Brooklands, where the hosts batted first, but seven wickets from A. D. Thomson, restricted them to 131. However, when Whalley Range batted, wickets quickly fell, and in the end they slipped to their fourth defeat of the season already, though 26 runs from W. S. Thornton batting at number ten, meant the final losing margin was just nine runs.

Whalley Range 1st XI 1935
R. N. Ainsworth, G. Rothwell, G. H. Isherwood, W. S. Thornton, G. B. Brookes, E. G. Widdows
S. Pilkington, J. P. V. Woollam, H. R. Classen (capt), A. D. Thomson, A. Horrocks

Next came the remarkable game against Stockport, where for the first time this season against a fellow team from the Association, the Whalley Range batting finally got into their stride, amassing 231-6 before declaring, with G. Rothwell, batting at number three, falling just short of his century, being run out for a superb 98. Amazingly, Stockport responded with exactly the same score, 231-6, where again their top-scorer was also just deprived of a century, with one of their openers (J. H. Briggs) scoring 98 before being caught behind by S. Pilkington off the bowling of A. Horrocks. It was actually a game the visitors perhaps should have won, since having drawn level, they lost their sixth wicket to what turned out to be the last ball of the game, before time ran out.

From here on in, from the start of June to the end of the season, Whalley Range played some supreme cricket, especially when batting second, as they chased down some imposing targets with apparent ease. The first of these successful run chases was at home against Knutsford, with the hosts responding with 157-6 after Knutsford had posted 125. Dolph Classen, again back in his role as opener, admirably led his troops with a fine 41. Admittedly the target set by Northwich (53 all out) in the next game wasn't too excessive, but W. Williamson (46) ensured there was no slipping up, as Whalley Range again closed on 157, this time for the loss of five wickets. On the following Monday, Whalley Range were without a few key players, including Classen the captain, and suffered as a result. Only two players made double-figures as the hosts were shot out for just 71. However the bowling of A. D. Thomson nearly rescued the game for Whalley Range, taking five wickets, though in the end, the visitors just scraped home on 73-9.

In the next reported game, at home to Cheetham Hill, Whalley Range again seemed to struggle when batting first, this time posting just 91. However, six wickets from A. Horrocks brought about a superb win with the visitors dismissed for just 73. Perhaps aware of their apparent fallibility when batting first, of the remaining 11 games reported on in the season, Whalley Range never ever batted first! One assumes they must have won the toss a few times during this period, so clearly Whalley Range were a lot more comfortable chasing targets, as indeed proved to be the case.

The next game saw visitors Castleton dismissed for exactly 100, with W. S. Thornton capturing seven wickets. Thanks to 67 from W. Williamson and 58 from J. P. V. Woollam, Whalley Range responded with an impressive 263-6, to claim a very easy win. Then came the visit of the strong Manchester team, who scored 175-4 before declaring. Williamson made it successive fifties with 52, and with 45 from E. G. Widdows, the hosts managed to ensure a draw, finishing on 148-6.

On Thursday 11th July 1935 at St. Margaret's Church in Whalley Range, Norman Alexander Barber married Constance "Connie" Mary Mark, the elder daughter of John Mark. Connie was the sister of Robert Mark, thus establishing a quite unique bond between the two families, since as mentioned previously, N. A. Barber would go on to be rewarded with an MBE, whilst Sir Robert Mark (along with being knighted of course!) would receive the GBE.

There then followed a brilliant run of six successive victories, where Whalley Range chased down the opposition totals of 150, 179, 139, 131, 173, and 171. It was a supreme team effort, though there'd be some fine individual performances as well, with two players scoring centuries. In the first of these games, at Cheadle Hulme (who'd go on to top the league and therefore win the Stockton Trophy this season), E. G. Widdows was again in fine form, this time with both bat and ball. His seven wickets helped remove the hosts for 150, before he followed this up with a score of 46. Also in the runs were Old Hulmeians, W. B. Stansby with a fine 55, and W. Williamson with 49, as Whalley Range finished on a winning total of 178-7. In the next game, South Manchester posted 179, but again this proved insufficient in the face of the rampant Whalley Range batting line-up who replied with 182-8 for a stunning win. The runs were fairly evenly distributed, with openers G. Rothwell (30) and H. R. Classen (38) getting them off to a good start before most other batsmen chipped in, including 35 from W. Williamson. The last game in July was at Brooklands where the hosts posted 139. This was superbly chased down with opener G. Rothwell contributing 52 out of a total of 142-8.

Almost a year to the day since R. N. Ainsworth got a century in the same match the previous season, it was the turn of another opener to register a century, as G. Rothwell continued his fine form scoring a brilliant 112, as Whalley Range replied with 203-3 after the visitors Northwich had scored 131.

Whalley Range v Northwich, at Whalley Range, Saturday 3rd August 1935
Whalley Range

H. R. Classen	lbw	b Mills	46
G. Rothwell	c Holland	b Schofield	112
J. P. V. Woollam		b Schofield	8
E. G. Widdows		not out	34
R. N. Ainsworth		not out	1
Extras			2
Total		(for 3)	203

Amazingly, there was another century for Whalley Range just two days later on the Bank Holiday Monday at Bowdon, where with a midday start, the hosts had batted first and posted a respectable 173. In reply, Whalley Range lost Rothwell (who'd earlier claimed five wickets), Woollam, and Widdows fairly cheaply, before a partnership began to develop between Classen and Ainsworth. When Ainsworth fell for 28, followed by a succession of cheap wickets, it seemed as if Whalley Range's supreme sequence of run chases was about to falter. However, opener Dolph Classen was still standing firm, and when he gained vital support from number ten batsman W. S. Thornton, this enabled him to not only go on and complete a brilliant and deserved unbeaten century, but guide his team to another sensational victory when batting second. At the ripe old age of 58, it really was a supreme effort from the long-standing Whalley Range captain :-

Bowdon v Whalley Range, at Bowdon, Monday 5th August 1935

Whalley Range

G. Rothwell		b J. Gilbody	7
H. R. Classen		not out	106
J. P. V. Woollam	c Dugdale	b A. Gilbody	10
E. G. Widdows		b J. Gilbody	1
R. N. Ainsworth		b Jackson	28
G. B. Brookes	c Pierson	b Jackson	1
G. H. Isherwood	c Eaves	b J. Gilbody	8
A. D. Thomson		b Kennedy	2
A. Horrocks		b A. Gilbody	0
W. S. Thornton		not out	15
S. Pilkington			-
Extras			7
Total		(for 8)	185

On the following Saturday, visitors Heaton Mersey posted 171, but again it wasn't sufficient to deny the irrepressible Whalley Range batting line-up, who replied with 173-6. Openers G. Rothwell and Dolph Classen got the home team off to a solid start, both scoring 35, before W. B. Stansby at number three, carried on the good work with 34. It was then left to G. H. Isherwood and W. S. Thornton to guide the team to their sixth successive successful run chase.

The sequence was ended when Castleton amassed 222-8 before declaring. For once, the Whalley Range batting wasn't up to the task, and settled for a draw. It was a similar story when Bowdon came visiting, before the arrival of Chorlton in early September saw Whalley Range return to winning ways in the most emphatic of fashions. Batting first, the visitors were unable to deal with A. Horrocks, as they were routed for just 26, with Horrocks finishing with an eight-wicket haul, to set up an easy win :-

Whalley Range v Chorlton, at Whalley Range, Saturday 7th September 1935

Chorlton				Whalley Range			
R. Berry	c Land	b Horrocks	7	J. P. V. Woollam		not out	15
G. H. Whittingham	c Williamson	b Horrocks	1	R. N. Ainsworth	lbw	b Bailey	0
J. L. Morland		b Horrocks	2	G. H. Isherwood	lbw	b Gates	12
A. H. S. Guthrie	c Williamson	b Horrocks	1	W. Williamson		not out	3
S. E. Clapham		b Grimshaw	6				
H. A. Lester		b Grimshaw	0				
M. Bailey	c Isherwood	b Horrocks	1				
F. Mather		not out	2				
J. H. Bond	c Isherwood	b Horrocks	0				
A. B. Maddocks	c Pilkington	b Horrocks	0				
G. Gates	lbw	b Horrocks	2				
Extras			4	Extras			0
Total			26	Total		(for 2)	30

The 1936 season kicked off with Whalley Range playing Chorlton-cum-Hardy at Hardy Lane. The Chorlton team comprised virtually the same side that had been bowled out for just 26 towards the end of the previous season, and A. Horrocks was once more in the Whalley Range team. However, on their own turf, Chorlton this time managed 180-6 before declaring. The visitors settled for a draw, closing on 77-5.

Again this season, Whalley Range cricket was blessed with a surfeit of players, so the Whalley Range 1st XI that won at Buxton in early May was just one of four teams that played that day, with E. G. Widdows scoring an unbeaten 50 as Whalley Range closed on 174-5 in reply to Buxton's 113. During the week, Whalley Range also entertained Hulme Grammar School, who were duly dismissed for 79 with A. Horrocks claiming 6-23. With a slightly weakened team, the home side then struggled to reach their target, doing so with just one wicket intact, before finally ending on 81 all out. Widdows was in the runs again the following Saturday, scoring 56, whilst R. N. Ainsworth scored 54, as the hosts replied with 171 after South Manchester had been bowled out for just 79. The following week witnessed Whalley Range's annual pilgrimage to Old Trafford, and having got off to a solid start through openers Classen (27) and G. Rothwell (24), the visitors finally posted a very respectable 186-9 declared with all of G. B. Brookes (22), A. Horrocks (28), and A. D. Thomson (23 not out) also doing well. As always, the Manchester batting line-up was quite a formidable one, and included the likes of Greenhalgh and Harry Makepeace. However the wickets soon started tumbling, and Whalley Range sensed another notable victory over their illustrious opponents. However, opener Garlick, who would go on to make 44 appearances for Lancashire over the coming seasons was immovable, and in the end Manchester hung on grimly, closing on 81-8.

Whalley Range's superb aptitude at chasing down targets that had really come to the fore the previous season, was still very much in evidence the following Saturday at Brooklands, where the hosts posted a respectable 194, only to see Whalley Range overhaul it with apparent ease. The main scorers in Whalley Range's reply of 198-6 were W. B. Stansby with 76, and Williamson with 49. Williamson made sure of his fifty in the following game, scoring 78 out of a total of 187-9, in a drawn game with Stockport.

Interestingly enough for this weekend, Whalley Range again fielded four teams, this time advertised as 1st XI, 2nd XI, 3rd XI, plus Whalley Range 'A'. Note that very few other teams at this time fielded three teams, let alone four, thus illustrating the considerable membership that the club was continuing to attract. In past seasons, where there had been four games on the Saturday, the handbook had invariably listed these as a 1st XI game, with the other three matches listed in the 2nd XI fixture list, with the 3rd XI fixture list generally reserved for just midweek evening matches. This season, apart from the case in early May already described, the tendency was to list any fourth game on a Saturday, as a 3rd XI fixture. Thus this season's 3rd XI fixture list in the handbook, comprised 21 games of which nine were on a Wednesday evening, eight were scheduled for Thursday evening, whilst the other games were normal Saturday games. The midweek fixtures, which all had a scheduled start time of 6:30pm, were local affairs against the likes of Bowdon, Brooklands, Cheetham Hill, Chorlton, Heaton Mersey, South West Manchester, and Stockport.

Whalley Range also made 187 against Cheadle Hulme, but the hosts responded with 206-9 in spite of a five-wicket haul from A. D. Thomson. Whalley Range lost the next match as well, as Knutsford chased down the visitors' total of 146 with three wickets to spare, though W. Williamson was again in fine form with the bat, scoring 57. Winning ways were restored in the return game the following weekend, with Whalley Range declaring on 154-6, with opener H. R. Classen top-scoring with 53. Knutsford were then removed for just 74 with E. G. Widdows claiming a seven-wicket haul.

Over the next few games, through most of July and August, Whalley Range didn't prosper too well with a series of draws and losses, and few if any performances of note, apart from a five-wicket haul from W. S. Thornton in the defeat at Bowdon. It was in the return game with Bowdon, at the end of August, that Whalley Range finally rediscovered their form. The visitors posted 163, but Whalley Range overhauled this comfortably, thanks mainly to the efforts of the two openers, G. Rothwell and R. N. Ainsworth, who contributed 61 and 77 respectively, to the Whalley Range reply of 171-2. It looks like the few remaining games in the season were adversely affected by the weather, since there were no further reports in the local press this season.

For the 1937 season, there was very much a "changing of the guard". After more than 20 years as 1st XI captain, a stint that had begun before the First World War, Dolph Classen finally relinquished his role as 1st XI captain, passing on the mantle to J. P. V. Woollam. Also, K. T. S. Dockray stood down as President of the club after several years in the role, and was replaced by Dolph Classen, who in taking up his new position, ceded his role of Honorary Secretary to W. W. Land, though he did maintain his position as Honorary Treasurer. A new position of Club Chairman was also introduced this season, with F. R. Leroy being the first to take on this role.

As was traditional, Whalley Range's 1937 season was supposed to begin at Hardy Lane against Chorlton, though no relevant reports appeared in the local press, so one assumes that the fixture, being so early in the year, again fell victim to the April showers. There was some activity in April though, with

Whalley Range overhauling Cheetham Hill's 97, with E. G. Widdows contributing 52 out of a total of 116-9, ably supported by Astin who scored 37 coming in at number eight.

Once more, this would be a season when the sport of cricket was really thriving at this level, and certain Saturdays would again witness Whalley Range fielding four teams, though this time the fourth side was always labelled as Whalley Range 'A' in the local press, even though the handbook would have these particular games listed in the 3rd XI fixture list, which again included Wednesday and Thursday evening games for the most part.

With such strength in numbers, the 1st XI started the season off in fine style. Following their victory over Cheetham Hill, they went on to win all of their first four games, with further victories over Buxton, Hulme Grammar School, and South Manchester, with the main highlight being an unbeaten 59 from W. B. Stansby in the game against the school. However, the following weekend saw Whalley Range lose by over 100 runs at Brooklands.

For the Bank Holiday Monday, neither of the 1st XI and 2nd XI games against Cheadle Hulme were subsequently reported on, though a further 2nd XI fixture at Ashley starting at 11:30 in the morning, did make the local press. The hosts were dismissed for just 63 with Rains capturing six wickets. Despite chasing such a low target, the fact that Whalley Range 2nd XI did win this game was virtually down to just one man, namely Peter Butler, who was less than a fortnight short of his 24th birthday. Of the first eight batsmen, five were out for ducks, but thankfully Ernest Charles Peter Butler (to give him his full title) scored 58 out of a final total of 86, to ensure victory. Peter was the son of John James Butler, who is the umpire in a couple of the Whalley Range 2nd XI team photos from the early 1930s (as previously shown) and who served on the club's General Committee from 1933 until his passing away in 1949.

Two days later on Whit-Wednesday came what appears to have been Whalley Range's first ever visit to Weaste (based in Salford, in the shadow of the Salford RLFC ground) where the hosts posted 172. Whalley Range's reply started confidently enough through openers G. H. Isherwood (27) and R. Astin (21), but in the end, despite 49 from E. G. Widdows, the visitors finished just nine runs adrift. Widdows' fine form continued into the next game, where he contributed 91 out of 183-7 declared, against Knutsford. The visitors were bowled out for 95, with W. W. Land taking seven wickets and a catch.

The Whit-Friday game against Heaton Mersey evaded the local press, but it is known from the handbook, that Ralph Astin scored 46. This was followed by a superb win at home against Knutsford, the following day on Whit-Saturday. The visitors declared having put 155-8 on the board, but this was not enough to deny Whalley Range victory, who countered with 163-5, thanks to 66 from Astin, and an unbeaten 40 from R. N. Ainsworth.

June was welcomed in with the return game against Weaste. Whalley Range notched up 179-8 before declaring, with A. J. Reeve top-scoring with 58, before Weaste replied with 105-7. Whalley Range had to be content with a draw the following Saturday as well, with Knutsford just hanging on with 95-9. Earlier, Whalley Range had posted 186-4 declared, thanks mainly to openers Ralph Astin and Jack Woollam, who scored 52 and 45 respectively. Ainsworth also had a good game, scoring an unbeaten 36, before capturing six wickets, and taking a stumping.

The following Saturday, one of the 2nd XI teams was up against Prestwich Mental Hospital, where one assumes they played against the staff, as opposed to the patients! Meanwhile the 1st XI were involved in a strange encounter at Cheetham Hill. Whalley Range appeared to be cruising along at one stage, with opener R. Astin having scored 69, and R. N. Ainsworth apparently well on his way to getting a fifty as well. However, the last six batsmen between them, made just six runs, including four ducks, and suddenly Ainsworth was stranded on 49 not out, with Whalley Range all out for 163, when a score in excess of 200 looked highly probable. This late collapse proved costly, as the hosts replied with 178-6 to win the game. Whalley Range saw out June with a second successive defeat, with Castleton responding with 173-6 after the hosts had scored 168, with opener Astin scoring 57, his fourth fifty of the season, and his third in succession. New recruit C. Gardiner claimed five of the six wickets to fall.

July started with draws against both Manchester and Cheadle Hulme, with R. N. Ainsworth scoring an unbeaten 63 in the former game, whilst W. B. Stansby scored exactly 50 in the latter. Later in the month, Whalley Range had a good victory over Brooklands, with Ralph Astin carrying his bat with an unbeaten 76 out of 131. Whalley Range ended the month with a second successive win, away at Northwich, with G. Rothwell top-scoring with an unbeaten 44.

As alluded to earlier, the handbook that survives from this season belonged to Ralph Astin, to which he added all of his batting scores. His five fifties from this season have already been highlighted, plus there would be a further four scores in the forties. The net result of all this consistent batting would be a very impressive tally of 729 runs at an average of 33.14 come the close of the 1st XI campaign.

Dolph's Farewell 1st XI Appearance

Two years earlier, the traditional August Bank Holiday Monday encounter at Bowdon, had witnessed the then 58-year-old Whalley Range captain Dolph Classen score a sensational century to guide his team to victory. This season, having now turned 60, Dolph decided that this same fixture would thus provide the most fitting and ideal opportunity to bring to a close his playing days for the 1st XI. To mark this truly momentous occasion, Dolph was presented with a bat by the Bowdon players inscribed as follows: *"To H. R. Classen, from a few friends at Bowdon, August 2nd 1937."* The bat is further decorated with the signatures of many of the players of both teams, though sadly the passing of time has rendered most of these now barely discernible.

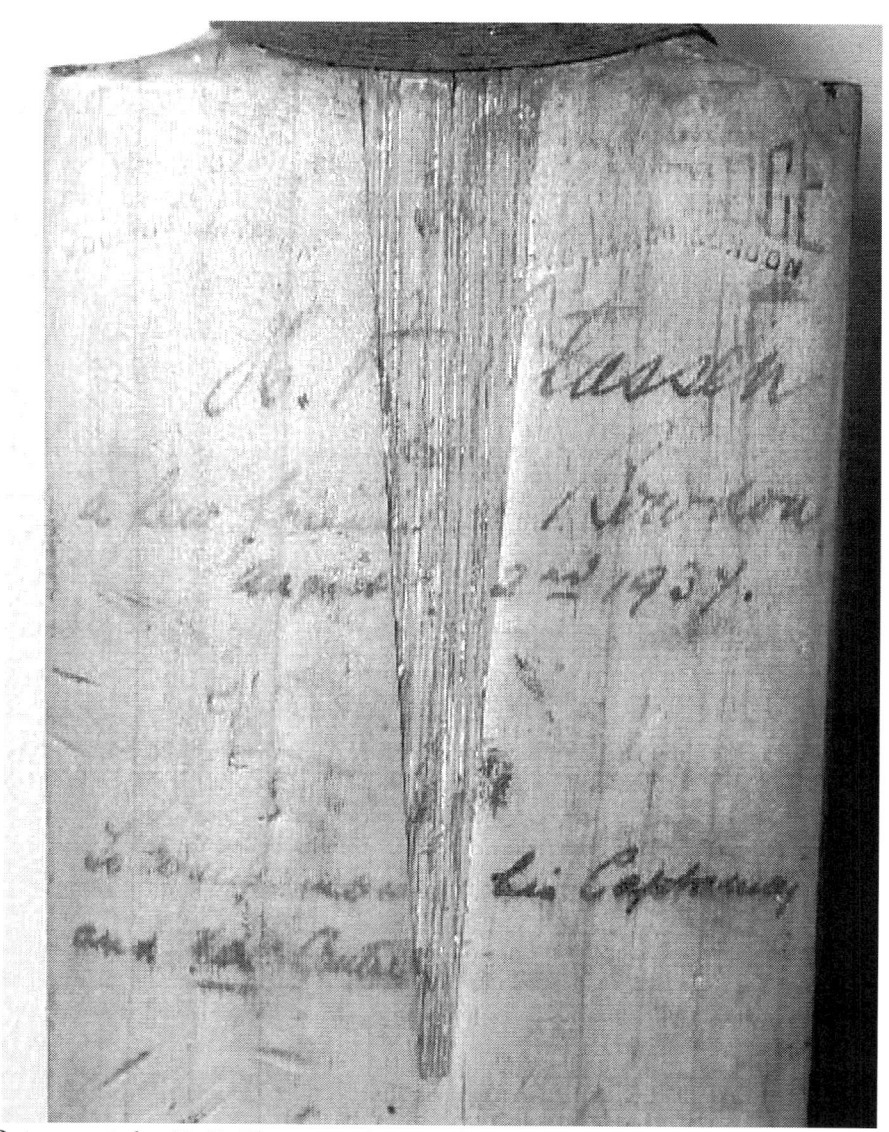

Bat presented to H. R. Classen on the occasion of his final appearance for the 1st XI

Having first played for the 1st XI at the back-end of the previous century, it really was a remarkable effort by Dolph to have represented the team for so many years, whilst also captaining them for most of that time. Dolph would still play for the 2nd XI in the next couple of seasons, whilst also continuing in the roles of both Club President and Honorary Treasurer. Ralph Astin would later replace him as Honorary Treasurer in 1955, though Dolph continued in his role as President for the best part of two decades, up until his passing away in 1956. As for the game with Bowdon itself, as the ensuing scoresheet illustrates, the hosts weren't quite as generous on the pitch, rattling up 241-7 declared, with G. K. Eaves scoring 110 before being caught and bowled by Widdows. Dolph then opened the innings for Whalley Range with Astin, though sadly in his last outing for the 1st XI, Dolph was run out for 20 and the visitors succumbed to a fairly heavy defeat.

Bowdon v Whalley Range, at Bowdon, Monday 2nd August 1937

Bowdon				Whalley Range			
A. G. Gilbody		b Horrocks	7	R. Astin		b J. Gilbody	16
W. Hanbidge		b Gardiner	42	H. R. Classen		run out	20
G. K. Eaves	c &	b Widdows	110	W. B. Stansby		b J. Gilbody	5
J. D. Worthington	c Gardiner	b Classen	7	W. Williamson		b J. Gilbody	29
G. F. Dugdale		b Widdows	35	E. G. Widdows		b A. Gilbody	19
G. P. Shaw	lbw	b Gardiner	5	R. N. Ainsworth		b A. Gilbody	2
K. A. Quas-Cohen	c Woollam	b Gardiner	0	G. B. Brookes	c Walton	b A. Gilbody	0
W. H. Booth		not out	3	J. P. V. Woollam	c Walton	b J. Gilbody	5
R. G. Shaw		not out	8	W. S. Thornton	c Walton	b A. Gilbody	28
D. N. Walton			-	A. Horrocks	lbw	b J. Gilbody	8
J. A. Gilbody			-	C. Gardiner		not out	4
Extras			24	Extras			8
Total		(for 7)	241	Total			144

The following week, it was Whalley Range who batted first and posted an imposing target, amassing 225-5 before declaring against Heaton Mersey. Openers R. Astin (46) and J. P. V. Woollam (43) got them off to a solid start before E. G. Widdows and G. Rothwell carried on the good work, and just as both were heading for their fifties, Widdows was out for 48. This wicket prompted the declaration, thus leaving the unfortunate Rothwell on 49 not out! Heaton Mersey replied with 148-1. It appears the rest of August was simply washed away, since no further reports appeared in the local press this month.

In the remaining games of the season, W. Williamson scored an unbeaten 71 in a comfortable win over Chorlton, whilst opener G. H. Isherwood scored exactly 50 in an enthralling game with Bury, who at the close were just four runs shy of the Whalley Range total with just one wicket remaining. Six wickets from C. Gardiner proved crucial in rebuffing Bury's endeavours to snatch victory, though not quite enough to help his own team be victorious.

During the season that had just concluded, N. E. Hawley had played alongside G. R. Vlies, in some of the Whalley Range 2nd XI games. Born in 1909, Norman Edgar Hawley was the son of Tom and Mary Evelyn Hawley, whilst Gordon Richard Vlies, who was born on 18th April 1914, was the son of Harry Huson Vlies and Blanche Lydia Vlies (nee Wood). In 1924-25, H. H. Vlies had actually been president of the Old Hulmeians Association, a position that G. R. Vlies would also be honoured with, nearly 50 years later in 1973-74. More pertinent to the affairs of N. E. Hawley though, was that G. R. Vlies had an elder sister, Nora Huson Vlies, born in about 1911, and one assumes that it was through his team-mate that he became acquainted with her, since on October 7th 1937, at St. Margaret's Church in Whalley Range, Norman Edgar Hawley and Nora Huson Vlies tied the knot. Following on from such a happy occasion, sadly the next significant event involving the club, was the passing away of one of Whalley Range's most beloved sons.

F. R. Leroy – RIP

Towards the end of the year, F. R. Leroy, one of Whalley Range's true stalwarts, having been a member of the club for 40 years, sadly passed away. He had first taken on the position of 2nd XI captain in 1901, a role he had maintained ever since, for an amazing span of 37 years in charge, and had only this past season, also taken on the new role of Club Chairman. The following obituary appeared in the Guardian on 21st December 1937 :-

The death, after a long and severe illness, of F. R. Leroy will come as a severe loss to sportsmen in Manchester and district. His genial personality will be greatly missed, and club cricket has lost one of its staunchest supporters. He was a member of the Lancashire County Cricket Club, and for 35 years he captained the Whalley Range Cricket Club second eleven. He was captain of South Manchester Hockey Club for many years, and represented Lancashire as long ago as 1901 and captained the side. His services to hockey earned him the presidency of the Lancashire County Hockey Association in 1920-1. He was also for many years a playing member of the Chorlton Golf Club. He was in his fifty-seventh year.

During the winter, the Old Hulmeians lacrosse team were again performing well, and in February 1938 beat Mellor, the holders for the past three years, 13-8 in the semi-final of the North of England Senior Flags competition at Heaton Mersey to reach their tenth final in this competition. However, they were unable to add to their tally of six previous titles, losing 6-8 in a close and keenly contested final against Old Waconians on 26th March at Fallowfield. Representing the Old Hulmeians in the final that day were Whalley Range members, G. W. Orr, G. R. Vlies, and N. A. Barber.

The start of the 1938 season found captain and opener J. P. V. Woollam in fine form. In the first game, at Chorlton, his 43 along with Stansby's 50 secured a comfortable win, whilst in the second game his innings of 88 ensured Whalley Range escaped with a draw against Cheetham Hill. The arrival of May then saw W. Williamson notch up another century. This was his third known century for the club, having previously scored unbeaten hundreds against South Manchester in 1928, and Castleton in 1933. Buxton had batted first and scored 151. Then after Woollam and Stansby had fallen cheaply, Astin and Williamson forged a brilliant partnership that was finally ended when Astin was run out, by which time the result was no longer in doubt. Williamson went on to complete his century, finishing on 101 not out, as Whalley Range closed on 176-5.

Whalley Range v Buxton, at Whalley Range, Saturday 7th May 1938

Whalley Range

J. P. V. Woollam	lbw	b Harding	8
R. Astin		run out	61
W. B. Stansby		b Rushworth	1
W. Williamson		not out	101
E. G. Widdows	c &	b Sowler	1
R. N. Ainsworth	c Locke	b Sowler	3
Extras			1
Total		(for 5)	176

After a draw against South Manchester, opener Astin was in the runs again, scoring an unbeaten 90 at Brooklands, out of a total of 210-4 declared. Whalley Range couldn't force the win though, with the home team finishing on 135-9. Next came the traditional trip to Old Trafford and what an exquisite exhibition of cricket was produced. Despite the early loss of four quick wickets, the visitors' middle-order batted superbly. Ainsworth was the first to steady the ship with 34, before G. B. Brookes with 59, and G. H. Isherwood with 58, really got the scoreboard moving. Whalley Range's final total was a superb 205. Playing for the Manchester side was A. Rhodes, who'd played for Whalley Range a few seasons earlier. Rhodes also possibly represented Lancashire, since someone called Albert Rhodes played for Lancashire between 1922 and 1924, but the Rhodes in question here, is perhaps more likely to be Cecil A. Rhodes, who represented the county between 1937 and 1938. Either way, there is too much uncertainty to state for definite, precisely which if any of the two Lancashire players, this was. As it happened, Rhodes had a big part to play against his former team-mates, scoring an unbeaten 58, as the hosts responded with an impressive 231-2 to claim a superb win. Earlier, opener Greenhalgh had scored 59 for the home team, before Fred Demetrius Beattie, who'd played five times for Lancashire in the 1932 season, along with Rhodes guided Manchester to victory with an unbeaten 66.

At the start of June, Whalley Range beat Northwich by over 100 runs, with the visitors bowled out for just 50, with E. G. Widdows doing most of the damage with six wickets. Two days later on the Bank Holiday Monday, Whalley Range enjoyed another resounding win, beating Cheadle Hulme by 97 runs, thanks to a five-wicket haul from Widdows. Whalley Range had batted first, and declared on 210-8. This was the second time in a few weeks that Whalley Range had declared on 210, regardless of any imminent individual milestones. On the previous occasion, it had been Astin who was denied the chance to go for his century. This time it was Williamson, who was 89 not out at the time of the declaration, though he at least had the satisfaction of already having scored a century this season. On Whit-Wednesday, Whalley Range scored 147, before Weaste were laid to waste for 77, to record another easy win, with A. Horrocks capturing five wickets. The following day, Wythenshawe were also well beaten by Whalley Range 2nd XI, with W. S. Grimshaw taking five wickets and scoring 90, a performance that would see him playing for the 1st XI at the weekend.

On Whit-Friday, Whalley Range rattled up 208 against Heaton Mersey, with former Hulme Grammar schoolboy Eric Boyd Jackson scoring 55, and A. J. Reeve scoring 52. However in spite of five wickets from A. D. Thomson, the home team hung on for a draw, finishing on 168-9. Whit-Saturday witnessed Whalley Range travelling to Knutsford where they removed their hosts for 92, with A. Horrocks taking six wickets, before winning easily with 152-5.

The next game saw Whalley Range draw against Weaste with opener G. H. Isherwood top-scoring with 45, before along came another game where Whalley Range's declaration again seemed a tad untimely. Not only were the team just one run short of a significant milestone, declaring on 199-5, but so was Widdows, who was left on 49 not out. The previous declarations this season would have been enforced by Jack Woollam, but he wasn't playing in this game, so presumably he can't be held accountable for this one as well! Earlier, opener Astin had top-scored with 72. Perhaps it was being deprived of his fifty that fired up Widdows for his bowling, as his six wickets helped dismiss Cheetham Hill for just 90, to leave Whalley Range victorious by over 100 runs.

At the start of July, Whalley Range drew with Castleton with Horrocks taking five wickets and opener Astin top-scoring with an unbeaten 46. After a couple of presumably wet weekends, Whalley Range's next reported game, was another where Horrocks captured five wickets, and opener Astin again top-scored with 46. The main difference this time though, was that Whalley Range were victorious, replying with 154, after South Manchester had been bowled out for 95. July was completed with a good win over Brooklands, with E. G. Widdows scoring 79.

A couple of days later, August was welcomed in with the traditional Bank Holiday visit to Bowdon, where the early start allowed the hosts to post a sizeable 253-5 before declaring. Opener Astin again led from the front, scoring 56 before being bowled, to help Whalley Range secure a respectable draw with a total of 206-7. Amazingly, for the second time this season, E. G. Widdows was left marooned on 49 not out. In what was now turning out to be a very successful season for Whalley Range, August witnessed further wins over Heaton Mersey and Castleton, with both Horrocks and Widdows taking five wickets in the latter game, with Castleton dismissed for just 59.

The last game in August saw another Whalley Range batsman seemingly on his way to a century when the declaration came. In fact, it was Jack Woollam himself who was the man in question this time, scoring an unbeaten 90 out of 177-7, though Buxton ultimately hung on for a draw. Having deprived others of personal milestones at the expense of the team's best interests, it seems only right and proper that he should adopt the same stringent policy for himself! In fact, at this time with teams batting second often continuing past their target with the game already won, it seems that there was more chance of getting a century when batting second, when the threat of an untimely declaration did not loom large!

Sadly at the start of September, one of Whalley Range's former stars, F. L. Steel, who was now in his eighty-fourth year, passed away, in Argyll, Scotland. Later in the month, Whalley Range lost to Chorlton having declared too early, though admittedly there were no batsmen deprived of personal milestones on this occasion. The following weekend saw a second-string Whalley Range team beating Ashley, with A. Davey taking five wickets.

Appearing for Whalley Range 2nd XI during the 1938 season was D. M. Arrandale. After the war, Dennis Matthew Arrandale would be a member of the Old Hulmeians lacrosse team that won the Iroquois Cup, and in later life, he would become Assistant Director for the Manchester Chamber of Commerce and Industry, and be awarded an MBE for services to export in 1980.

The 1939 season would see Whalley Range at the pinnacle of their game, having continued to blossom into a really potent and brilliant team. Throughout the season, of the nineteen 1st XI games that were reported on, just two would end in defeat, as the Whalley Range batsmen invariably put the opposition bowlers to the sword, including a wonderful Whit-Week which saw them sail past 250 on three separate occasions. However, the season would end on a much more sombre note, with the onset of the Second World War at the start of September. Thus for many players at the club, this season would prove to be their last, and tragically for some, this would be in the worst way imaginable.

The season started at Chorlton-cum-Hardy, where Whalley Range batting first, amassed 210-6 before declaring. Opener J. P. V. Woollam scored 50, whilst W. Williamson scored an unbeaten 71. The hosts were then dismissed for 108. Maybe Whalley Range were aiming to declare on their favourite declaration score again in the second game, but the fall of a wicket, prompted the closure on 206-8. The main scorers were opener R. Astin with 59, and W. B. Stansby with 79, though Cheetham Hill comfortably secured a draw. The next game, at home against Buxton, was also drawn.

Whalley Range's superb season continued as they again scored in excess of 200, replying with an impressive 221-3 to South Manchester's total of 170. Widdows took six wickets but the main star of the show was R. N. Ainsworth with yet another century for Whalley Range, to guide them to victory :-

Whalley Range v South Manchester, at Whalley Range, Saturday 13th May 1939

Whalley Range

J. P. V. Woollam	b Brunt	18
R. Astin	run out	48
R. N. Ainsworth	not out	100
W. Williamson	st Sharp b Derbyshire	43
E. G. Widdows	not out	1
Extras		11
Total	(for 3)	221

Also in the runs in May were A. I. Robinson (94) and J. G. Davenport (50) who shared a fourth-wicket partnership of 123 out of 206-7 declared, for the 2nd XI when beating Hulme Grammar School by over 100 runs. James Gradwell Davenport had played a few seasons for Manchester YMCA in the late 1920s, before joining Whalley Range in 1930, a club he remained faithful to for quite some years to come, and appears in the 2nd XI team photo from 1946 that is hanging in the clubhouse. The following weekend, a defeat at Brooklands for the 1st XI proved to be only a temporary blip, as they bounced back with a series of fine wins and draws. The first of these games was at Knutsford, where the hosts were bowled out for 142 with both A. D. Thomson and A. Horrocks capturing five wickets, before opener Ralph Astin's fine knock of 74 not out, guided the team to an easy six-wicket win. During Whit-Week, Whalley Range then rattled up a superb total of 254-6 before declaring against Cheadle Hulme. Stansby was the main contributor with a fine 83, whilst Williamson with 55, and G. B. Brookes with 40 also joined in with the run feast. In the end, the visitors earnt a draw, closing on 143-8. Meanwhile, in a 2nd XI game at Ashley, we see the name of J. Buckland on a Whalley Range scoresheet for the first time.

John Buckland – The Club's Third Olympian

John Buckland was the son of Ron Buckland, and therefore nephew of George Frederick Buckland, who'd represented Great Britain at lacrosse in the 1908 Olympics. Thus, it would become an amazing double for the Buckland clan, when John Buckland would also represent Great Britain at lacrosse in the Olympic Games that were held in London in 1948. With only USA also submitting a team for this demonstration sport at the Games, there was just a single match, played at Wembley Stadium, which ended 5-5, after Great Britain had trailed 2-4 at the end of the first of four periods. John Buckland was also a member of the Old Hulmeians lacrosse team that enjoyed much success after the war, winning the Iroquois Cup in 1949 and 1950, and was still playing for them in the early 1960s. He also represented Lancashire and England. With regard to his association with the Whalley Range club, this continued for many years after the war, where he had the dubious honour of keeping wicket to the Reverend Alan Godson (sic), one of the fastest bowlers ever to play for the club.

The impressive form of Whalley Range, and W. B. Stansby in particular, continued on Whit-Wednesday, at Weaste, where they posted an imposing total of 272-5. Stansby was again the top scorer, with an unbeaten 95, before the declaration deprived him of a much-deserved century. Weaste replied with 113-6.

The start of June saw a massive win at home to Northwich. Batting first the visitors were soon dismissed for just 62, with B. D. Bailey claiming seven wickets. Basil Dinnis Bailey (born in 1912) had first appeared for Whalley Range about five seasons previously, and would continue to play for the club after the Second World War, and at the time of his passing, aged in his late eighties, was still associated with the club, as an honorary life member. Whalley Range then batted out the rest of the afternoon against Northwich, finally finishing on 264-6. Both Geoff Widdows, who notched another fifty, and E. B. Jackson batted well, but the main batting star was undoubtedly G. B. Brookes with a superb unbeaten century. With his baking business now well established, one wonders whether he got the sustenance for his lengthy innings from tea-time sandwiches made from Mother's Pride bread!

Whalley Range v Northwich, at Whalley Range, Saturday 3rd June 1939

Whalley Range

A. J. Reeve		b Robinson	5
W. S. Grimshaw		b Carlon	17
E. G. Widdows	st Riley	b Carlon	56
E. B. Jackson		b Robinson	35
G. B. Brookes		not out	110
T. M. Tillotson	st Riley	b Robinson	2
R. Hawley	c Dudley	b Griffiths	12
B. D. Bailey		not out	18
Extras			9
Total		(for 6)	264

Two weeks earlier, Ralph Astin had opened against Knutsford and scored an unbeaten 74. This time, in the return game, with Knutsford having been bowled out for just 73, opener Astin carried on from where he'd left off last time, again keeping his wicket intact, as his 68 not out helped guide Whalley Range to an easy win, ably supported by an unbeaten 56 from J. P. V. Woollam. Following a midweek jaunt to Old Trafford where rain had deprived them of getting a bat against Manchester, captain Woollam then made it back-to-back fifties on the Saturday with his 53 being the main score in a total of 185-5 declared. Whalley Range were then assured of another easy win, thanks to six wickets from B. D. Bailey, as Weaste were dismissed for 93.

The superb sequence of recent performances came to an abrupt halt against Cheetham Hill who knocked up an insurmountable 235-6, though Whalley Range hung on for a draw with 107-7. Rain appears to have accounted for the next couple of games. However when they did finally take to the field again, it was to engage in what turned out to be an absolutely classic encounter with the champions-elect. Batting first at Cheadle Hulme, Whalley Range got off to a great start through Astin and Ainsworth, though Astin was out soon after getting his fifty. However, Ainsworth went on to record yet another century, with this being at least his sixth for the club, with Whalley Range eventually all out for 212. When Cheadle Hulme batted, W. S. Grimshaw captured all of the first seven wickets to fall, and the game seemed all but over. However, with the kind of spirit that would later see them acquire the Stockton Trophy this season, Cheadle Hulme fought back valiantly, especially through P. Howarth batting at number eight. However, Horrocks then accounted for numbers nine and ten, and in an exhilarating finish, Cheadle Hulme's last man was run out when they were just four runs away from Whalley Range's total. It was a sensational win for Whalley Range, and one that illustrated, not for the first time, that if Whalley Range had been competing for points at this time, the Stockton Trophy would probably have been heading in their direction, rather than to Cheadle Hulme!

Cheadle Hulme v Whalley Range, at Cheadle Hulme, Saturday 15th July 1939

Whalley Range				Cheadle Hulme			
R. Astin	c Dodge	b Collinge	51	A. Sanderson	c Horrocks	b Grimshaw	14
R. N. Ainsworth	c Scarboro'	b Collinge	105	D. Ratcliffe	c Ainsworth	b Grimshaw	13
W. B. Stansby		b Sanderson	9	T. Connolly		b Grimshaw	0
G. B. Brookes		b Sanderson	1	A. Crossley		b Grimshaw	0
J. P. V. Woollam	c Hough	b Collinge	6	G. Scarborough		b Grimshaw	33
W. Williamson		b Collinge	21	W. Dodge		b Grimshaw	8
E. G. Widdows		b Collinge	11	T. P. Hough		b Grimshaw	7
E. B. Jackson		b Sanderson	2	P. Howarth		not out	78
W. S. Grimshaw	lbw	b Sanderson	0	D. O. Collinge		b Horrocks	28
G. H. Isherwood		not out	2	M. S. Harrison	c Widdows	b Horrocks	9
A. Horrocks		b Sanderson	1	P. Jeans		run out	4
Extras			3	Extras			14
Total			212	Total			208

The rest of July was virtually washed away by the rain, before the start of August heralded another superb Whalley Range performance. At Northwich, the hosts declared on 199-5. However, with Ainsworth still in such wonderful form, this target was surpassed for the loss of just three wickets, as the opener smashed a superb 93, in a sizeable partnership with E. B. Jackson who scored 67, out of the total of 202-3. Whalley Range then lost their Bank Holiday Monday clash with Bowdon, before drawing with Heaton Mersey and Castleton, the main highlight of which was 65 from Jack Woollam against Heaton Mersey.

Sadly the game against Castleton, on Saturday 19th August, was the last reported game involving Whalley Range before the outbreak of the Second World War.

Cricket at Whalley Range did continue throughout the War, with a 1940 fixture list showing the usual array of games, though understandably these went unreported. There are no surviving handbooks for 1941 and 1942, with the following fixture lists coming from the 1943 handbook :-

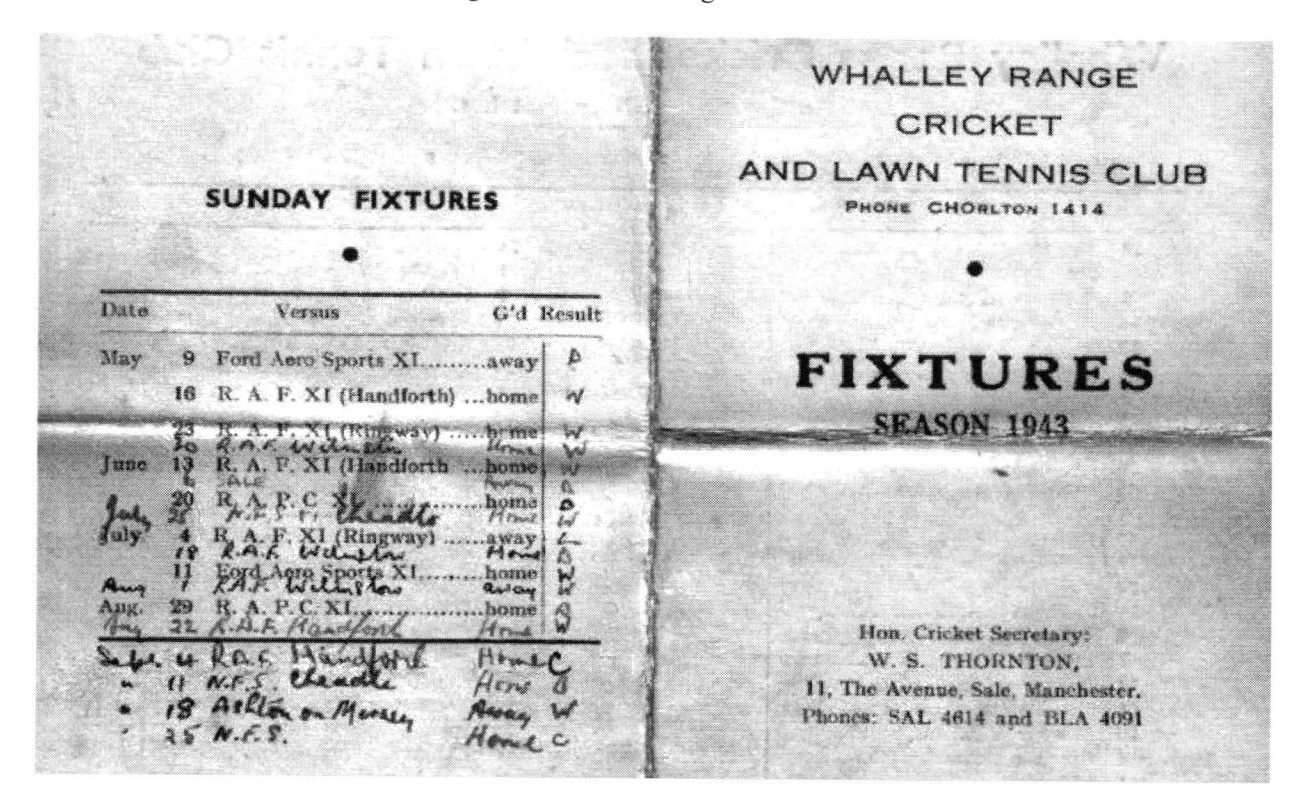

Fixture Lists from 1943 handbook

Though going unreported in the local papers, as can be seen, the outcomes have been added to the handbook. These fixture lists provide the earliest evidence of Whalley Range cricket being played on a Sunday, with a lot of these games being against the likes of RAF teams, e.g. Ringway (now Manchester Airport). Further handbooks exist for 1944 and 1945 which again illustrate a full list of fixtures for the 1st and 2nd XI teams, and Sunday fixtures which once more were mainly against military teams. The following section is devoted to those Whalley Range heroes who paid the ultimate sacrifice in serving their country.

Second World War Heroes

Memorial tablet adorning the clubhouse wall

As can be seen above, there were seven members of the club who lost their lives during the Second World War, namely F. Clarke, J. Hargreaves, R. Hawley, G. H. Isherwood, P. S. Preston, J. C. Scammell, and J. E. L. Woollam.

Fred Clarke was born on 27th April 1920, and attended Hulme Grammar School between 1930 and 1938, where he played for the 1st XI cricket team in his last three years there, and also represented the school at lacrosse and rugby. He then studied at Brasenose College, Oxford, where he obtained a war degree in English History, European History and Political Science. He was called up to train for the Infantry in 1940, and was commissioned in 1941. He was killed on 17th July 1943 in Sicily, and is buried in Catania War Cemetery in Sicily.

It is believed that J. Hargreaves is **John Charles Walker Hargreaves**, who was born on 2nd February 1921, and also attended Hulme Grammar School between 1930 and 1938. He was a Leading Airman with the Royal Navy Fleet Air Arm, HMS Goshawk, and was reported missing on active service at sea, on 17th January 1941. He is commemorated on the Lee-on-Solent Memorial.

Rupert Hawley, who is featured in one of the preceding scoresheets for the 1939 season, was born in 1918, to Richard and Isabel Mary Hawley. Sergeant Rupert Hawley was thus in his mid-twenties, when he too was killed in action in Sicily. The groundsman's hut was subsequently bought as a memorial to him, with the ensuing picture showing the commemorative plaque that graced it :-

Commemorative plaque for Rupert Hawley who lost his life in the Second World War

George Herbert Isherwood, who is pictured in several of the preceding team photos from the 1930s, first played cricket for Whalley Range in the 1929 season, and played in all of the ensuing seasons leading up to the war. Lieutenant G. H. Isherwood was killed in 1943, aged 32, and is buried in Burma (now known as Myanmar).

Philip Stansfield Preston was born on 27th October 1919 and attended Hulme Grammar School between 1930 and 1937, where he excelled at most sports, including cricket, rugby, and lacrosse. He was called up in 1941, eventually rising to the position of Captain, and was attached to 301 Field Regiment East Africa Artillery. He was killed on 12th February 1944 in transit from Mombasa to Ceylon, when the troop ship he was on, SS Khedive Ismail, was torpedoed by a Japanese submarine, resulting in the loss of many lives. He is commemorated on the East African Memorial in Nairobi, Kenya.

John Cosson Scammell was born on 12th March 1909 and attended Hulme Grammar School between 1919 and 1927, at which time he lived on Albany Road in Chorlton-cum-Hardy. His father, Bertram, was a tailor. During the war, he was a Sergeant Observer with the RAF Volunteer Reserve, and died on 2nd October 1943, as a result of an aircraft accident. He is commemorated at Manchester Crematorium.

James Edward Lucas Woollam was born in 1922, the son of Eddie and Stella Frances Woollam. He enlisted with the Royal Air Force Volunteer Reserve, but died on 10th March 1943, aged just 20. Sergeant J. E. L. Woollam is commemorated on the Runnymede Memorial.

The memorial tablet only pays tribute to those who were club members at the time of the War, and so does not include former club members who also perished during the conflicts. One such former member was David Stanley Bonner Vincent who represented Whalley Range 2nd XI during the 1935 season. He was born in 1917, and educated at Hulme Grammar School, and in his last year there in 1934, he opened the batting for the School 1st XI. Thus, perhaps in search of further 1st XI cricket, he only played the one season for Whalley Range, spending the rest of his cricketing days before the forthcoming war, playing for Brooklands.

Raid on Cologne

Late in the evening on 20th May 1942, before they'd even completed their training, Sgt. D. S. B. Vincent and four others, were sent on their first operation, as part of a formidable squadron of Wellington bombers flying out of RAF Gravely in Huntingdon. In total, Operation Millennium, as it was codenamed, witnessed over a thousand aircraft heading out over the North Sea that evening, towards occupied Europe. The original choice for the operation had been Hamburg, but various factors including poor weather, meant that Arthur "Bomber" Harris eventually chose Cologne as the mission's target. However, German radar detected the unusually large force approaching, and the Luftwaffe scrambled its night fighters to await the incoming bombers. Shortly after midnight, the plane that Sgt. D. S. B. Vincent was in, was shot down and crashed at Alem in the Dutch province of Gelderland. The pilot survived and was taken prisoner, but the other four members of the crew, including Sgt. D. S. B. Vincent, lost their lives that day, and were buried in Uden War Cemetery.

Following the outbreak of war, the committee was empowered to elect temporary members from the likes of HM Forces, ARP, ATS, and WNS, who were resident in the area. The LDS (Lad's Army) were allowed to use the ground for parades, and members of the Home Guard slept in the visitors' changing room which was fortunate because in March 1941, incendiary bombs fell on the pavilion and it was only their prompt action that saved the structure. Following the scare, the committee decided to purchase two new fire buckets, making four in all! For a while, matches had to be played without sightscreens, because they had been borrowed by the RAF to protect barrage balloons.

Though not directly connected with the War, several significant former Whalley Range players, who had all gone on to play first-class cricket, also passed away during these troubled times, all aged in their seventies. H. C. L. Tindall, who was once heralded as the greatest runner in his day, died in June 1940, aged 77. The following year in July, E. E. Steel, one of Whalley Range's best ever players, also died aged 77. Then in March 1944, J. F. Arnold passed away, aged 75. Later in the year, Whalley Range's greatest ever cricketing son, the legendary A. C. MacLaren died, aged 72. In 1939, Archie MacLaren had actually appeared, albeit briefly, in a Hollywood film called The Four Feathers, which starred Sir Charles Aubrey Smith, a friend and former cricketer. Following this, in the last few years of his life, Archie's health began to deteriorate, a situation not helped by being hurt in a car crash. He then contracted cancer, and sadly passed away on 17th November 1944.

Lest the cricket chapters conclude on too sombre a note, as was previously highlighted with the surviving handbooks from this period, the club did survive during the hostilities, with social sport at the club, continuing to be played during these troubled times. After the war, official cricket matches began again in the summer of 1946, and the club continued not only to survive, but to thrive, though alas such post-war stories are for the second volume of the club's history.

Tennis (1881-1945)

The reporting in the local press of Whalley Range's cricket teams before the Second World War was little short of incredible, with almost blanket coverage once the club had become well established. However, the same can not be said about Whalley Range tennis during this same period, when the amount of coverage could at best be described as minimalistic. Fortunately, one very significant event that was captured, was what appears to have been the first-ever Whalley Range tennis tournament, which was concluded on Friday 5th August 1881. Thus, even though the Whalley Range Cricket & Lawn Tennis Club sign proudly boasts that the club was founded in 1845, this does just relate solely to the cricket aspect, with lawn tennis not even having been invented at this time.

It is worth bearing in mind that 1881 was the same year that the U.S. Open was first held, with Wimbledon having first been contested just four years earlier. This inaugural Whalley Range tennis tournament was reported in the Manchester Guardian on Monday 8th August under the headline of "Whalley Range Cricket and Lawn Tennis Club", with the opening paragraph reading as follows :-

> *The first tournament in connection with this club was concluded on Friday evening. The competition consisted of doubles and singles, for which there were fair entries. The double-handed competition was won by Messrs. S. H. Fourdrinier and W. Lund, and the single by Mr. G. S. Welsh.*

The full list of results was as follows :-

Singles :-

First round :-

F. Radford beat G. A. Brown 3-6, 6-1, 6-3
D. J. Fitzgerald beat Rev. H. T. Jones 6-1, 6-1
G. S. Welsh beat W. H. Radford 6-1, 6-2
S. H. Fourdrinier beat G. G. Kendal 6-0, 6-2
G. H. Wood beat W. R. Richardson 6-5, 3-6, 6-4
T. W. Bridgford beat J. W. Botsford 6-1, 6-2
W. Lund – bye
C. M. Wood and W. Welsh both walked-over

Second round :-

D. J. Fitzgerald beat T. W. Bridgford 6-3, 4-6, 6-0
S. H. Fourdrinier beat W. Welsh 6-3, 4-6, 6-0
Rev. G. F. Coombes beat C. M. Wood 6-3, 6-2
G. H. Wood beat W. Lund 4-6, 6-0, 6-3
G. S. Welsh beat G. A. Brown 6-2, 6-0

Third round :-

G. S. Welsh beat D. J. Fitzgerald 6-2, 6-1
Rev. G. F. Coombes beat G. H. Wood 6-1, 6-1
S. H. Fourdrinier – bye

Fourth round :-

G. S. Welsh beat Rev. G. F. Coombes 6-1, 6-5

Final round :-

G. S. Welsh beat S. H. Fourdrinier 6-1, 6-2

Doubles :-

First round :-

S. H. Fourdrinier & W. Lund beat G. A. Brown & Rev. H. T. Jones 6-1, 6-2
G. H. Wood & T. W. Bridgford beat G. S. Welsh & J. W. Botsford 6-5, 5-6, 6-5
W. R. Richardson & Rev. G. F. Coombes beat W. Welsh & J. Magnall 6-1, 6-2
D. J. Fitzgerald & W. H. Radford – bye

Second round :-

W. R. Richardson & Rev. G. F. Coombes beat D. J. Fitzgerald & W. H. Radford 6-4, 6-3
S. H. Fourdrinier & W. Lund beat G. H. Wood & T. W. Bridgford 6-3, 6-2

Final round :-

S. H. Fourdrinier & W. Lund beat W. R. Richardson & Rev. G. F. Coombes 3-6, 6-4, 6-2

These are the results exactly as published, with the singles draw appearing a tad over-complicated, with G. A. Brown also strangely progressing further in the competition at the expense of his victor, F. Radford. Quite a few of the aforementioned players also played cricket for Whalley Range, e.g. G. A. Brown, J. W. Botsford, D. J. Fitzgerald, S. H. Fourdrinier, Rev. H. T. Jones, W. H. Radford, W. R. Richardson, C. M. Wood, G. H. Wood, and W. Lund, with the latter also playing cricket for Owens College.

The most notable name is undoubtedly W. R. Richardson, who played cricket for Whalley Range between 1878 and 1887. William Ryder Richardson was born in Chorlton in 1861, and by the time he played in the 1881 Whalley Range tennis tournament, he had already represented his country earlier in the year, at rugby. On 5th February 1881, Richardson made his one and only appearance for England against Ireland, with the match being staged in Whalley Range, as it happens, thus presumably being played at the Manchester Rugby Club's ground on what is now called Upper Chorlton Road. It was a game that England won, by a margin of two goals. On 22nd June 1887, he married Alice Jane MacLaren, a younger sister of James MacLaren, and therefore aunt of Archie. By doing so, he was following in the footsteps of another of the tennis combatants mentioned above, since on 4th June 1885, William Harold Radford had married Annie MacLaren, an elder sister of Alice Jane. Having moved to St. Anne's-on-Sea on the Fylde coast, sadly W. H. Radford would die fairly young, passing away in 1900, aged just 39. His younger brother, Francis Herbert Radford, passed away even younger, aged just 22 in 1885, and is presumably the F. Radford who also featured in this inaugural tennis tournament in 1881.

As can be seen above, it wasn't just the cricket side of the club that attracted members of the clergy, with Rev. G. F. Coombes competing in this inaugural tournament, along with Rev. H. T. Jones. George Frederick Coombes was born in Stockport on 7th March 1856 to Harriet and Rev. Jeremiah Coombes, who was the vicar of St. Paul's Church in Portwood, Stockport. Having studied at Manchester Grammar School and Cambridge University, like his father, Rev. G. F. Coombes also worked at Portwood, between 1881 and 1883, before Winnipeg in Canada beckoned, where he spent most of the rest of his life. Over there, he worked at such establishments as St. John's Cathedral, and was also the Dean of Rupert's Land at one point. In 1885 he married Mary Elizabeth Eagles of Rushall, England, and had three sons and a daughter. His sister, Annie Gertrude Coombes, married Sir George Harry Holcroft, 1st Baronet, who was a Justice of the Peace for Worcestershire, a Member of Parliament for Staffordshire, and also the High Sheriff of Staffordshire for a short time. For the last few weeks of his life, ill-health caused Rev G. F. Coombes to move to Santa Monica in California, where he died at the age of 66 on 22nd September 1922.

Whalley Range's First Tennis Finalists

As mentioned above, the two people who contested the first ever Whalley Range singles final were G. S. Welsh and S. H. Fourdrinier. George Strafford Welsh was born to George and Mary Welsh, in Whalley Range in 1859, and would thus have been in his early twenties when he became the club's inaugural tennis champion. Also featured in the competition was his younger brother

William Welsh, who lost to S. H. Fourdrinier in the second round, so G. S. Welsh managed to gain revenge on his brother's behalf in the final. In 1886, G. S. Welsh married Elizabeth Selina.

As for the beaten finalist, Samuel Harding Fourdrinier was born on 13th June 1842, the tenth of 14 children to George Henry Fourdrinier and Jane Harding, and would thus have been 39 at the time of the final. The Fourdrinier family emanated from Normandy in France, and like G. S. Welsh, 1886 was also the year that saw S. H. Fourdrinier tying the knot, marrying Marion Pearson Crosland in Huddersfield. Despite being of a big family, he only had one child himself, namely Grey Crosland Fourdrinier. In business life, S. H. Fourdrinier was for several years the assistant superintendent of the Great Central Railway, before retiring in 1905. He passed away three years later, on 18th July 1908.

Perhaps some insight as to precisely where in Whalley Range the 1881 tennis tournament was held may be gained from an advertisement that appeared in the local press at the start of 1884. The full classified ad read as follows :-

> *To be let, Royston Lodge, Whalley Range, now in the occupation of James MacLaren; tennis ground attaching to same can be had on certain conditions. – For full particulars apply Jas. MacLaren, 18, George Street.*

Royston Lodge was on Carlton Road, whilst James MacLaren (father of Archie) had a long association with Whalley Range cricket club, and sport in the area, though perhaps even at this point, he was contemplating retirement, since he handed over his business to his nephews at the age of just 44 in 1889, before retiring to Guernsey, where he lived out the rest of his days until his death in 1900. (Note that back then, Jas was an abbreviation for James, and not Jason.) Royston Lodge was also of course the childhood home of both Archie and James Alexander MacLaren, though sadly is no longer extant. Today, we find the likes of Royston Avenue (see photo below) built in the gardens and on the tennis court, and Royston Court on Carlton Road (which can also be seen in the background in the photo below).

Royston Avenue and Royston Court now occupying the area where Royston Lodge once stood

Over the next few years, there were no more specific references to Whalley Range Lawn Tennis Club, though there was mention of further tennis activity in the area. The Carlton Club was often reported on from 1885 onwards, and though based nowadays at Rowan Lodge on Carlton Road, may too be a candidate for those who played tennis at Royston Lodge at this time. However there were no similarities between those who represented the Carlton team, and those who played in the 1881 Whalley Range tournament, so there is no evidence to suggest any connection between the two. The Carlton team at this stage, played against such opponents as Broughton, Priory, Longsight Liberal Club, Longford Institute (Stretford), Sale, and Cheetham Reform.

At the start of June 1886, a tennis match between Lancashire Independent College and Monton was reported on, being played at Whalley Range, though the visitors won by "*14 setts to 6, or 103 games to 74*". At this point in history it seems the protocol for publishing the match results was not quite standardised, and often the result would be expressed in terms of overall matches, sets, and games won. Also sets were quite often referred to as 'setts'.

A. H. Hartwig, who would be playing cricket for the Whalley Range club the following year, was a member of the Longford Institute team that played against Carlton at Whalley Range on Saturday 21st July 1888, though his team lost narrowly by 76 games to 74 apparently (though in fact drew, if just the matches, or even sets, were taken into account!).

In July 1891, a match between Victoria (Seedley) and Chorlton Road (Whalley Range), played at Seedley, also made the local press. It was a match that the Whalley Range outfit won by 21 sets to 2, and 148 games to 84, though again there would appear to be no connection to those who had represented Whalley Range Lawn Tennis Club, a decade earlier. July 1894 then witnessed the first mention of a tennis team called Southolme (Whalley Range), who in a match played on a Wednesday lost heavily to H. W. Kelly's Team. Playing for the Southolme team were F. Molyneux, G. Oddy, H. Werner, and Taylor. George Oddy also played cricket for Manchester, and was the father of Stephen Roberts Oddy, who though more renowned for his subsequent lacrosse exploits, would go on to play cricket for Whalley Range between 1899 and 1912. Both also played golf for the Chorlton-cum-Hardy club, with Stephen winning their annual tournament in 1925, and being appointed their club captain in 1936. Both are also reported as having occupations in the Grey Cloth trade, though later in life, George served as a Liberal councillor. In April 1912, when he was chairman of the South-West Manchester Liberal Association, George is quoted as saying that one of his closest personal friends was amongst the passengers unaccounted for, following the sinking of the Titanic.

On 27th August 1892, F. Clay featured in a match for Carlton against Sale, in what was described as "miserable tennis weather", and eventually the match had to be abandoned with Carlton declared the winners by 5 setts to 3. One assumes this is the same F. Clay who before the century was out, was playing cricket for Whalley Range, and who would also later captain them. In mid-June 1893, F. Clay represented a tennis team called Manchester Athletic at their home ground in Fallowfield, which interestingly enough, as described earlier in the book, correlates with how the Whalley Range cricket team were sometimes referred to, so perhaps there was some remnant of a connection here, though none of the other names (A. H. Hackett, W. T. Hill, C. Hooper, and F. J. Sutcliffe) were familiar. Later in the month, F. Clay was back representing Carlton.

At Whalley Farm in Whalley Range, there was a tennis match between The Range and Moss Side on Saturday 20th June 1896. Playing for The Range were Miss E. Simpson, Miss Colwell, J. Vanderveen (sometimes spelt as Van der Veen in other reports), C. Tait, G. B. Cox, R. A. Leech, Mr. Werner, and Mr. Mumford. The home team was reported as winning by 7 matches to 3, 16 setts to 7, and 128 games to 91. A name common to both this team and that of the Southolme team two years earlier is Werner. During the 1890s, H. E. Werner also played in goal for the South Manchester hockey team, and in November 1891 he was trying to fend off a Didsbury attack that inclued Whalley Range cricketers H. W. Tindall and J. F. Arnold, a role he seems to have performed fairly well, since this particular game ended in a one-all draw, with only J. F. Arnold managing to get the ball past him.

On Saturday 11th July of the same year, there was a match between Southolme and Heaton Park, which Southolme won by 7 matches to 6, 17 sets to 16, and 170 games to 159. The match exclusively comprised doubles encounters with the Southolme team having such pairs as Tait and Vanderveen, and G. Oddy and S. R. Oddy. Later in the same summer, a match between The Range and Hawthorn Bank (Sale) was played at Whalley Range on 22nd August. Again, the contest solely comprised doubles matches and the team from Sale emerged victorious by 18 setts to 14, and 144 games to 128.

The pairings for The Range comprised Vanderveen and J. Tait, C. Tait and Stiven, Holgate and Oddy, Misses E. Simpson and Colwell, and Misses Riley and M. Simpson. Thus, there appears little doubt of a strong connection between The Range and Southolme clubs, to the point where one suspects that they are indeed one and the same. Furthermore, with the connections to the Oddy family, and lack of any further direct references to Whalley Range Lawn Tennis Club since 1881, one also has to wonder whether The Range club isn't also some form of incarnation of the club that first emerged in 1881. Admittedly, there are no similarities with the names of those who played in 1881, but now 15 years downstream, this wouldn't necessarily be the case anyway.

The following season, on Saturday 17th July 1897, Hawthorn Bank again beat Southolme, this time by the margin of 21 sets to 5, and 142 games to 97. The Southolme pairings were S. R. and G. Oddy, Vanderveen and R. Clarke, H. Clarke and F. Holgate, and Misses Wilkins and Garraway. One of the games reported on for Southolme in 1899, involved a trip to Southbank in Southport. According to the report in the local press, the match was played in delightful weather, but somewhat marred by a strong wind. The Southolme team were victorious, winning 8 matches to 3, 17 setts to 11, and 167 games to 145, with two matches being drawn owing to failing light. The Southolme pairings comprised Caw and Johnes, Tyrer and Evans, Hessey and Constance, Miss M. Simpson and Miss E. Simpson, and Miss Littlewood and Miss Makin.

The following summer in July 1900, Southolme again travelled to face Southbank in Southport to the accompaniment of delightful weather, and this time won a much closer affair by 7 matches to 6, 15 setts to 14, and 148 games to 145. The Southolme pairings comprised W. N. Caw and H. H. Price, C. Tyrer and J. H. Evans, W. Hessey and R. Constance, Miss Maclurkin and Miss N. Booth, and Miss Hunt and Miss Cann. W. N. Caw is William Newton Caw, and as will be seen later, his younger sister Agnes Graham Caw would definitely be associated with Whalley Range tennis, whilst his brother John Graham Caw also played cricket for the club and would later serve on the committee. Their father, John Caw (who married Sarah Ellen Newton in 1873) was born in Scotland and worked as a bank manager, a profession that both William and John would also adopt.

There were further reports of tennis in the Whalley Range area in July 1900, with a team from Manley Park losing fairly heavily at West Didsbury, but then trouncing Moorfield (Stockport) in a game played at Whalley Range, by 12 matches to 1, 24 setts to 4, and 153 games to 76, with the report stating that both teams suffered from absentees (though it seems like the visitors were presumably more afflicted than their hosts, judging by the score!).

The following month, the local papers reported on Southolme closing their match season with a fixture against Winnington Park (Northwich). It was a contest that they won by 5 matches to 3, 13 sets to 9, and 109 games to 102, with one match drawn owing to failing light. As always at this time, the match consisted of just doubles contests, and in this particular match, these were exclusively male affairs, with the Southolme pairings comprising J. Johnes and M. Johnes, C. Tyrer and W. Hiller, and J. H. Evans and W. Hessey.

From 1900 onwards, club handbooks are available, and these indicate quite clearly that at the turn of the century, the club is solely devoted to cricket. Thus, bearing this in mind, together with the lack of any further local press coverage, it certainly seems a possibility that the 1881 tennis tournament was a one-off event, and that with regard to the Whalley Range club, tennis and cricket went their separate ways for many years after this.

In June 1903, for the first time since 1881, we see a tennis team being referred to specifically as Whalley Range, with Whalley Range (Ladies) beating Owens College by 3 matches to 1, and 7 matches to 3. The Whalley Range ladies were listed as Miss Budenberg and Miss Mecs, and Miss Robinson and Miss Dockray. With such an unusual surname, one imagines that the latter is related to K. T. S. Dockray who can be seen in the 1910 Whalley Range cricket team photos, and who would later become the President of the club. However, further evidence suggested that this probably related to a school team.

A team called Whalley Range Old Girls is then reported as beating Carlton in mid-July 1903, by 4 matches to 0, 8 sets to 1, and 50 games to 29, though sadly the team details were not printed. Over the ensuing few years or so though, the only mention of tennis in the Whalley Range area relates solely to the Manley Park and Carlton clubs. However there would still be some familiar names appearing, with the likes of W. N. Caw, Miss Dockray, and Miss D. Mumford and Miss N. Mumford (Mr. Mumford had appeared for The Range in 1896) all representing the Manley Park club. One wonders if the Mumfords are related to Dr. Percival Brooke Mumford who later played cricket for the club.

As mentioned earlier in the book, significant events then happened which would ultimately lead to the cricket and tennis parties becoming reunited. In 1911, the cricket team were forced to relinquish their College Road ground that they'd enjoyed for more than half a century, and spent the season down to one team, solely playing away fixtures. For the following season, they managed to acquire the use of

Hough End Playing Fields, at which point the club again embraced both sports, with the new ground presumably able to also accommodate tennis, unlike the previous ground.

As mentioned in previous chapters, Hulme Grammar School was founded in 1887, and had a profound impact on the Whalley Range Cricket Club. In 1891, Whalley Range High School was founded on the corner of Withington Road and Burford Road, on the site of what is now St. Margaret's Primary School. Its playing fields backed onto the cricket ground, and tennis was played at the school. It is likely that, as with cricket, the adoption of the game by local girls and women from the burgeoning middle classes took this social sport out of the back-gardens and grounds of the big houses and increasingly into the more organised world of local clubs.

The question of what happened to the relationship between the cricket club and tennis after the 1881 competition could be that the lack of space at the College Road ground frustrated the establishment of permanent tennis section. Meanwhile, the friends and families of the cricketers played tennis where they could when they could, until the forced move of the ground to Hough End allied to the growth of the game in the Edwardian period allowed the tennis section to be formed in 1912.

Inside of 1912 club handbook

As can be seen from the picture of the inside of the 1912 handbook, the club was now known as "Whalley Range Cricket & Lawn Tennis Club", probably for the first time since 1881, though the cover of the handbooks would not reflect this until 1914. In fact, actually within the 1912 handbook, there was nothing else to acknowledge the fact that the club now comprised both tennis and cricket. However, being their first season, it is certainly a possibility that the tennis members merely competed against each other.

For the 1913 season, the handbook contains a list of mixed doubles fixtures, with home and away matches against Edge Lane, Broughton, and Carlton. However, as can be seen from the added note within the handbook, it would appear that the Whalley Range club did not commence their season with a victory! Also listed in the handbook was the fact that Charles Henry Fox (i.e. the goalkeeper of the all-conquering Old Hulmeians lacrosse team) was the Honorary Tennis Secretary and that he belonged to a tennis committee which also comprised Miss A. Caw, Miss H. Wood, S. Fox, F. A. Mitcheson, C. Smart, and A. Worthington.

As alluded to earlier, Miss A. Caw was Agnes Graham Caw. However about a week before the final match of the season was scheduled to be played, Agnes sadly passed away at the tender age of just 25, on 29th August 1913. Lamentably, Arthur Worthington would be another whose life would be cut short far too early, and as mentioned earlier in the book, is featured on the memorial tablet that adorns the clubhouse wall. F. A. Mitcheson is Frederick Arundel Mitcheson, an accountant, who had married Marion Bullough back in 1901. The following year they had a son, Maurice Arundel Mitcheson, though sadly their son was another who would die young, aged just 22.

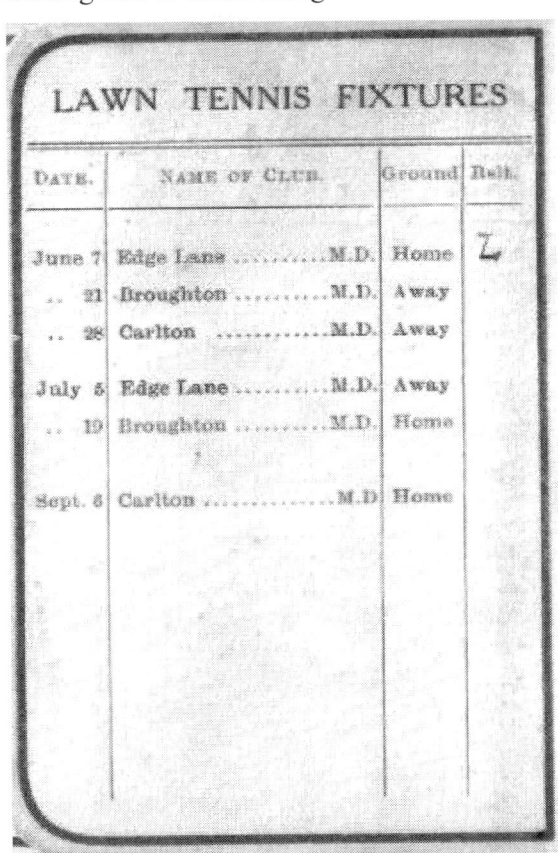

1913 tennis fixtures

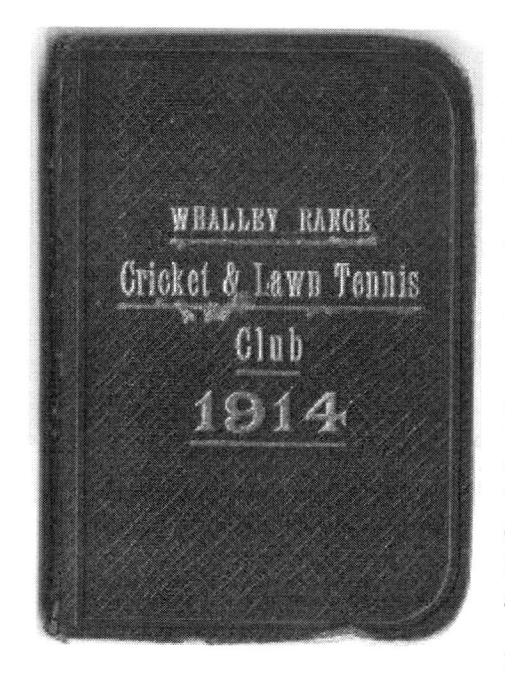

The 1914 handbook was the first that acknowledged the new name of the club on the actual cover. Again for this season, the fixture list comprised solely of six mixed doubles matches, with home and away matches against Broughton, Edge Lane, and Brantingham.

Reports of both of the matches against Edge Lane appeared in the local press. The first encounter was played at Whalley Range on June 13th with Edge Lane winning by 7 matches to 2, 15 sets to 5, and 102 games to 64. The Whalley Range pairings were H. Evans and Mrs. Howard, S. Fox and Miss G. Robinson, and C. Stuart and Mrs. Harvey. The return match at Edge Lane (whose own courts were in Chorlton-cum-Hardy) was on July 4th and was an encounter which Edge Lane won easily by 8 matches to 1, 17 sets to 3, and 114 games to 64. The Whalley Range pairings this time were H. Evans and Miss G. Robinson, S. Fox and Mrs. Harvey, and C. H. Fox and Miss Fox. Just as Whalley Range Tennis Club had finally got going again, tragically the First World War came along.

As described earlier in the book, immediately after the First World War, the Whalley Range club was again homeless, and it wasn't until 1923 that it was back up and running again, at their new and still current ground on Kingsbrook Road. In the early days, there were seven tennis courts, four grass and three hard courts (according to the Lancashire County LTA handbook from 1936, which also stated that Sunday play was allowed). However, in the 1980s, with the club struggling financially, it was decided to sell off the grass courts for housing development.

Tennis is a sport that is inherently a very social game, and certainly at this point in time, provided one of the more accessible and socially acceptable occasions for young people to get acquainted. The fact that seven courts were available certainly implies that a lot of tennis was played, with ample opportunities to socialise. As is evident throughout its entire history, there have been many who met their future partners because of associations forged within the convivial environs of the club!

The first available handbook from this new era is from the 1924 season, and shows that the Tennis Secretary is A. Clarke (living on College Road), whilst the rest of the tennis committee comprised G. Greenup (who'd been involved in the sweepstakes scandal the previous year), C. Jones, W. M. Stone, J. S. Whitehead, Miss D. Stanley, and Miss E. Watts. The opening fixture was a mixed doubles away at Chorltonville, whilst the second fixture was an internal affair pitching "Tennis v Cricket" at men's doubles. Apart from the return fixture against Chorltonville, the only other scheduled matches were against Carlton, though they do indicate an increased tennis membership with both 1st and 2nd teams competing against them, at both men's and ladies' doubles.

C. Jones is in fact George Cyril Mansell Jones, though he was known by his second name of Cyril. At the start of the year (on New Year's Day itself!) he'd married Dorothy Lucy Oddy, a younger sister of S. R. Oddy, and daughter of George Oddy (senior), who was a vice-president of the club at this time. Cyril was born in 1893, the son of George Reginald Jones, who was a physician at the Manchester Homeopathic Institute. It seems his father was a bit of a wit, being compelled to reply to someone's query in a monthly publication called The Homeopathic Recorder as follows :-

> *...under the head of 'Personal' there is a question by Freshman as to any occult physiological connection between the Calves and the Corn. The only connection is the ankle that is placed where it is, to prevent the calf coming down and eating the corn.*

W. M. Stone is William Moses Stone who was born in 1890, and worked as a chartered accountant in Manchester. At one point he worked for the firm of David Smith, Garnett & Co., for whom one of the main partners was John Philip Garnett, and in 1919, William married his daughter, Dorothy Garnett. William continued to contribute to various Whalley Range committees up until the Second World War, and after the war, was made a vice-president in 1954 and an honorary life member in 1956. He passed away in 1968, aged 78.

For the 1925 season, James Stanley Whitehead was now the Tennis Secretary, though for whatever reason, this would appear to be the last season he was involved with the club, and A. Clarke would again take over the following season. Stanley, as he was known, was born in 1896 to Jessie and James Smallpage Whitehead. On 10th October 1946, he married Gertrude Elizabeth Shone, who within a year had given birth to a daughter. He was another who lived into his seventies.

Listed on the tennis committee for the first time this season was John Stanley Ardern, who also played cricket for the club. He was born in 1885 to Emily and John Henry Ardern. His father was listed as a vice-president from the club from as early as 1900 (the earliest surviving handbook) until his death in the early part of 1936, whilst he himself would be granted honorary life membership in 1958, though passed away the following year, aged 73. The fixtures for the 1925 season were much the same as the previous season, with the addition of home and away matches against Brantingham at mixed doubles.

Other people new to the tennis committee this year included Miss G. Blaikie and Miss M. Blaikie. Grace Blaikie was born in 1894 and was named after her mother who'd been born in India, whilst her father hailed from Scotland. However, since she had sisters called Marian and Margaret, it is not possible to distinguish which of these two was also on the committee.

The 1926 season would witness the welcoming of L. S. Pidd to the tennis committee (of whom more anon). The scheduled matches for this season comprised mixed doubles against both Brantingham and Chorltonville, and men's and ladies' doubles against Carlton, for both 1st and 2nd teams again.

In August 1927, the Criccieth (North Wales) annual open lawn tennis tournament featured players from all over the country, including the pairing of G. V. Oddy and G. W. Orr, who were listed as coming from Manchester. George Vernon Oddy, the son of S. R. Oddy, was born in 1906, whilst his tennis partner, Geoffrey Wallace Orr, was born in 1907. Also listed as belonging to a Manchester club were H. and J. Connolly, the latter of whom also competed in the singles tournament, though he lost in the first round to L. Henn (Bedford), in straight sets, in what was described as "*boisterous weather*".

The 1927 and 1928 handbooks are not available, but in the 1929 handbook, G. W. Orr is on the tennis committee, as is S. R. Oddy, so it seems fairly certain that at least G. V. Oddy and G. W. Orr were in fact Whalley Range members at the time of this Criccieth tournament.

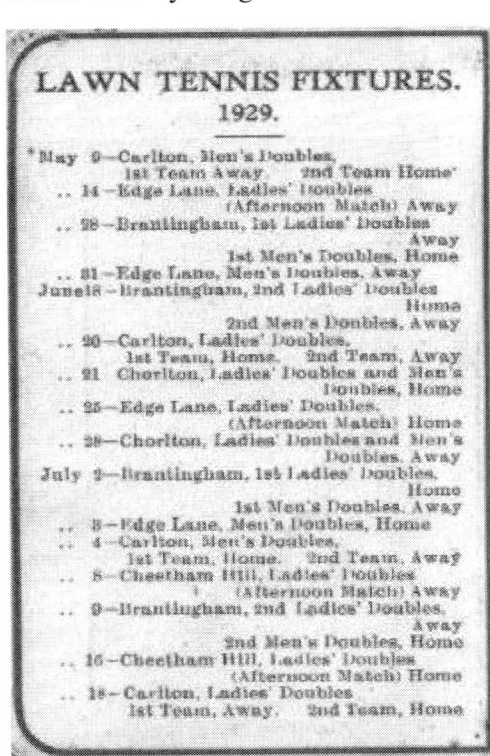

With Cyril Jones now installed as secretary, in 1929 the fixture list was really beginning to expand with matches scheduled for most weeks from early May to mid-July, and the following season would be further augmented with fixtures against Didsbury for the first time.

In August 1930, G. W. Orr and G. V. Oddy are again seen competing in the Criccieth tournament, and this time are listed as representing Whalley Range. However, G. W. Orr lost in the first round of the men's handicap singles to T. Dunlop (Ealing) who beat him 6-2, 6-2, whilst in the same event, G. V. Oddy also lost in the first round, despite winning the first set, with V. Seligman (Queen's, London) beating him 2-6, 10-8, 8-6. At the same tournament, G. W. Orr also competed in what were described as the men's level singles, but he was knocked out in the second round by the Rev. H. M. Johnson (Chatham) who beat him 6-4, 6-4.

In the men's doubles, G. V. Oddy and G. W. Orr got to the third round before being beaten by V. Seligman and H. Nelson, 6-1, 10-8. This doubles match occurred on the fifth day's play of the Criccieth tournament with hard courts being used some of the time in the morning, due to rain, though the afternoon play was favoured with glorious sunshine, according to the report. The following day, G. W. Orr also played in the third round of the mixed doubles (handicap) where he partnered Miss Hatch (Farnham) in beating S. J. Jagger and Miss Podmore 6-0, 6-2, though sadly subsequent rounds of this event didn't appear to make the local papers. The following winter witnessed G. W. Orr playing lacrosse for the Old Hulmeians.

In June 1931, G. W. Orr played in the men's singles handicap at the Chorltonville tournament (Chorltonville being a garden village dating from 1911 within Chorlton). The opening day had what was described as "*its usual rainy accompaniment*", and since the grass was therefore too wet for play, all the matches were decided on hard courts, in the evening. In hindsight, one suspects that G. W. Orr might have wished for the original surface, since he failed to win a single game on the Chorltonville hard courts that evening, being beaten 6-0, 6-0 by E. Locke!

Later in the week, in the (normal) men's singles event, G. W. Orr reached the third round before being beaten 6-1, 6-2 by P. E. Riley, whilst in the mixed doubles event, he partnered Miss J. Butler, but they were beaten in the second round 6-0, 6-4, by S. E. Rocca and Miss C. M. Sankey. The two were also paired together in the mixed doubles handicap event but again lost in the third round, this time to P. E. Riley and Miss M. Brown. In the same event, G. V. Oddy partnered Miss C. M. Swann (who also appeared on the tennis committee for various seasons in the 1930s), and got to the semi-finals, where they were beaten by N. Goodbrand and Miss N. Jones. It seems a distinct possibility that the Miss J. Butler referred to above, and Miss E. J. Butler who features later, are one and the same person.

The following month, G. W. Orr was competing in a tournament at Brooklands, and in the first round beat N. Bury 5-7, 7-5, 6-4, though he was beaten in the very next round by F. R. Monkhouse who beat him in straight sets, 6-0, 6-2. Regular sports players in South Manchester will recognise that last name, as F. R. Monkhouse is the name of the sports shops and school uniform suppliers based in Stockport and elsewhere, and every year they still come to the Whalley Range tennis open day with racks of tennis clothing and footwear, racquets and other kit.

For the 1932 season, L. S. Pidd became Tennis Secretary, and would fulfil the role for five seasons, whilst G. V. Oddy would also join his father on the committee for the first time this season. In August this year, G. W. Orr was back in Criccieth in North Wales where he performed particularly well in the mixed doubles handicap event. In the semi-final, he and partner Miss Sandiford (Bury), beat J. G. Leaf and Miss Leaf (Bowdon) 6-1, 6-4. The score in the final was also 6-1, 6-4, but unfortunately this time they were on the receiving end, beaten by J. Briggs (Blundellsands) and Mrs. H. S. Fox. A year later in August 1933, G. W. Orr and G. V. Oddy were again in Criccieth, partnering each other in the men's doubles event of the North Wales Championships. In the first round they beat D. H. Anderson and C. J. MacLaren in a very tight game, 6-4, 4-6, 8-6. The following day witnessed showery weather and another very close game that went to 8-6 in the deciding set, but this time they were defeated 1-6, 6-2, 8-6 by Maurice Brown and Brian Berey.

The next mention of Whalley Range players unearthed in the local press, was again at the tournament that was held in Criccieth in August 1935, which this year was billed as the 48th annual open lawn tennis tournament for the North Wales championships Admittedly G. V. Oddy was listed with Northern after his name, though one assumes this was a mistake since he was on the Whalley Range tennis committee this season! At the same tournament, G. W. Orr (who was listed as representing Whalley Range) partnered Miss M. Law (Hoylake) in the mixed doubles but they lost 6-2, 6-3 in the third round to E. T. Hollins and Miss E. P. Hollins (Alderley Edge).

At the start of July 1936, Fred Perry won what would prove to the last of his three Wimbledon men's singles titles, beating Gottfried von Cramm in a one-sided final 6-1, 6-1, 6-0. Later that month, G. V. Oddy was again competing in the men's singles handicap at the Northern in West Didsbury, with his first round result being reported as "*A. R. Ainsworth (15/1) beat G. V. Oddy (15/2), 6-4, 6-2*", where the figures in brackets presumably bore some relation to the handicapping system.

The following year, in July 1937, G. V. Oddy played in the Brooklands tournament, beating J. L. Lacayo 6-3, 4-6, 7-5 in the first round. In the second round he was then up against R. V. Fontes, who was described in the local press as a "*violent foot-faulter*", though it was further reported that Brooklands had "*a nice disregard for the front-foot rule, treating it with the contempt it deserves*"! Thus, it seems like G. V. Oddy was somewhat up against it in this match, and so it proved, with R. V. Fontes winning 7-5, 6-3. In spite of the rather unflattering appraisal, Raymond Victor Fontes was actually a very accomplished player, and regularly represented his home county of Cheshire around this time in his career, and had actually appeared at Wimbledon the month before, though he was knocked out in the first round of the singles by Raymond Tuckey, winning just four games. In 1935, R. V. Fontes had married Nancy Kidson from Knutsford, and after the war, he would make his second (and last) appearance at Wimbledon in 1947, partnering his wife, though again experienced defeat in the first round, losing in straight sets to a Hungarian pair.

In the 1935 season, a new role of Tennis Match Secretary had been introduced, and the first person to fill the position had been E. D. Croft. For the 1937 season this role now belonged to H. C. Webber, with E. D. Croft instead filling the role of Tennis Secretary that had been admirably occupied by L. S. Pidd for the past few seasons. Thus it seems quite fitting that the 1937 season would see the introduction of both the L. S. Pidd Trophy (for ladies' doubles) and the G. V. Oddy Trophy (for men's doubles), the oldest surviving tennis silverware relating to the Whalley Range club (see ensuing photos).

It also seems quite expedient, that the first winners of the G. V. Oddy Trophy were J. P. V. Woollam and G. V. Oddy himself. Thus not only was Jack Woollam a fine cricketer and a superb lacrosse player, but not a bad tennis player either. The winners of the L. S. Pidd Trophy for 1937 were Miss E. J. Butler and Miss P. Marlow.

The names of W. B. Stansby and H. C. Webber are inscribed on the G. V. Oddy Trophy for 1938, again illustrating the close links between the tennis and the cricket sections at the club. In fact, W. B. Stansby was on both the cricket and tennis committees this season, and the following year would also be on the general committee. A former Hulme Grammar schoolboy, Walter Bennett Stansby first played cricket for the club in 1929, and continued to represent the club, up to and after the war, eventually going on to become Club Chairman between 1964 and 1967. He won the G. V. Oddy Trophy three further times following the war, in successive years from 1951 to 1953 when he partnered G. B. Appleby on each occasion.

The winners of the L. S. Pidd Trophy in 1938 were Miss P. Marlow again, this time partnering Miss E. G. Pickering, who together retained their title the following season. As for the men's doubles, G. V. Oddy again laid claim to his own trophy in 1939, this time partnering L. W. N. Fogg, who had previously been a member of the Chorltonville club for the last decade or so, and who had also represented Lancashire. Even though he was known as Laurie Wilfred Newell Fogg, the name Laurie does not appear on any official documentation, i.e. his birth, marriage and death records refer to him as Wilfred Newell Fogg. In October 1943, he married Rotha Marjorie Lucas Maiden in Altrincham, and in later life, moved down south to Helston in Cornwall. He passed away in 1976, aged in his late sixties.

Miss E. G. Pickering is Enid Grace Pickering (born in 1904 to Harold and Charlotte Glover Pickering) who after the war, would serve on the tennis committee for one season. In the 1920s and 1930s she regularly appeared at the Northern's open tournament at West Didsbury with her older sister Dorothy, though for most of this time, she was a member of the Chorltonville club.

L. S. Pidd, or Leslie Stubbs Pidd to give him his full name, continued to serve on both the tennis and general committees up until the Second World War. His father, a cotton goods merchant, emanated from Crowle in Lincolnshire, though he'd moved to Whalley Range by the time of Leslie's birth. Sadly, Leslie died suddenly whilst on holiday in the Lake District in September 1941, aged just 44. The following extract is taken from his obituary :-

> ... the death of Mr. Leslie Stubbs Pidd, of 'Axholme', 288 Wilbraham Road, Manchester 16, occurred suddenly whilst on holiday at Keswick, on September 11, at the age of forty-four years. Mr. Pidd was the son of the late Mr. Eli West Stubbs Pidd of the above address. Born in Whalley Range, his youth was spent at the Hulme Grammar School, in connection with which in later years he was a member of the General Committee of the Old Hulmeians. He was keenly interested in sport and was closely connected with the lacrosse team until his death. He was also secretary of the tennis section of the Whalley Range Cricket and Tennis Club for many years. From boyhood he had taken an active part in the Whalley Range Methodist Church and his fondness for children is exemplified by his fourteen years' connection as superintendent of the primary department. He joined William Mather, Ltd., medical and surgical plaster manufacturers, Manchester, in 1915, and on the death of his uncle, Mr. A. J. Pidd, M.P.S., in 1930, he became chairman of the board of directors, a position which he filled until his death. He had an active interest in business and in his own many social activities, and the numerous friends who attended the funeral service testify to the esteem in which he was held. At the Manchester Crematorium the service was conducted by the Rev. Metcalf, of the Whalley Range Methodist Church. Amongst those present were representatives of the Whalley Range Methodist Church, Whalley Range Cricket and Tennis Club, Old Hulmeians Association, Manchester Pharmaceutical Association, The Medical Plaster Makers' Conference, and all the directors, office and works staffs of William Mather, Ltd.

Amazingly enough, the Axholme property on Wilbraham Road still has connections to the Tennis section of the club, with Paul Schofield, a recent former tennis coach and first team player, having in-laws who currently live there.

The following two photos show the L. S. Pidd trophy for ladies' doubles, and the G. V. Oddy trophy for men's doubles :-

L. S. Pidd Trophy, for Ladies' Doubles Open champions

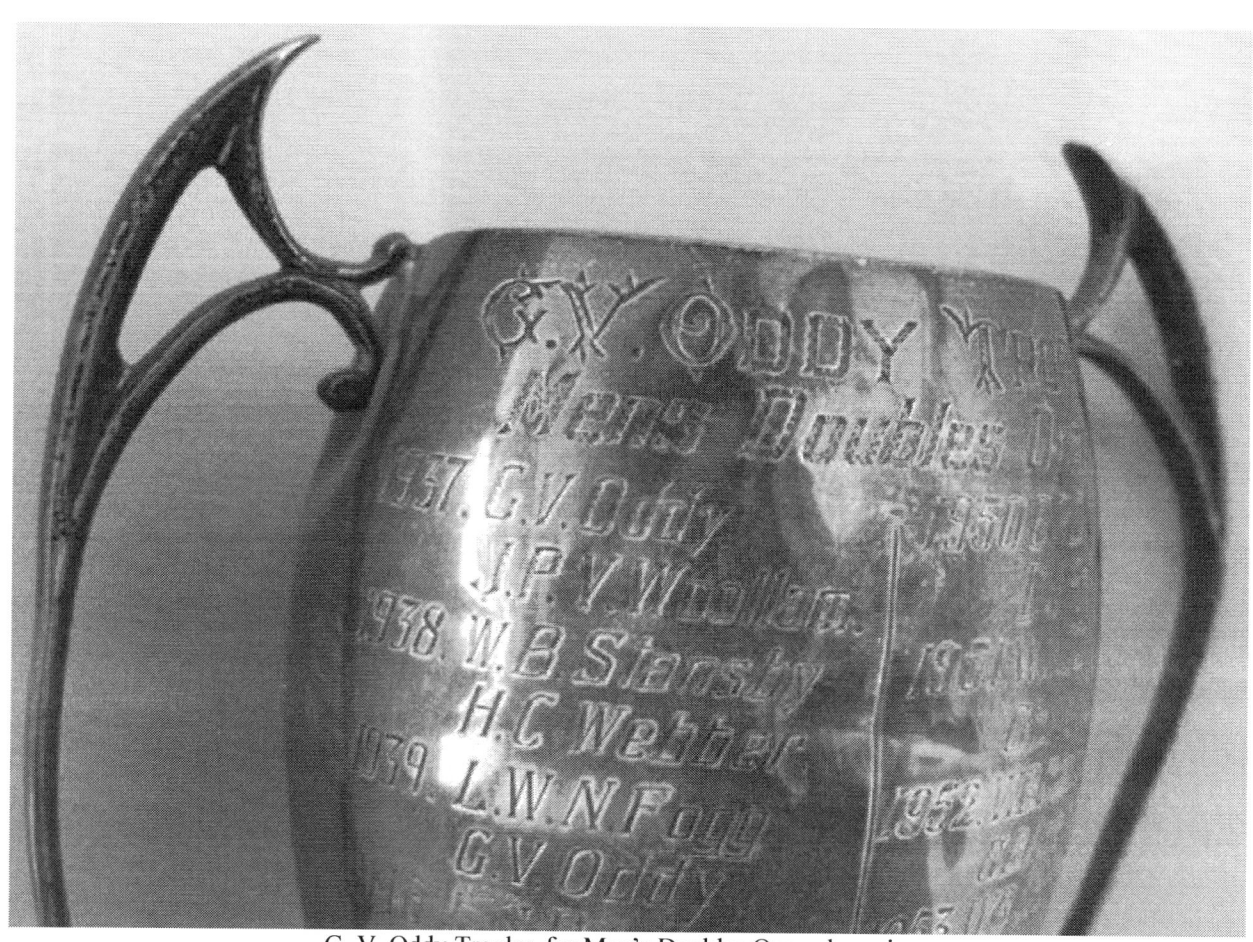

G. V. Oddy Trophy, for Men's Doubles Open champions

In 1914, just before the start of the First World War, the reporting of a Whalley Range Tennis Club match had made a rare appearance in the local press. Strangely enough, in 1939, perhaps as an uncanny portent of imminent events, we witness the next reporting of a Whalley Range Tennis Club match, with a headline in the Manchester Guardian of July 26th 1939 proclaiming *"Whalley Range Beat Northern"*. As it happens, the result was 3-all with regards to matches, but Whalley Range won **8** sets to **7**, and **88** games to **86**. The results are listed below, with the scores being shown exactly as they were printed, with the Whalley Range players appearing on the right-hand side :-

W. T. Shewell and L. Gilbert	beat L. W. N. Fogg and G. V. Oddy 7-5, 6-6
	beat L. S. Brittain and J. H. Wright 6-6, 6-2
	beat W. Stansby and J. Fergie 6-2, 7-5
V. Fletcher and T. Willans	lost to L. W. N. Fogg and G. V. Oddy 3-6, 4-6
	lost to L. S. Brittain and J. H. Wright 6-6, 2-6
	drew with W. Stansby and J. Fergie 6-3, 5-7
J. Merritt and E. V. Horne	drew with L. W. N. Fogg and G. V. Oddy 1-6, 6-0
	lost to L. S. Brittain and J. H. Wright 1-6, 3-6
	drew with W. Stansby and J. Fergie 6-3, 5-7

At this level of tennis, sets were often deemed to be shared if the score reached 6-6, and so as can be seen, it was possible to win a match by the score of 6-6, 6-2, for instance. Sadly, this was the last report relating to Whalley Range tennis before the onset of the Second World War.

Tennis at the club did continue throughout the war, with the fixture list from 1940 showing matches against Bramhall Lane, Brooklands, Carlton, Didsbury, Edge Lane, Gatley, and West Heaton, though admittedly the other surviving club fixture lists from the war years, illustrate just cricket fixtures. As is known though, following the war, tennis at Whalley Range has continued to thrive with new courts and even floodlights being installed in recent years, though again such tales belong in the second volume of this book.

Appendix A – Notable Alumni

The following notable people all represented Whalley Range prior to the end of WWII, and are listed in order of their first recorded appearance for the club, with the years in brackets relating to their known playing seasons for the club.

J. (James) MacLaren (1864 - 1879) – Honorary Treasurer of Lancashire Cricket Club (1881 to 1900). President of the Rugby Union committee in 1882. Father of J. A. MacLaren, A. C. MacLaren, and G. MacLaren, who would all play cricket for Lancashire, with A. C. MacLaren also going on to captain not only his county but also his country.

C. A. G. (Campbell Arthur Grey) Hulton (1868 - 1888) – Played 8 times for Lancashire between 1869 and 1882, and was also a Lancashire committee member at one time, before going on to serve on the MCC committee in later life. Was A. C. MacLaren's godfather, and thus gave Archie his second name. Also represented his county at rugby according to one report. Direct descendant of King Henry VII.

W. (William) Grave (1868 - 1869) – Inaugural Hon. Sec. and Treasurer of Lancashire rugby union. Played rugby for Lancashire, and also represented the North of England (v South).

W. (William) MacLaren (1869) – Played for England in the world's first ever rugby international in 1871, against Scotland. Cousin of James MacLaren.

D. B. (David Bannerman) MacLaren (1869 - 1879) – Played rugby for Lancashire. Younger brother of James MacLaren, and uncle of Archibald Campbell MacLaren

H. E. (Henry "Harry" Ernest) Carter (1874 - 1879) – Represented North of England at Lacrosse in 1877 alongside P. W. Kessler.

P. W. (Philip William) Kessler (1874 - 1891) – Represented North of England at Lacrosse in 1877 alongside H. E. Carter, H. Eller, and his brother E. Kessler.

A. M. (Andrew Marcus) Bulteel (1874) – Represented England against Ireland in a rugby international in 1875.

J. C. Low (1876 - 1878) – Represented Lancashire at rugby. Note that his name was spelt as J. C. Lowe, on several occasions.

H. (Harry) Eller (1876 - 1879) – Represented North of England at Lacrosse in 1877 alongside P. W. Kessler and E. Kessler

E. (Edward) Kessler (1877 - 1887) – Represented North of England at Lacrosse in 1877 alongside P. W. Kessler and H. Eller.

D. A. (David Alexander) Bannerman (1877 - 1883) – Died tragically young at the age of 29 following a swimming pool accident. His son, David Armitage Bannerman, was born just 5 days after his burial, a son who would go on to become one of the world's most prominent and renowned ornithologists, winning many awards, including an OBE. Also related to Sir Henry Campbell-Bannerman GCB, who was Prime Minister of the UK between 1905 and 1908.

A. G. (Allan Gibson) Steel (1877) – England cricket captain. Played in 13 test matches between 1880 and 1888, scoring 600 runs and taking 29 wickets. In 162 first-class matches (including 47 for Lancashire), scored exactly 7000 runs, and captured 789 wickets at an average of only 14.78, between 1877 and 1895. Scorer of the earliest discovered century for the Whalley Range club. Came from a remarkable cricketing family, with three other brothers representing Lancashire, including E. E. Steel, who also played for Whalley Range.

T. P. (Thomas Percy) Bellhouse (1877 - 1891) – Won inaugural Amateur Boxing Association Middleweight Championship in 1881. Secretary of the Manchester Amateur Gymnastic Club, a club devoted to boxing.

A. M. (Alfred Mortimer) Nesbitt (1878 - 1882) – Played one game for the MCC in 1879. Then emigrated to Australia and played for a Queensland team of 18 against a touring English team that included A. G. Steel in 1882. Related to the famous Nesbitt/Nisbet (various variants of the name) family of artists.

W. R. (William Ryder) Richardson (1878 - 1887) – Played one rugby international for England, against Ireland on 5th February 1881, in Whalley Range, as it happens. Married Alice Jane MacLaren (Archie's aunt) in 1887.

F. D. (Frederic Ducange) Gaddum (1879 - 1896) – Played one game for Lancashire in 1884.

E. F. (Edward Ffooks) Woodforde (1879 - 1895) – Played rugby for Lancashire. He didn't actually have a middle name, with the 'F' in his name, solely relating to his former surname which was changed from "Ffooks" (having already previously been changed from "Fooks") to Woodforde.

A. (Alan) Railton (1880 - 1891) – Played hockey for Lancashire. His elder sister, Emily Railton, married David Bannerman MacLaren.

W. G. (Walter George) Mills (1882 - 1891) – Played 6 times for Lancashire between 1871 and 1877, before joining Whalley Range. His son, Walter Henderson Mills, played for Whalley Range in the 1913 season.

F. (Frederick) Delius (1883) – One of Great Britain's greatest ever composers played for Whalley Range in 1883.

Rev R. P. (Robert Peel) Willock (1883 - 1891) – Called Robert Peel because of his family connection to Rt. Hon. Sir Robert Peel, who was twice Prime Minister, and after whom the police bobbies are named after.

R. W. (Reginald William) Sharp (1883 - 1894) – Played hockey for Lancashire, and also represented the North (v South).

C. N. (Charles Nigel) Stewart (1884 - 1887) – Like C. A. G. Hulton, was a direct descendant of King Henry VII.

H. C. L. (Henry Charles Lenox) Tindall (1884 - 1891) – One of the greatest runners of his time, over all distances between 100 and 1000 yards. Won the AAA Championship quarter-mile in both 1888 and 1889, and also the half-mile in 1889. Played cricket twice for Kent in 1893 and 1894. Brother of S. M. Tindall and H. W. Tindall.

E. E. (Ernest Eden) Steel (1885 - 1887) – Played 40 times for Lancashire between 1884 and 1903. Came from a remarkable sporting family that boasted four brothers in total that played cricket for Lancashire, with one of them, A. G. Steel, also going on to captain his country.

S. M. (Sidney Maguire) Tindall (1885 - 1896) – Played 42 times for Lancashire between 1894 and 1898, and was captain as well at one point. Regarded as one of the best hockey players in the country. As such, represented both his county and the North (v South), where he played alongside J. F. Arnold and his brother H. W. Tindall. Also brother of H. C. L. Tindall.

H. W. (Herbert Woods) Tindall (1885 - 1897) – Played 2 times for Lancashire 2nd XI in 1897 and 1898. Represented his county at hockey, and also represented the North (v South), appearing in the same team as J. F. Arnold, and his brother S. M. Tindall. Also brother of H. C. L. Tindall.

E. H. (Edward Hoare) Hardcastle (1886) – Played 2 times for Kent in 1883 and 1884. Son of Conservative politician Edward Hardcastle, he was the Archdeacon of Canterbury between 1924 and 1939.

J. N. (James Nesfield) Forsyth (1887) – Played just the once for Whalley Range, in the final game of the 1887 season. The son of a sculptor, he followed in his father's footsteps, earning much recognition in the art world.

A. C. (Archibald Campbell) MacLaren (1888 - 1890) – Undoubtedly the greatest ever cricketer to have played for Whalley Range, who went on to captain not only Lancashire but England as well. Played 307 games for Lancashire between 1890 and 1914, scoring 15772 runs at an average of 33.34. Scored 47 first-class centuries (five of which were for England), including a score of 424 (a record at the time) for Lancashire against Somerset at Taunton in 1895. In all, played 35 times for England, captaining his country in 22 of those matches. Son of James MacLaren and brother of James Alexander MacLaren.

J. A. (James Alexander) MacLaren (1888 - 1893) – Played 4 times for Lancashire between 1891 and 1894. Son of James MacLaren and brother of Archibald Campbell MacLaren.

C. F. (Charles Frederick) Butterworth (1889 - 1896) – Renowned amateur astronomer whose main interest lay in the observation of "variable stars", for which work he gained much recognition and several awards. In his honour, the British Astronomical Association now presents the Charles Butterworth Award to those who excel in this particular field of astronomy.

J. F. (James Frederick) Arnold (1890 - 1897) – Played 3 times for Lancashire in 1896. Represented his county at hockey, and also represented the North (v South) appearing alongside both S. M. Tindall and H. W. Tindall. Was honorary secretary and treasurer of the Lancashire County Hockey Association and also served on the Northern Counties Hockey Association committee.

H. T. (Harry Temple) Mawson (1891 - 1897) – Played for South of Argentina at cricket between 1906 and 1919.

E. W. (Ernest Walter) Bellhouse (1891 - 1892) – Played in a couple of football matches for Derby County in January 1889, in the first ever season of the Football League.

L. A. (Lewis Alfred) Orford (1892) – Just played the once for a team that was billed as F. D. Gaddum's XI against Bilton Grange in Rugby, though in all but name, this was a Whalley Range team. He was the Uppingham School cricket captain in 1883, and played in seven first-class cricket matches for Cambridge University in the 1886 and 1887 seasons, playing against the likes of W. G. Grace.

D. H. (Douglas Harold) Brownfield (1892) – He may have only made one guest appearance for the club in 1892, when they travelled to Rugby in 1892, but he did play for an England XI against the touring Australians in 1888, and made occasional appearances for MCC between 1874 and 1907.

E. B. (Ernest Butler) Rowley (1892) – Played 16 times for Lancashire between 1893 and 1898.

A. J. (Alfred James) Arnold CBE (1893 - 1896) – Awarded CBE for his military efforts. Brother of J. F. Arnold who played for Lancashire.

W. R. (William Rothschild) Deakin (1893 - 1898) – Was Chairman of Manchester United Football Club from 1909 until his death in 1919.

F. E. (Francis Edward) Hildyard (1894) – Another Whalley Range player who could claim to have royal connections, and who had no fewer than ten knights amongst his forefathers.

W. N. Fletcher (1894) – Played hockey for Lancashire and the North of England (v South).

J. C. (John Charles) Bythell (1895) – Played hockey for Lancashire. Also very good tennis player who played in tournaments as far afield as Hamburg, and played in the Lancashire County Championship doubles tournament with his younger brother, William James Storey Bythell.

A. G. (Arthur George) Baker (1895 - 1910) – Played once for Cheshire in Minor Counties Championship in 1912. Brother of C. S. Baker.

H. R. C. (Henry Ralph Champion) Partridge (1895) – Married Lilla Gwendolen Morris who was a direct descendant of King James I.

F. R. (Ferdinand Raymond) Leroy (1897 - 1937) – represented Lancashire at hockey, captaining them at one point. He was also president of the Lancashire County Hockey Association in 1920-21.

C. S. (Charles Shaw) Baker (1898 - 1906) – Played over 200 times for Warwickshire, scoring close to 10,000 runs. According to one source, also played football for Aston Villa. Brother of A. G. Baker.

J. E. G. (John Edward Gunby) Hadath (1898 - 1899) – Prolific author of over 100 books. One of his tales, "Fortune Lane" was filmed by Elstree Independent Films in 1947. He also wrote a number of songs.

S. R. (Stephen Roberts) Oddy (1899 - 1934) – Member of the all-conquering Old Hulmeians lacrosse team who were champions of England on several occasions, and was their captain in 1908. Also played tennis for the club, and played golf for Chorlton.

G. F. (George Frederick) Buckland (1901 - 1914) – Represented Great Britain at lacrosse in Olympic Games in 1908. Also played lacrosse for England and Lancashire. Member of the all-conquering Old Hulmeians lacrosse team who were champions of England on several occasions, and was their captain in 1910. Brother of Herbert and Ronald Buckland.

H. (Herbert) Buckland (1903 - 1914) – Member of the all-conquering Old Hulmeians lacrosse team who were champions of England on several occasions. Also played lacrosse for Lancashire. Brother of George and Ronald Buckland.

R. (Ronald) Buckland (1905 - 1931) – Member of the all-conquering Old Hulmeians lacrosse team who were champions of England on several occasions. Also played lacrosse for Lancashire. Talented athlete as well. Brother of George and Herbert Buckland, and father of John Buckland.

R. (Reginald) Sykes (1906 - 1914) – Represented Lancashire at rugby on several occasions. Sadly, he was killed in the First World War.

J. H. (John Haslam) Walker – The exact years of John's association with the club are unknown. His name didn't appear in any cricket scoresheets, but this was at a time when only 1st XI matches were reported on, so he could well have solely played 2nd XI cricket around this period, since he certainly played cricket at Hulme Grammar School in his final year there in 1905. He was a member of the successful pre-War Old Hulmeians lacrosse team who were champions of England, and also represented Lancashire. Sadly, he was killed in the First World War.

W. A. (Wilfred Alston) Hobbins (1907 - 1908) – Member of the all-conquering Old Hulmeians lacrosse team who were champions of England on several occasions, and was their captain in 1914. Also played lacrosse for Lancashire and England.

F. (Frank) Fairbank (1908 - 1910) – Played for Yorkshire 2nd XI, and also played for Cheshire in Minor Counties championship in 1912 and 1913.

S. E. (Samuel Edward "Eddie") Woollam (1911 - 1945+) – Chairman of the Lancashire & Cheshire Amateur Football League for an amazing 38 years, with the S. E. Woollam Aggregate Trophy being named in his honour. Older brother of J. P. V. Woollam. His father, Samuel, was Lord Mayor of Manchester (1934-35).

C. H. (Charles Henry) Fox (1913 - 1914) – Goalkeeper of the all-conquering Old Hulmeians lacrosse team who were champions of England on several occasions.

J. A. (James Arthur) Barber (1914 - 1928) – Member of the all-conquering Old Hulmeians lacrosse team who were champions of England on several occasions, and also represented Lancashire. Father of N. A. Barber, who also represented Lancashire at lacrosse.

H. L. (Hubert Leslie) Palmer MBE (1915 - 1933) – Served with distinction in both world wars. Commissioned in 1916 in the Lancashire Fusiliers, and awarded the MBE in 1917.

J. P. V. (John "Jack" Victor Philip) Woollam (1915 - 1945+) – Hailed as one of the best lacrosse players in the country, Jack was a member of the successful post-WWI Old Hulmeians lacrosse team who were champions of England, and also represented Lancashire, and North of England at lacrosse. Also part of the Great Britain squad that competed in a lacrosse demonstration event at the 1928 Olympics in Amsterdam. Younger brother of S. E. Woollam.

N. A. (Norman Alexander) Barber MBE (1923 - 1929) – was a member of the successful post-WWI Old Hulmeians lacrosse team who were champions of England, and also represented Lancashire at lacrosse. Married Constance (Connie) Mark, the sister of Sir Robert Mark GBE. Son of J. A. Barber who also represented Lancashire at lacrosse.

A. J. (Alexander James) Leggat (1924 - 1929) – President of Lancashire County Cricket Club in 1992, and close friend of L. S. Lowry.

G. F. (George Frederick) Henson OBE (1924 - 1945+) – President of the Manchester Division of the Grenadier Guards Comrades Association, and won an OBE in the 1954 New Year Honours.

A. G. (Archibald Gordon) Campbell (1925 - 1927) – Represented Lancashire at lacrosse.

K. (Kenneth) Rains (1926 - 1937) – Member of the successful post-WWI Old Hulmeians lacrosse team who were champions of England, and also represented Lancashire, and North of England at lacrosse. Also toured America in 1930, as did R. N. Ainsworth, as part of what was in effect a touring England lacrosse team, that won the Flannery Cup. Related to Samuel Rains (of Reeds Rains fame) who founded his estate agency company in 1868. Affectionately known as Tubby.

T. L. (Thomas Leslie) Brierley (1928 - 1931) – Played 181 games for Glamorgan between 1931 and 1939, and 46 times for Lancashire between 1946 and 1948. He also represented the Canadian national team in the 1950s, which included a tour of the UK in 1954. He was also a fine lacrosse player.

A. R. (Alan Roy) Merchant (1929 - 1938) – was a member of the successful post-WWI Old Hulmeians lacrosse team who were champions of England.

G. B. (Gordon Bertram) Brookes (1930 - 1945+) – was co-founder of W. J. Barton, the baking company that introduced the "Mother's Pride" white bread brand to the British public.

R. N. (Raymond Nichols) Ainsworth (1930 - 1939) – Represented Lancashire at lacrosse. Also toured America in 1930, as did K. Rains, as part of what was in effect a touring England lacrosse team, that won the Flannery Cup.

W. E. F. (William Edwin Forsyth) Stockton (1933 - 1934) – Member of the prestigious Stockton family. His uncle was Sir Edwin Forsyth Stockton, who was LCCC President and Chairman at various times, and after whom the Stockton Trophy (awarded to the league champions of the Manchester & District Cricket Association) is named, whilst his father was Albert Forsyth Stockton who as Sale captain was the first to receive the Stockton Trophy. Albert also held various LCCC positions including treasurer and honorary secretary.

B. C. K. (Brian Charles Keene) Ballinger (1933 - 1945+) – Goalkeeper of the Old Hulmeians lacrosse team who won the Iroquois Cup after WWII. Also represented Cheshire at lacrosse.

D. M. (Dennis Matthew) Arrandale MBE (1938) – Member of the Old Hulmeians lacrosse team who won the Iroquois Cup after WWII. In later life, he was the Assistant Director for the Manchester Chamber of Commerce and Industry, and was awarded an MBE for services to export in 1980.

J. (John) Buckland (1939 - 1945+) – Member of the Great Britain squad that competed in a lacrosse demonstration event at the 1948 Olympics in London. Also represented Lancashire and England. Son of Ronald Buckland. His uncle, George Frederick Buckland, competed at the 1908 Olympics, to make it an amazing double for the Buckland clan. Also part of the Old Hulmeians lacrosse team that had much success in the 1940s, 50s and 60s.

L. W. N. (Laurie Wilfred Newell) Fogg (1939 - ?) – Played tennis for the Whalley Range club in 1939 (at least), having previously played tennis for Lancashire. Prior to playing for Whalley Range, he was a member of the Chorltonville club for about a decade. Note that the name Laurie did not appear on his birth and death records, so it seems like his official name was Wilfred Newell Fogg.

Sir R. (Robert) Mark GBE QPM (1942 - 1945+) – Played tennis for the Whalley Range club. Member of the post-war Old Hulmeians lacrosse team that won the Iroquois Cup, and also represented Lancashire at lacrosse. More famous though for being the Commissioner of the Metropolitan Police from 1972 to 1977, and his involvement in an advert during this period when he endorsed a certain make of tyre with the catchphrase *"I'm convinced they're a major contribution to road safety"*. His sister, Constance "Connie" Mark, married N. A. Barber.

Appendix B – List of Officers

Presidents (1900-1945)

1900-1904   W. G. Thompson
1904-1914   H. Worrall
1914-1929   J. J. Leroy
1929-1937   K. T. S. Dockray
1937-1945+ H. R. Classen

In addition to the above information which has come from the club handbooks dating back to 1900, it is known that H. Dunnill was the President in 1861.

Chairmen (1937-1945)

1937   F. R. Leroy
1938-1945+ W. J. Mountain

The position of Chairman did not come into force until 1937, when F. R. Leroy became the first to fulfil that role, though sadly he passed away before the year was out.

Honorary Treasurers (1869-1945)

1869-1899   J. H. Beckett
1900-1929   K. T. S. Dockray
1929-1945+ H. R. Classen

As can be seen above, as well as the club handbooks providing information back to 1900, it is also known that J. H. Beckett was the Honorary Treasurer for a long period immediately prior to this.

Honorary Secretaries (1900-1939)

1900-1902   A. F. Walley
1902-1904   I. Melling
1904-1906   A. C. Elderton
1907-1937   H. R. Classen
1937-1939   W. W. Land

In 1900, there were joint-secretaries with A. F. Walley being joined in the role with H. J. Amos. The 1906 handbook is not available, so it is not known precisely when H. R. Classen took over from A. C. Elderton. There were some club handbooks during WWII but these did not list the secretaries, and in the season immediately after the war, W. W. Land was no longer in the role, so it is not possible to state how much longer his tenure lasted beyond 1939.

1st XI Captains (1899-1945)

1899-1904   A. G. Baker
1905   F. Clay
1907-1910   A. G. Baker
1912-1913   G. F. Buckland
1914-1936   H. R. Classen
1937-1945+ J. P. V. Woollam

From reports it is known that A. G. Baker's captaincy began at least as early as 1899. He may well have been acting captain for a lot of the 1905 season, since F. Clay was absent for most of that season. The handbooks are missing for 1906 and 1911 so the 1st XI captain for these seasons is unknown. However, it is also known from the 1884 team photo, that P. W. Kessler was the captain for that particular season.

Appendix C – Notable Vice-Presidents

The club handbooks also illustrate a number of notable personnel fulfilling the roles of vice-presidents, though it should be noted that there were over fifty vice-presidents listed some seasons, with most of the more prominent names seemingly having little or no connection to the club, other than to allow their names to be associated with the club. These notable vice-presidents are listed in order of their first known association with the club, with the years in brackets relating to their years as vice-president.

Sir J. W. (John William) Maclure, 1st Baronet (1900) – was a Conservative politician. He was educated at Manchester Grammar School and Brasenose College, Oxford. He served as President of the Conservative Association of South and East Lancashire, and held the seat of MP for Stretford (a constituency which included Whalley Range at the time) from 1886 until his death in 1901, aged 65.

Rt. Hon. W. R. W. (William Robert Wellesley) Peel, 1st Earl Peel, GCSI GBE TD PC (1903-1905) – was a politician who held various roles throughout his career, including MP for Manchester South between 1900 and 1906. He was the grandson of Prime Minister Sir Robert Peel, and therefore related to Rev. R. P. Willock who played cricket for Whalley Range.

Rt. Hon. C. A. (Charles Alfred) Cripps, 1st Baron Parmoor, KCVO PC QC (1903-1907) – was a politician who started out with the Conservative Party though later switched allegiance to the Labour Party. He was MP for Stretford from 1901 to 1906, succeeding Sir John William Maclure, whilst he himself was succeeded by Harry Nuttall.

Rev. W. J. (William John) Canton (1903-1907) – was the vicar of St. Margaret's Church in Whalley Range. With the help of his wife and fellow local people, he helped purchase the land on Brantingham Road that is now used as the playing fields of the local school. Father of John Talbot Canton and William Bashall Hick Canton who both played cricket for Whalley Range.

H. (Harry) Nuttall (1905-1913) – was a Liberal politician and MP for Stretford from 1906 to 1918. He was born in Manchester in 1849 and attended Owens College. An export and import merchant, he became President of the Manchester Chamber of Commerce in 1905. He died suddenly on September 25th 1924.

G. B. (George Beatson) Blair (1905-1914) – was an extremely wealthy businessman in the local area, and (with his brother James) a great collector of art, with over 30,000 artefacts (including 5000 paintings) filling the five entertaining rooms, twenty bedrooms, and various other rooms of his brother's house. Sadly, George was killed in WWII, a victim of the Manchester Blitz in December 1940. Many of the art items have now been acquired by the Manchester Art Gallery.

Sir A. A. (Arthur Adlington) Haworth, 1st Baronet (1905-1913) – was a Liberal politician. He was born in Eccles, and educated at Rugby School. In 1902 he was appointed a director of the Manchester Royal Exchange, becoming a chairman of the board in 1909. He was MP for Manchester South between 1906 and 1912, succeeding William Robert Wellesley Peel.

Dr. F. D. (Fred Duke) Woolley (1905-1912) – was a prominent physician and surgeon, who worked alongside Henry Beecham and Sir Thomas Beecham.

Ven Archdeacon N. L. (Noel Lake) Aspinall (1907-1934) – was Archdeacon of Manchester from 1916 up until his passing away in 1934. He was also rector of St. Edmund's Church in Whalley Range from 1902 to 1922.

B. B. (Bridge Baron) Peters (1934-1939) – performed as a baritone in the early part of the 20th century. He was born in 1882 in Accrington, Lancashire, and lived for most of his life in and around the Manchester area. He later moved down south and passed away in Honiton, Devon, in 1949.

Dr. J. B. (John Bowling) Holmes (1937-1938) – Was Chairman of Lancashire County Cricket Club for five years, before becoming the President in 1954. He was also a director of Manchester City Football Club for a quarter of a century, prior to being LCCC chairman. He passed away in January 1956.

Appendix D – Highest Totals

By Whalley Range :-

The following match results are all the known occasions when Whalley Range reached 300 prior to WWII, all of which occurred before the invention of declarations in 1889. All but one of these were scored at their home ground at College Road, with the notable exception being a total of 322 at Old Trafford.

Date	Result	Venue
03/8/1878 (Sat)	Athletic 1st XI 307, Wanderers dnb	College Road, Whalley Range
24/8/1878 (Sat)	Athletic 1st XI 322, Manchester dnb	Old Trafford
28/7/1883 (Sat)	Whalley Range 1st XI 315, Mr. C. Malcolm Wood's XI 33-8	College Road, Whalley Range
18/8/1883 (Sat)	Whalley Range 1st XI 328, Kersal dnb	College Road, Whalley Range
09/8/1884 (Sat)	Whalley Range 1st XI 345, Alderley Edge dnb	College Road, Whalley Range
02/8/1886 (Mon)	Whalley Range 1st XI 312, Huyton 60	College Road, Whalley Range
23/7/1887 (Sat)	Whalley Range 1st XI 362, Bowdon 71-2	College Road, Whalley Range

Against Whalley Range :-

The following match results are all the known occasions when Whalley Range conceded 300 or more, prior to WWII. The first of these was in 1883, a season which witnessed the 300 barrier being reached three times at the College Road ground, with Whalley Range amassing totals of 315 and 328 later in the season. As can be seen below, all of the first three 300+ totals conceded by Whalley Range, were against the powerful Cheetham Hill side, who were bolstered by the Holt family brewery business. This included both the home and away fixtures in 1887, as the Cheetham Hill side amassed a record 659 runs in total without reply that season! The next team to score over 300 against Whalley Range were Longsight, though Whalley Range got their revenge just two seasons later, when the same fixture saw Longsight being bowled out for just 25, with G. A. H. Jones taking 9-12, including a hat-trick. Saturday 7th July seems to be a particularly bad day for Whalley Range, conceding 300+ totals in both 1883 and 1894.

Date	Result	Venue
07/7/1883 (Sat)	Cheetham Hill 302, Whalley Range 35-3	College Road, Whalley Range
25/6/1887 (Sat)	Cheetham Hill 339, Whalley Range dnb	Cheetham Hill
13/8/1887 (Sat)	Cheetham Hill 320-9, Whalley Range dnb	College Road, Whalley Range
30/6/1888 (Sat)	Longsight 320-7, Whalley Range dnb	Longsight
07/7/1894 (Sat)	Manchester 307-2 dec, WR 188-5	Old Trafford
03/8/1896 (Mon)	Huyton 334, Whalley Range 128	Huyton
17/6/1899 (Sat)	Manchester 303-6, WR 128-7	Old Trafford
27/5/1912 (Mon)	South Manchester 327, Whalley Range 165	Withington
21/6/1913 (Sat)	Earlestown 304-5 dec, Whalley Range 164	Earlestown

Appendix E – Lowest Totals

1st XI

With regard to the 1st XI, there would appear to be only one occasion where Whalley Range failed to reach 20 prior to WWII, when they were dismissed for just 17 by Longsight on Saturday 18th April 1903, with no individual batsman making more than 4. Going back to 1864, when Whalley Range games very rarely made the local press, there was one game against Pendleton 2nd XI where they possibly scored 16, but the print is not especially clear, and this was in their second innings, having already won the game, based on the first innings totals.

The lowest total by the opposition in a 1st XI match was 21 by Knutsford on Saturday 25th August 1894, when both F. D. Gaddum and G. A. H. Jones captured 5 wickets. Boughton Hall were also bowled out for 21, on Saturday 9th May 1885, but this was in their second innings having being bowled out for 24 in the first innings. The bowlers doing all the damage here were E. E. Steel and F. L. Steel who claimed 19 wickets between them. Alderley Edge were also bowled out twice for less than 30 (25 & 27) the following season, on Saturday 21st August 1886. Again, the bowlers doing all the damage were the Steel brothers, who claimed another 19 wickets between them.

2nd XI

As for the 2nd XI though, they were once dismissed for a mere 1, and that was an extra, with not one batsman scoring a single run in the game against Chorlton-cum-Hardy on Saturday 14th May 1887. The 2nd XI team have twice dismissed their opponents for single figures though, with Timperley 2nd XI scoring just 5 on Saturday 17th May 1902, and Knutsford 2nd XI being bowled out for just 6 on Saturday 30th May 1931, with A. S. Bell capturing 5 wickets, L. L. Cooper 3 wickets, whilst the other two were run outs.

Appendix F – Centuries

Date	Name		Fixture	Venue	Pos
06/8/1877 (Mon)	A. G. Steel	115	1st XI v Western	Eccles	4
03/8/1878 (Sat)	A. M. Nesbitt	110	1st XI v The Wanderers	WR (College Rd)	2
23/7/1881 (Sat)	E. Woodforde	117	2nd XI v Castleton 2nd XI	Castleton	1
28/7/1881 (Thu)	A. M. Nesbitt	150	1st XI v City Police	WR (College Rd)	1
04/8/1883 (Sat)	W. G. Mills	105	1st XI v Alderley Edge	Alderley Edge	3
18/8/1883 (Sat)	W. G. Mills	165	1st XI v Kersal	WR (College Rd)	3
13/6/1885 (Sat)	S. M. Tindall	101	2nd XI v Alderley Edge 2nd XI	Alderley Edge	1
27/6/1885 (Sat)	S. M. Tindall	109	2nd XI v Cheetham Hill 2nd XI	Cheetham Hill	1
31/7/1886 (Sat)	E. E. Steel	146	1st XI v South Manchester	WR (College Rd)	1
02/8/1886 (Mon)	E. E. Steel	140	1st XI v Huyton	WR (College Rd)	1
11/9/1886 (Sat)	E. E. Steel	110	1st XI v Castleton	WR (College Rd)	1
23/7/1887 (Sat)	W. G. Mills	114	1st XI v Bowdon	WR (College Rd)	3
01/8/1887 (Mon)	S. M. Tindall	115	1st XI v Huyton	WR (College Rd)	2
20/7/1889 (Sat)	H. W. Tindall	106	1st XI v Boughton Hall	Chester	6
26/7/1890 (Sat)	J. A. MacLaren	119	1st XI v South Manchester	Withington	4
20/6/1891 (Sat)	H. W. Tindall	104	1st XI v Alderley Edge	WR (College Rd)	3
10/9/1892 (Sat)	S. M. Tindall	105	1st XI v South Manchester	Withington	1
10/6/1893 (Sat)	H. W. Tindall	115	1st XI v Knutsford	WR (College Rd)	5
30/6/1894 (Sat)	J. F. Arnold	128	1st XI v Broughton	Broughton	2
15/6/1895 (Sat)	C. E. Dunderdale	102*	2nd XI v Alderley Edge 2nd XI	Alderley Edge	4
25/5/1896 (Mon)	H. W. Tindall	108	1st XI v Huyton	WR (College Rd)	6
07/8/1897 (Sat)	G. Dale	103*	2nd XI v Western 2nd XI	WR (College Rd)	2
10/6/1899 (Sat)	C. S. Baker	100	1st XI v Alderley Edge	WR (College Rd)	1
02/6/1900 (Sat)	A. G. Baker	121	1st XI v Kersal	Kersal	1
04/6/1902 (Wed)	C. S. Baker	100*	1st XI v Owens College	Fallowfield	4
05/7/1902 (Sat)	S. R. Oddy	100	2nd XI v Kersal 2nd XI	Kersal	4
19/7/1902 (Sat)	C. S. Baker	127	1st XI v Castleton	Castleton	4
03/8/1903 (Mon)	D. M. Peacock	157	1st XI v Castleton	WR (College Rd)	1
20/6/1908 (Sat)	A. G. Baker	101*	1st XI v Rusholme	WR (College Rd)	3
20/6/1908 (Sat)	S. Nixon	100*	2nd XI v Rusholme 2nd XI	Rusholme	1
04/7/1908 (Sat)	F. Fairbank	102	1st XI v Sefton	WR (College Rd)	1
08/8/1908 (Sat)	H. Buckland	100*	1st XI v Castleton	WR (College Rd)	2
08/5/1909 (Sat)	A. G. Baker	101	1st XI v Macclesfield	WR (College Rd)	1
17/6/1910 (Fri)	L. Oliver	105*	1st XI v Yorkshire Gentlemen	York	4
09/7/1910 (Sat)	A. G. Baker	106*	1st XI v Prestwich	Prestwich	5
13/8/1910 (Sat)	F. Howard	150*	1st XI v South Manchester	Withington	2
18/4/1914 (Sat)	H. Buckland	103*	1st XI v Northwich	Northwich	3
21/7/1923 (Sat)	H. R. Classen	104*	1st XI v Cheadle Hulme	WR (Kingsbrook Rd)	1
12/5/1928 (Sat)	H. R. Classen	115	1st XI v South Manchester	WR (Kingsbrook Rd)	1
12/5/1928 (Sat)	W. Williamson	100*	1st XI v South Manchester	WR (Kingsbrook Rd)	2
16/5/1928 (Wed)	A. J. Leggat	112*	1st XI v Hulme Grammar Sch	WR (Kingsbrook Rd)	2
29/6/1929 (Sat)	T. L. Brierley	110*	1st XI v Castleton	WR (Kingsbrook Rd)	5
13/7/1929 (Sat)	A. Pitt	105*	2nd XI v Cheadle Hulme 2nd XI	WR (Kingsbrook Rd)	7
09/6/1930 (Mon)	H. L. Palmer	152*	2nd XI v Ashley	Ashley	1
26/7/1930 (Sat)	R. N. Ainsworth	114*	2nd XI v Brooklands 2nd XI	Brooklands	5
30/7/1932 (Sat)	R. N. Ainsworth	116	1st XI v Northwich	WR (Kingsbrook Rd)	1
13/8/1932 (Sat)	R. N. Ainsworth	116	1st XI v Castleton	Castleton	1
19/8/1933 (Sat)	W. Williamson	109*	1st XI v Castleton	Castleton	4
04/8/1934 (Sat)	R. N. Ainsworth	105	1st XI v Northwich	WR (Kingsbrook Rd)	1
03/8/1935 (Sat)	G. Rothwell	112	1st XI v Northwich	WR (Kingsbrook Rd)	2
05/8/1935 (Mon)	H. R. Classen	106*	1st XI v Bowdon	Bowdon	2
07/5/1938 (Sat)	W. Williamson	101*	1st XI v Buxton	WR (Kingsbrook Rd)	4
15/5/1939 (Sat)	R. N. Ainsworth	100*	1st XI v South Manchester	WR (Kingsbrook Rd)	3
03/6/1939 (Sat)	G. B. Brookes	110*	1st XI v Northwich	WR (Kingsbrook Rd)	5
15/7/1939 (Sat)	R. N. Ainsworth	105	1st XI v Cheadle Hulme	Cheadle Hulme	2

Notes on Centuries:

These are all of the Whalley Range centuries that were discovered whilst researching the book, though undoubtedly there'll be others that evaded the local press for whatever reasons, or went undetected.

A. G. Steel's century is the earliest discovered century for the club (named Athletic at the time), with his 115 coming out of an all-out total of 186, on the August Bank Holiday Monday in 1877.

E. E. Steel's first two centuries for the club were scored in consecutive innings just two days apart.

For H. W. Tindall's century on 25th May 1896, the final digit of his score is not totally clear in the paper, but fairly sure it is 108.

L. Oliver was a guest player from Ashton-under-Lyne who came along for the North Yorkshire tour in 1910.

A. J. Leggat's century against Hulme Grammar School appeared in the local papers on Thursday 17th May 1928, so this midweek game would probably have taken place the day before.

H. R. Classen and W. Williamson both scored centuries when opening for Whalley Range against South Manchester on Saturday 12th May 1928.

T. L. Brierley's century is not very clear in papers, but is probably 110 not out.

Spookily, R. N. Ainsworth's two innings of 116 were just a fortnight apart, and both formed part of a total of 207-6.

Appendix G – Best Bowling Performances for 1st XI

No occurrences of a bowler taking all ten wickets in an innings were discovered prior to WWII, though there were quite a few occasions when brothers E. E. Steel and F. L. Steel captured all ten wickets in an innings between them, including twice in the same match! As such, the lists below cover all the known occasions when a bowler captured nine or eight wickets in an innings. In most cases the exact bowling figures were not given, but an idea of their performance can be gauged to a certain extent from the opposition total, so the match result is also provided in the lists below. In the second-earliest discovered 9-wicket occurrence, one of E. E. Steel's nine victims was his elder brother A. G. Steel who had previously played for Whalley Range, and who of course, would go on to become the England captain. In the second occurrence, G. A. H. Jones's figures were 13 overs, 7 maidens, 9-12, including a hat-trick. F. D. Gaddum captured his 9-5 from just 4 overs, and were the best ever recorded figures for the club, in the period covered by this book.

9 Wickets in an Innings :-

Date	Name		Result	Venue
19/8/1882 (Sat)	J. M. Cowie	9w	WR 133, City Police 52 & 18-1	WR (College Rd)
27/8/1887 (Sat)	E. E. Steel	9w	WR 128, Liverpool 110	WR (College Rd)
17/5/1890 (Sat)	G. A. H. Jones	9-12	Longsight 25, WR 73	Longsight
09/8/1890 (Sat)	F. D. Gaddum	9w	Western 173, WR 122	Eccles
30/5/1891 (Sat)	F. D. Gaddum	9-5	South Manchester 23 & 35-1, WR 135	WR (College Rd)
24/4/1897 (Sat)	H. C. Butterworth	9w	Cheetham Hill 132, WR 29	WR (College Rd)
10/6/1905 (Sat)	C. A. Wicks	9-31	Knutsford 75, WR 107	Knutsford
05/6/1926 (Sat)	H. T. Eke	9-78	WR 202-8, Knutsford 135	WR (Kingsbrook Rd)

8 Wickets in an Innings :-

Date	Name		Result	Venue
27/6/1874 (Sat)	J. M. Cowie	8w	Athletic 65 & 68-6, Heaton Norris 48	WR (College Rd)
24/6/1876 (Sat)	H. E. Carter	8w	Athletic 79, Lymm 67	WR (College Rd)
10/6/1882 (Sat)	J. M. Cowie	8w	Western 145, WR 45-4	Eccles
07/8/1882 (Mon)	F. D. Gaddum	8w	WR 111 & 168-4, Kersal 68	Kersal
02/9/1882 (Sat)	G. A. H. Jones	8w	Alderley Edge 138, WR 59-3	WR (College Rd)
13/6/1885 (Sat)	E. E. Steel	8w	Alderley Edge 63, WR 118	WR (College Rd)
21/8/1886 (Sat)	E. E. Steel	8w	Alderley Edge 25 & 27, WR 195	WR (College Rd)
01/8/1887 (Mon)	F. L. Steel	8w	Huyton 176, WR 295	WR (College Rd)
18/8/1900 (Sat)	H. J. Amos	8-11	WR 125, Alderley Edge 40 & 22-5	Alderley Edge
24/8/1901 (Sat)	C. S. Baker	8w	Longsight 110, WR 49	WR (College Rd)
24/5/1902 (Sat)	W. H. Ashton	8w	WR 141-9, Urmston 72	Urmston
27/8/1904 (Sat)	H. C. Butterworth	8w	WR 75, Knutsford 144	Knutsford
23/6/1906 (Sat)	C. A. Wicks	8w	WR 136, Urmston 104	Urmston
08/9/1906 (Sat)	C. A. Wicks	8w	Manchester Clifford 36, WR 138	WR (College Rd)
26/6/1909 (Sat)	S. R. Oddy	8w	Earlestown 160, WR 136	Earlestown
25/6/1910 (Sat)	F. Fairbank	8w	Earlestown 164, WR 126-7	Earlestown
16/7/1910 (Sat)	F. Fairbank	8-25	Didsbury 107, WR 143-9	WR (College Rd)
18/7/1925 (Sat)	W. H. Thornton	8-32	WR 117, Cheadle Hulme 99	Cheadle Hulme
27/7/1929 (Sat)	H. B. Brooks	8w	Brooklands 138, WR 291-7	WR (Kingsbrook Rd)
03/6/1933 (Sat)	W. S. Thornton	8w	Knutsford 69, WR 147-5	Knutsford
16/6/1934 (Sat)	W. S. Thornton	8w	WR 210-7, Northwich 96	Northwich
07/9/1935 (Sat)	A. Horrocks	8w	Chorlton 26, WR 30-2	WR (Kingsbrook Rd)

Note that for the first 8w occurrence above, the match was billed as Athletic v Heaton Norris Club & Ground, but the opposition scorecard was headed with a title of Heaton Chapel. Against Alderley Edge in 1886, E. E. Steel took a further 5 wickets in their second innings, for a total haul of 13 wickets in the match, having also taken 8 wickets in an innings in the same fixture the previous season. H. J. Amos took a hat-trick in his figures of 8-11.

References

Written Physical Material

Archie A Biography of A C MacLaren, Michael Down
Frederick Delius: Memories of My Brother, Clare Delius
LCCC Yearbook 2005 (for article Mr Leggat and Mr Lowry, Barrie Watkins)
Manchester & District Cricket Association Centenary 1892-1992 booklet
Manchester & District Cricket Association handbooks
Manchester Courier archived newspapers
Manchester Guardian archived newspapers
Manchester Times archived newspapers
Old Trafford, John Marshall
OS Map of Chorlton 1907
South Manchester Remembered, Graham Phythian
The History of Lancashire County Cricket Club, Peter Wynne-Thomas
The Story of Chorlton-cum-Hardy, Andrew Simpson
Whalley Range Cricket & Lawn Tennis Club handbooks

Online Websites

The vast majority of the research for this book has been done online, with literally hundreds of websites being perused. Thus, it would be impossible to list all of these websites that have been visited, but it does seem prudent to make reference to some of the more salient ones that have proved especially useful :-

adsabs.harvard.edu (re C. F. Butterworth)
ancestry.co.uk
backwatersman.wordpress.com/2013/03/24/frederick-delius-yorkshire-cricketer
beeston-notts.co.uk/wesleyan_1876.htm (re G. F. Henson)
bbc.co.uk
bradlibs.com/localstudies/delius/pages/schooldays.htm (re F. Delius)
bridportnews.co.uk/news (re C. F. Butterworth)
britishnewspaperarchive.co.uk (for access to Manchester Courier archived newspapers)
chorltonhistory.blogspot.co.uk
cottontown.org
cricketarchive.com
espn.co.uk
findmypast.co.uk
geni.com
iomtoday.co.im/news/isle-of-man-news (re C. F. Butterworth)
lan-opc.org.uk
landc.org.uk (re S. E. Woollam)
lostaircraft.com
maccastro.wikispaces.com/file/view/Whats+Up+April+2008+Final. (re C. F. Butterworth)
mocavo.co.uk/Lancashire-Biographies-Rolls-of-Honour
myprimitivemethodists.org.uk (re H. E. Sanby)
oldhulmeians.org
oldhulmeianswarmemorial.yolasite.com
playcricket.com
proquest.com (for access to Manchester Guardian archived newspapers)
rcplondon.ac.uk (re Dr. P. B. Mumford obituary by William Brockbank)
simostronomy.blogspot.co.uk (re C. F. Butterworth)
spinningtheweb.org.uk (re Bannerman family)
telegraph.co.uk
thefamouspeople.com/profiles/frederick-delius-385.php
thepeerage.com
thompsonian.info/delius-cyclopedia-bio.html

Index (of Whalley Range personnel, including guest players, featured in the book)

Ackroyd, Cyril Brewood 128-129
Ainsworth, Raymond Nichols 144-173, 194, 200-201
Allen, Ernest Cecil 86-89
Allen, H 16-21
Allen, Samuel Joseph 48
Amos, Harold Joseph 56, 72-90, 115-119, 196, 202
Angel, L E 129
Appleby, G B 187
Arden/Ardern, S 97
Ardern, John Henry 185
Ardern, John Stanley 109, 185
Arnold, Alfred James 61, 192
Arnold, Henry Charles 45, 57-68
Arnold, James Frederick 56-78, 177, 181, 191-192, 200
Arnold, Willie Alfred 60-62
Arrandale, Dennis Matthew 171, 195
Ashton, William Henry 79-99, 202
Ashworth, H 86
Aspinall, Noel Lake 197
Astin, Ralph 5-6, 141, 147-173
Austin 102
Bailey, Basil Dinnis 172-173
Baker, Arthur George 59, 66, 69-106, 114, 115-119, 152, 193, 196, 200
Baker, Charles Shaw 74-94, 117-119, 152, 193, 200, 202
Ballinger, Brian Charles Keene 6, 159, 195
Banks, S R 152
Bannerman, David Alexander 26-28, 39, 45, 190
Barber, James Arthur 108-109, 121-126, 135, 141, 194
Barber, Norman Alexander 135, 144, 155-156, 164, 170, 194-195
Barlow, C M 14, 16
Barnes, C E 90
Barnes, Eric 147, 152
Barnes, William Theodore 131
Barnes-Lawrence, Herbert Cecil 30-35
Beckett (possibly J H Beckett) 18
Beckett, J H 18, 42, 196
Beeching, Edward Vernon 52-59
Bell, A S 154, 199
Bellhouse, Ernest Walter 58-60, 192
Bellhouse, Thomas Percy 24, 29-59, 66, 71, 77-82, 88, 191
Bertenshaw, James Alec 159-160
Blaikie, A 36
Blaikie, Grace (Miss) 185
Blaikie, M (Miss) 185
Blair, George Beatson 197
Botsford, Arthur 33, 47, 59, 62, 66-70, 75
Botsford, Charles Wright 33, 67, 72
Botsford, James Wall 30-50, 178-179
Botsford, John William 30-48, 178-179
Bowden-Smith, Edmund Philip 23
Bowman 24
Bradbury, Austen 104-110
Bradbury, Ross James 108
Bradshaw, William Platt 85-89, 118
Bridgford, T W 178-179

Brierley, Thomas Leslie 138-155, 194, 200-201
Brittain, L S 189
Brookes, Gordon Bertram 6, 151-173, 194, 200
Brooks, Harold Buckley 136-160, 202
Broughton, F D 19
Brown 102
Brown, G A 178-179
Brownfield, Douglas Harold 60, 192
Buckland, George Frederick 6, 84-124, 172, 193, 195-196
Buckland, Herbert 90-110, 120-125, 193, 200
Buckland, James Edward 29, 84, 118, 144
Buckland, John 6, 172, 193, 195
Buckland, Ron 93-114, 120-147, 172, 193, 195
Bull, Archibald Louis Alfred 73
Bulteel, Andrew Marcus 22-23, 190
Bulteel, Edward 22-23
Burd, S 17-18
Burton, George Frederick Ellinthorpe 35-50
Burton, H 109
Bury, J 30-31
Butler, Ernest Charles Peter 167
Butler, E J (Miss) 186-187
Butler, J (Miss) (possibly Miss E J Butler) 186
Butler, John James 154, 159, 167
Butterworth, Charles Frederick 53-56, 71, 192
Butterworth, R 22-23
Butterworth, Harry Clement 53, 67-92, 104-107, 202
Butterworth, Joseph Francis (senior) 53, 71
Butterworth, Joseph Francis 53, 71
Bythell, John Charles 69, 193
Campbell, Archibald Gordon 133-139
Campbell, Charles Douglas 133, 144, 152
Cannell, Doug 5
Canton, John Talbot 87, 197
Canton, William Bashall Hick 87-88, 197
Canton, William John 87, 197
Carter, A 129, 135
Carter, Charles Clement 22-25
Carter, Henry Ernest 22-32, 190, 202
Carver, Alfred John 20
Carver, C 17
Carver, Frank Henton 20-24, 155
Carver, Frederick William 20-28, 155
Carver, H 16-24
Casebourne, Frederick 89, 93
Caw, Agnes Graham (Miss) 182-183
Caw, John Graham 182
Chapman, W C 51-59
Chronnell, Gerald Bernard 139-147, 158
Clarke, A 184
Clarke, Fred 175
Classen, Ernest 74, 95, 106
Classen, Geoffrey 74, 129, 132, 144
Classen, Harry Rudolph 7, 74-169, 196, 200-201
Clay, F 81-94, 181, 196
Colburn, C 16
Coombes, George Frederick 178-179
Cooper, Leonard Lawton 154, 199
Cowie, John McRae 22-73, 202
Cowie, Thomas Scott 24, 34-40, 49, 64

Crankshaw 24
Crawford, A B 131-132
Cripps, Charles Alfred 197
Croft, E D 186
Crompton, Alfred Bernard 3, 5
Cummins, J A 86-103
Dale, G 72, 200
Dale, J M 72, 77
Daniel, J E 72
Darbyshire, J A 129-132, 159
Darwent 17
Davenport, James Gradwell 172
Davey, A 171
Dawson, Frederick Francis 97, 101-103
Deakin, William Rothschild 67, 69, 192
Delius, Frederick 6, 36-39, 191
Denison, Joseph Glasson 32-33
Dennis, Trevor 129, 133
Dixon, Roy 5
Dockray, Francis Smalley 78
Dockray, Kenneth Titus Smalley 78-86, 100-102, 166, 182, 196
Donald, W 21
Dorrity, David 52-70, 79-83, 91
Douglas, Stewart Keith 28, 34
Downing, S R 48
Dunderdale, Charles Edward 69, 200
Dunkerly/Dunkerley, J 16-17
Dunnill, Henry 6, 14-15, 196
Eke, Herbert Thomas 108-114, 129-155, 202
Elderton, Arthur Cecil 90, 140, 196
Elderton, Henry Edward 140
Eller, Harry 31, 190
Elliott, G 21
Emeris 25
Escombe, J 59, 62, 65
Evans, H 184
Fairbank, Frank 96-106, 193, 200, 202
Farbridge, Edward Brisco Owen 60
Farbridge, Frank Holliday 60
Farbridge, Robert Cridland 60-62
Farbridge, Stanley Brisco Owen 60
Farquhar, W R 30-31
Fawssett, Henry Barnard 35-36
Fennell, Theodore Llewellyn 70
Fennell, William Whately 70
Fergie, J 189
Fisher, G R – see Russel-Fisher
Fitzgerald, D J 35, 178-179
Fletcher, Norman 99-100
Fletcher, W N 69, 192
Fogg, Laurie Wilfred Newell 187, 189, 195
Forsyth, James Nesfield 51, 192
Forsyth, W F 55, 57
Foster 17
Fourdrinier, Samuel Harding 31, 178-180
Fox (Miss) 184
Fox, Charles Henry 96, 107-108, 121-126, 183-184, 194
Fox, S 183-184
Fox, W 21
Furnival, F 133-134, 136, 140
Gaddum, Frank Ernest 59-60

Gaddum, Frederick Ducange 7, 32-71, 81-82, 89, 191-192, 199, 202
Gardiner, C 167, 169
Garnett 100
Gates, C 97
Gilliat, George Nicholas Earle 86, 97
Godson, Alan 172
Gow, John Biggart 83, 85, 100
Grave, William 21, 190
Graves, C L 39
Greenup, George 131, 135, 144, 154-162, 184
Greenup, John William 135, 137, 144, 154
Gregson, E C 109
Gresham, James Neville 130, 142, 155
Gresham, Samuel Rowland 129-130
Grey, A 138
Grimshaw, W S 154, 165, 170, 173
Hadath, John Edward Gunby 6, 76-79, 193
Hardcastle, Edward Hoare 45, 48, 192
Hargreaves, John Charles Walker 175
Hartwig Von Der Lahr, Alfred Hayman, 54-62, 181
Harvey, W B 35
Harvey (Mrs.) 184
Hawley, Norman Edgar 154, 157, 159, 169
Hawley, Rupert 173, 175-176
Haworth, Arthur Adlington 197
Headley 31
Henson, George Frederick 135, 139, 150-152, 158, 194
Hesketh, J 87, 97
Hildyard, Francis Edward 67-68, 192
Hiller, W 86, 182
Hilton, Kenneth Boyd 154, 158
Hobbins, Wilfred Alston 95-96, 107, 118-125, 193
Hodgkinson, G F 152
Hodgkinson, P 154
Holden, William Leak 109-110
Holliday, C J 21
Holt, C A 56
Horrocks, A 136-173, 202
Howard, C M 102
Howard, F 72, 77-114, 128-153, 200
Howard, George Guest 97-98
Howard, T 83
Howard (Mrs.) 184
Hudson 24
Hulton, Campbell Arthur Grey 19-32, 40, 190-191
Hulton, J 21
Hulton, R W 48
Hunt, R 30-31
Isherwood, George Herbert 151-176
Jackson, Eric Boyd 170-173
Jackson, F 93
Jackson, F J 48
Jameson, A S 22, 28, 30
Jones 28
Jones, A 33-34
Jones, George Albert Hamilton 29-75, 198-199, 202
Jones, George Cyril Mansell 184-185
Jones, G C M (Mrs) – see Miss Dorothy Lucy Oddy
Jones, H T 178-179
Jowett, G A 57
Joy, George Percy 79

Kelly, Cuthbert Bede 84-103
Kelly, Francis James 85
Kendal, C 35
Kendal, G G 178
Kessler, Edward 25-47, 190
Kessler, George Albert 43
Kessler, Philip William 22-50, 190, 196
Kiernan, S S 137, 141, 144, 147
Kilminster/Kilmister, C H 107
Kirkman, J 95
Kitcat, Walter Parry de Winton 66-67
Knapp, Thomas Lloyd 24-25
Knapp, William Kenyon 25
Knowles, C J 62, 65
Land, William Walker 129-137, 159, 165-167, 196
Laurie 18
Leggat, Alexander James 132, 141-147, 151, 155 194, 200-201
Leigh, A 21
Leroy, Ferdinand Raymond 7, 74-113, 128, 135-166, 169, 193, 196
Leroy, Jules Joseph 77, 108, 196
Lindley, H 30
Lomax, Harry Douglas 86
Low/Lowe, J C 24, 28
Ludlow, J 16
Lund, W 50, 178-179
Lyon, Charles Sturges 39-47
Macalister 17
Macfie, D 54
Mackeson, W J 31
MacLaren, Archibald Campbell 8, 17, 21, 27-28, 51-57, 60, 66-69, 81, 93, 177, 179-180, 190-192
MacLaren, David Bannerman 21-24, 28, 34, 190-191
MacLaren, James 16-33, 81, 179-180, 190, 192
MacLaren, James Alexander 17, 28, 52-59, 66, 81, 88, 180, 190, 192
MacLaren, William 20-21, 28, 190
Maclure, John William 81, 197
Magnall, J 179
Mantle 21
Mark, Kathleen Mary (Mrs., nee Leahy) 162
Mark, Robert 161-164, 194-195
Marlow P (Miss) 187
Marrian, Harry Platt 136-137, 140
Marriott, Hail 18-19
Marriott, Percy Henry 18-19, 81
Marshall 16-17
Mason, T 56
Matteson, William Ord 22-23
Mawdesley, J 139, 140
Mawson, Harry Temple 67, 70-71, 192
Mayall, Edward Arthur 69, 70-71
McEwen, A P 21
McLachlan, William 34
Melling, Isaac 81, 83, 90, 196
Mellor 29
Merchant, Alan Roy 155-156, 161, 194
Miller, J 86
Mills, Walter George 35-59, 66, 69, 71, 88, 107, 191, 200
Mills, Walter Henderson 107, 191
Mitchell 16, 18

Mitcheson, Frederick Arundel 183
Moore, Harry Farr Bradley 41-50
Mountain, William John 86, 100-105, 114, 130-131, 137-138, 144, 154, 159, 196
Mountain, George Talbot 101, 138, 144-154, 162
Mumford, Percival Brooke 148-149, 182
Muth, Hermann Bernhard Lionel 79-82, 88-89, 94, 97, 107-108, 119
Nelson, John 109-110
Nesbitt, Alfred Mortimer 29-36, 191, 200
Nicholson 16
Nixon, S 97, 200
Nuttall, Harry 197
Oddy, Dorothy Lucy (Miss) 184
Oddy, George 181-184
Oddy, George Vernon 87, 185-189
Oddy, Norman Lee 97
Oddy, Stephen Roberts 87-90, 97-103, 121-124, 181-185, 193, 200, 202
Oldfield, Henry Keeler 83, 86, 93, 99-108, 135, 140
Oldfield, Leonard 86, 101
Oliver, L 100, 104, 200-201
Openshaw, Charles Herbert 34, 40-44
Orford, Lewis Alfred 59, 192
Orr, Geoffrey Wallace 170, 185-186
Palmer, Hubert Leslie 109, 132-159, 194, 200
Palmer, John Raymond 134, 150, 154
Palmer, Sydney James 150
Parker 86
Pattison 24
Peacock, Douglas Mason 89-90, 200
Peacock, John Pender 39, 89
Pearn 17-18
Pearson, R 97
Peel, William Robert Wellesley 197
Pennington, H 114, 128-130, 134
Peters, Bridge Baron 197
Pickering, Enid Grace (Miss) 160, 187
Pickering, H 159-160
Pidd, Leslie Stubbs 185-188
Piercy 17
Pilkington, S 136-137, 141-145, 153, 157, 163-165
Pitt, A 139, 142, 144, 147, 154, 159, 200
Pitt, D 147
Pope, Henry Newbery 21-23
Preston, Philip Stansfield 175-176
Proctor, Frederick Burdett 141, 147, 150, 154, 158
Radford, F 178-179
Radford, William Harold 33, 35, 178-179
Railton, Alan 34-35, 40, 48-56, 191
Railton, Joseph Arthur 34-35, 71
Rains, Kenneth 132-157, 167, 194
Rawlinson, Edward Cuthbert Brookes 35-40
Ray, R 65
Reeve, Alfred Joseph 134-173
Reynolds, R 99
Rhodes, A 161-163, 170
Richardson, H 22-23
Richardson, William Ryder 29, 35, 44, 50, 178-179, 191
Rickards 18
Rickards, Arthur Benjamin 23, 33
Rippon, J M 35

Robinson, A I   172
Robinson G (Miss)   184
Rodgers, H   16
Rogers, W   41, 46-48
Rothwell   34
Rothwell, G   161-169, 200
Rowarth   17-18
Rowbottom/Rowbotham, A E   86
Rowlands   99-100
Rowley, Ernest Butler   61, 70, 192
Russel-Fisher, Graham   135, 158
Russell, S A   77
St. Lawrence, Thomas Kenelm Digby   30-31
Sanby, Harold Ernest   109-110
Sarkis, C K   162
Saunders, A M   36, 39
Saxelby, Sydney Walter   79-94, 116-119, 126
Scammell, John Cosson   175-176
Schiele, W   57
Schofield, C   33, 35
Schofield, J R   96
Schofield, Paul   187
Scott, C H   36, 39-40
Sewell   18
Shanks, Henry Pearson   106-107
Sharp, Charles Arthur   35, 39-40, 45, 48-49
Sharp, Reginald William   40, 48-49, 55, 60, 62, 67, 69, 191
Sharp, Walter Ainsworth   49
Shelmerdine   29
Skinner, L   159
Smart, C   183
Smith, A   21
Smith, B   22
Smith, E A   82
Smith, H   141
Smith, S   21-22
Smith, William Cecil   95, 109
Sowler, Frank   65, 72
Spear, Harold   139, 158
Spear, Holwell Walshe   139
Stanley, D (Miss)   184
Stanley, E   158
Stansby, Walter Bennett   6, 138, 141, 154-158, 164-173, 187, 189
Steel, Allan Gibson   6, 25-34, 38, 43, 50, 60, 155, 190-191, 200-202
Steel, Ernest Eden   26, 43-51, 58, 77, 82, 155, 157, 177, 190-191, 199-202
Steel, Frederick Liddell   25-28, 43-51, 55, 66, 77, 171, 199, 202
Stephenson, J   88
Stewart, Charles Nigel   40-41, 44, 47, 50, 191
Stewart, M J   24
Stockton, William Edwin Forsyth   158, 194
Stone, William Moses   184
Stuart, C   184
Stubbs, F R   135, 139-140, 144, 154
Style, J   31-32, 34
Sudlow   17
Suttle, J   17-18, 21
Swain, William Gilbert   131
Swann, C M (Miss)   186

Sykes, Reginald   95-96, 99-103, 107, 109, 111, 193
Tarr   17
Thompson, W G   81, 90, 196
Thomson, A   59
Thomson, A D   134, 139-151, 161-166, 170, 172
Thomson/Thompson, H   47-48, 54
Thornton, John Talbot   148
Thornton, William Herbert   108-109, 129-138, 148, 202
Thornton, William Sydney   6, 148, 154-169, 202
Tillotson, Tom Mackenzie   152, 154, 158, 161, 173
Tindall, Henry Charles Lenox   41-51, 65, 177, 191
Tindall, Herbert Woods   43-82, 113, 181, 191-192, 200-201
Tindall, Sidney Maguire   43-72, 114, 191-192, 200
Trafford, Alan Shaw   140, 143
Turner   42
Turner, F B   95
Turner, J   21, 22
Varbetian, N   72, 74, 79, 89
Vincent, David Stanley Bonner   176-177
Vlies, Gordon Richard   169-170
Walker, George Stanley   109-111
Walker, John Haslam   109, 111, 122-125, 193
Walker, R   21
Walley, Archibald Frederick   75, 79, 81, 83, 196
Walton, William Lees Percival   109, 111
Watson, C S   21
Watson, R S   101
Watts, E (Miss)   184
Webber, H C   186-187
Welsh, George Strafford   178-180
Welsh, William   178-180
Whitehead, James Stanley   184-185
Whittaker   16-18
Wicks, Charles Alfred   90-96, 107, 202
Widdows, Ernest Geoffrey   5, 138, 147-148, 152, 157, 160-173
Williamson, Winston   114, 129, 132-173, 200-201
Willock, Robert Peel   6, 36, 38, 48-59, 191, 197
Wilson   18
Wilson, W H   86
Winchester, John Lee   83, 87-90, 92
Winson, John Barrie   129, 131
Wood, C M   178-179
Wood, G H   23, 178-179
Wood, H (Miss)   183
Wood, W H   106, 130
Woodforde, Edward (Ffooks)   32-54, 59, 191, 200
Woodforde, Woodforde Beadon   32-34
Woollam, James Edward Lucas   175
Woollam, John Philip Victor   7, 106-110, 126-173, 187, 193-194, 196
Woollam, Samuel Edward   7, 105-106, 135, 139-144, 151-154, 158, 161, 176, 193-194
Woolley, Fred Duke   197
Worrall, Edward   18, 21, 23
Worrall, Henry   23, 81, 87, 90, 108, 196
Worthington, Arthur   109, 111, 183
Worthington, F   49
Wright, C   16
Wright, J H   189
Wrigley, A W   129-130, 139, 141

Acknowledgements

The compilation of this book was made a whole lot easier by the efforts of many people. In particular, Mike Hill and Pete Simpson would like to thank all of the following people, who have assisted with providing information for this or the subsequent volume with regard to the history of the Whalley Range Cricket & Lawn Tennis Club : Anthea Arnold; Len Balaam (re Manchester Rugby Club); Chris Battle; Thomas Beckett; Wayne Belston; Duncan Broady; Simon Butterworth (re Butterworth family background); Dick Chandler (re J. E. G. Hadath); Shibaji Dasgupta; Paul Davies; Malcolm Edwards; Gill Frigerio; Anne Gamble; Sarah Gillam; Ken Grime; Frances Harris; Gary Kewin (for much information about C. F. Butterworth) who himself acknowledges the invaluable assistance of Tony Cross, Kevin Kilburn, Glyn Marsh, Melvyn Taylor, and the Manx Museum; Waqas Malik; Ros Menzies; Robert Oxley; Graham Palmer (re Palmer family background); Keith Robson; Dave Rushforth; Tony Smith (re Manchester Rugby Club); Ken Walsh; Barrie Watkins (LCCC Hon. Librarian); Peter Williams; Pat Winfield.

Of the people mentioned above, a special mention to Keith Robson who undoubtedly has provided the most assistance with regard to the research for this book.

Appeal for Information for Second Volume

If anyone has any material for the second volume (post-War to modern-day), then please feel free to contact the club or authors by phone (Mike Hill 07894 961530, club 0161 881 1414), by email (petersimpsonnh@talktalk.net, m.hill@prospects.ac.uk), or via the club's Facebook page. Any additions or amendments to this first volume will also be included as an addendum to the second volume.

Other Cricket Books by Peter Simpson

A History of the Ashton Cricket League

This book charts the complete history of the Ashton Cricket League from its inception in 1907, through to its sad demise following the end of the 2011 season. At its height, prior to the Second World War, the League attracted over sixty teams, though a steady decline in numbers thereafter, saw just four teams competing for the league title in 1968. The League then recovered over the ensuing years, and really thrived in the 1980s and 1990s with Clayton Methodist in particular experiencing unparalleled success, winning the title on no less than nineteen occasions. Some famous names were associated with the Ashton Cricket League down the years, with Lord Beaverbrook serving on the cricket committee in the 1920s, and a certain Gordon Taylor (of PFA fame) topping the batting averages in 1962. The book is published by Tony Brown and is available from Tameside Local Studies & Archives Library, Old Street, Ashton-under-Lyne, OL6 7SG

A History of Newtonhurst Cricket Club

This book chronicles the history of Newtonhurst Cricket Club from its emergence in the early part of the twentieth century, right through to the present day. Up until the early 1970s, the team was known as Newton Mill Cricket Club, having been formed from employees of the Newton Mill company in Hyde. Down the years, the team has played in numerous leagues, including the Hyde & District League, the Glossop & District League, the High Peak League, the Denton & District League, the Ashton Cricket League, the Ashton & Oldham Cricket Alliance, and even the heady heights of the North Western League for a short period in the 1950s. Currently, the team plays in the Greater Manchester Amateur League. The book is available online as an eBook from www.lulu.com.